THE LEGISLATION OF DIRECT ELECTIONS TO THE EUROPEAN PARLIAMENT

To Jane and Roger, Clytie and Virginia.

The Legislation of Direct Elections to the European Parliament

edited by

VALENTINE HERMAN
Erasmus University, Rotterdam

and

MARK HAGGER
Kingston Polytechnic

Gower

Published by
Gower Publishing Company Limited,
Westmead, Farnborough, Hants., England.

British Library Cataloguing in Publication Data

The legislation of direct elections to the European
   Parliament.
   1. European Parliament — Elections
   2. Election law — European Economic Community
      countries
   I. Herman, Valentine   II. Hagger, Mark
   328'.37   JN36
   ISBN 0-566-00247-7

Printed in Great Britain by
Biddles Ltd, Guildford, Surrey

ISBN 0 566 00247 7

Contents

Editors

Valentine Herman is a Senior Lecturer in Political Science at Erasmus University, Rotterdam. He is author of *Parliaments of the World: A Reference Compendium*; co-author of *The European Parliament and the European Community*; *Direct Elections to the European Parliament: A Community Perspective*; and *Workbook for Comparative Government*; co-editor of *The Backbencher and Parliament*, *Cabinet Studies* and *The European Parliament and The National Parliaments*, and has written many articles on comparative, European and British politics. His current research interests include an empirical study of governments and coalitions, and the relationship between political symbols and political ideologies.

Mark Hagger is a Senior Lecturer in Political Science at Kingston Polytechnic, and Visiting Lecturer at the Institut d'Etudes Politiques, Grenoble. He is the author of a number of articles and chapters on the European Parliament, the House of Commons, and the French National Assembly. He is currently directing a project on 'The Transformation of the European Parliamentary Elite, 1958-1979', and working on a study of change in the French National Assembly since 1962.

Contributors

Karl-Hermann Buck is at present a functionary in the General Secretariat of the European Council, previously an Assistant at the University of Tubingen. He has written a doctorate on the Chilean Socialist Party, and has published a book on Greece and the EC, *Griechenland und die EG*; contributed to a reader in Eurocommunism, *Eurokommunismus und die Zukunft des Westens*, and written various articles on left-wing parties in Mediterranean Europe, on direct elections and the enlargement of the EC, and on problems of development.

Maurizio Cotta is Associate Professor of Political Science in the Faculty of Law and Political Sciences of the University of Siena. He was previously Assistant in the University of Florence. He is author of *Classe politica e instituzione parlamentare: L'esperienza italiana del dopoguerra*, and articles on parliamentary institutions, political élites and participation. He is working on a data archive of Italian MPs, and has undertaken a research project on the historical development of the Italian party system.

Derek Hearl is currently at the University of Essex where he is researching for a PhD on the party systems of Belgium and the Netherlands. He has contributed chapters to books on theories of party alignments and links between the European and the National Parliaments. His research interests include coalition-formation, comparative electoral behaviour and the politics of the Grand Duchy of Luxembourg.

Juliet Lodge is Lecturer in Politics at the University of Hull. She is author of *The European Policy of the SPD*, and *New Zealand and the European Community* and co-author of *The European Parliament and the European Community*, and *Direct Elections to the European Parliament: A Community Perspective* and author of many articles on European politics and international relations. Her research interests include the politics of the European Community and political terrorism.

Edward Moxon-Brown is a Lecturer in Political Science at Queen's University, Belfast. He is the author of *Relations between the Oireachtas and Irish Members of the European Parliament after Direct Elections*, and several articles on the European Parliament, Ireland and the European Community, and political terrorism. His research interests include politics in Northern Ireland, and the European Community.

Dominique Remy is an Assistant in the Department of Political Science at the University of Paris I (Sorbonne). She is researching the influence of political parties on the functioning of the French Parliament, and on the political logics of legislative production. She has published articles on parliamentary information, coalitions and political parties, and bicameralism.

Rinus van Schendelen is a Senior Lecturer in Political Science at Erasmus University Rotterdam. He is author of *Parlementaire, informatie, besluitvorming en vertegenwoordiging; Terugtred van de wetgever*, and *Regering en Parlement in crisistijd*; co-author of *Ministers, ambtenaren en parlementariërs in Nederland; Openbaar bestuur: organisatie beleid en politieke omgeving* and *Proces van wetgeving*; editor of *Kernthema's van de politicologie*; co-editor of *The European Parliament and the National Parliaments* and author of many articles. His research interests include the parliamentary and administrative systems in The Netherlands, and relationships between normative and empirical political theory.

Tove Lise Schou is a Senior Lecturer in international politics at the Institute of Political Studies, University of Copenhagen. She has written 'A Study of External Factors Influencing Denmark's Market Policy' (Institute of Political Studies, University of Copenhagen) and has been awarded a Doctorate for a thesis on: 'Norway and the EC: A Study of External and Internal Factors Influencing the Norwegian Parties' Positions towards the EC Issue' (Institute of Political Studies, University of Copenhagen). Her research interests lie in integration theory; the international relations of small states, and Danish policy towards the European Community.

Martin Wing is a Research Associate at Henley Staff College. He is the author of a number of articles and chapters on committees and legislative roles in the European Parliament. His research interests include the politics of the European Community and he is currently working on a study of 'The Transformation of the European Parliamentary Elite'.

Acknowledgements

The research for this study was carried out by a team of European political scientists under the auspices of the Anglo-Dutch Institute of Parliamentology and Parliametrics. Three research conferences were held to develop the research project. We are particularly grateful to the Nuffield Foundation, to the European Commission and to the home institutions of each participant, for financing these meetings, without which this study would not have been possible. Our thanks also go to Robert Atkinson for editorial assistance, and to many secretaries who so kindly helped with organisation and typing.

1 Introduction

Mark Hagger and Valentine Herman

On 20 September 1976 the Member States of the European Community signed the 'Act concerning the election of the representatives of the Assembly by direct universal suffrage'. The signing of the Act represented the culmination of a process of negotiation in the EC, that had begun two decades earlier, when a clause was included in the Treaty of Rome that pointed to the eventual introduction of direct elections to the European Parliament.[1] The fact that this EC level decision took 20 years in the making, and that a further 33 months — including the postponement of the original May—June 1978 target date — were to pass before the eventual implementation of the elections on 7-10 June 1979, testify to the saliency of the issues and the complexity of the decision processes in the nine Member States. So also does the fact that no common electoral system was used for the first supranational election, but instead a compromise that involved a framework for the elections being defined at the EC level, and the details of each country's own electoral system being defined at the national level.

The passage of electoral legislation through nine national parliaments at the same time provides an unusual and exciting subject for the political scientist. The opportunity to focus on the more or less simultaneous making of laws dealing with the same subject in nine different national political systems provides a unique occasion to study the similarities and differences between those legislative processes and between the laws that eventually emerged. Moreover, the chapters of this book provide a series of case studies of nine European parliaments at work, that are not otherwise available.

For the politician and the political observer, the legislation of direct elections has a special importance. The first direct elections to the European Parliament in 1979 were not held according to a single uniform electoral system, but instead according to provisional electoral systems determined separately by each nation specifically for the elections. The implication both of the Act of 20 September 1976 and of Article 138 of the Rome Treaty, is that a uniform electoral system would be created subsequently. Indeed Article 7(1) of the Act requires the Assembly to draw up such a proposal. The lessons that can be

1

learnt from the passage of the first set of laws will be an invaluable guide to the problems and obstacles that will inevitably be encountered in any move toward the adoption of a uniform electoral system.[2]

Three features make the legislation of direct elections an admirable subject for comparative study. Firstly, the process occurred in nine countries which are all established western liberal democracies. All nine have the institutional framework of this type of political system: universal suffrage, free elections, a competitive party system, an elected parliament and an executive dependent on majority support in parliament. All nine also share the value system underpinning this type of regime. Although the 'rules' are not clearly defined, it is apparent that membership of the EC 'club' is restricted to countries not only supporting the principles of liberal democracy but also putting these into practice.[3] In addition to political homogeneity, the social and economic structures of the nine states are of a similar type. When comparisons are made with other political systems, the high levels of similarity between the political systems and the socio-economic contexts of the nine, ensures that the similarities and differences relevant to the legislative processes within them are highlighted.[4]

Secondly, the subject to be dealt with by the national legislatures is identical. The same two issues — the principle of holding direct elections, that is the 'ratification' of the EC Act of 20 September 1976, and the 'implementation' of this principle through the passage of the necessary electoral legislation — were faced by each of the nine political and parliamentary systems. Much recent legislative research has shown that policy processes vary considerably across different policy areas.[5] The passage of direct elections legislation in nine countries enables us to compare the way in which different legislatures, and legislative processes, handled a common issue.

Thirdly, the legislative processes all occurred within the same short time period. This began with the signing of the Act of 20 September 1976 — before which there was a low level of national parliamentary activity on the subject — and ended with the holding of the first direct elections. Exogenous forces that might otherwise have influenced the national legislative processes — such as the energy crisis or the economic recession — were, therefore, more or less similar for each Member State.

Thus we have a situation as controlled as any in the world of comparative politics. With the same issue being legislated in nine different polities at the same time, and with factors external to the political systems controlled, it becomes possible to focus attention on differences between the legislative processes themselves, which are attributable to factors endogenous to each political system. As will be seen in the national case studies which follow, these differences mani-

2

fest themselves in a number of ways including the timing of the legislative stages; the relative emphasis on different institutions; the level of institutionalisation of the legislative process; the roles of political parties and other political actors; the influence of interest groups; the parliamentary tactics and procedures employed; and differences in the legislative outputs — in this case the laws themselves. In more substantive terms, our comparison will also elucidate the nature of the issues that arose in different nations, the manner in which they presented themselves, and the way in which they were handled by political parties, party leaders and governments.

Comparing legislative processes: methodological and substantive issues

In recent decades, research on legislative studies has expanded considerably in quantity and has embraced important new areas, such as the role of the legislature in developing countries, as well as new methodologies, such as survey research and roll-call analysis. One consequence has been an increased specialisation and a narrowed research focus onto highly specific elements of the legislative process: for example, on the role of committees in policy-making, or the role of the individual legislator in representing constituency opinion. This has resulted in a diversion of attention from an earlier research approach, the case-study of a single legislative process. The unique advantage of this latter approach is that, in analysing the different actors and activities involved in the making of a single policy item, the relative importance of the different institutional and political elements of that process is established.

Very often the legislative case-study has adopted a descriptive — historical and institutional approach. It is perhaps this characteristic that hastened its fall from favour in the 1950s and 1960s, when attention turned to the development of more sophisticated methodological and analytical techniques, both in political science as a whole and, especially, within the field of legislative behaviour. These techniques were concerned with evaluating attitudes of legislators, or on certain limited and privileged moments in the life of a legislature — such as roll-calls, the initiation of legislation or the formation or termination of a government. Typically, they would be located within a case-study, but they would not necessarily contribute greatly to the more general goal of that study — the role of the legislature in the policy process.

The study of the law-making process also escapes much of the intensive theory development and concept formation that occurred in other areas of political science during recent years. Not only did the

3

legislature itself fail to represent a dynamic element in the policy-making process, but broad acceptance of the 'decline of legislatures' thesis resulted in political power being seen as having shifted to governments, bureaucracies and interest groups. Thus in a recent review of almost a hundred articles and books published in the period 1965-1978, Malcolm Jewell included only four items that were concerned with the analysis of a single law-making process or policy area, and this approach warranted neither separate consideration nor recommendation as a research focus.[6]

The reaction that has occurred amongst political scientists in the late 1970s, stimulated by the critique of philosophers such as Popper and Toulmin, has led to reappraisal of the traditional methods of research. In the words of Gabriel Almond, one of the spiritual leaders of the 'behavioural movement': 'Knowledge of political substance in its institutional, historical and philosophical aspects has to be re-established on an equal footing with sophisticated methodologies and reductionist knowledge . . .'.[7] The case-study approach that occupies the bulk of this volume is consistent with this appeal. But we should also note that an increased awareness of the complexity and un-predictability of the political process has been created both as a direct product of the research developments indicated above, and as a result of substantive political changes that have occurred, some of which have implied an explicit rejection of the decline of legislatures.

Given the existence of over 70 national legislatures — as indicated by membership of the Inter-Parliamentary Union — the lack of a strong comparative approach in legislative studies is surprising. The call for a comparative focus appears regularly in the reviews of research in legislative studies, but it seems that these pleas are thicker on the ground than the actual comparative studies.[8] Indeed the famous critique by Macridis published in the early 1950s can effectively be applied to legislative studies today:

> Essentially noncomparative . . . essentially descriptive . . . essen-
> tially parochial . . . essentially static . . . essentially monographic
> . . . the traditional approach to the study of comparative politics
> is centered on the description of the formally established institu-
> tions of government, . . . the study of the legal instrumentalities
> of government; . . . it is in general singularly insensitive to informal
> factors and processes such as the various interest groups.[9]

The absence of cross-national comparisons is particularly evident in the study of the legislative process, a fact that is surprising given that many national or sub-national parliaments frequently treat similar issues. The widespread absence of comparative legislative studies is

4

especially apparent in the co. ...nt of European legislatures. However, two recent research endeavours are notable exceptions to this; one a comparison of 'The Role of European Parliaments in Managing Social Conflict' in Belgium, Italy and Switzerland;[10] the other, 'The Power of the Purse', a study of the budgetary processes in nine European parliaments.[11] These studies provide some indication of the problems of comparative analysis, but it is apparent that the handling of financial and deep-rooted social problems by these parliaments is different in many respects from their handling of other areas of policy-making. These studies, therefore, provided no real basis for developing either a comparative theory, or even comparative propositions, about the functioning of (European) legislatures.

In consequence of the absence of anterior studies, and concomitant with this theoretical weakness, there exists no clearly defined methodology for the comparative analysis of the legislative process. At the outset, the modest goal of this study was, therefore, seen to be the provision of a set of 'comparable' case-studies, which might both enable and encourage reflection on the methodological problems in this area. This might eventually contribute to the development of a framework for a more rigorous and systematic comparative analysis of law-making.

In order to ensure that the set of case-studies would provide the body of comparable data necessary for such a goal, a common 'indicative' framework was established for the nine case-studies. The structural basis of this framework requires no apology. Its indicative function allowed researchers to explore fully the particular characteristics of their own national law-making experience, and to illuminate their study with the richness of their national traditions of political science. The set of case-studies would enable a 'comparable cases' analysis to be conducted, following the advocacy of Arendt Lijphart.[12]

Apart from the theoretical and methodological difficulties which precluded the adoption of a more 'rigorous' comparative framework, there were a number of substantive features that helped to define our comparative approach. Firstly, it was apparent that the relationship between the parliament and the legislative process varied considerably in the nine countries. In some contexts, an issue may be handled for years or even decades by some part of the political system, yet it may receive only peremptory treatment by the legislative institution during, or at the end of, this period. Adapting a concept developed for a different purpose,[13] we consider this to represent a low level of *institutionalisation* of an issue. Traditionally, the United Kingdom is regarded as having a high level of issue-institutionalisation, with parliament providing the key focus in the political process. But the difficulties experienced in the United Kingdom in the 1970s, over the two major constitutional issues of devolution and Britain's continued membership of the European Community, indicate that the level of institutionalisation may vary from one issue to another. On both of these issues governments resorted, exceptionally, to referenda in attempts to achieve wider legitimacy for decisions which would 'normally' be taken by parliament. The second feature indicated by the British experience of parliamentary difficulties in the 1970s is that the level of institutionalisation may vary over time: a country, whose parliament successfully handled issues for centuries, experienced a sharp decline in the level of issue-institutionalisation in this period.

From this and other examples it was evident that a study of the legislation of an issue must embrace the evolution of that issue outside parliament as well as within it. Indeed the relative importance of pre-parliamentary stages, as well as of extra-parliamentary performance, is discussed in each case-study. The level of institutionalisation of the legislative process is also a fundamental element of the analysis in the concluding comparative chapter.

Within the general framework of a liberal democracy there is a certain variation between the basic political structures of the nine European polities (see table 1.1), and these differences inevitably affect the character of the legislative process in each.[14] The first structural characteristic considered concerns the number of chambers in the parliament.[15] Apart from Denmark and Luxembourg, all the countries had a bicameral system, though Luxembourg has a Council of State which plays a role that falls between a second chamber and a constitutional court. The power of the second (or upper) chamber is difficult to evaluate in practice: in the field of law-making, the Belgian, French, Italian and Dutch upper chambers all have constitutional powers that are equal to those of the lower chamber. But in real terms, we can only seriously consider the Italian and the German second chambers as having a generally powerful role in the political system, though in the case of direct elections it was the French and Italian Senates which were to play the leading role amongst second chambers.

The relationship between the executive and the legislative is our second structural variable. The conventional distinction between presidential and parliamentary systems has no utility in Western Europe where parliamentary systems are the norm, and where France's hybrid system is commonly referred to as 'semi-presidential'. Nevertheless, there is an important variation in the extent of executive domination of the political system. Thus we have dichotomised into categories of 'more executive dominance' and 'less executive dominance' — expressed, perhaps euphemistically, in the table as 'parliamentary dominance' — with Denmark, Italy and the UK falling into the second category. One of the more interesting findings of the case-studies was in fact that these normal patterns of dominance were disturbed in at least two countries — Britain and France — during the legislation of direct elections.

Thirdly, the location of ultimate authority is defined by the existence or absence of judicial review by a constitutional court. Parliamentary control over constitutionality is retained in the UK, Luxembourg, Denmark and Belgium. In the four most recently established regimes (France, the Federal Republic, Ireland and Italy), together with the Netherlands, a constitutional court is used to provide an independent adjudication of constitutionality. We should note that both Belgium and Luxembourg have advisory courts.

On the other hand, all countries except the UK have a written constitution. Most of these are in legal and political terms, 'difficult' to change — insofar as they involve complex procedures such as a referendum. Although it may not be politically 'easy' to change a constitution by a special parliamentary majority, which is the procedure required in Italy and the Federal Republic, one should not assume that an unwritten constitution provides *ipso facto* a flexible constitutional form. There is evidence to suggest that major constitutional changes in the UK involve procedures that are equivalent to the referendum, and indeed this procedure has been used twice in recent years to influence or legitimise, issues seen as being of special constitutional importance.

The level of decentralisation of the polity may also be an important factor affecting the legislative process. Conflict between centre and periphery has been part of the conventional analysis of political development in a number of states. In the EC, only the Federal Republic has a fully fledged federal system. The powers of the Italian regions are such, that Italy is tantamount to being federal; and the reforms actually being created at the time in Belgium were aimed at this goal. Decentralisation had occurred elsewhere, particularly in the 1970s, but it was not sufficiently important to warrant classification alongside the Federal Republic and Italy.

The final structural factor, chosen for its specific relevance to direct elections, is the nature of the electoral system. Apart from Britain and France, all countries use a 'proportional representation' (PR) system for national elections, although the Federal Republic uses a mixed PR—plurality system. However, the use of constituencies smaller than the nation is common, and only the Netherlands has a national list system for parliamentary elections. The details of the national electoral systems in comparison to those eventually adopted for the European elections are discussed in chapter 12; but it is important to note the general characteristics, which are consistent with established national traditions except in France, where more proportional systems were used before 1958. France was to prove the only country which did not closely follow existing national practice in the direct elections.

Table 1.1
Some structural/political characteristics of 9 European polities in 1978

Variable	Values	Belgium	Denmark	France	Federal Republic of Germany	Ireland	Italy	Luxembourg	Netherlands	Great Britain
a. No. of Chambers	1 or 2	2	1	2	2	2	2	1	2	2
b. Power of Second Chamber	Weak		—	X		X		—	X	X
	Strong	X	—		X		X			
c. Extent of Executive Dominance	Exec.-dominance			X	X	X				X
	Parl.-dominance	X	X				X	X	X	
d. Adjudication of Constitutionality	Constitutional Court			X	X	X	X			
	Parliament	X	X					X	X	X
e. Constitution	Written	X	X	X	X	X	X	X	X	
	Unwritten									X
f. Decentralisation	Federal				X					
	Regional	(X)					X			
	Unitary		X	X		X		X	X	X
g. Electoral System	Plurality			X	X					X
	Regional PR					X		X		
	National PR	X	X		X		X		X	
h. Government Status	Majority	X		X	X	X		X	X	X
	Minority		X				X			
i. Coalition Structure	No. of parties in government	4*	1	4	2	1	1	2	4	1
	No. of parties in majority	5*	3-7†	4	2	1	6	2	4	2
j. Government ideology	L = Left / C = Centre / R = Right	C	L	C-R	C-L	R	C-R	C-L	C-L	L
k. Party System in Parliament	No. of parties (large and small) [Large 10%, small 1-10% of seats]	3+4*	3+8	4+3	2+2	2+1	2+5	3+2	4+10	2+3

*These figures refer to Parliamentary Groups, which in Belgium are not equivalent to political parties.

†No fixed majority coalition

Apart from the structural factors discussed above, it is also necessary to consider some political factors that affect the legislative process. There were three countries that had minority governments during 1977/78. Whilst this situation is not uncommon in Western Europe — indeed the proportion corresponds precisely to the proportion of years in which all European governments have been in minority since 1945[16] — it evidently makes a government-centred legislative process more difficult. Five of the governments were formed of a coalition of parties, and in most cases that coalition corresponded to the parliamentary majority. Italy and the UK were the notable exceptions, both having 'minority governments' with an agreement from additional parties to provide majority support in parliament. In both of these countries, the legislative process was to prove difficult, in part because of the governments' inability to exercise firm control over a parliamentary majority. Similarly, the Danish minority government formed its majority coalition for this issue with the support of pro-European parties, whose support conditioned the outcome. An indication of the government's ideological orientation is also given and the nature of the party system is shown in terms of the number and relative size of the parties in parliament.

Normality: controlling for national characteristics

An important element in the comparative method used in the case-studies is the definition of the 'normal' characteristics of the legislative process in each country. This provides a yardstick against which the national legislative processes on direct elections can be measured, so that comparisons can be made in relation to national norms. Appropriate caveats are necessary, since the concept of the 'normal bill' is in many senses on a par with that of the 'average man'. As a preliminary criterion, the normal process provides a 'statistical average' of government bills, and thus defines a general or probabilistic context. Since the variations in the treatment of bills by any one parliament are considerable, such an analysis locates the direct elections legislation on the range of legislative processes utilised within each country.

From this preliminary base it is necessary to qualify the analysis by taking into account a number of 'abnormal' features of the direct elections issue. In the first instance the issue is a part of the EC policy area, which bridges uneasily the divide between foreign and domestic policy. It is commonplace that the foreign policy area is 'different' from other policy areas. There is a particular emphasis on executive action, in negotiating treaties and conducting relations between states; and in most European polities it is accepted that the parliamentary role

9

in foreign policy is limited. Two classic examples illustrate this; the case of Prime Ministerial decision-making by Eden during the Suez crisis in 1956,[17] and the analysis by Prime Minister Chaban-Delmas in 1959 of the defence and foreign affairs sectors of policy-making as 'reserved' for Presidential decision.[18] However, EC policy does not fall neatly into the foreign affairs category at all, for its impact is on various sectors of domestic policy, notably agriculture, but also industry, trade, transport, social policy, etc.

In terms of the way in which policy is made, the EC sector borrows both from the 'international negotiation' style of the foreign policy area, and builds on the 'network of interest groups' which domestic departments consult to create a viable policy. In the case of direct elections, one important feature arising from the EC nature of the policy area was the nature of the legislative initiative. For domestic policy it is normal for the government to introduce the overwhelming majority of public legislation in response to party policy or interest group pressure. Concerning the direct elections legislation decisions taken at the EC level by the European Council were critical in launching the process, and additional stimuli were provided by another Community institution, the European Parliament (see chapter 2).

One consequence of this for the legislative process was that, in most countries, the first step that was required was the ratification — by standard treaty procedure — of the decision of the European Council. In Denmark, Ireland, and the UK, however, ratification was accomplished by the passage of the electoral law. In many European countries, ratification is carried out by a different, simplified procedure than that used for domestic legislation. The difference may be merely behavioural — that the bill is treated in a more rapid way — or it may be constrained by formal rules, as in France where the Parliament cannot amend treaties during their ratification.

In many Member States, EC matters have a second important effect on politics: they disturb the 'normal' balance of political forces. A distinctive ideological dimension is introduced, that contrasts with the left—right division that is usually the basis for political cleavage. The 'EC dimension' proved to be particularly important in Britain and France, where the traditionally dominant left—right cleavage was threatened during the passage of the direct election legislation to an unusual extent.

The law-making process was also profoundly affected by the constitutional nature of the issue. Indeed the separate parts of the direct elections issue acquired constitutional significance in different ways: the principle of direct elections threatened — or was perceived by some parties or groups as threatening — national sovereignty in Britain, Denmark and France; whilst the implementation bill, in defining an electoral system, automatically elevated the issue to the constitutional level. It is evident that items of similar importance reach the policy-makers' agenda only on rare occasions, and this enhanced the potential for contention.

The fact that the issue relates to elections is also of importance. If there is one policy area in which all MPs see themselves as experts, it is that of electoral law. This is sufficient to ensure that electoral bills receive special treatment, particularly where there is dissonance between the views of parliamentarians, the electoral proposals and the national electoral system. In practice, it was only in the UK that a major political issue emerged over this; but in Italy, for example, dispute over the electoral system was the major reason for delay in passing the legislation.

The implications of the legislative process

The legislation of direct elections took about four and a half years to complete, with a wide variation both in the pattern of legislative process and in the resulting outputs. Whilst our aim in carrying out this research was to further the understanding of legislative behaviour, the results of the research are not merely of academic and scholarly interest. Without a full understanding of the difficulties involved in placing the legislation for the 1979 direct elections on the statute books, it will be impossible to properly evaluate and develop policy toward a uniform electoral system for subsequent elections.

The proponents of a uniform electoral system have put forward a variety of idealistic blueprints which have considerable technical interest and which may be viable as electoral mechanisms. However, the acceptance of these schemes depends on the successful surmounting of the real political obstacles that have been demonstrated in the Member States between 1974 and 1979. In a move toward a common electoral system, the debate at the supranational level outlined in chapter 2 will have to be re-opened, in order to reach agreement on the issues of size, distribution of seats between Member States, incompatibilities, and so forth. Whilst the rehearsal of these issues in the negotiations prior to the Council Act of September 1976 may facilitate future debate, agreement at this level should not be assumed to be easy. The common electoral mechanism itself presents a fundamental problem. It is also clear from the 1974-79 process that many Member States may face constitutional obstacles which will need to be overcome by amendment of the Treaties of Paris, Rome and Brussels, and by national referenda. The conflicts within the party systems, within parliaments and within governments will re-emerge. Finally, it is likely that the policy process

11

will be based on an enlarged Community of 12 members, or at least it will need to take this eventuality into account.[19]

It is not our aim to express pessimism in regard to the common electoral system, but it is important to emphasise that the holding of direct elections in 1979 was but the first step along the thorny path that the Member States must tread before the second (or subsequent) elections can be held under a common electoral law. Our purpose in presenting this book is to emphasise the importance of the five years of policy debate which gave birth to the first supranational elections in 1979. A careful analysis of the process as it occurred in nine nations will help both scholar and politician to measure the path toward a common electoral system, and the speed at which it should be traversed.

Notes

1   Article 138(3) of the Treaty of Rome required that 'the Assembly should draw up proposals with a view to implementing direct elections according to a uniform electoral system'.
2   One might also note that one of the electoral laws of Belgium is valid only for the first direct elections and further legislation of some sort will be necessary for subsequent elections.
3   Indeed it was made clear to Spain, during her preliminary negotiations to join the EC, that she should 'make progress' toward this goal.
4   The importance of 'minimising the variance in the control variables', notably by choosing countries of a similar cultural and environmental context, so as to 'maximise the variance of the independent variables', is discussed further below. The rationale is developed by A. Lijphart, 'The Comparable Cases Strategy in Comparative Research', *Comparative Political Studies*, vol.8, 1975, pp 158-77.
5   See, for example, D. Damamme et al, 'Etudes sur le processus legislatif en France', ECPR, Louvain-la-Neuve, 1976.
6   M.E. Jewell, 'Perspective on Legislative Studies', *Legislative Studies Quarterly*, vol.3, 1978, pp 537-54.
7   G. Almond and S.J. Genco, 'Clouds, Clocks and the Study of Politics', *World Politics*, vol.29, 1977, pp 489-522, at p.522.
8   M.L. Mezey cites 5 other articles which made such a plea in reviewing legislative studies between 1966 and 1973. 'Legislatures in Western Democracies', *Legislative Studies Quarterly*, vol.3, 1978, pp 335-52 at p.345. The recent appearance of comparative studies by M.L. Mezey, *Comparative Legislatures* (Duke U.P., Durham NC, 1979); G. Loewenbert and S.C. Patterson, *Comparing Legislatures* (Little Brown, Boston, 1969). J.D. Lees and M. Shaw (eds) *Committees in Legislatures* (Duke U.P., Durham NC, 1979) are recent exceptions.
9   R.C. Macridis, *The Study of Comparative Government* (Doubleday, New York, 1955), pp 7-21.
10 Special issue of: *Legislative Studies Quarterly*, vol.3, 1978, pp 1-186.
11 D. Coombes et al, *The Power of the Purse* (Allen and Unwin, for PEP, London, 1976).
12 A. Lijphart, 'Comparative Politics and the Comparative Method', *American Political Science Review*, vol.65, 1971, pp 682-93; and 'The Comparable Cases Strategy in Comparative Research', op.cit.
13 N.W. Polsby, 'The Institutionalization of the U.S. House of Representatives', *American Political Science Review*, vol.62, 1968, pp 144-68; S.C. Huntington, *Political Order in Changing Societies* (Yale U.P., New Haven, 1968); S.N. Eisenstadt, 'Institutionalization and Change' *American Sociological Review*, vol.29, 1964, pp 235-47.
14 The analysis of political systems presented here is of necessity highly interpretative. Of the many studies available, we would commend: G. Smith, *Politics in Western Europe* (Heinemann, London, 1976); M.O. Heisler (ed.) *Politics in Europe* (Mackay, New York, 1974) and M. Dogan and R. Rose (eds) *European Politics* (Macmillan, London, 1971).
15 The existence of Economic and Social Connects in most EC countries might lead one to introduce the motion of tricameralism. However, these 'third chambers' were not involved in

the legislation of direct elections.

16 V. Herman and J. Pope 'Minority Governments in Western Democracies' *British Journal of Political Science*, vol.3, 1973, pp 191-212.

17 J.B. Christoph, 'The Suez Crisis', chapter 4 in: J.B. Christoph and B.E. Brown (eds), *Cases in Comparative Politics* (Little Brown, Boston, 1969).

18 The conception of a Presidential *'domain reserve'* was proposed by J. Chaban-Delmas in a speech to the UNR Congress in 1959. The analysis was superceded by subsequent political developments; see E. Cahm, *Politics and Society in Contemporary France* (Harrap, London, 1972) pp 134-41, 199-204.

19 At the time of going to press, a sub-committee of the European Parliament's Political Affairs Committee had been established. Its strategy was *minimalist*: it would endeavour to determine a minimum of items for EC agreement, including the electoral formula and the enfranchisement of EC residents; leaving other items to be determined by Member States, including the constituency/national basis and matters of electoral organisation and campaigning.

2 Direct Elections: The Historical Background

Valentine Herman

The commitment to a directly elected European Parliament is as old as the European Communities. Article 21 of the Paris Treaty, which established the European Coal and Steel Community,[1] (signed on 18 April, 1951) stated:

> The (Common) Assembly shall consist of delegates whom the parliaments of each of the Member States shall be called upon to appoint once a year from among their own membership, or who shall be elected by direct universal suffrage, according to the procedure determined by each respective High Contracting Party.

In practice, however, no Members of the Common Assembly were directly elected, although the Assembly set up a subcommittee (under the chairmanship of Mr Bernard Dehousse) to see how Article 21 might be put into effect. When the European Community was established on 25 March, 1957, the commitment to an elected Assembly was more strongly renewed in Article 138(3) of the Treaty of Rome:

> The Assembly shall draw up proposals for elections by direct universal suffrage in accordance with a uniform procedure in all Member States.
> The Council shall, acting unanimously, lay down the appropriate provisions, which it shall recommend to Member States for adoption in accordance with their respective constitutional requirements.

Immediately after the constitution of the European Parliament in March, 1958, its Political Affairs Committee began considering the question of direct elections. A special working party, again chaired by Mr Dehousse, was set up to undertake a detailed examination of the problems associated with such elections. Consultations took place in the six Member States with Ministers and party leaders, and in March, 1960, the Political Affairs Committee adopted a draft Convention which it submitted to the European Parliament for its approval.[2] The

Convention was accompanied by a report in four parts: a general report drafted by Mr Dehousse; a report on the composition of the Parliament by Mr Maurice Faure; a report by Mr Willem Schuyt on questions relating to the electoral system; and a report on the representation of overseas countries and territories drafted by Mr Metzger. As the Dehousse Report provided a framework within which later discussions of direct elections took place, it is worthwhile to consider some of its proposals in detail.

Concerning the electoral procedure to be adopted, the difficulty of drawing up a completely uniform electoral system was recognised. Accordingly, the draft Convention proposed that the details of the electoral procedure should initially be determined at the Member State level until the European Parliament prepared and introduced a uniform electoral procedure. The 1960 draft Convention also proposed that direct elections would be introduced by stages, and that during a transitional period — which would run parallel with the transitional period for establishing the European Communities (and ending at the latest by 1970) — two-thirds of the Members of the European Parliament would be directly elected, while the remaining third would continue to be nominated from the national Parliaments. At the end of the transitional period, it was expected that outstanding questions of electoral procedure would be settled. Another recommendation of the draft Convention was that the elections would be held on the same day: the first direct elections to the European Parliament were to be held six months after the ratification of the Convention by all the Member States. The 1960 proposal also recommended that the directly elected Parliament would triple in size and contain 426 Members, and each nation's quota of Members would be increased three-fold, irrespective of the size of the country. Concerning the question of increasing the powers of the European Parliament, it was suggested that these should be dealt with separately from direct elections: increased powers were not seen as a prerequisite for direct elections.

Following a debate on the draft Convention, on 17 May, 1960, the European Parliament adopted the following resolutions:[3]

1 resolution on the adoption of a draft Convention introducing elections to the European Parliament by direct universal suffrage;

2 resolution on the procedure to be adopted in respect of the draft Convention;

3 resolution on the electoral procedure during the transitional period;

4 resolution on the strengthening of the Parliament's powers;

5 declaration of intent on participation by parliamentary representatives of the overseas countries and territories in the work of the European Parliament;

6 resolution on the preparation of public opinion for European elections by direct universal suffrage.

Although the European Parliament had acted promptly under Article 138(3) of the Rome Treaty on the question of direct elections, and had attempted to draft a Convention which would be acceptable to all of the Member States, little action was taken on the matter by the Council of Ministers. When the Convention was presented to the Council it was not given serious attention. General de Gaulle, then President of France, would not accept direct elections to the European Parliament, which he saw as inevitably leading to an increase in the power of the Parliament and a concomitant erosion of French sovereignty. The Governments of the other five Member States were more enthusiastic about the idea of direct elections, but easily grasped how great was the difference of opinion between themselves and the French: this was apparent in the two summit conferences held in 1961 which discussed the question of political union. Periodically, the Parliament or the Governments of the Five would make faint-hearted attempts to resurrect the matter, and the Council or its subordinate bodies would give it brief consideration. No progress was made: although there were serious disagreements concerning the distribution of seats in the Parliament, the length of the transitional period, and the absence of a common electoral system, the major objection was to the principle of supranationality that would be enshrined in a directly elected European Parliament. A number of bills and motions were introduced by MPs in the national Parliaments proposing that, pending a Community decision, the Member States should introduce direct elections for their own delegations to the European Parliament (see table 2.1). Although none of these measures were enacted — and other parliamentary devices such as questions, agenda motions, and adjournment debates were used — they served to keep the issue of direct elections alive at the national level during the 1960s and early 1970s.

The European Parliament also maintained its interest in the matter. In a resolution of 27 June, 1963, on the powers and competences of the European Parliament, it stated that the direct election of the European Parliament was essential to the democratisation of the Community, and urged the Council of Ministers and national Governments to assume full responsibility for the early entry into force of the draft Convention.[4] A new summit conference was proposed by the Italian Government in November, 1964. It was also suggested that, as a pre-

Table 2.1
Legislative initiatives on direct elections in national parliaments, 1961-75

	1961	1962	1963	1964	1965	1966	1967	1968	1969	1970	1971	1972	1973	1974	1975	Total
Belgium								x		x	x		x	x	x	6
Denmark																0
Federal Republic				x												1
France			x	x				x								3
Ireland																0
Italy	xx				xx	x		xx	xx				x			10
Luxembourg									xx		x				x	4
Netherlands					x			x		x						3
United Kingdom																
Total	2	0	1	2	3	1	0	5	4	2	2	0	2	1	2	

liminary to the conference, serious consideration should be given to the draft Convention with a view to holding elections before 1970. However, the Community was soon to enter a crisis with France withdrawing from the Council of Ministers, and in such circumstances — and also in the aftermath of the 'Luxembourg compromise' — it was apparent that there could be little or no progress on direct elections.

Some years later, frustrated by the Council of Ministers' inaction, the Parliament threatened to take the Council of Ministers before the Court of Justice. On 12 March, 1969, the following resolution was agreed to:

> The European Parliament, having regard to the fact that Article 138(3) of the EEC Treaty provides for the election of its Members by direct universal suffrage, having regard to the fact that Parliament submitted as long ago as on 17 May, 1960, a draft convention on elections to the European Parliament by direct universal suffrage, having regard to the fact that the Council has to date taken no decision on this draft convention and has not considered the matter for six years, instructs its President to call upon the Council without further delay the procedure laid down in the Council in Parliament's draft, and to refer the Council to Article 175(1) and (2) of the EEC Treaty.'[5]

The Council of Ministers replied quickly to the Parliament's threat of judicial action. On 12 May, 1969, it announced:

> The Council has held a searching discussion on certain aspects of its relations with the European Parliament. With regard to the resolutions adopted on 12 March by the European Parliament on its election by direct universal suffrage, the Council has instructed the Committee of Permanent Representatives to report to it on this draft Convention, and has sent a letter on this subject to the President of the Parliament. Moreover, after hearing a report from its President on a conversation held by him with the President of the European Parliament in Strasbourg on 7 May, the Council instructed the Committee of Permanent Representatives to make preparations for the Council's discussions on the various questions raised by the President of the Parliament.[6]

On 12 May the Council instructed the Committee of Permanent Representatives (COREPER) to report to it on the question of elections by direct universal suffrage: this strategy enabled the Council to evade the threatened legal action. However, the Committee could not reach agreement on the main items of the 1960 draft Convention: the main difficulties concerned the electoral procedure for the European Parliament; links it would have with the national Parliaments; provisions concerning the incompatibility of occupations and professions with membership of the Parliament; the size and distribution of seats in the elected Parliament; and transitional arrangements concerning it. In spite of these problems, the final communiqué of the meeting of the Heads of State or Government in The Hague on 1-2 December, 1969, stated that, 'The question of direct elections shall be given further consideration by the Council'.[7]

The open-ended nature of this commitment did not assuage the Parliament's impatience with the Council. On 3 February, 1970, it adopted a resolution based on a report by Mr Dehousse. This:

1. note(d) that the Heads of State or Government, while inviting the Council to give further consideration to the question of direct general elections, laid down no timetable or time-limit for such consideration;
2. urge(d) the Council to complete its work on this question as quickly as possible;
3. call(ed) for the creation by mutual agreement of a suitable consultation procedure between Parliament and the Council, in order to define concrete provisions on the basis of the draft drawn up by Parliament in 1960 to enable Article 138 of the EEC Treaty, Article 108 of the EAEC Treaty and Article 21 of the ECSC Treaty to be implemented.[8]

Under the terms of this consultation procedure three meetings were held in June and December, 1970, and March, 1972, between a delegation from the European Parliament, or its Political Affairs Committee, and the President-in-Office of the Council. However, it was apparent that the Council's working party had neither reached unanimous agreement on the European Parliament's proposed plan, nor been able to agree on an alternative to it. Additional meetings took place between the Presidents of the Council of Ministers and the European Parliament in December, 1970, in which the Parliament mentioned the likelihood of national projects for the elections being adopted and the danger of a part-elected, part-appointed Parliament coming into existence. The question of the enlargement of the Community was also mentioned at these meetings, especially as to how it would affect the Parliament. In April, 1971, COREPER again considered direct elections, but no progress was made. Proposals for a joint Council-Parliament committee on direct elections were made, but vetoed by the French in July and September, 1971.

The European Parliament was unwilling to have its will further thwarted by the Council of Ministers and tried another strategy. At the same time as it was urging that the Council should adopt its 1960 proposal, it also contacted the authors of the national bills for the introduction of European elections. A meeting of these was held with the Political Affairs Committee on 6 October, 1971, where it became apparent that there were considerable differences between the details of the various national schemes which the Parliament had little chance of bridging.

Given that no immediate action by the Council of Ministers was likely, in a resolution of 5 July, 1972, on the forthcoming Paris Summit Conference, the European Parliament recommended that:

> The request first made by the European Parliament in 1960, and emphatically repeated on several occasions since for its Members to be elected by direct universal suffrage in accordance with Article 138(3) of the EEC Treaty, still stands. The search for ways and means of removing the practical and political obstacles which have so far postponed implementation of this measure must be begun immediately and pursued resolutely.
>
> The widening of Parliament's powers is not linked with the issue of its direct election, and cannot be postponed until such elections are held.[9]

When the Summit failed to adopt a position on the question of direct elections — or even mention the elections in its communiqué — Parliament stated on 14 November, 1972, that,

> It regrets that no definite dates have been laid down for the general and direct election of Members of the European Parliament and no instructions given to solve the remaining difficulties.[10]

The intense activity on direct elections (compared to what had preceded it between 1960-69) of 1969-72, produced no results. However, three somewhat contradictory developments in the Community during that period combined to create an atmosphere in which direct elections came to be given serious consideration by the Council of Ministers. First, the enlargement of the Community drew attention to a range of problems inherent in the structure and functioning of the Community's institutions, and also provided the impetus for a measure of institutional reform and adaptation. The sceptical attitude (by the British and Danes) to a number of the Community's institutional arrangements — especially to the absence of democracy, legitimacy and parliamentary control — provided a fresh opportunity for the reconsideration of direct elections. Second, it was apparent that a measure of institutional reform in the Community to strengthen the powers and competences of the Parliament was already under way: these included the Treaty of Luxembourg of 22 April, 1970, which increased the Parliament's budgetary powers; the Vedel Report of 1972; and the Treaty amendments of July, 1974, which established the concertation procedure Direct elections were seen by many as a logical corollary of these developments. Third, it was equally apparent that, in an enlarged Community, French intransigence to the idea of direct elections would be mollified; at the same time French fears of the erosion of national sovereignty would be shared by the British and Danish Governnments. The election of M. Giscard d'Estaing to the French presidency in March, 1974, subsequently led to major changes in French policy towards both the Community and the Parliament.

Mr Dehousse, the author of the 1960 proposals and rapporteur of the Political Affairs Committee, left the Parliament in 1970. On 14 May, 1971, Mr Hans Lautenschlager was appointed rapporteur of the Committee, and charged with the task of determining whether the conclusions reached by the Parliament on direct elections eleven years earlier should be revised. The enlargement of the European Communities on 1 January, 1973, also presented the Parliament with an opportunity to adapt its earlier draft to changing circumstances. On 4 June, 1973, the Parliament decided to draw up a new report on the introduction of elections by direct universal suffrage. Mr Schelto Patijn was appointed rapporteur of the Political Affairs Committee on 13 September, 1973, in succession to Mr Lautenschlager. During 1974, Mr Patijn consulted spokesmen from the national Parliaments, other political leaders and experts in the field, and produced a report for the Political Affairs Committee. The main provisions of the report[11] eventually adopted by the Committee were:

— the European Parliament should have 550 Members,[12] elected by direct universal suffrage for a five-year term;

— the elections should be held on the same day or days within the Member States;
   the first direct elections should be held not later than the first Sunday of May, 1978;

— each Member State would determine the electoral system it would use for the first direct elections;

— by 1980, the European Parliament would draw up a proposal for a common electoral system;

— membership of the European Parliament would be compatible with membership of a national Parliament;

- provisions governing the admissibility of political parties to elections in each of the Member States would apply to the European Parliament;
- vacancies in the European Parliament would be filled by the Member States.

The Report also contained provisions concerning the incompatibilities of membership and the verification of credentials of Members of the Parliament.

The Political Affairs Committee's report was also considered by the Parliament's Legal Affairs Committee, and an opinion on it was drawn up by the rapporteur, Mr Lautenschlager. The Legal Affairs Committee proposed two amendments to the report: first, that the elected Parliament should have 355 Members (as originally proposed by Mr Patijn); second that the dual mandate could only be held until the Parliament was elected by a common electoral system.

While the Patijn report was awaiting debate by the Parliament, the nine Heads of State or Government met at a Summit Conference in Paris on 9-10 December, 1974. In the Conference's communiqué[13] they established a target date for the elections:

> The Heads of Government note that the election of the European Assembly by universal suffrage, one of the objectives laid down in the Treaty, should be achieved as soon as possible. In this connection, they await with interest the proposals of the European Assembly, on which they wish the Council to act in 1976. On this assumption elections by direct universal suffrage could take place at any time in or after 1978.

This appeared to give the green light to the principle of direct elections. But it was not clear how this was to be achieved: moreover, the issue was intermingled with the question of increasing the Parliaments' power:

> The Head of Government will not fail to take into consideration the points of view which, in October, 1972, they asked it to express on this subject. The competence of the European Assembly will be extended, in particular by granting it certain powers in the Communities' legislative process.

However, the Governments of both the United Kingdom and Denmark inserted reservations into the communiqué. That of the

United Kingdom read:

> The Prime Minister of the United Kingdom explained that Her Majesty's Government did not wish to prevent the governments of the other eight Member States from making progress with the election of the European Assembly by universal suffrage. Her Majesty's Government could not themselves take up a position on the proposal before the process of renegotiation had been completed and the results of the renegotiation submitted to the British people.[14]

The reservation of the Danish Government stated that, 'The Danish delegation is unable at this stage to commit itself to introducing direct elections by universal suffrage in 1978'.[15]

In January, 1975, the European Parliament debated the new draft Convention.[16] In presenting his report, Mr Patijn stressed that any issues likely to cause controversy had been left to one side. In other words, the whole aim of the Convention that he had drafted was to ensure that direct elections would take place as soon as possible. He emphasised that:

> If, with the vote on my report this evening, we take a further step on the long and difficult road to European elections, it will not be an occasion for jubilation, since it will mean that we are again submitting proposals to the Council which, in 15 years, has done nothing about European elections. We shall therefore have to make it very clear to the Council that we are not prepared to tolerate another delay of this kind. We shall insist that the Council adheres to the terms of the communiqué issued by the Paris Summit, i.e. a decision in 1976 and elections in 1978. The European Parliament will therefore begin work tomorrow . . . (W)e shall have to put pressure on the Council in the immediate future to compel it to take a swift decision on direct elections to the European Parliament. The European Parliament must not and cannot tolerate another 15 years of unbroken silence on the part of the Council.[17]

The Parliament's debate focussed on two issues. First, consensus was reached on the amendment of Mr Lautenschlager that the elected Parliament should have 355 Members. Second that the European mandate should be regarded as compatible with a national mandate, even though the dual mandate would eventually be phased out. According to Mr Peter Kirk, European Conservatives' spokesman, '. . . this Parliament cannot continue to function for very much longer on the basis of a dual mandate. . That is quite clear to all of us who take part in it. It is quite clear, or should be quite clear, to all of those who observe it'. Mr Kirk also expressed the desire to maintain links between the national Parliaments and the European Parliament.[18] One hundred and six Members voted in favour of the Convention: 35 Christian Democrats, 33 Socialists, 13 Liberals, 17 European Conservatives, 6 European Progressive Democrats (5 Irish and 1 Danish), and 2 Independents. Two Danish Socialists voted against it; and there were 17 abstentions, 9 Communists, 6 European Progressive Democrats (all French), and 2 Danish Liberals.[19]

In June, 1975, the referendum in the United Kingdom confirmed Britain's membership of the Community.[20] When the Italian Government took over the presidency of the Council of Ministers in July, a working party on direct elections was established. Its report, which was ready by October, identified a number of items on which different national positions existed: although it made some progress on the main outstanding issues, it was unable to reach agreement on the size of the elected Parliament. The British argued that Scotland's representation should not be significantly lower than that of Denmark or Ireland. Both the latter two countries argued that proportionately they should retain their existing representation in an enlarged Parliament, and the Irish Foreign Minister (Mr Garret Fitzgerald) pledged his Government to this demand. On 5 November, a delegation from the European Parliament participated in preliminary discussions on the draft Convention in the Council of Foreign Ministers. Here the Danish Government formally withdrew its general reservations, but continued to reserve the Danish position on the dual mandate and a single election date: Denmark was anxious to avoid a situation in which the party balance in the European Parliament would be different from that in the Danish Parliament. On 11 December, the Danish Folketing confirmed this position by 110 votes to 29, with 10 abstentions.

On 1-2 December, 1975, the Heads of State or Government met in Rome and, once again discussed the matter of direct elections. They agreed that the election should take place on one date only in the period May-June, 1978. Any country which could not hold direct elections on that date could nominate its own representatives from among the elected Members of its own national Parliament. The meeting also noted that the British Government needed a further period for consultation before finally adopting a position on the date fixed.[21] As Prime Minister Wilson reported to the House of Commons on 4 December,

I made it clear that we accept in principal the commitment to direct elections in the Treaty of Rome. This issue was decided by

24

the referendum: Article 138(3) of the Treaty of Rome is mandatory. But I added that we required a further period for consultations with political parties in this House and for consideration of the matter by Parliament before we could adopt a final position about holding direct elections ourselves as early as 1978.[22]

The conditions of the Danish Prime Minister were also noted in regard to the need for a compulsory dual mandate in Denmark and for European elections to be held there on the same date as national elections.

The European Council instructed its Council of Ministers to submit a report on the outstanding problems which would enable it to finalise the Convention at its next meeting. The major outstanding problems were whether the dual mandate should be optional, as laid down in the draft Convention, or compulsory; and what the size and composition of the Parliament should be. It was known that the Irish Government had proposed a Parliament of 384 Members, a figure achieved by adding three seats to the number for each country in the draft Convention, except for Ireland, which would receive five extra seats. The French proposed a Parliament of 284 with a higher proportion of seats given to the four larger Member States, and a reduction in the number of seats held by Belgium, Denmark, Ireland, and Luxembourg. During the early months of 1976, the Council of Ministers' Committee of Permanent Representatives and the Council of Foreign Ministers continued detailed discussions on the Parliament's draft Convention. Certain controversial matters were referred to the European Council meeting in Luxembourg on 1-2 April. Two issues in particular were decided by the Council. First, concerning the timing of the poll and the count, it was agreed that the first direct elections would take place over a four day period from a Thursday morning to the following Sunday evening. The Member States could choose when they would vote, but the count would not take place until the close of the poll on Sunday. The target date of May-June, 1978, was confirmed. Second, against all expectations, the Council failed to reach agreement on the size of the elected Parliament. At the last moment, the French President suggested its size should remain at 198 Members.

Following the Luxembourg Summit, the Council of Foreign Ministers held further discussions on direct elections in an attempt to break the deadlock on the number of seats. At an unofficial meeting of Foreign Ministers on 12 June, the field was reduced to three or four proposals and, following the French President's visit to the United Kingdom in the week of 21-25 June, it was reported that the 'Giscard Plan' had been withdrawn. Final agreement was reached in Brussels on 12 July, 1976, when the European Council decided that the directly-elected Parliament should have 410 seats: the Federal Republic, the United Kingdom, Italy and France would have 81 seats each; the Netherlands 25; Belgium 24; Denmark 16; Ireland 15; and Luxembourg 6.[23] For the benefit of a unanimous decision, the Belgium Prime Minister (Mr Tindemans) agreed to yield one of the proposed Belgian seats to Denmark: this extra seat was immediately reserved for Greenland.[24]

The Council decision implementing Article 138(3) was finally taken on 20 September, 1976, with the signing of the 'Act Concerning the Election of the Representatives of the Assembly by Direct Universal Suffrage'. The Act fell into three main parts. The first was a brief formal text announcing that the Council has 'laid down the provisions annexed to this Decision which it recommends to the Member States for adoption in accordance with their respective constitutional requirements.' It also announced the Council's intention 'to give effect to the conclusions that the election of the Assembly should be held on a single date within the period May-June, 1978' (although this date was not mentioned in the Act). Second, in sixteen Articles the Act contained details of the number and distribution of seats; the term of office of the Parliament; the dual mandate; incompatibilities; the electoral register; the timing of the elections and the holding of the first elections; the validation of elected Members' credentials; the filling of vacancies in the Parliament; and the procedure for further measures should they be necessary to implement the Act. Concerning the electoral system to be used, Article 7 charged the elected Assembly with the task of drawing 'up a proposal for a uniform electoral system': for the first direct elections, however, 'the electoral procedure (should) be governed in each Member State by its national provisions.' Third, the Annexes to the Act dealt with the position of Greenland; the Isle of Man and the Channel Islands (to which the Act did not apply); and the details of the Parliament-Council conciliation procedure mentioned in Article 13 of the Act. Also attached to the Act was a declaration by the Government of the Federal Republic on the representation of Berlin.

Thus a quarter of a century after the establishment of the European Coal and Steel Community, the European Community was brought to the brink of direct elections. The Council of Ministers' decision of 20 September, 1976, can be seen as neither a logical outcome of the developments we have chronicled above nor a simple honouring of the legal commitment of Article 138(3). Numerous reasons have been advanced as to why the Council of Ministers finally acquiesced to the holding of direct elections. We have already drawn attention to the parts played by the enlargement of the European Community, the strengthening of the powers and competences of the European Parliament, and the changing attitude of the French Government, in influencing the Council's final decision.

Two additional explanations of the Council of Ministers' decision deserve brief consideration. One is that it was a reflection of public opinion in the Member States (especially the new ones) which was strongly in favour of direct elections (see Appendix). However, although the results of polls conducted by the European Community showed that by the Autumn of 1976 a majority of the public viewed the elections as 'an event with important consequences which is certain to make Europe more politically united', there is no evidence whatsoever to suggest that the Council of Ministers was influenced on this matter by public opinion in the Member States, nor that the decision of 20 September, 1976, could in any way at all be attributed to popular feelings. A second explanation of the Council's decision is that the Council hoped that the holding of direct elections would draw the press' and publics' attention away from the pressing economic and political problems of the European Community, and focus it instead on the election of the European Parliament. To the Council, elections were seen as a device which would increase the saliency of the European Community and involve the public at large in its functioning, without incurring much financial expense nor changing the nature of the Community's institutional arrangements.[25]

Following the Council of Ministers' decision of 20 September, 1976, each Member State was obliged to complete the necessary procedures for the adoption of the European election Act 'in accordance with their respective constitutional provision'. This was undertaken in two stages: firstly, the Member States had to ratify the Council decision and the Act, and notify the Council of this ratification; secondly, the Member States had to enact their electoral laws and, where necessary, associated implementing legislation. In the next nine chapters we examine how each Member State legislated for direct elections to the European Parliament and examine the reasons why the elections were postponed from May-June 1978 to 7-10 June, 1979. The final two chapters offer an analysis of the electoral laws passed by the Member States, a consideration of the problems the elected European Parliament will face in drawing up a uniform electoral procedure, and a comparison of the legislative processes in the nine Member States.

Notes

1   A similar provision was contained in Article 108 of the European Atomic Energy Community Treaty.
2   Doc 22/60.
3   OJ no.37, 2 June, 1950, pp 834-60.
4   Doc 31/1963.
5   Doc 214/1968-69.
6   Communiqué para.14.

7   Final Communiqué, Meetings of the Heads of State or Government of the EC, The Hague, 1-2 December, 1969.
8   Doc 210/1969-70.
9   Doc 73/1972.
10 Doc 194/1972.
11 Doc 368/1974.
12 Mr Patijn's original proposal was that the Parliament should have 355 Members.
13 Final Communiqué, Meetings of the Heads of State or Government of the EC, Paris, 9-10 December, 1974.
14 'Statement by the UK delegation', ibid.
15 'Statement by the Danish delegation', ibid.
16 OJ Annex no.185, 14 January, 1975.
17 Ibid., pp 34-6.
18 Ibid., pp 47-9.
19 Ibid., p.92.
20 See D. Butler and U. Kitzinger, The 1975 Referendum, St Martin's Press, New York, 1976, and A. King, Britain Says Yes, American Institute for Public Policy Research, Washington, 1977.
21 Final Communiqué, Meetings of the Heads of State or Governments of the EC, Rome, 1-2 December, 1975.
22 The Times, 5 December, 1975.
23 Final Communiqué, Meetings of the Heads of State or Government of the EC, Brussels, 12-13 July, 1976.
24 See L. Neels, 'Preparations for Direct Elections in Belgium', Common Market Law Review, vol.15, 1978, pp 337-45.
25 M. Pöhle, 'Direktwahl des Europaischen Parlaments: Ein Ablenkungsmanöver? Zehn skeptischen Thesen zu den möglichen Wirkungen', Zeitschrift für Parlamentsfragen, vol.7, 1976, pp 222-6.

Appendix

Since the Autumn of 1973, 'Eurobarometre' public opinion polls have asked representative samples in each of the Member States whether they were for or against the election of the European Parliament by direct universal suffrage. The following table reports the main findings of Eurobarometre.

	B	DK	D	F	IRL	I	L	NL	UK[1]	EC[2]
	%	%	%	%	%	%	%	%	%	%
'For'										
Autumn 1973	52	36	69	51	45	64	67	62	33	54
Autumn 1975	53	32	73	69	56	78	75	59	41	64
Autumn 1976	69	42	76	69	63	77	77	74	57	69
Autumn 1977	63	54	73	70	74	79	76	77	69	72
Spring 1978	64	54	74	67	71	77	82	80	65	71
Autumn 1978	62	54	70	67	75	80	80	82	63	70
Spring 1979	62	58	80	71	72	85	86	84	61	74
'Against'										
Autumn 1973	14	43	12	18	31	12	12	16	49	23
Autumn 1975	9	43	11	13	23	8	7	11	42	18
Autumn 1976	9	37	10	13	14	8	9	11	22	14
Autumn 1977	12	29	11	14	11	9	14	10	18	13
Spring 1978	14	22	7	12	10	7	11	9	17	11
Autumn 1978	13	22	7	11	7	7	12	8	21	11
Spring 1979	16	17	6	13	8	6	8	6	17	11
'Don't know'										
Autumn 1973	34	21	19	31	24	24	21	22	18	23
Autumn 1975	38	25	16	18	21	14	18	30	17	18
Autumn 1976	22	21	14	18	23	15	14	15	21	17
Autumn 1977	25	17	16	16	15	12	10	13	13	15
Spring 1978	22	24	19	21	19	16	7	11	18	18
Autumn 1978	25	24	23	22	18	13	8	10	16	19
Spring 1979	22	25	14	16	20	9	6	10	22	15

1 Great Britain only in 1973.
2 Weighted average.

Source: *Eurobarometre*, no.11, May 1979, p.20.

3 Belgium: Two into Three will go[1]

Derek Hearl *

Introduction: 'A Joyous Entry'

As befits the country which not only plays host to most of the principal European Community Institutions but which has also spawned perhaps more 'European' statesmen than any other — from Paul-Henri Spaak to Léo Tindemans — it was only to be expected that Belgium would unreservedly welcome the decision to implement Article 138 of the Rome Treaty providing for direct elections to the European Parliament.

Certainly this was the Government's position on 20 September 1976 (when the European Act concerning Direct Elections was finally signed by the Foreign Ministers of the Nine) as well as that of virtually every politician and commentator in the country. Indeed, Belgians generally have always been among the most ardent of 'Europeans' ever since the Coal and Steel Community's foundation in 1950.[2] As the Government pointed out in its Explanatory Memorandum attached to the Bill ratifying the European Act[3]

> By their active participation in the decision of various European Councils and Councils of Ministers, Belgian Governments have shown that they have been vigorously attached to the realisation of direct elections. The interest of Members of Parliament is shown by the fact that Private Members' Bills were introduced on 27th June 1969, 14th May 1970 and 2nd May 1974 envisaging the holding of an electoral consultation by direct universal suffrage for the appointment of the Belgian Members of the European Parliament.

As a matter of fact, *four* Private Members' Bills had been introduced since 1969[4] all seeking to institute what may be termed 'unilateral'

*Although a number of people in Belgium gave me considerable help and information in connection with this chapter, I would like to single out Mijnheer Guido de Sutter of the Chamber of Representatives' Documentation and Study Service for special mention. The speed, efficiency and courtesy with which he and his colleagues supplied me with vast quantities of parliamentary documents and other information were models of their kind.

direct elections in Belgium. All four were couched in very similar terms. Each proposed that there should be a single national constituency; that only serving MPs and Senators would be eligible to stand; that the elected delegation be drawn equally from the two Houses of the Belgian Parliament; and that the elections be held by proportional representation. Two of the bills proposed to extend the franchise to all EEC countries' nationals resident in Belgium while two did not.

Of the four bills, the one submitted to the Chamber on 2 May 1974 by Messrs Nothomb and Martens made the most progress. Like its predecessors, this bill too proposed that there should be a single national constituency, but this time this particular concept was challenged. Three separate amendments were submitted; two seeking to divide the country into three constituencies for European electoral purposes and one, prophetically as it turned out, providing for two constituencies corresponding to the two main language regions, with voters in Brussels being given the opportunity to vote in which of the two they pleased. Nor were these the only amendments put down to the Nothomb/Martens Bill; there were five more dealing with various other aspects — a sign, perhaps, of the greater seriousness with which this particular Bill was taken in contradistinction with those that had gone before. Indeed, had it not been overtaken by events at the European level, it is quite possible that the 1974 initiative might well, in due course, have become law in Belgium.

In short, in September 1976, it was not really to be expected that Belgium — of all countries — would experience any serious obstacles either to the rapid ratification of the European Act or to its translation into domestic legislation. Yet, in the event and for a variety of different reasons some of which will be examined here, not only was Belgium the last country to ratify the 20 September decision, but it was also very nearly the last to carry the necessary implementing legislation at home.

However, this is not to imply that the Government was dragging its feet in the wake of the 20 September decision — although its successor was to do so later. The Bill for the ratification of the European Act was submitted to the Chamber of Representatives on 14 February 1977 and there is every reason to suppose that it would have had an easy passage through both Houses of Parliament had the Prime Minister, Mr Tindemans, not requested the King to dissolve Parliament some three weeks later following a revolt by one of the parties forming his coalition government.

Legislative elections were held on 17 April and Mr Tindemans took office as Prime Minister of a new four-party coalition on 3 June. The new Government received parliamentary approval one week later. The Ratification Bill was reintroduced on 2 December[5] just three days before Mr Tindemans was to chair the European Council in Brussels. Consisting of a single Article,[6] it was rushed through the Chamber the very next day by 122 votes to nil (with the two Communist Members abstaining). It passed through the Senate two weeks later on 23 February – this time unanimously – to become law on 28 March 1978.[7] Apart from the somewhat unusual haste with which it was dealt, itself clearly associated with the timing of the European Council (see below), the Ratification Bill's passage through Parliament was entirely uneventful and it will not be considered further here. The passage of the Implementation Bill, however, was not to be anything like so straightforward.

Political environment: Babel revisited

Virtually as soon as direct elections had been agreed to by the Nine, the Belgian political world began to consider how they were to be organised. There was virtually unanimous agreement upon a number of important points. Firstly, as has already been pointed out, the principle of direct elections was not merely accepted by almost everyone concerned, it was positively welcomed by virtually all shades of political opinion. In Parliament, only the two Communist Members were less than enthusiastic supporters of direct elections and as we have already seen, even they abstained rather than vote against the principle when the opportunity arose for them to do so on the ratification bill.

Similarly, there was general agreement upon the use of the d'Hondt List system of proportional representation for the European elections. This system has been used for national elections in Belgium since 1920 since when it has scarcely been seriously questioned.[8] However, the number and extent of the constituencies in which the d'Hondt system was to be applied did present something of a problem. As we have seen, earlier attempts at legislation had been framed in terms of a single national constituency and, indeed, this was the solution eventually to be adopted in all four of Belgium's neighbouring countries also.

The single national constituency was supported by a number of people, including it is said,[9] Léo Tindemans himself, since it would have enabled the tricky question of the distribution of seats between the various language Communities to be ignored. The matter could simply be left to the electorate to resolve by its votes. However, in the event, the political environment in general, and the negotiations which preceded the formation of the new Government in particular, were to render such a simple solution politically impossible.

In March 1977, following the defection of the Rassemblement Wallon ministers from his government, Mr Tindemans had advised the

King to dissolve Parliament. Fresh legislative elections were held on 17 April and resulted in significant gains for his own Christian Social Party, especially in Flanders; modest gains for the Socialists; and a shift in support from the Flemish Liberals to their Walloon partners. Of the regionalist/linguistic parties only the Brussels-based FDF held its ground (indeed, it gained one seat) while the Volksunie and the Rassemblement Wallon, both suffered very significant setbacks (see table 3.1).

Table 3.1
Parties in the Chamber of Representatives, April 1977

	Party	Abbreviation	Vote %[1]	Seats(N)[2]
	Communists (Parti Communiste de Belgique — Kommunistische Partij van België)	PCB-KPB	2.9	2
G	Socialists (Parti Socialiste Belge — Belgische Socialistische Partij)	PSB-BSP	26.9	62
(G)	Walloon Regionalists (Rassemblement Wallon)	RW	2.9	5
G	Brussels Regionalists (Front démocratique des Francophones bruxellois)	FDF	4.3	10
G	Flemish Regionalists (Volksunie)	VU	10.0	20
G	Christian Socials (Parti Social-Chrétien/ Christelijke Volkspartij)	PSC/CVP	35.9	80
	Liberals (Parti des Réformes et de la Liberté en Wallonie/Parti libéral/Partij van Vrijheid en Vooruitgang)	PRLW/PL/PVV	15.6	33
	Others		1.5	–
	Total		100.0	212
	Turnout		95.1%	

1 Share of valid votes cast in General Election, April 1977
2 Seats in Chamber of Representatives, April 1977

G Party forming the Government
(G) Member of the Majority — not in Government

A new coalition government under Léo Tindemans' leadership comprising the Christian-Social Party, the Socialists and the two main regionalist parties, the Brussels FDF and the Volksunie took office some seven weeks later. The basis of the agreement between the four parties was the now famous — or infamous — 'Egmont Pact', so-called after the Egmont Palace in Brussels where the negotiations had taken place.

This technique of an inter-party 'Pact' has been used once or twice before in Belgium with a view to taking certain very controversial and fundamental problems out of politics — most notably, of course, the 'Schools Pact' of 1958.[10] Unlike its predecessors, however, the new Pact did not obtain all-party support, being opposed by the Liberals who, together with the Communists, now became the official Opposition in the new Parliament.

The Egmont Pact, aimed at nothing less than an agreed settlement to the so-called 'Communities Question'[11] which has bedevilled Belgian politics since the middle 1960s. The Pact was the very corner-stone of the new Government and fundamentally influenced much of its programme. The issue of European elections was considered during the negotiation of the Pact and, as a result, the bill when finally adopted by the Cabinet in the autumn of 1977, was strongly influenced by the Pact's provisions.

Briefly,[12] these were that three directly-elected Regional Councils dealing with economic and related matters were to be established, one each for Flanders, Wallonie and the bi-lingual Brussels Agglomeration. In addition, there were to be two new Cultural Councils each composed of one of the two main Regional Councils augmented by those members of the Brussels Council speaking the relevant language. The Regional Councils were to have territorial competences including planning, regional development etc., while the Cultural Councils would administer so-called 'personalisable' matters such as education, social services and, of course, cultural and linguistic affairs.

A compromise was reached over the difficult problem of Brussels and its periphery. The present position is that full bi-lingualism is confined to the nineteen Boroughs (*Communes/Gemeenten*) of the Brussels Agglomeration while certain 'facilities' are provided on a personalisable basis to the French-speaking inhabitants of six further Boroughs outside the Agglomeration itself which are otherwise part of the Flemish-language Region proper. The French-speaking minority living in other parts of the periphery has at present no such facilities. However, they are able to vote for French-speaking candidates in Provincial and National elections since the entire area, i.e. the Brussels Agglomeration together with the Halle-Vilvoorde Administrative District, forms a single vast Parliamentary constituency within which candidates from both language communities compete for the votes of the inhabitants of the entire constituency (see figure 3.1).

This situation compounded as it is by the continuing migration of French-speakers into the communes of the Flemish periphery, has now become perhaps the single most intractable problem of the entire community issue and now finds itself at the very centre of Belgian politics. The French-speakers quite naturally demand not only the conversion of

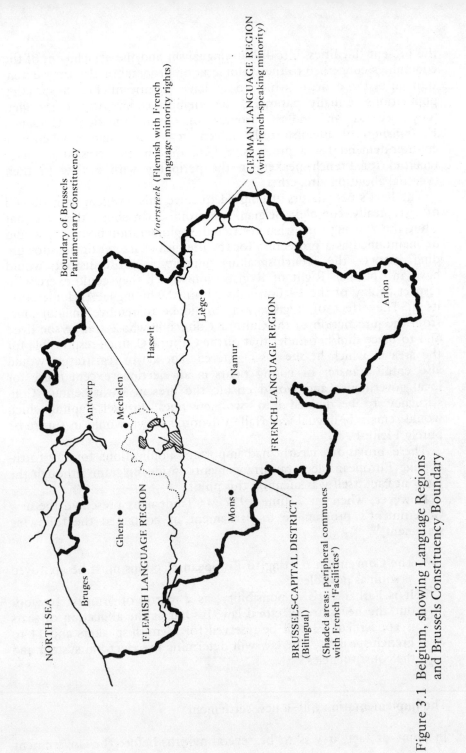

Figure 3.1 Belgium, showing Language Regions and Brussels Constituency Boundary

NORTH SEA

Bruges •

Ghent •

Antwerp •

Mechelen •

FLEMISH LANGUAGE REGION

Mons •

Hasselt •

Liège •

Namur •

Arlon •

FRENCH LANGUAGE REGION

Boundary of Brussels Parliamentary Constituency

Voerstreek (Flemish with French language minority rights)

GERMAN LANGUAGE REGION (with French-speaking minority)

BRUSSELS-CAPITAL DISTRICT (Bilingual)

(Shaded areas: peripheral communes with French 'Facilities')

the present 'facilities' into full bi-lingualism and the attachment of the communes concerned to the agglomeration proper, but also their extension into those areas which now have significant French-speaking populations. Equally naturally, the Flemish community resists what they see as an endless process of 'Frenchification' (Flemish: *Verfransing*) of Flemish soil. Indeed, many of them now enter a counter-demand for a progressive *reduction* in the present language facilities for French-speakers in the periphery with a view to their eventual abolition altogether.

The Pact's negotiators attempted to solve this problem with the aid of a typically complex Belgian compromise. In short, this was that while the existing somewhat restricted Agglomeration boundary would be maintained as a protection for the Flemish character of the surrounding districts, the French-speaking minority in those districts would have an optional 'Right of Registration' which they could exercise in respect of any of the 19 Boroughs within the bi-lingual Agglomeration itself. The effect of 'registration' would be to remove an individual from the jurisdiction of the Cultural Council in whose area he/she lived and to place him/her under that of the Cultural Council responsible for the area in which he/she has registered. The act of registration would also entail transfer of voting rights in all elections except those for local government and would enable the present Parliamentary Constituency to be divided into two new ones: Brussels-Capital which would remain bi-lingual and Halle-Vilvoorde which would in future be purely Flemish.

These provisions clearly had important implications for the forthcoming European electoral arrangements inside Belgium although the Egmont Pact itself was silent on this point.

However, when on 7 June 1977 Mr Tindemans presented the new Government's programme to Parliament, it contained the following statement,[13]

> The Convention relating to European elections must be approved as soon as possible.
> It is Parliament's responsibility, as a matter of priority, to work out the necessary electoral law. Insofar as the allocation of seats is concerned, 13 will be reserved for Flemish-speakers and 11 to French-speakers. The law will determine the electoral system and the constituencies.

The Implementation Bill: a new settlement

In point of fact, it was to be several months before the Government showed its hand although the reasons for this are not wholly clear. In view of the Prime Minister's own personal commitment to the cause of European Union, however, it is unlikely that any unnecessary delay can be attributed to that source. Indeed, it seems to have been no accident that the Bill was eventually published only three days before Mr Tindemans was to chair the European Council in Brussels on 5 December. This, it will be remembered was the Council Meeting at which it was expected that pressure would have to be brought by Belgium among others, upon certain other Governments — notably the British — to expedite *their* procedures. Since Belgium, traditionally among the staunchest supporters of direct elections, was *already* going to be the last to ratify the Convention, it would have been intolerably embarrassing for her Prime Minister to have had to admit that she was going to among the laggards in enacting the detailed internal legislation as well.

However, while it may be that the imminence of the European Summit on 5 and 6 December forced the Government to produce its bill, it is still unclear why it delayed so long. However, one explanation may be that there was internal disagreement within the Government on such questions as the number and extent of the constituencies; whether or not some form of national *apparentement* (see below) should be applied; the question of some guaranteed representation for the small German-speaking minority in the east of the country; and of course, arrangements in linguistically-mixed areas such as the Voerstreek and (especially) Brussels. Since these issues were subsequently among the most hotly disputed when the bill was finally debated in Parliament, it seems in retrospect almost inconceivable that the Government, given its unusually heterogeneous composition, could have been immune from significant disagreement on the same and similar issues.

Whatever the reason, the Cabinet took the final decision on 14 October and the bill was transmitted to the Council of State for an advisory opinion in accordance with normal practice before being presented to Parliament on 2 December 1977.

The main provisions of the bill[14] were as follows: the twenty-four seats allocated to Belgium were to be divided between the two main language communities on the basis of thirteen to the Flemish-speakers and eleven to the French-speakers. No separate provision was made for the German-speaking community nor for the linguistically mixed Voerstreek. Voters throughout the existing Parliamentary Constituency of Brussels were to be permitted to vote *either* for Flemish-speaking or for French-speaking lists according to their individual choice and special double ballot papers would be issued there in order to make this possible.

This latter provision, however, was subject to modification following the subsequent introduction of the 'Right of Registration' and the splitting of the Brussels Constituency as envisaged by the Egmont Pact.

The voting age was to be eighteen in line with practice in other Member States and with local government elections in Belgium.[15] The bill changed the requirement for electors to have six months' residence in the same Commune. In place of this provision, it would in future be sufficient to be registered as resident in Belgium although the actual place of voting would be that in which the voter was registered three months before the European election. The bill introduced a new term to Belgian electoral law; 'electoral college' (*college électorale/ kiescollege*). There were to be two of these: one composed of electors who live in existing parliamentary constituencies *entirely* contained within the Flemish-speaking region together with those in the Brussels constituency voting for Flemish candidates in the election, and a corresponding French-speaking 'college' consisting of the French and German language regions and those in the Brussels constituency voting for French-speaking candidates.

Territorially speaking, therefore, the bill divided the country into three areas, Flanders, Wallonie and Brussels. Unlike other administrative divisions in Belgium however, which usually coincide with the Constitutionally enshrined linguistic regions, the boundaries of the three European electoral areas were to be based upon existing parliamentary constituencies which, in north west Brabant at least, take no account of the language 'frontier'. The bill introduced new terms for these areas as well, they were to be known as *circonscriptions électorales* in French and *kieskringen* in Flemish. In the Brussels electoral area special 'double' ballot papers were to be issued containing the Flemish lists on one half *and* the French-speaking lists on the other. Voters in this area could then vote on whichever half, and therefore in whichever 'college' they wished. Elsewhere, of course, only the lists of the appropriate language group would appear.

Candidates had to be Belgian nationals and at least twenty-one years of age. They had themselves to be members of the 'college' for which they wished to stand and needed to be nominated *either* by 10 parliamentarians, *or* by 5,000 electors. In the latter case, the 5,000 electors had to be distributed 1,000 to each of the five provinces involved and in all cases proposers had themselves to be members of the appropriate 'college'.

The bill provided for the establishment of two new tiers of election authority to be superimposed upon the existing hierarchy of 'local electoral bureau', 'cantonal bureau' and 'constituency bureau'. In the capital of each Province, a 'Provincial Bureau' was to be set up charged with the task of printing ballot papers and with drawing up election returns at the provincial level. In the cities of Mechelen and Namur respectively, the Flemish and French-speaking 'colleges' were each to have their 'college bureau' whose task would be to compile the final figures for the entire college, to divide the seats between the lists and to designate the elected candidates.

Other details of the election procedure were based upon the existing Electoral Code governing national elections in Belgium. The polling stations would be open from 8 a.m. to 1 p.m. on a Sunday. The vote would be compulsory and electors could cast their votes either for a list or for an individual candidate. The bill continued the provision for the simultaneous election of 'substitutes' (*suppléants/opvolgers*) to fill any casual vacancies which might occur between elections.

Insofar as the vexed question of the 'dual-mandate' was concerned (which has been the subject of as much debate in Belgium as in the other Member States and has covered much the same ground), the bill came down on the side of compatibility between the membership of the Belgian and European Parliaments but only for the first five year period. The Government stated that it was, in principle, opposed to the dual-mandate but had decided it should be retained temporarily in order that the links between the two Parliaments should not be broken-off too suddenly.

Reactions and passage: legislative over-indulgence, constipation and purgative

The bill received considerable press publicity, meeting with less than unanimous approval. Many Flemings objected to the fact that the area in which voters were to be given a choice of electoral college would extend to the whole of the Brussels Parliamentary Constituency (and hence to the uni-lingual Flemish District of Halle-Vilvoorde). Secondly, the 13:11 seats distribution was said to unfairly benefit the French-speaking community. The correct ratio, it was argued, would be 14:10.[16]

Predictably, protests were raised by French-speakers on behalf of the inhabitants of the *Voerstreek* (or in French, *Fouron*). This is a mixed-language area whose transfer from the French-speaking Province of Liège to the Flemish one of Limburg in 1962 has never been accepted by French-speaking militants who demanded that the inhabitants of the Voerstreek, too, be given the right to choose in which college they wished to vote.

However, it was the fate of the 65,000 German-speakers of Eastern Belgium which aroused most disquiet, particularly among moderates on all sides. The bill made no provision for separate representation for the German-language community at all, subsuming it into the Walloon constituency and, hence, into the French-speaking college. Many people felt this to be manifestly unfair and morally unjustifiable in a multi-cultural state where the mutual acceptance and, as far as possible, equal treatment of the different cultures is seen as a *sine qua non*.[17]

It was against this background that the Implementation Bill, thirty-five Articles in length, was presented to the Chamber of Representatives over the signature of the Minister of the Interior, Hendrik Boel. As a Government Bill (*Projet de loi/Wetsontwerp*),[18] it was automatically referred to Committee and thereby began what was to prove a long and arduous passage through the Belgian legislative machine.

In the ordinary way, Belgian parliamentary procedure in respect of Government Bills is quite straightforward. A bill is presented to one of the two Houses and is immediately referred to the appropriate Com-mittee (or Committees) of that House. Following its consideration and possible amendment in Committee, the bill is then reported to a Plenary Session of the House where it is first subject to a general dis-cussion (*Discussion Generale/Algemene Bespreking*). There then follows a discussion of the individual Articles of the bill at which stage additional amendments may be introduced. Finally, the House votes upon each article (and any amendments thereto) in turn and then upon the Bill as a whole. If passed, it is then transmitted to the other House where the same stages are repeated before the bill is ultimately sent to the King for Royal Sanction and Promulgation as a Law.

However, the 'Bill relating to European Elections' as it was then known,[19] was not, in the event, to follow this normally fairly uncom-plicated procedure, for a number of reasons, some directly connected with the bill itself and some resulting from the general domestic politi-cal situation in Belgium during 1977 and 1978.

Initially, following its submission to the Chamber on 2 December 1977 and in accordance with normal procedure, the bill was auto-matically referred to Committee. In this case, following the precedent established for the ratification bill before it, this was in fact *three* Committees (Interior Affairs; Foreign Affairs and Development Co-operation; and European Affairs), sitting in joint session. However, unlike the ratification bill, in this case only members of the Interior Affairs Committee had the right to vote. The chairman of the latter, Mr Beauthier (PSC, Brussels) presided over the joint Committees and Mr Van Lent (BSP, St Niklaas) was appointed as Rapporteur.

Even before the Committees met for the first time on 7 December 1977, however, it was already becoming clear that they were in for a long haul. By that date, some twenty-four amendments to the bill had already been submitted and there were to be many more over the ensuing seven months.[20] By the time Mr van Lent was able to make his first Report to the Chamber on 10 July 1978, he estimated the total number of amendments then received at over eighty.[21]

The general discussion occupied the remainder of the 10 July Sitting and the discussion and vote on the individual Articles (including a large number of amendments thereto) was set for Thursday, 20 July. However, in the event and in spite of virtually the whole of that day's business being devoted to the European Elections Bill, the Chamber had still not been able to move to votes on the various Articles and amendments by the time it rose at 8.00 p.m. (It is normal Parliamentary practice in Belgium as elsewhere for *all* votes to take place at a pre-arranged time following the entire debate instead of as and when each Article and amendment is discussed.) What was presumably still expected to be the final vote, therefore, had to be put back again, this time until the following Tuesday, 25 July, 1978. On that occasion, however, there was something of a surprise; Mr Karel Blanckaert (CVP, Antwerp) the (Flemish) Co-President of the Christian-Social Group in the Chamber asked leave to make a statement before the voting began.[22] He said that, in his view it had become apparent in the course of the previous week's discussion that the text of the bill as it stood could still be the object of 'textual improvements of a technical nature'. Accordingly, he proposed that the bill be sent back to the committee for further consideration.

He was immediately followed at the rostrum by his French-speaking counterpart, Mr Desmarets (PSC, Brussels) who acquiesced in his colleague's proposal while at the same time warning Members that the PSC could not accept that the move should permit the Egmont (and the associated Stuyvenberg) agreements to be called into question, and particularly not the proposed electoral arrangements for the Brussels area.

Following short statements by spokesmen for each of the other Groups in the Chamber all supporting Mr Blanckaert's proposal (although as Mr Clerfayt, the FDF spokesman pointed out, not all for the same reasons), the President of the Chamber declared that the bill be returned to the joint Committees for one further marathon meeting which took place on 31 October following the summer recess. In the course of this meeting, Mr Boel, the Minister, moved an amendment on behalf of the Government to add a new thirty-sixth clause limiting the bill's application to the first European election only. No other changes were accepted by the Committees and the bill returned to Plenary Session on Friday, 3 November, 1978.

In the meantime, however, the political crisis of October 1978 had taken place and with it the fall of the Government and Mr Tindemans' departure from office. A 'new' Government under the premiership of Paul Vanden Boeynants but with otherwise precisely the same composition as its predecessor took office pledged to deal with urgent legislative business and then go to the country to seek powers to amend the Constitution. Among the items of 'urgent legislative business' was the European Elections Bill.

Presumably because, in this new situation, the Government's attention was now concentrated upon the bill in a way that it had not been before, events now began to move very rapidly indeed. The bill was debated for the last time in the Chamber of Representatives on 3 November and the voting took place the same day. The bill was approved with Mr Verroken voting against and the Opposition abstaining and was immediately transmitted to the Senate where it was dealt with almost as expeditiously as had been the ratification bill in February.

Following consideration by the Senate's Interior Affairs Committee (which made no changes to the text), the bill was considered in plenary session of the Upper House on 14 November 1978 during which one last attempt was made by Senator Evers to insert a clause providing for guaranteed representation for German-speaking Belgians. The attempt failed and the bill was passed by 127 votes to 7 abstentions later the same day. It received the Royal Assent a mere two days later, and became law following its publication as the Law of 16 November, 1978, in the *Moniteur Belge/Belgisch Staatsblad* of 23 December.[23]

Issues: the glory and impotence of the backbencher

As has already been pointed out, the bill had been the subject of a very large number of amendments, some 151 in the Chamber and 9 in the Senate, although not all of them were moved.

These amendments were concerned with a wide variety of issues and varied from the huge 'packages' submitted by the PRLW Leader, André Damseaux whose vast Verviers Constituency includes the whole of the German-language Region (and many of whose amendments were designed to safeguard the interests of German-speaking Belgians) to one of Mr Galle's (BSP, Aalst) designed merely to correct the linguistic style of the Flemish text of the bill without thereby effecting any change in its meaning.

Mr Galle also sought, successfully, to change the words 'European Assembly' wherever they appeared in the bill to 'European Parliament' on what were essentially 'public relations' grounds; Mr Dejardin (PSB, Liège) failed in his attempt to extend voting rights to other EC Member States' nationals resident in Belgium (of whom there are estimated to be some 550,000); Mr De Croo, the Flemish Chairman of the Liberal Group in the Chamber tried but failed to have serving Government Ministers disqualified as *candidates* (they are of course, under the terms of the European Act, disqualified from *sitting* as MEPs) although this particular attempt may have had a more 'political' motive since, if carried, it would have prevented Mr Tindemans from heading the European Peoples' Party List in Belgium as was widely believed to be his intention, at least for as long as he were to remain Prime Minister. Nor were Messrs van Cauwenberghe (PSB, Charleoi) and Dejardin any more successful in their attempt to have the dual mandate prohibited. On the other hand, the two Communist Members of the Chamber, Mr van Geyt (Brussels) and Mr Levaux (Liège) *were* successful in persuading the Committees to accept an amendment reducing to five (from ten) the number of Belgian Parliamentarians' signatures necessary to nominate candidates for the European Parliament. This change was of particular importance from the point of view of the Belgian Communist Party which at that time had only three Parliamentarians of its own (one Senator and two Representatives).

The Government, too, submitted a number of relatively minor amendments to the bill during its first Committee stage. The most important of these was one removing references to Article 147 bis of the Belgian Electoral Code which provides for proxy voting for certain categories of persons in national elections. The effect of this, therefore, was to deny proxy voting facilities altogether insofar as European Elections were concerned. No significant opposition to this move was raised in the Committees, although it may be assumed from the fact the Government submitted two *alternative* amendments[24] to the proxy voting provision (to be moved if its primary amendment was not accepted), that it had anticipated parliamentary opposition to an outright ban. In the event, however, there was no such opposition and this seems to have been due to the almost universal recognition that proxy voting (which is new in Belgium, having only been introduced in 1975) had been the subject of some abuse in the previous legislative elections in 1977 and was better not extended to the European Election.

However, not only the largest number of amendments, but also the most important and controversial, were those relating to Articles 4 and 5 of the bill. These were the Articles which established the 'three-constituency/two-college' electoral system and which, consequently formed its very heart. Some thirty-two amendments to these Articles were submitted to the joint Committees between December 1977 and June 1978 which devoted eight of their thirteen meetings to them. Over half — thirty-five pages out of a total of seventy-five — of Mr van Lent's Report[25] was concerned with these two Articles alone and their associated amendments.

Several distinct and highly controversial issues were contained within the various amendments to Articles 4 and 5. Generally speaking, however, they fell into two types; those concerned with the principle of linguistic 'colleges' and the implications of this principle on the one hand, and those relating to the status and extent of the special arrangements for the Brussels area on the other.

Basically, the first group included amendments designed to create a third German linguistic college with its own representation, to extend the special 'double ballot' concession to the Voerstreek, and to provide for some form of national *apparentement/apparentering* as in Belgian elections. This is a device whereby surplus votes cast for a list in one area and which might otherwise be wasted, can be added to those of an associated list in another thereby improving the proportionality of the overall result. This particular change was particularly desired by the Liberals and the Communists who would probably have had most to gain from it. Also under this first heading must come the long series of wrecking amendments submitted by Mr Jan Verroken (CVP, Oudenaarde).

Mr Verroken is a senior backbencher in the Flemish wing of the Christian Social Party and has a well-deserved reputation as a rebel within its Parliamentary Group in the Chamber. He is also something of a militant on language-related issues and appears to have been particularly incensed by what he saw as the Egmont Pact's unwarranted concessions to French-speakers' demands particularly in the Brussels' periphery. It was Jan Verroken's single-handed opposition to the European Elections Bill which, more than any other factor, delayed its passage for so long.

Of the 151 amendments submitted at the various stages of the bill's passage through the Chamber, no less than fifty-two were submitted by Mr Verroken while of the many thousands of words spoken in the various plenary debates, nearly half were his. In short, it was a massive — and impressive — filibuster, illustrating vividly how an experienced and determined backbench Member can, given the right circumstances, severely delay legislation in spite of a large and disciplined Government majority.

There were very many other amendments of varying importance submitted in respect of Articles 4 and 5, notably by Mr André Damseaux, the Leader of the Walloon Liberals. Mr Damseaux was particularly exercised about two issues: the right of his German-speaking constituents to have separate representation of their own and the right of the inhabitants of the Voerstreek to have the same facility as the people of Brussels to vote in either the Flemish or the French-speaking college as they might individually wish.

Insofar as the remainder of the bill was concerned, the innovation of a 'language declaration' to be made by candidates as a condition of eligibility was opposed by Mr De Croo (PVV, Oudenaarde) on grounds of principle and by his fellow MP from the same constituency,

Mr Verroken, on grounds of unenforceability. There were also several amendments of a drafting/technical nature many of which were accepted by the Minister without discussion. Insofar as the Brussels problem was concerned, controversy centred around two issues; firstly, the extent of the area in which French-speaking and Flemish Lists would appear on the same ballot papers (predictably, Flemish opinion generally favoured its restriction to the nineteen Boroughs) and its inclusion with, or separation from, the remainder of the French-speaking college. Fears were expressed (not least by Mr Verroken!) that unless Brussels was separated from Wallonie, the latter Region might find itself represented in the European Parliament exclusively by candidates from the capital who might be expected to garner more preferential votes than candidates from the rest of the Walloon Region proper whose support would not be concentrated in one place. Finally, Mr Clerfayt of the FDF put forward an amendment designed to ensure state finance for those political parties which, like the FDF, would not be in receipt of European Parliamentary funds through their membership of Party Federations at the European level. He was unsuccessful in this attempt. The foregoing does not, of course, represent more than the briefest sketch of the numbers and variety of amendments submitted to the Implementation Bill. There were many others, but lack of space precludes their being examined in the present chapter.

Conclusion: sovereign parliament or rubber stamp?

Writing on the United Kingdom Parliament, Gordon Smith points out that:

> The efforts of, say, the Opposition in Britain are geared to fighting controversial government legislation step-by-step, clause-by-clause, on the floor of the Commons and in committee, even though the final product may not look much different from what the government had originally intended. The apparent 'failure' to secure this control in its direct sense does not preclude the Opposition from securing indirect successes.[26]

Most observers of the Belgian Parliamentary scene, too, would readily recognise parallels between what Smith describes at Westminster and the situation which unfolds almost every day of the Parliamentary session at the Palace of the Nation in Brussels. Even a cursory glance at the *Annales parlementaires/Parlementaire Handelingen*, Belgium's Hansard, will show many instances of the official Opposition vainly trying to obstruct Government business, amend its bills and generally to present alternative policies and personnel to the public, at least in the Plenary Sessions of the Chamber. (The Senate, like Upper Houses the world over, tends to be rather more decorous in its behaviour.) Certainly this view of the Belgian Parliament as an executive-dominated, gladiatorial battleground is one that has become almost traditional among its scholars. Jules Gérard-Libois, for example, comments that:

> More and more, Parliament gives the impression of being simply a rubber stamp for decisions taken elsewhere, by those who have the ability to manipulate the Parliamentarians and take their place.[27]

Against this traditional view, however, it must be admitted that Dewachter et al have recently shown that this is not the whole picture and that Opposition parties do, in fact, often realise quite significant policy goals in legislative terms.[28]

While this, of course, is not the place to go into this question in any depth, it might nevertheless be interesting to consider what light, if any, the passage of the European Elections Bill throws upon it. Consequently, an attempt has been made below to classify the various amendments to the bill which were submitted for Committee consideration, both by degree of importance and by origin. Before considering the findings, however, it is necessary to make a couple of methodological points.

Anyone who has ever tried systematically to count legislative amendments knows that it is never as simple as it might appear at first sight. There is usually a wide variety of ways in which an amendment can be drafted to achieve the same or similar effect. To take a rather simple example, one man may write a single amendment to change a certain word or phrase *whenever* it occurs throughout the bill which is the subject of the amendment, while another may achieve exactly the same object by putting down a whole series of identical amendments, one for *each occurrence* in the original text of the word or words it is desired to change. Then again, certain amendments are the logical consequences of others; are they to be considered as distinct amendments in their own right or as integral parts of those others that they are the consequence of? The way(s) in which such questions are answered can often significantly alter the findings of even the simplest quantification of this kind.

In the case of the European Elections Bill, I have employed the rule of counting the *Articles of the original bill* which each amendment or set of amendments seeks to alter. This method has the merit that it is (a) relatively simple, (b) relatively rigorous and (c) tends to produce answers which are intuitively plausible. Insofar as the classification of the various amendments by degree of importance is concerned, I have taken my cue from Herman's study of amendments to Government legislation in the British Parliament.

Although it is very difficult to make exacting distinctions between amendments, it is possible to place them into four somewhat crude but analytically useful categories according to the extent of departure, or change, they intended to make from the original text of a bill.[29]

Herman distinguishes between major, important, minor and technical amendments which are, respectively, those intended to make fundamental changes in or to negate a bill; those which seek to make substantial changes within the general principles of the bill; those which would change only relatively unimportant details of a bill; and, finally, those which are merely concerned with correcting errors, clarifying the text and so forth.

In the present case, where no-one was opposed to the principle of the Belgian direct elections bill, Herman's major amendments category is of little value and can be subsumed into his important amendments classification. Apart from this, I have chosen to stay with his method. The results of the classification are shown in table 3.2.

Table 3.2
Numbers of amendments to Direct Elections Bill submitted by
Members of Chamber classified by origin and degree of importance

Origin of amendments	Important	Minor	Technical	Total
Government	–	9	1	10
Government MPs	46*	30*	6*	82*
Opposition MPs	21†	19†	19†	59†
Totals	67	58	26	151

*including 37 Important, 13 Minor and 2 Technical amendments submitted by Mr Verroken.
†including 10 Important, 11 Minor and 16 Technical amendments submitted by Mr Damseaux.

As was only to be expected, the Government submitted only a very few amendments, none of which could by any strength of the imagination be classified as important in Herman's terms. In addition, eleven[30] Government backbenchers submitted amendments to the bill as did five[31] Members of the Opposition. However, it is important to note that more than half of the total number of amendments submitted came from only two Members of the Chamber, Messrs Jan Verroken and André Damseaux, the Leader of the Walloon Liberals.

However, of the total of 151 amendments submitted by Members of the Chamber, only a very few were eventually successful. In fact, nearly half — sixty-two to be precise — were never moved at all while a further eight were withdrawn after being moved. In the vast majority of cases this was either because they were associated with (or were dependent upon) earlier amendments which had already been lost, or in the case of minor and technical amendments mostly, following assurances given by the Minister. Of those amendments which *were* moved, sixty-three were rejected either in committee or in plenary session. A mere eighteen were accepted, none of them in the important category and only one of these (Mr Galle's changing 'Assembly' to 'Parliament' mentioned above) was opposed by the Government.

Table 3.3 shows the eighteen successful amendments classified as before by origin and importance and also shows them as percentages of amendments actually *moved*.

Table 3.3
Successful Amendments classified by origin and importance
(with percentages of those moved in brackets)

Origin of amendments	Important	Minor	Technical	Total
Government	—	6 (100%)	1 (100%)	7 (100%)
Government MPs	0 (0%)	6 (42%)	1 (33%)	7 (19%)
Opposition MPs	0 (0%)	3 (33%)	1 (9%)	4 (12%)
Totals	0 (0%)	15 (20%)	3 (20%)	18 (23%)

It will be immediately seen from this table that the Government achieved a 100 per cent 'success rate' in that all seven amendments moved by it were accepted by the Chamber for incorporation into the final text of the bill. Backbench Members had considerably less success by this criterion, however, although Members of the Majority did do rather better than their Opposition colleagues.

The ratio of successful amendments originated by the Government to those emanating from backbench MPs, however, is at variance with what previous research leads us to expect. Meeusen, for example, found that in the period 1961 to 1965, 67 per cent of successful amendments introduced in the Chamber came from the Government and only 33 per cent from MPs.[32] By contrast, of the eighteen successful amendments to the European Elections Bill, only 39 per cent were put down by the Government and 61 per cent came from MPs on the backbenches.

However, in view of the fact that the Government raised (half-hearted) objections to only one successful backbench amendment — and that of no substantive importance — no inference can be drawn from this contrast. At first sight, therefore, and taking the above into consideration, the picture presented by table 3.2 does not seem an unlikely one even allowing for the fact that the figures relate to only one bill, and an untypical one at that. The general impression certainly, is one of governmental dominance of the legislative process and this is in accord with the widespread view that the Belgian Parliament — like so many others — no longer possesses any real rule-making power even if, as is perhaps somewhat doubtful, it ever did.

On the other hand, it must not be forgotten that the very long delay which the Chamber was able to impose upon the bill, especially in Committee, was clearly an example of the exercise of at least a modicum of Parliamentary power. (To say this, though, is not to contradict Gérard-Libois' point since a generalisation of that kind is not really susceptible to disproof on the basis of evidence from a single rather exceptional bill.)

On balance, therefore, insofar as the bill relating to European elections was concerned, it seems very clear that Parliament (or at any rate the Chamber of Representatives) behaved very much according to the Government versus Opposition model of Belgian political folklore. On practically every issue in Committee as far as one can tell[33] voting was on Government vs. Opposition lines (except where Mr Verroken was acting as a one man Opposition on his own!) and this was certainly the case in the Plenary Sessions. The bill, of course, was a highly contentious one in its details, if not in its broad principles, and the fact that it had already had to be negotiated *inside* the Governmental Coalition before even being published meant that there could be no possibility of the Government's making any but the most minor concessions to the official Opposition. The latter's motive in putting down so many amendments, particularly in the important category, therefore, can be presumed to have had more to do with its role *qua* Opposition than to the intrinsic merit of its proposed alternatives.

And this is what one would expect. Herman van Impe notes,

> Moreover, the Opposition generally puts down more amendments than the Majority. The chances of seeing such amendments adopted are so very minimal that parliamentarians from minority groups come to the point of introducing a large number of amendments which they would not want adopted, and which they would even reject, were they in Government.[34]

However, this does not seem to have been true of the two Communist Members, Messrs Levaux and van Geyt who constituted the only other political group in the Chamber not forming part of the Majority. This is presumably because the Belgian Communist Party is not seen as a potential coalition partner by any other group and consequently is not seen as playing the same role as a traditional party having a governmental 'vocation' but temporarily out of office. Indeed, it may be no coincidence that it was the Communists who achieved practically the only significant concession to their own partisan interest (the reduction of the number of MPs needed to nominate Eurocandidates from ten to five). Unlike the Liberals, the Communists may have been seen as not engaging in 'opposition for Opposition's sake' and may therefore have reaped the benefit of their more sincere attitude towards the various amendments proposed by them.

Some further mention should also be made of the part played by Mr Verroken in the passage of the Belgian direct elections bill. There is no doubt whatever that his was the decisive influence in causing the very long delay which the bill suffered in Committee. The rapporteur, Mr van Lent, was either amazingly tactful or heavily sarcastic on this point when introducing his first Report to the Chamber on 10 July:

> It was in respect of Article 4 more than any other that the bill was strongly criticised by a number of Members. A surfeit of amendments that we may describe as of . . . [linguistic] . . . community origin were introduced and, on occasion, passionately defended. Here I would like above all to thank our colleague Verroken who, with considerable conviction, tried to give the bill an entirely different foundation and content.[35]

When the bill did eventually emerge from the joint Committees for the plenary discussion of the Articles, again it was Jan Verroken who stole the limelight by delaying its passage. Indeed, the greater part of the debate was reduced to nothing more than a dialogue between Mr Verroken and Mr Boel who, as Interior Minister, had the thankless task of defending the bill's provisions literally line-by-line in the face of the former's relentless onslaught. In short, the experience of this one bill shows graphically the extent to which the Belgian parliamentary system can still on occasion provide opportunities for its Members to engage in filibusters of which a United States Senator might well be proud! However, the fact that Mr Verroken has a safe seat in his Oudenaarde Constituency (including one of the highest personal votes in Belgium) and appears to have long ago given up hope of front-bench office should not be overlooked. Another less colourful and more ambitious personality would certainly be much more vulnerable to party discipline than is Jan Verroken.

In the last analysis, therefore, the accepted view of an executive-dominated legislative process is not invalidated in any significant way by the experience of the direct elections bill. As we have seen, the bill was eventually enacted in almost exactly the same form as that in which it was presented to Parliament in spite of strong opposition (and Opposition) to some of its most fundamental provisions. Even when the bill appeared to be bogged down by the time-wasting tactics of Verroken and others, it could be and was forced through very quickly once the Government had made up its mind that this should happen. On the evidence of this legislation at least, the Belgian Parliament did in the end act as the 'rubber stamp' described by Gérard-Libois and others in spite of loud but ritual noises to the contrary.[36]

Notes

1   Throughout this chapter I have tried, as far as possible, to employ English language equivalents in translation of Belgian political and Parliamentary terminology. Generally, I give the original terms in both Belgian languages in the (arbitrary) order French/Flemish immediately following their first use in the text.

I have elected to use the word 'Flemish' in place of the confusing 'Dutch' which in recent years has become more fashionable as an English translation of the official term 'Nederlands'. Although this must remain largely a matter for individual preference, for a number of reasons I consider it the better solution.

Place names are given in the form which is locally official except where there is a recognised English form.

References to Belgian Parliamentary Papers etc. are (again arbitrarily) in the French language form except for dates which are in English.

2   See Appendix, chapter 2.

3   Doc. Ch.205 (1977-1978) no.1.

4   Doc. Ch.454 (1968-1969 no.1; Doc. Ch.680 (1969-1970) no.1; Doc. Ch.24 (1971-1972) no.1 and Doc. Ch.15 (S.E. 1974) no.1.

5   Doc. Ch.205 (1977-1978) no.1.

6   'The Decision of the Council of the European Communities of 20 September 1976 and the provisions annexed thereto . . . shall enter into full effect' (my translation).

7   Law of 28 March 1978, *Moniteur Belge*, 30 September, 1978.

8   Although modifications to its detailed working are of course suggested from time to time.

9   *Agence Europe*, no.2547, Brussels, 26 October, 1977.

10 J. Meynaud et al, *La décision politique en Belgique*, (A. Colin, Paris, 1964).

11 F. Coppieters, *The Community Problems in Belgium*, (INBEL, Brussels, 1971).

12 For full text of Egmont Pact see Annex I to Governmental Declaration of 7 June 1977, Ann. Parl. Ch. (S.E.1977) p.29, 7 June, 1977.

13 Ann. Parl. Ch. (S.E. 1977) p.47, 7 June, 1977 (my translation).

14 Doc. Ch.195 (1977-1978) no.1.

15 The reduction of the voting age was also in anticipation of a similar reduction for national elections. This latter change however, although established Government policy, requires a Constitutional Amendment which at the time of writing (February 1979) has still to be enacted.

16 See, for example, *De Standaard* of 17/18 December 1977.

17 Although there is no formal provision for German speakers to be represented *as such* in the Belgian Parliament either.

18 A Private Member's Bill is known as *Proposition de Loi/Wetvoorstel* and follows a slightly different procedure. See V. Herman, *Parliaments of the World*, (Macmillan, London, 1976), esp. table 50.

19 The Committees renamed it 'Bill relating to European Parliament Elections'.

20 Doc. Ch.195 (1977-1978) nos.1 to 18 inclusive.

21 Doc. Ch.195 (1977-1978) no.19.
22 Ann. Parl. Ch. (S.O. 1977-1978) p.3164, 25 July, 1978.
23 Law of 16 November, 1978 (*Moniteur Belge*, 23 December, 1978).
24 Doc. Ch.195 (1977-1978) no.18.
25 Doc. Ch.195 (1977-1978) no.19.
26 G. Smith, *Politics in Western Europe*, (Heinemann, London, 1972) p.189.
27 J. Gérard-Libois, 'The Belgian Parliament within the Political System' in *Report on Symposium on European Integration and the Future of Parliaments in Europe*, (European Parliament, Luxembourg, 1975).
28 W. Dewachter, E. Lismont and G. Tegenbos, 'The Effect of the Opposition Parties on the Legislative Output in a Multi-Party System', *European Journal of Political Research*, vol.5, 1977, pp 245-65.
29 V. Herman, 'Backbench and Opposition Amendments to Government Legislation' in D. Leonard and V. Herman, *The Backbencher and Parliament*, (Macmillan, London, 1972), pp 141-55.
30 That is Messrs. Bertrand, De Vries, Verroken and van den Brande of the PSC/CVP; Messrs. Dejardin, Dupon, Moock and van Cauwenbergh of the PSB/BSP; Messrs. Valkeniers and Belmans of the Volksunie and Mr Clerfayt of the FDF.
31 That is, Messrs. Bertouille, Damseaux and De Croo of the Liberals and the two Communist Members, Messrs. Levaux and van Geyt.
32 Cited by Dewachter et al, op.cit.
33 Voting figures in Committees are not published.
34 H. van Impe, *Le Régime Parlementaire en Belgique*, (E. Bruylant, Brussels, 1968), p.206 (my translation).
35 Ann. Parl. Ch. (S.O. 1977-1978) p.2568, 10 July, 1978 (my translation).
36 In May 1979, after this chapter had been written and during the European election campaign, the Belgian Parliament was called upon to pass a third bill modifying certain provisions of the implementation Law. This third bill was adopted by the Senate on 17 May 1979 and by the Chamber six days later. It came into force on publication in the *Moniteur Belge/Belgisch Staatsblad* on 2 June just eight days before the election. Consisting of two Articles, the new Act made certain changes in the Electoral Code in order to allow the count to be delayed until the time agreed by the nine Governments. Presumably, this matter was overlooked at the time of the passing of the principal Act.

The Belgian Parliament: some readings

F. Debuyst, *La fonction parlementaire en belgique: mécanismes d'accès et images* (Crisp, Bruxelles, 1967). A comprehensive work on the Belgian parliamentary process.

J. Gérard-Libois, 'The Belgian Parliament within the political system', in *Report on Symposium on European Integration and the Future of Parliaments in Europe*, (European Parliament, Luxembourg, 1975).

H. van Impe, *Het Belgische Parlement* (also in French as *Le Parlement Belge*) (Heule, Brussels, 1968) is a good short introduction, albeit somewhat formal and legalistic.

H. van Impe, *Le Régime Parlementaire en Belgique* (E. Bruylant, Brussels, 1968) is an excellent and comprehensive book containing a wealth of detail, particularly on procedure, but not always very analytical.

V. Lorwin, 'Belgium: Religion, Class and Language in National Politics' in R. Dahl, *Political Oppositions in Western Democracies* (Yale University Press, New Haven, 1966) pp 147-87. A brief description and analysis of the contemporary political scene; remains quite the best so far written in English.

T. Luyckx, *Politieke Geschiedenis van België van 1789 tot heden*, (Elsevier, 3rd edition, Brussels/Amsterdam, 1973) is a monumental work cataloguing virtually every significant political event in modern Belgian history: an indispensable work of reference.

X. Morbille and V. Lorwin, 'Belgium' in S. Henig, ed., *Political Parties in the European Community*, George Allen and Unwin, London, 1979).

R. Senelle, *Political and Economic Structures of Belgium*, (Ministry of Foreign Affairs, External Trade and Co-operation in Development, Brussels, 1966) is a useful factual introduction to Belgian public life in general.

G. Weil, *The Benelux Nations*, (Holt, Rinehart and Winston, New York, 1970) contains a useful chapter on the position of Parliament within the Belgian political system.

4   Denmark: The Functionalists

Tove Lise Schou

Introduction

In this chapter, the legislative process on direct elections will be described, in order to evaluate the influence of various factors, both internal and external to the Danish Parliament (the Folketing), on the direct elections legislation. The principal actors on whom the analysis will focus are the political parties represented in the Folketing and the government — in particular the two Social Democratic minority Governments of Prime Minister Anker Jørgensen, 1975-77 and 1977-78, that were responsible for steering the direct elections legislation through parliament.

The main questions that we will attempt to answer are: what pattern of activities emerged in the Folketing in the direct elections legislative process? How does this compare with the 'normal' legislative pattern? How did the political environment condition the behaviour of parliamentary actors?

In order to answer these questions, it will be necessary to consider the structure of the legislative institution and the way in which it normally processes legislation; the structure of partisan cleavages with particular reference to recent development and the European Community issue; the relevant aspects of the structure of Danish society; and the international roles of Denmark within the several overlapping international economic and political systems of the Atlantic nations, the Nordic countries and the European Community. It will also be necessary to examine the evolution of Danish attitudes toward the direct elections issue, as expressed in parliamentary debates in the decade prior to the referendum, in relation to party conceptions of integration and the role of EC institutions; the legislative strategy of the Government; the relationship between this legislative proposal and the competing body of legislation on the agenda of the Folketing at the same time; and the interplay between the Folketing and other elements in the political system, particularly interest groups and public opinion.

The method used for the study of the government and of the political parties in relation to the direct elections legislation is 'structure conditioned behavioural analysis'. In this sociological-historical method, a qualitative content analysis of the parliamentary declarations of government and party spokesmen is used to determine the roles of these actors,[1] and to analyse the influence of sociological and other environmental factors in shaping the evolution of their parliamentary behaviour over time.

The 'normal' legislative process

The Danish Parliament is unicameral. The Folketing has 179 MPs: four North Atlantic MPs (two each from the Faroes and Greenland), the remainder from the rest of the country. The electoral system is proportional representation with party lists. A party can only participate in an election if it is already represented in the Folketing, or if it has collected the signatures of not less than 1/175 of the votes cast at the last election.[2]

The main parties represented in the Folketing between 1953 and 1973 were the Conservatives, the Agrarian Liberals, the Radical Liberals and the Social Democrats. These parties are in broad agreement on Denmark's foreign policy. In 1958, a new party opposed to the official foreign policy was formed, the Socialist People's Party. In the 1971-73 governmental period all of the seats in the Folketing were held by these five parties.

The 1973 election dramatically changed this pattern. The five established parties won only 64 per cent of the votes, a decrease of 29 per cent from their combined vote in 1971. Two new parties on the right and centre, the Progressive Party and the Centre Democratic Party together collected 24 per cent of the votes, and four minor parties, the Christian People's Party, the Justice Party, the Communist Party and the Left Socialist Party together won a further 12 per cent.

The Progressive Party bases its appeal on opposition to increasing tax burdens, growth of bureaucracy, and alleged misuse of social welfare money. The Centre Democratic Party was formed when a 'right-wing' member of the Social Democrats left that party as a protest against the 'leftist' policies of both the Social Democrats and the Socialist People's Party, particularly in the area of property taxes on house ownership.[3] The Communist Party and the single-tax free-trade Justice Party existed before the 1973 election. By contrast the small Christian People's Party was new and, as its name indicates, it stands for traditional Christian values in society.

Thus eleven parties were represented in the Folketing[4] when a single bill was passed on 2 December, 1977, which dealt with the issues of the principle of holding direct elections to the European Parliament and of the features of the electoral law to be used (see table 4.1).

Studies of parliamentary voting in Denmark in the 20 years preceding the 1973 election have revealed that the left-right dimension was the only salient voting dimension.[6] These studies also showed that this left-right model was used in a wide variety of specific issue-areas, especially foreign affairs and defence, throughout this period.[7] The positions of the parties toward the EC before the 1972 referendum could also be placed along the left-right dimension with the Agrarian Liberals as the most pro-EC party, followed by the Conservatives, Social Democrats and the Radical Liberals — also pro-EC — whilst minorities within the Social Democrats, the Radical Liberals, and the Socialist People's Party opposed the EC. That the Agrarian Liberal Party was more pro-EC than the Conservative Party shows, however, that dimensions other than the left-right ones were important. At the time of the referendum on joining the EC there was a high level of congruence between mass and elite attitudes in terms of the analysis presented above.

The election in 1973 showed a massive change in voting behaviour, and studies of the voters' perceptions of the party system have revealed a two-dimensional party cleavage structure. While the left-right dimension was still the most important dimension, a second dimension — a protest against the established parties — was completely new.[8] Studies of voting behaviour in Parliament in the first half of 1974 revealed two dimensions: the left-right dimension, and a second dimension representing a 'consensus and co-operation' view of politics. Thus there seemed to be a fundamental difference between how the elites and the voters viewed the party cleavage structure and protest against the established parties seemed to be stronger at the mass level. Studies of the voters' attitudes and behaviour in the 1977 election have shown that 'protest against the establishment' attitudes were still important especially for voters of the Progressive Party.[9]

A left-right ordering of the parties in the 1977 Folketing is shown in table 4.1. While this dimension remained the most important, other dimensions seemed also to be important at the parliamentary level, especially 'the protest against the establishment' dimension. The question that arises is whether the fragmentation of the party system, and its ramifications in the Folketing, have narrowed the traditional 'broad-based agreement' on Danish foreign policy. A study of voting behaviour on foreign policy in the Folketing has indicated that the inter-party agreement on foreign policy had not narrowed despite the proliferation of parties in the Folketing.[10] More specifically, this study showed that legislation concerning EC matters had a particularly broad support. It is therefore especially interesting to try to determine whether the direct elections issue confirmed this picture of 'foreign policy stability', in spite of the generally unstable situation in the

Folketing in other policy areas and contexts.

Table 4.1
Parties in the Folketing, February 1977

	Party	Abbreviation	Vote (%)*	Seats†
	Communist Party (Danmarks Kommunistiske parti)	CP	3.7	7
	Left Socialist Party (Venstresocialisterne)	LS	2.7	5
	Socialist People's Party (Socialistisk Folkeparti)	SP	3.9	7
G	Social Democratic Party (Socialdemokratiet)	SD	37.0	65
	Radical Liberal Party (Det Radikale Venstre)	RL	3.6	6
	Justice Party (Retsforbundet)	JP	3.3	6
	Centre Democratic Party (Centrum-Demokraterne)	CD	6.4	11
	Christian People's Party (Kristeligt Folkeparti)	CPP	3.4	6
	Agrarian Liberal Party (Venstre)	AL	12.0	**21**
	Conservative Party (Det Konservative Folkeparti)	C	8.5	15
	Progressive Party (Fremskridtspartiet)	PP	14.6	26
Total			100.0	175
Turnout			88.9%	

*Share of valid votes cast in the parliamentary election, February, 1977.
†Seats in the Folketing, February, 1977.

G = Government Party.

The adaption of the Folketing to environmental change

It may be assumed that the structural changes in the Folketing concerning the party system and the dimensions of ideology described above, can be partly explained by changes in the structure of economic interests in society, due to the process of economic growth. In particular, the primary and secondary sectors have declined, whereas the relative importance of the tertiary sector is increasing.

Another important trend is the change in the role of the state, both as regards its scope (as measured by the increasing share of gross domestic product used for public expenditure) as well as the character of its interventions in society. A consequence of this development has been a co-operation between the private and public sectors for the steering and planning of the economy. A corporatist decision-making system has been created through the direct participation of interest groups in the making of public policy.[11]

Structural adjustments in the Folketing have accompanied this expansion of the role of the state. The incorporation of the interest organisations of each sector in steering and planning mechanisms, and the specialisation of labour in the administrative structure, have led to sectoral specialisation in the Folketing; this is revealed by the composition of committees and by the speeches of MPs other than official party spokesmen in parliamentary debates. The assumption has been made that this kind of adjustment of the Folketing may in turn lead to sector autonomy and a relative weakening of political leadership.[12] The legislature comes under increased pressure as the number of laws passed increases, and as the content of bills becomes both more complex and broader in scope. In addition to the laws passed, the legislature must also deal with Private Members Bills, resolutions, interpellations, reviews and questions; MPs are also often appointed to serve on committees which prepare new legislation, and are also involved in the executive stage. Furthermore, the growing involvement of the legislature in foreign policy matters has meant that MPs have had to participate in meetings of a number of international organisations.[13]

One type of structural adjustment to these developments is a division of labour amongst MPs, so that issues are handled by those members who have specialised knowledge, experience or interest in various areas. Other types of adjustments concern time-saving, such as limitations on debating time, and increases in staff and other support resources. There has also been an increase in the use of permanent, specialised committees in the legislative process, which are now used more frequently than ad hoc committees.[14]

These structural adjustments have lead to the following characteristics of the 'normal' legislative process: in the 1973/74 Parliament (when the fragmentation of the party-system initially occurred) each bill was debated in plenary for 3.13 hours.[15] Of the bills in this period, 95.5 per cent were Government bills and only 4.5 per cent were Private Members' bills.[16] In 60 per cent of the parliamentary votes in this year there was conflict, compared to 19 per cent in the previous year, as a consequence of the fractionalisation of the party system. Most bills were referred to the permanent, specialised committees for consideration.

Membership of the EC led to the creation of a new type of committee — the Market Relations Committee (MRC) — as an instrument of parliamentary control over the Government's EC policy. The Danish Law of Accession to the EC stated that the Government must report to the Folketing on developments in the EC, and also give information to the MRC about proposals for decisions in the Council of Ministers that are immediately applicable in Denmark. The importance of this information provision became clear soon after accession, when the Government accepted an 'agenda motion' to extend the role of the MRC.[17] From then on the Government had to ensure in advance that the basis for negotiation in the Council of Ministers was not in conflict with a majority of the Folketing, as represented by the MRC. This control system was a pragmatic innovation, introduced under a minority government in an area full of conflict. It is also in accordance with the theory of parliamentarism as regards the relationship between Government and Parliament, although such theoretical views have not been found in a study of the Folketing.[18]

The Minister is politically obliged to follow the opinion of the MRC. Such a 'delegation' is in line with the traditions of the Folketing. Members of the MRC normally consult their groups and they are usually party leaders who can speak on behalf of their parties. By custom, the parties in any case accept commitments made by their representatives in committee. The mandate to the Minister is often general, but may in certain cases go into detail: conditions on the conduct of direct elections is an example of such a mandate.[19]

The MRC occasionally has joint meetings with the Foreign Affairs Committee. The latter has a semi-autonomous status like the MRC though it does not consider legislation. Another committee of the Folketing, the External Affairs Committee is also concerned with foreign policy: it may give the MRC an opinion, but the MRC alone retains the right to mandate Ministers.[20]

The MRC is frequently described as the most effective example of national parliamentary control in any Member State. However, anti-marketeers demand greater control and more advance information about the very complex package deals commonly used in EC policy-making. Pro-market parties seem to consider the present system satisfactory. Thus even though the MRC is a new type of committee, it is not so unique[21] that the whole area of EC policy can be considered as 'non-normal', and indeed the legislation of direct elections can be compared to the 'normal' legislative process.

The formal steps in the legislative process are as follows: a bill is introduced by the Government or an MP. At the first reading the Folketing discuss the central issues in the bill, and the parties make statements on their positions of principle. After that the bill normally is referred to a committee for scrutiny and the consideration of amendments. At the second reading both the principle and the details are debated, and amendments are introduced. The bill is then normally referred to the committee again, and the third reading follows the same pattern as the second; however, it is usually very short, as it is rare for any new elements to appear at this stage. The third reading is concluded by a vote on the bill as a whole.

Thus even if the Market Relations Committee is an innovation of the legislative system it is neither formally nor in practice sufficiently different from the traditions of the Folketing that the whole EC policy area can be considered as abnormal. We can therefore proceed to analyse the legislation of direct elections in terms of the normal legislative procedure employed by the Folketing and the Danish political system.

Political background

In order to describe and explain the positions of parties and groups in Denmark towards direct elections, it is necessary to see this issue in relation to their conceptions of integration and of the role of the EC institutions in the integration process, and in relation to the theoretical frames of reference ('theories of action') within which they formulated their EC policy in the period before the referendum on 2 October, 1972.

One of the most prominent features of the EC debate in Denmark in that period was the EC supporters' attempt to 'fractionalise' Denmark's external relations, and to treat each sector separately.[22] The EC supporters, especially the Social Democrats, maintained that the EC was an arrangement for economic co-operation, and that foreign policy co-operation was not a legitimate EC function. The Agrarian Liberals, the most 'European' of the Danish parties, expressed a positive attitude to political co-operation in the EC but reassured their more sceptical supporters that it was improbable that Europe would 'speak with one voice' in the foreseeable future.[23] The Agrarian Liberals thought 'that the only possibility of a small power securing its freedom and autonomy' was to 'lay its so-called sovereignty in a common pool — without thereby losing its national identity'.[24]

In the period from Denmark's first application for membership of the EC in 1961, until the referendum in 1972, a 'broad agreement' was established on foreign policy between the Social Democrats, the Agrarian Liberals, the Radical Liberals and the Conservatives. Apart from small anti-EC groups in the Social Democrat and Radical Liberal Parties, which publicly opposed the official EC policy of their parties during the debates in the Folketing in 1971, these four parties were all strongly in favour of Danish membership of the EC. Differences between them related to their conceptions of integration: ranging from the Social Democrats functionalist conception of pragmatic co-operation in economic matters and opposition to the idea of strong institutions; to the Agrarian Liberals federalism, which underlined the need for strong institutions in the EC and the importance of mobilising mass support for these institutions especially for the European Parliament. In the 1968-71 Parliament, the Social Democrats held 62 of the 179 seats in the Folketing, the Conservatives had 37, the Agrarian Liberals had 34 and the Radical Liberals 27. All of these parties had been in government: the Social Democrats formed three minority governments; and between 1968 and 1971, the three non-socialist parties formed a majority coalition government. In one respect, the anti-EC minority within the Social Democratic parliamentary group followed the party line on EC policy: they accepted the 'fractionalisation' of Denmark's relations with other international actors, thereby implying that it was possible to consider the relationship with other members of the EC as a purely economic one.

The other opponents of the EC in the Folketing — the minority within the Radical Liberal Party, and the Socialist People's Party — tried hard to persuade voters that the political aspects of EC membership were the most important. The Socialist People's Party was unanimous in its opposition to EC membership, and argued that the enlarged EC was planned as a supplement to NATO. It did not think it possible to consider the EC in any other way, nor did it share the opinion of pro-market groups that it would be possible for new members to bring about essential changes to the EC during policy negotiations. The Party considered it dangerous for Denmark to become a member of the EC since the country's economic autonomy and freedom of action in international politics would be jeopardised.

It also feared that an independent Danish fiscal policy would be virtually impossible in the EC and that it would be very difficult to control the development of social policy because of the influence of large multi-national companies.[25]

For the Agrarian Liberal Party as well as for the Socialist People's Party, there was a clear relation between Market policy and defence policy. While both based their conception of Denmark's European role explicitly on the fact that Denmark is a small power, each party adopted opposite positions towards EC membership, as a result of their different value systems and 'theories of action'. The small group of Radical Liberal EC opponents also saw a connection between Market and defence policy.[26] The small parties not represented in the Folketing before the referendum and the Folkebev ægelsen mod EF (People's Movement against the EC, an organisation cutting across party lines), stressed their fears of EC membership in the debate outside the Folketing.

The Social Democrat's EC supporters emphasised that the EC issue was a question of economic co-operation, and the party explicitly declared that it could not accept that parts of defence policy be transferred to the EC.[27] The Conservative Party, which is strongly Atlanticist in its orientation, also maintained that security problems belonged to NATO and not to the EC.[28] The EC supporters succeeded in ensuring that economic problems were the dominant feature of the debate in the period just before the referendum.

Following the publication of the Werner report on the EC economic and monetary union in 1970, the Social Democratic Party expressed doubts as to Denmark's autonomy, as an EC-member, in regard to the economic development of society.[29] Apart from the small anti-EC group formed in 1971, the Social Democrats in the Folketing overcame their doubts on EC membership, and the debate preceding the referendum centred around the EC as an instrument for economic growth and a weapon to fight recession and unemployment. The opposing parties and groups expressed their fears as to the consequences of EC membership for control over national economic development and they warned against optimistic expectations of the economic consequences of Danish membership.

In the referendum there was the highest turnout ever seen in Denmark: 90.1 per cent. For the whole nation, 63.3 per cent of those voting supported entry to the EC. But in Greenland there was an overwhelming rejection with 70.3 per cent of participants voting 'no'; and in the Greater Copenhagen area there was a slight 'no' majority. However in nearly all constituencies outside the Copenhagen area the ratio of 'yes' to 'no' votes ranged from 2:1 to 4:1.[30]

Studies of the Danish voters' attitudes and behaviour have shown that support for the EC was overwhelming amongst workers in agriculture and fisheries, and those in secondary and tertiary occupations in rural municipalities tended to follow suit. A majority of the voters believed that EC membership would be an advantage for industry. Most of the voters expected that EC membership would lead to higher income for farmers, and feared serious consequences for Danish agriculture if Denmark remained outside the EC.[31]

For most Danes, at both elite and mass levels, a positive attitude towards the EC was thus closely connected with expectations of economic growth, against which they offset expectations of only minor change in external economic relations and a modest diminution of control over the domestic economy. No strong ideological or political arguments were advanced by EC supporters to counter possible disappointments in regard to economic development, or to justify a transfer of sovereignty from national institutions to the EC in certain areas.

To understand Danish attitudes toward direct elections in the light of

62

the referendum debate, one must also examine the parties' conceptions of European integration and of the role of the European Parliament, as expressed in the Folketing. Here again the Agrarian Liberal Party and the Socialist People's Party adopted positions different from the other parties. Both parties conceived of European integration as an ongoing development toward European union, and they ascribed great importance to the institutions of the EC, including the European Parliament. The Agrarian Liberals expressed their position in both federalist and neofunctionalist terms,[32] and argued that the European Parliament was an important element in the development of closer co-operation and democratic control in the EC. The party also believed that strong institutions would be in the interest of Denmark as a small state.[33]

In contrast, the Socialist People's Party had a conception of integration that reflected neofunctionalist ideas, and they warned of the dangers of spill-over effects from one issue area to another. In the economic area, it was seen to be an inevitable consequence of the structure of the EC that the very large firms would dominate, and it would therefore be dangerous for Denmark to give up all obstacles to the movement of capital.[34] The Party also attached great importance to the EC institutions and warned against the consequences of transferring power of decision from national to EC institutions. The anti-EC factions within the Social Democratic and Radical Liberal Parties expressed the same fears. However the dominant argument in the debate arose from the majority of the Social Democratic Party, which pushed economic issues to the fore, and presented a functionalist argument for co-operation on welfare goals and opposition to the strengthening of institutions.[35]

The main issues of the 1972 debate in the Folketing were: firstly, was it possible to consider co-operation in the EC as purely economic? Secondly, could institutional development of the EC be limited? The supporters of entry — the Agrarian Liberal and Conservative Parties, and the majority groups within the Social Democratic and the Radical Liberal Parties — answered 'yes' to both questions, even though the Agrarian Liberals expressed positive attitudes to political co-operation in the EC and to the ideas of strong institutions. The EC opponents — the minority groups within the Social Democratic and Radical Liberal Parties and the Socialist People's Party — all rejected the possibility of limiting institutional development. All except the anti-EC Social Democratic group — which in this instance followed the majority of the Party — also rejected the possibility of co-operation in the EC being purely economic.

Two further issues were of importance in the 1972 debate. First, all pro-EC parties except the Agrarian Liberals made British entry a condition for Danish membership. The second issue was the condition that the other Nordic countries should obtain 'satisfactory arrangements' with the EC.

All Danish parties were — and still are — very 'Nordic' in orientation. Overlapping membership of a close Nordic co-operation system and at the same time of the EC was considered a high priority by most EC supporting parties. It was again only the Agrarian Liberals that deviated from the position of the other EC supporters, being lukewarm to the NORDEK plan during the negotiations in 1968-1970. The anti-EC parties and groups considered a closer economic co-operation among the Nordic countries a realistic alternative to EC membership for Denmark as a part of a more comprehensive arrangement for economic co-operation in Europe.[36]

To the electorate, the most important argument offered by EC supporters was that entry would strengthen the national economy and benefit agriculture.[37] A second important argument was that it was impossible to oppose 'the forces of history'. The EC opponents' most important argument was that as an EC member Denmark would be 'run by outside forces'. Nordic considerations also played a part in the anti-EC voters' thinking, although neither these, nor economic considerations, were as important at this level as in the debate among the parties in the Folketing. During the last months before the 1972 referendum, both the parliamentary elite and the voters focussed on the same arguments.[38]

Between 1961-1970, the electorate's attitude to membership was very stable. About 50 per cent supported membership, 10 per cent were against and 40 per cent didn't know. In 1971 the opposition grew to about 30 per cent, and at the same time support for membership dropped to 35 per cent. Then the trend of support again moved upward to about 57 per cent just before the referendum.[39] In the referendum of 2 October, 1972, 63 per cent voted for and 37 per cent against EC membership. With the debate on joining the EC extending over ten years, the public was well informed, particularly in regard to the institutions of the EC, the question of future development towards political co-operation and economic and monetary union. The referendum gave no mandate for a strengthening of the EC institutions, nor for transferring new responsibilities from the Danish Government and the Folketing to the EC.[40]

The political situation in 1975 and 1977
in relation to direct elections legislation

The EC issue has remained alive in Denmark both inside and outside the Folketing. It has been shown that attitudes in Denmark have been persistently negative towards traditional Europeanism.[41] Anti-market forces have remained mobilised, and have placed a highly restrictive interpretation on the mandate given by the referendum.

In 1975, when the principle of holding direct elections was debated in the Folketing, three of the ten parties were anti-market parties: the Communist Party with seven members, the Socialist People's Party with nine members and the Left Socialist Party with four members. An 'agenda motion',[42] tabled by the Social Democratic Government, was passed 118-29 with ten abstentions, thus ratifying the Government's assent to the Council decision on direct elections. It is evident that members from outside the three anti-EC parties (twenty members) declared their opposition to further development of the EC. On the other hand, the Socialist People's Party abandoned its policy of withdrawal from the EC, and adopted a new policy of 'constructive opposition'.[43] The issue remained highly politicised, and the anti-marketeers interpreted direct elections as a step to further development of the Community.

The Folketing plays an active role in foreign policy making. On foreign policy issues such as NATO and the EC, the Social Democrat minority governments have had to seek support from the 'old' non-socialist opposition parties. There is, as mentioned earlier, a tradition of seeking a broad consensus on foreign policy issues. The two Social Democrat minority governments of 1975 and 1977 also sought support from across the centre of the political spectrum, in order to find solutions to severe domestic economic problems. A number of pacts on economic measures were concluded with various opposition parties. These agreements attempt to strengthen the political leadership through a period of acknowledged economic crisis, which was further complicated by signs of a political crisis: fragmentation of the party system, corporatist traits and sector autonomy toward political leadership.

In terms of her international economic and political relations, Denmark had by this time acquired an almost neutralist foreign policy, as a result of the loosening of the Atlantic system. The failure of the NORDEK plan in 1970 presaged a weakening of ties in this direction. Whilst in relation to the EC, co-operation had proved successful in both economic and political terms — though of course it had not provided either full employment or a trade surplus.[44]

The debate on principle

For the majority of EC-supporters in 1972, direct elections to the European Parliament was not something that would become a reality in the foreseeable future. When only a little more than two years after the referendum the question of direct elections appeared on the agenda of the Council of Ministers, the Agrarian Liberal Government believed that the time was not yet ripe for carrying out direct elections. However, the Social Democratic Government accepted the principle by supporting the decision in the European Council to aim to hold direct elections by May-June 1978. It tabled two reservations to the agreement: (1) The dual mandate should be compulsory for Danish representatives, (2) European and Folketing elections should take place on the same day. However, when it appeared that a majority of the Market Relations Committee was against these reservations the Government withdrew them.

The principle of holding direct elections was debated on 11 December, 1975, when a Government 'agenda motion' was passed,[45] stating that the Folketing 'took note' of the Government's agreement in the European Council that direct elections would be held in 1978, and that the Government would introduce the electoral bill as soon as the Council's draft convention was available. The Government maintained that the passing of a single bill for the election of Danish representatives would imply ratification of the Council's decision. The bill was presented to the Folketing almost two years later, on 6 October, 1977. In the interim, modest parliamentary pressure was exerted formally by two pro-EC members' questions[46] and the **Progressive** Party tabled a private bill on 14 October, 1976.

The principle of holding direct elections to the European Parliament was discussed on 11 December, 1975, in a debate on an inquiry to the Foreign Economy Minister concerning the EC. Four 'agenda motions' were tabled: one from the Social Democratic Party and three from the opposition. The parties' **positions** towards the principle of holding direct elections were presented only during this debate. During the passage of the Government's bill, the debate focussed on the details of the bill and only occasionally touched on the principles.

The Social Democratic Government supported the principle, but at the same time wanted to emphasise its functionalist, pragmatic attitude to co-operation in the Community. Its spokesman pointed out that the role of the European Parliament was to control the decision-making institutions in the EC, and not to be its legislature. He also stressed that the Social Democrats wanted to keep the dual mandate for Danish representatives, in order to obtain a better co-ordination of work in the Folketing and the European Parliament; and that elections to Folketing and the European Parliament should take place on the same day in order to avoid too great differences between the representation in the two assemblies.[47]

The spokesman for the Agrarian Liberal Party declared that his Party opposed the Government's reservations and would not vote for them.

The Party found it unacceptable and incomprehensible that Denmark should be leading an attempt to prevent an elected assembly from gaining influence over the political aspects of co-operation in the EC.[48] The spokesman for the Progressive Party also clearly stated his Party's hostility to the Government's reservations. He found the dual mandate awkward, and thought that simultaneous elections would reduce the voters' interest in the European elections to a low level.[49] Mogens Glistrup's Party thus indicated a pro-European position, which was to be confirmed a year later by its tabling of a Private Bill.

The Radical Liberal Party spokesman doubted that the Government's reservations were consistent with Denmark's acceptance of the principle of direct elections, and he considered — contrary to the Government's claim — that direct elections would inevitably change the European Parliament's competences. He reproached the Government for not having insisted on the immediate liquidation of illegal national subsidies from the other EC members as a condition for extending the EC.[50]

The Conservative Party's spokesman welcomed the decision of direct elections, arguing that it would stimulate public interest in the EC. He thought that direct elections were a pre-condition for the strengthening of political co-operation between EC countries in the long term. He pointed out the logical inconsistency of the Government's two reservations: with a compulsory dual mandate and the same day for the two elections, it would not be possible to know who was eligible for membership until the election had taken place. The Conservative Party was satisfied with an opportunity to discuss the whole problem on the firm basis of an election bill; its spokesman could not recall that the Radical Liberal Party's spokesman had ever given in the MRC the advice to the Government presented here in plenary.[51]

The Christian People's Party spokesman said that his Party had not finished its considerations of direct elections, but thought that the advantages of the Government's reservations outweighed their disadvantages. He found it more important to ensure that a candidate for the European Parliament would be nominated by a party already represented in the Folketing. The Centre Democratic Party spokesman declared that he held the same views as the Socialist People's Party regarding the consequences of direct elections — namely future increases in the competences of the European Parliament — but he considered this to be a virtue. The Centre Democrats accepted the need for a common election day. Regarding the dual mandate, the Party expected that in the long run it would be necessary to abandon it, as it placed too heavy a burden of work on Members.

Hence the seven pro-EC parties all had positive attitudes to the principle of holding direct elections, and only the Social Democratic

Government Party supported the Government's reservations. In some of the pro-EC parties there were minorities sceptical to the further development of the Community. This was revealed in the vote on the Social Democratic agenda motion which was passed by 118–29 votes, with ten abstentions. The agenda motions introduced by the Socialist People's, Communist, and Left Socialist Parties were not debated. As these three anti-EC parties had twenty MPs, nineteen MPs from the pro-EC parties must also have expressed their hostility to direct elections. The anti-EC forces in the Folketing thus had more support than the size of the anti-EC parties would indicate, and opinion polls showed that anti-EC forces were even stronger at the level of the electorate.

All of the anti-EC parties considered direct elections to the European Parliament to be a threat to Denmark's autonomy. The Socialist People's Party spokesman saw direct elections as part of the plan for a European union. The Party opposed direct elections because it thought that they would bring about an increase in the competences of the European Parliament. The Party thought that a strengthening of this supranational institution would weaken the veto power of the Member States. The Party was also opposed to any increase in the Parliament's budgetary powers, an issue which it felt should be seen in relation to the elections. The spokesman pointed out that in September, 1972, the majority in the MRC had commented in regard to the elections that '. . . a transformation of the institutions ought not to be an end in itself, but should originate in a desire by politicians and the population for greater co-operation.' He also pointed out that the present Market Minister had voted against direct elections in January 1975 in the European Parliament. On behalf of the Socialist People's Party he introduced an agenda motion.[52]

The Communist Party's spokesman quoted the Patijn report's view that direct elections were 'an absolutely necessary link in the accomplishment of further progress on integration'. He reminded the Folketing of the Government's reservations against the carrying out of direct elections only one year earlier, and maintained that the Government had been persuaded to abandon its objections to the transformation of the EC into a political union. He found the Government's current position insincere, and stated that there was only one way in which the Government could defend Danish interests, namely to insist that the time had not yet come to implement direct elections. The Communist Party, therefore, supported the agenda motion moved by the Socialist People's Party: it also introduced an agenda motion of its own.[53]

The spokesman for the Left Socialist Party also thought that direct elections would mean an important step toward political union. He drew the Folketing's attention to the fact that leading Social Democrats had continuously maintained that foreign policy co-operation was not an EC function and that the Social Democrat's Market policy had been a series of steps towards integration, contradicting the promises that the Party gave before the 1972 referendum. At that time the Social Democratic Party had said that the EC issue concerned economic but not political co-operation – whereas the Agrarian Liberal Party had said that it was also about political co-operation, which it wanted. The Left Socialist Party introduced another agenda motion.[54] The general debate on the EC was extensive, lasting six hours with twelve MPs and two Social Democratic Ministers speaking in it. The principle of direct elections was commented on by ten MPs – all party spokesmen – and by the Minister of International Economic Affairs, Ivar Nørgaard.

The passage of the Government's Bill

The Government's Bill for the election of Danish representatives to the European Parliament was presented to the Folketing on 6 October, 1977. It was eventually signed by the Queen on 14 December, 1977. The basic provisions were that sixteen Danish representatives were to be elected in two constituencies, one for Greenland (1 representative), the other for the rest of the country (15 representatives). The franchise for the European elections was extended to persons eligible to vote in Folketing elections, and to Danish citizens with a permanent address in one of the other Member States. Persons permanently resident in the Faroe Islands were not able to vote. Those eligible to become members of the European Parliament were those eligible to vote, unless previously convicted of an offence which made a person unworthy of being an MEP.

Parties represented in the Folketing could submit lists of candidates for the election to the Minister of the Interior. New parties could participate in the elections only if they collected the signatures of at least 2 per cent of the voters in the last Folketing election.[55] A provision in the bill that the parties could make election alliances was important, because it opened up the possibility of the anti-EC parties forming an alliance with the 'Folkebevaegelsen mod EF' – the People's Movement against the EC.

The Government Party's spokesman declared, in the First Reading debate, that the Party did not want to participate in a general discussion about Denmark's membership of the EC. The Party agreed with the Government's withdrawal of its reservations concerning the dual mandate and the simultaneous holding of European and national elections, which nearly all the other parties in the MRC were against. The Social Democrats appealed to the Folketing to investigate the possibilities of creating a close relationship between the directly elected MEPs and the Folketing. The Party maintained that direct elections to the European Parliament would have no consequences for the distribution of competences between the EC's institutions, and that the veto right of the Member States would be unaffected.

The Progressive Party supported the proposal, expressing the belief that the elections would lead the EC in a more democratic direction. But the Party opposed the proposal to give Greenland one MEP, and favoured the whole country forming a single constituency. The Agrarian Liberal Party declared that the Council of Minister's decision of 20 September, 1976, opened the road for 'the citizen's Europe alongside the Member States' Europe'. They strongly supported the Government's proposal, and expressed the hope that the elections would give the European Parliament a more important role. The Party preferred a larger number of constituencies which it thought would bring about more 'grassroots' activity in the elections.[56]

The Conservative Party was doubtful about the possibilities of persons who were not connected with the parties in the 'Folketing' being elected to the European Parliament. The problem of establishing a connection between such MEPs and the Folketing had to be solved, as did their relationship to the MRC. Apart from these doubts, the Conservative Party strongly supported the Government's proposal. The Centre Democratic Party also expressed appreciation of the Government's dealing with the issue which, with a single exception it supported: it wanted to make it easier for groups outside the 'Folketing' to participate in the elections. The Party did not expect great changes to come about as a consequence of the elections, but believed that the development of greater unity in the EC was highly desirable. The Christian People's Party thought that the direct elections would make the EC more democratic, and asked what alternatives to the elections the anti-EC parties had.

The Radical Liberals declared that there were varying opinions of the value of direct elections inside the Party, and that it would participate in the elections on the basis of its own programme, not that of the Federation of Liberal Parties. The Party found it valuable that the elections would involve an open debate, and emphasised that the competences of EC institutions could not be altered without changing the Treaty.

The Justice Party was strongly against the bill, but recognised that it was a positive development that the issue of the EC should again be extensively debated. The Party feared the elections would mean a step in the direction of European union, and referred to the Tindemans Report. The Party demanded a referendum concerning Denmark's representation in the directly elected European Parliament.

The Socialist People's Party protested against the Government's handling of the issue. The Party thought that it was wrong that the passage of an election bill implied a ratification of the Council of Ministers' decision. The Party did not agree that direct elections would mean a step in a more democratic direction; on the contrary they expected that the European Parliament would be strengthened at the expense of the national Parliaments. The Socialist People's Party also feared the development of a European union and a loss of Danish sovereignty. The Communist Party argued along the same lines as the Socialist People's Party, but declared that it would take up the challenge, and entered into a debate on the features of the election law. The Party compared the seat provided for Greenland with the poisoned apple given to Snow White. The Left Socialist Party declared that the elections would strengthen the supranational element in the EC, and maintained that there was an anti-EC majority in the electorate.[57]

The bill was scrutinised in four meetings of the MRC. Amendments to the bill were discussed among the parties in the Committee. Forty amendments were moved — nine by the Justice Party, eight by each of the Progressive and Socialist People's Parties, seven by the Communist Party, two by the Centre Democrat Party, and three by each of the Radical Liberal and Christian People's Parties. A majority of the MRC — the Social Democratic, Agrarian Liberal and Conservative Parties — recommended that the proposed bill be passed unchanged.[58]

At the second reading of the bill in the Folketing, the amendments were introduced.[59] Eleven votes were taken on the amendments, none of which were adopted. The Social Democratic spokesman congratulated the MRC for its thorough investigation of the question of increased competences of the European Parliament; the Minister had confirmed that the bills related only to election procedures, and that a change in the Treaty of Rome would be necessary before the competences could be changed. Moreover, the MRC had rejected the analysis that the European Parliament could 'legislate via the EC budget'. In proposing that Denmark and Greenland form a single constituency, the Progressive Party argued against some Danish inhabitants having special privileges because they lived in Greenland. Amendments that would make it easier for parties to participate in the elections were moved by all of the minor parties. The Radical Liberal Party's spokesman found it unfortunate that, under the bill, it would be more difficult to collect the necessary number of signatures for European elections than it was for Folketing elections.

In the second reading debate a majority of the Folketing — drawn from the Social Democratic, Agrarian and Conservative Parties — recommended that the Government's Bill be passed unchanged. When their amendments had been rejected, the Progressive, Centre Demo-

71

cratic, Radical Liberal and Christian People's Parties, also recommended the passage of the bill. The Socialist People's, Justice, Communist, and Left Socialist Parties all recommended the rejection of the bill. Once more the bill was referred to the MRC, where a single amendment — on the provisions for Greenland — was moved by the Justice Party.

At its third reading, the bill was passed unchanged by 120—25 votes with nine abstentions.[60] As the four anti-EC parties — the three Socialist parties and the non-socialist Justice Party — had twenty-five members between them, the vote shows that some MPs from the pro-EC parties had reservations on, or were hostile to the bill. The Justice Party's amendment to the bill concerning Greenland was rejected by 103—46 votes, with nine abstentions. Finally, the separate bill for Greenland was passed by 104—48 votes, with nine abstentions.

Conclusion

The passage of the direct election act through the Folketing had all the characteristics of a 'normal' legislative process. The plenary debate lasted four hours, compared to the average in 1973-74 II of 3.13 hours. It was a Government Bill, as were 95.5 per cent of the bills in the session. Like 60 per cent of the other bills in 1973-74 II, there was opposition at the final vote; and like most bills it was referred to a permanent, specialised committee.

Looking at the issues in the debates, it is possible to see a pattern in the parties' positions. There were seven main issues: the principle; the European Parliament's increased competences; the number of constituencies; links between MEPs and the Folketing; conditions for parties to participate in the elections; the conditions of eligibility for membership; and the question of a referendum for Greenland. The left—right division can explain the positions of all the parties to the principle of direct elections, with the exception of the Justice Party. As regards the issue of the European Parliament's increased competence, the previously discussed 'protest against the establishment' dimension seemed to play a role since some of the non-socialist parties, the Progressive and Christian People's Parties, were against the change. The issues connected with the new details of the elections divided the parties along established versus new, or large versus small lines.

In the light of the debate before Denmark's accession to the EC about ensuring strong national control of the Government's EC policy, it is surprising that the passage of the direct election legislation was so speedy and relatively uncomplicated. The fear of losing national control over EC policy-making had been so strong that the MRC was granted unusually large control powers. Legislation, that many feared would extend the competence of an EC institution, was influenced by the MRC in such a way that the Government had to withdraw its two reservations (on the compulsory dual mandate, and on the simultaneous holding of Folketing and European elections) in spite of the fact that these reservations aimed at forging a close connection between the Folketing and Danish MEPs. The Government had to do this, not just because there was pressure to do so from the EC, but also because it became clear that there was not a majority for the reservations in the MRC.

The members of the MRC were of course influenced by an interplay of factors outside the Folketing, both domestic and international. Judging from the debates in the Folketing, some of the EC supporting parties were concerned about the impression of uncertainty in Denmark's EC policy, which the Danish government's reservations might give to other members of the EC; and all parties were no doubt influenced by the negative mass attitudes to further institutional progress. The common ground where the EC supporting parties could meet was a functionalist conception of the co-operation in the EC.

It could also be expected that the fragmentation of the party system since 1973, and the new 'protest against establishment' dimension, would narrow the agreement behind the Government's EC policy. However, a study of voting behaviour in the Folketing has shown that this has not happened. In the case of direct elections, broad agreement was eventually obtained in support of the Government's proposals.

The structural adjustments of the Folketing to the changing environment and especially to EC membership, seem to have been adequate. This analysis reveals that the Folketing played an active role in the direct elections legislation, particularly through its Market Relations Committee. It influenced the Government to give up its 'reluctant European' position, and to seek agreement with parties which had no reservations on the direct elections. The voter's reluctant attitudes, however, remained to be seen.

Notes

Acknowledgement is due to the University of Copenhagen and the Danish Foreign Policy Institute for financial support.

1 It is assumed that 'theories of action' (i.e. the theoretical frames of reference, within which parties formulate their foreign policy) are concealed beneath economic and ideological elements in the parties' positions towards EC membership. Ole Karup Pedersen has developed a method for examining these 'theories of action' (Ole Karup Pedersen: *Udenrigsminister P. Munchs opfattelse af Danmarks stillng i international politik*, (København, Gads, 1970) English summary pp 634-42). The method is sociological-historical and 'the role concept' is used in the study

of public declarations of statesmen about the relationship of their states with other states. It is assumed that such strong restrictions are laid upon a representative of a state by his organisational role, when he is speaking as a representative in parliament or in an international organisation or in other similar situations, that the *role* is decisive and individual-psychological factors have only marginal importance. It is argued that in such situations the statements of the representatives will contain 'signals' to other actors indicating the limits within which the solution to the political 'game' may be found. For this reason contemporary records and papers to which the public has full access are valuable material for defining the general conceptions of active participants in political negotiations.

2 By 15 February, 1977, this amounted to not less than 17,751 persons. *Folketinget 1977 Handbog* (Folketinget, Copenhagen, 1977).

3 Erik Damgaard, 'Stability and Change in the Danish Party System over Half a Century', *Scandinavian Political Studies*, vol.9, 1974, pp 103-25.

4 H.J. Nielsen, 'Politiske holdninger og partivalg' in O. Borre et al, *Folketingsvalget 1977* (Akademisk Forlag, Copenhagen, 1979), pp 27-39.

5 One member represented the Greenland party, Atassut. The other member of the Folketing elected in Greenland was a member of the Socialist People's Party. One of the two members of the Folketing elected in the Faroe Islands was a member of the Social Democratic Party; the other represented the Faroe party, Sambandspartiet, and was a member of the Agrarian Liberal parliamentary group.

6 E. Damgaard and J.G. Rusk, 'Cleavage Structures and Representational Linkages: A Longitudinal Analysis of Danish Legislative Behaviour' in I. Budge et al, *Party Identification and Beyond* (Wiley, London, 1976), p.166.

7 Ibid, p.172.

8 H.J. Nielsen, 'Protestholdninger i 70'ernes vaelgeradfaerd' (Institute of Political Studies, University of Copenhagen, Arbejdspapir 1977/12).

9 Ibid, p.12.

10 I. Faurby, 'Partiafstande og udenrigsøkonomi. En dansk illustration' (Aarhus University, Bergen Conference paper, August 1978).

11 D. Dahlerup et al, 'Korporatismebegrebet og studiet of samspillet mellem politiske institutioner', *Økonomi og Politik*, no.4, 1975; L.N. Johansen et al, 'Corporatist Traits in Denmark 1946-76', (ISA Conference paper, Uppsala, August 1978).

12 E. Damgaard, *Folketinget under forandring* (Samfundsvidenskabeligt Forlag, Copenhagen, 1977) pp 312-4.

13 Ibid, pp 286-8.

14 Ibid, pp 290-3.

15 Ibid, p.116.

16 Ibid, p.114.

17 Ibid, p.247.

18 Ibid, p.248.

19 J. Fitzmaurice: 'National Parliaments and European Policy Making: The Case of Denmark', *Parliamentary Affairs*, vol.XXIX, 1976, p.288.

20 Ibid, p.289.

21 The Finance Committee — which served as a precedent for the MRC — also has delegated decision powers.

22 The analysis of the debate in Denmark before the 1972 referendum is taken from: Tove Lise Schou, 'En undersøgelse af ydre faktorers pavirkning af Danmarks markedspolitik' (Institute of Political Studies, University of Copenhagen, 1972) and: Tove Lise Schou 'Norge og EF. En undersøgelse af ydre og indre faktorers pavirkning af de norske partiers stillingtagen til sporgsmalet om Norges forhold til EF' (Institute of Political Studies, University of Copenhagen, 1978). The analysis of the 1961-1972 parliamentary debates in Denmark and Norway has been made through a qualitative content analysis of the Folketing and Storting records. The persons selected for the study were the representatives in 'roles' as speakers on behalf of government, or of a party, or of an opposition group within one of the parties that were split over the EC issue.

23 Folketingstidende (FT.) 11 May, 1967, col.4090; 18 May, 1971, col.6677. P. Federspiel (AL) spokesman.

24 FT. 4 August, 1961, col.4704. P. Federspiel (AL), spokesman.

25 FT. 11 May, 1967, col.4151-55. G. Petersen (SP), spokesman; FT. 11 November, 1970, col.1126. M. Lange (SP), spokesman.

26 FT. 24 April, 1972, col.5990. O. Nielsen (RL), EC opponent.

27 FT. 11 November, 1970, col.1057. I. Nørgaard (SD), spokesman.

28 FT. 11 November, 1970, col.1067. H. Clemmensen (C), spokesman.

29 FT. 11 November, 1970, col.1056ff. I. Norgaard (SD), spokesman.

30 J. Elklit and N. Petersen, 'Denmark Enters the European Communities', *Scandinavian Political Studies*, vol.8, 1973, p.208.

31 H. Valen, J. Elklit and O. Tonsgaard, 'Economic Conflicts and Orientation towards Europe in Denmark and Norway', *ECPR Paper*, London, 1975.
32 Cf. R.J. Harrison, *Europe in Question* (Allen and Unwin, London, 1974).
33 FT. 18 May, 1971, col.6675. P. Federspiel (AL), spokesman.
34 FT. 11 November, 1970, col.1125ff. M. Lange (SP), spokesman.
35 Cf. D. Mitrany, *The Functional Theory of Politics* (M. Robertson, London, 1975).
36 T.L. Schou, 'A Study of External Factors influencing Denmark's Market Policy' (Institute of Political Studies, University of Copenhagen, 1972).
37 P. Hansen, M. Small and K. Siune, 'The Structure of the Debate in the Danish EC Campaign' (University of Aarhus, 1974).
38 Ibid.
39 J. Elklit et al, op.cit., pp 203-4.
40 J. Fitzmaurice, 'National Parliaments and European Policy Making: The Case of Denmark', *Parliamentary Affairs*, vol.29, 1976, p.285.
41 See Appendix to chapter 2.
42 An agenda motion is formally a motion for the Folketing to pass on to the next point of the agenda, or to continue the treatment of the point under consideration. It also contains an opinion, and its function is to express the opinion of a majority supporting the policy of the Government or of an opposition suggesting a change of the policy of the Government. T. Worre, *Det politiske system i Denmark* (Akademisk Forlag, Copenhagen, 1973), p.82.
43 J. Fitzmaurice, op.cit., p.286.
44 C.L. Sørensen, *Danmark og EF i 1970 erne* (Borgen Forlag, Copenhagen, 1978), pp 241, 265.
45 FT. 11 December, 1975.
46 The questions were asked by Maigard (SPP), 9 July, 1975 and Junior (PP), 23 June, 1976. The basic provisions of the Progressive Party's Bill were: One constituency for the whole country (Denmark and Greenland). The franchise open to persons, who have reached the age of 20, and who have had permanent address in Denmark for two weeks. Candidates must have signed a list containing their name, which must be delivered to the Ministry of the Interior between 60 and 30 days before the election.
47 FT. 11 December, 1975, col.2924-5. The Social Democratic agenda motion read as follows: 'As the Folketing has taken note that the Government in the European Council has accepted that direct elections to the European Parliament be held in 1978, and that a proposal for the electoral law concerning the particular rules for the carrying out of this election in Denmark will be produced as soon as the Council of Ministers' draft convention is available, the (Folke)tinget passes on to the next point of the agenda' FT, 11 December, 1975, Col.2985.
48 FT. 11 December, 1975, Col.2931.
49 Ibid, col.2932-3.
50 Ibid, col.2939-40.
51 Ibid, col.2942-6.
52 'As the Folketing is turning against the actual plans under consideration for direct elections to the European Parliament, the Folketing passes on to the next point of the agenda'. FT. 11 December, 1975, col.2956.
53 Concerning proposals from the EC Commission and Parliament for a European union, among other things stating that '. . . the carrying through of such proposals goes far beyond the surrender of sovereignty, which was decided in 1972, and must therefore be subjected to a referendum . . . '. FT. 11 December, 1975, col.2966.
54 'Dissociating itself from the plans for introducing direct elections to the European Parliament as a step on the way to a political union, furthermore dissociating itself from the EC Commission's further plans for the construction of a supranational EC state with a common economic policy, a common foreign policy and a common European army, and stating that the plans contravene the conditions for the Danish referendum on 2 October 1972, the Folketing passes on to the next point of the agenda'. FT. 11 December, 1975, col.2976.
55 FT. 20 October, 1977.
56 The term 'naerdemokrati' means 'decentralised decision making' ('naer' = near the 'grassroots').
57 Cf.. Appendix to chapter 2.
58 The 17 members of the MRC were: 6 from SD, 2 from AL, 2 from PP, 1 from C, 1 from RL, 1 from CD, 1 from CPP, 1 from JP, 1 from SP and 1 from CP. The LS Party was not represented in the Committee. The chairman was Arne Christiansen (AL) and the deputy chairman was Erik Holst (SD).
59 FT. 29 November, 1977, col.2711-38.
60 FT. 2 December, 1977.

The Danish Folketing: some readings

E. Damgaard, *Folketinget under forandring* (Samfundsvidenskabeligt Forlag, Copenhagen, 1977). A study of the evolution of the Folketing, with English summary.

J. Fitzmaurice, 'The Danish system of parliamentary control over European Community policy', chapter 9 in: V. Herman and R. van Schendelen, *The European Parliament and the National Parliaments* (Saxon House, Farnborough, 1979). A study of the Danish Market Relations Committee.

T. Worre, *Det politiske system i Danmark* (Akademisk Forlag, Copenhagen, 1973). A recent general text on the Danish political system.

E. Damgaard, 'Stability and change in the Danish Party System over Half a Century', *Scandinavian Political Studies*, vol.9, 1974, pp 103-25.

C.L. Sorensen, *Danmark og EF i 1970 'erne* (Borgen Forlag, Copenhagen, 1978). The standard work on Denmark and the European Community.

N.J. Haagerup, Dänemark: 'Direktwahlen un Schatten wirtschaftlicher under sozialer Probleme', *Europa Archiv*, vol.24, 1978. A study of the economic and social context of direct elections.

5 Germany: Modell Deutschland

Juliet Lodge

Introduction[1]

By 1976, direct elections to the European Parliament was not really a political issue in the Federal Republic of Germany (FRG). The major parties welcomed them and were, by and large, intent upon setting an example to the other European Community (EC) Member States by passing legislation to hold the elections as quickly and amicably as possible. That the Germans failed to be the first to complete the requisite legislative processes was not simply due to the disagreement between the SPD-FDP governing coalition and the CDU/CSU opposition over the relative merits of holding elections according to federal as opposed to Land lists. Rather, the tardiness of other Member States, coupled with the uncertainty over the year of direct elections, and the Nine's failure to agree to Members of the European Parliament (MEPs) receiving a common salary, meant that any urgency to complete the legislative process was dissipated. This is not to deny the fact that because three separate but simultaneously submitted bills had to secure the Bundestag's and Bundesrat's approval the process was somewhat protracted. However, this was not used as an excuse by the parties to attempt to thwart the holding of direct elections by either the original target of May/June, 1978 or the later one of June, 1979.

Public opinion was largely favourable to direct elections, and the European Movement in conjunction with the Länder governments — some of which faced elections in 1978 — began to establish special committees to promote enthusiasm for the direct elections.[2] The absence of controversy over the principle of direct elections, their expected impact upon the European Parliament's powers, or relations between MEPs and Members of the Bundestag, did not imply an absence of inter-party, government-opposition, argument. However, this was marked by pragmatism rather than acrimony; and even though the Bundesrat contested the Government's view that mandatory approval of the legislation could not be inferred, the legislative process operated normally and smoothly in respect of the direct elections bills.

In order to appreciate the normality of the direct election legislative process it will be useful to begin by outlining briefly the key features of the legislative process. The attitudes of the Federal Governments towards the EC and direct elections since the Communities' inception will then be examined prior to an analysis of the legislative process on direct elections.

The legislative process

The Parliament of the Federal Republic of Germany has two chambers based on different forms of representation. The Budestag, to which the Government is responsible, is elected by a mixed plurality and proportional electoral system (d'Hondt). The Bundesrat consists of representatives from the Länder (States) within the federation, appointed by each Land government. Both chambers include non-voting representatives appointed by the West Berlin House of Representatives.

The Government was led by the Social Democratic Party (SPD) in coalition with the smaller Free Democratic Party (FDP). The Christian Democratic Union (CDU) and its Bavarian sister party, the Christian Social Union (CSU), comprised the opposition in the Bundestag, but in some Länder formed the government and held a majority in the Bundesrat.

Legislative authority is shared by the Federation and the Länder. The Länder have legal authority wherever the Basic Law does not expressly confer it on the Federation (Article 70(1)). The Basic Law differentiates between the exclusive legislative power of the Federation on questions of foreign affairs, defence, currency and citizenship; the concurrent legislative competence of the Federation and Länder covering matters of civil law, public welfare and labour laws; and skeleton legislation where the general provisions enacted by the Federation are implemented in detail by Land legislation.

All Government bills are submitted first to the Bundesrat which may state its views within six weeks. The direct elections bills, being Government bills, were submitted to the Bundesrat before the Bundestag. In general, at the first passage or reading of a bill, the Bundesrat may either approve, reject, or recommend amendments and additions to Government bills. Bills are then returned to the Government which transmits them to the Bundestag with its own views on any Bundesrat opinions. Following a Bundestag vote on the bill, it returns to the Bundesrat for a second reading. The bill goes through the same procedure again but its position depends on the type of bill it is. So-called 'simple' bills (representing 50 per cent of all bills) do not require the Bundesrat's approval to become law. In these cases, the Bundesrat may table objections to the draft and require the Bundestag to reconsider its earlier decisions. Bundesrat objections can only be rejected by qualified majorities in the Bundestag. Other draft bills require the Bundesrat's approval to become law because they are deemed to directly affect the Länders' interests (because they have to be administered by them or affect their revenue).

The Bundesrat can invoke the Arbitration Committee (Vermittlungsausschuss) — consisting of eleven Bundesrat and eleven Bundestag members — in all cases where the Bundesrat disagrees partly or wholly with the Bundestag's decision on a bill. The Government or Bundestag may invoke the Arbitration Committee in cases of the Bundesrat withholding approval to a bill, though this is a rare occurrence. The Arbitration Committee's task is to promote compromise between the Bundestag and the Bundesrat. Its proposals are subject to approval by both chambers.

Background

Aspects of European integration have been an issue in German politics since the founding of the FRG in 1949. Since the FRG's accession to the EC as a founding member, there has been a basic commitment on the part of the major parties — CDU, CSU, SPD and FDP — to both the principles of the EC and to the realisation of parliamentary democracy at the supranational level.[3] Such commitment has been tempered by critical evaluations as to how European integration can serve the FRG's political status in the international arena.[4] Even today, the SPD uses the EC in an instrumental way when 'Europeanising' goals and policies which are difficult to enact domestically. The Europeanisation of policy goals is a means both of heightening the credibility and respectability of those goals, and to some extent legitimising and disguising the FRG's potentially powerful position in Western Europe.[5] The legacy of the past has conditioned the FRG's attitudes towards European integration. Space limitations preclude a discussion of the background to the parliamentary parties' current enthusiastic support for direct elections, the accretion of the European Parliament's powers, and the intensification of the integration process. Some of the attempts made by the FRG to advance the goal of direct elections will therefore be noted.

The Germans have been reticent about agitating for direct elections because they have perceived, at least during the 1960s and early 1970s, a need to play a modest political role in the EC, and to cede prominence to France; and to advance other priority goals — such as the EC's enlargement in 1973. However, sporadic attempts have been made to facilitate direct elections. In an attempt to prompt action on direct elections by the Six, the German Government had, on 11 November

79

1969, put forward a compromise, interim proposal on direct elections, designed both to avert unilateral action in individual Member States, and to expedite the gradual introduction of direct elections.[6]

The Government's failure to advance direct elections appreciably, led to the Chairman of the SPD's Working Party on direct elections, Klaus Peter Schulz, resigning in protest in October 1971.[7] The Brandt-Scheel government, concentrating on securing the accretion of the European Parliament's budgetary powers and image, made constructive proposals to these ends but was unable to advance direct elections. In March 1973, Brandt argued that direct elections were unrealistic given the differing electoral systems of the Nine. However, the SPD — supported by the FDP and CDU/CSU — continued to call for the EC's democratisation: first, by extending the European Parliament's powers; and second, by directly electing it.[8] The first having been conceded by its EC partners, the German Government called for MEPs' direct accountability to the people and was supported by the Opposition over the matter of direct elections. Indeed, the CDU advocated transnational party solidarity and the production of a common manifesto for direct elections.[9] However, the SPD accorded the extension of the European Parliament's powers precedence over direct elections and did not support the CDU/CSU's proposal in December 1973 to devise an interim German solution to direct elections.[10]

By contrast, in November 1974, the SPD enthusiastically supported the proposals of the Dutch Socialist MEP Schelto Patijn on direct elections against those of CDU MEP, Egon Klepsch, secure in the knowledge that Britain's 'renegotiation'[11] was progressing satisfactorily and that direct elections were more acceptable to its EC partners than hitherto. All the major German parties saw and continue to see direct elections giving the EC political impetus and direction; providing the rationale for reappraising the EC's institutional balance; increasing the European Parliament's powers, and involving citizens in the construction of Europe.[12] The political climate of opinion towards direct elections was, therefore, highly favourable by the time of the Council of Ministers' decision of 20 September, 1976, to hold direct elections to the European Parliament.

Shortly after the Nine had endorsed the principle of holding direct elections, the Federal Ministry of the Interior, which has responsibility for electoral matters, began drafting (and by December 1975 had completed preparations for) the provisions necessary to facilitate the holding of direct elections. Discussions were begun on the consequences of the decision to hold direct elections. Well before the Council of Ministers' decision of 20 September 1976, the FRG had taken steps to introduce direct elections. On 27 January 1976, the SPD's and FDP's working parties on direct elections adopted 'Principles of a European

Table 5.1
Parties in the Bundestag, October 1976

Party		Abbreviations	Vote %*	Seats(N)†
G	Social Democratic Party	SPD	42.6	213
G	Free Democratic Party	FDP	7.9	39
	Christian Democratic Party and Christian Social Union	CDU CSU	48.6	244
	Others		0.9	0
	Total		100.0	496
	Turnout		90.7%	

*Share of valid votes cast in General Election, October 1976
†Seats in the Bundestag, October 1976
G Parties forming the Government.

electoral law' which were approved by the party executives on 10 February 1976, and subsequently adopted by the parties. These principles formed the basis of the Federal Ministry of Internal Affairs' bills to facilitate the holding of direct elections in the FRG.

The Bills

When the Council Act was signed on 20 September 1976, the FRG Government stipulated, in an appendix, that those of the FRG's quota of seats in the European Parliament allotted to Berlin should be filled by members selected from Berlin's House of Representatives, according to the strength of its parties. Significantly, this appendix acknowledged the special rights and responsibilities of Great Britain and Northern Ireland, the USA and France for Berlin. The USSR protested because the provisions for Berlin's MEPs — who were to have full rights in the European Parliament, although having only limited powers in the Bundestag — acknowledged, as did the Rome Treaty, that Berlin was part of the FRG and EC.[13]

Given all-party consensus on direct elections, and agreement over electing MEPs according to the existing d'Hondt system of proportional representation, few problems were anticipated vis-à-vis the adoption of the three draft laws. Originally, it was hoped that they could be adopted as a package before the Bundestag went into summer recess in 1977 in order to adhere to the Council's target date of May/June

1978 for direct elections. Despite intentions to avoid confrontation over the draft laws, it proved impossible to adopt them as a package although presented as such to the Bundestag.

Although ratifying the Council Act and Decision was to prove straightforward, partisan controversies surfaced in the all-party committees of the Bundesrat and Bundestag over the Election Bill (the Europawahlgesetz) and the Legal Status Bill (the Europaabgeordnetengesetz) when they were submitted to them for scrutiny. Consequently, the FRG's hopes that it would present a model or good example for the EC in legislating for direct elections were to be disabused.

The role of Parliament in the ratification of the Council Act

Under the Basic Law, there is a division of competence between the Federation and the Lander concerning their exclusive and concurrent legislative powers. In matters within the exclusive legislative competence of the Federation, the Länder may legislate only if a federal law explicitly authorises them to do so. In matters within concurrent legislative powers, the Länder may legislate as long as the Federation does not exercise its right. Under Article 73(i), the Federation has exclusive power to legislate in foreign affairs' matters; but concurrent legislative powers extend, under Article 74, *inter alia*; to civil law, residence and establishment of aliens, citizenship in the Länder, and to laws of association and assembly. In these respects, measures governing direct elections, residence and eligibility requirements may have been seen to affect the Länders' interests. However, as will be shown, the Government's bill was not one that required the Bundesrat's consent to become a federal law.

The Ratification Bill[14] presented by the Government to the Bundestag and Bundesrat was an 'Einspruchsgesetz'. This meant that although the Bundesrat could enter an objection against it at the second reading stage within two weeks of its adoption by the Bundestag, the latter could reject the Bundesrat's objection. Under Article 77(iv) of the Basic Law, if the Bundesrat adopts an objection by a majority, it can be overruled by a majority in the Bundestag. If the Bundesrat adopts an objection by a majority of at least two-thirds of its votes, its rejection by the Bundestag also requires a two-thirds majority. Thus, the Bundesrat had the right and opportunity to enter objections against the bill, but its consent was neither essential providing that the bill could command the Bundestag's support; nor was it in this case necessary — a point contested by the Bundesrat in respect of the two bills submitted to it simultaneously with the Ratification Bill — the

Election and Legal Status Bills.

The Government transmitted the Ratification Bill to the Bundesrat on 1 April 1977. For the first reading, the bill was sent to the Committee on EC Questions and was discussed also by the Committees for Internal Affairs, and Legal Questions. They advised the Bundesrat against entering an objection to the bill, as it was entitled to do under Articles 76 and 77 of the Basic Law.

Only the Committee on EC Questions considered the bill again for the second reading. Thus, there was no deviation in the Bundesrat procedure from normal practice. Because the Bundesrat desisted from putting forward amendments, it was able to complete the first reading of the bill within the six week period provided for by the Basic Law. On 6 May 1977, the Bundesrat decided against entering objections against the Ratification Bill but registered objections in respect of the other two bills.[15] Its opinion was transmitted immediately to the Bundestag.

The Bundestag considered the Ratification Bill simultaneously with the Election[16] and Legal Status[17] Bills on 26 May 1977. The Ratification Bill had been transmitted to the Committees for Internal Affairs, Legal Affairs, Foreign Affairs and for the Budget. The Election and the Legal Status Bills were transmitted, additionally, to the Committee for Elections Vertification, Immunity, and Procedure. The parliamentary parties also asked for the three bills to be referred to the Committee for Inner-German Relations.

The passage of the Ratification Bill

The Legal Affairs Committee discussed the bill on 25 and 27 May, and unanimously recommended its adoption to the Committee for Internal Affairs. On 25 May, the Foreign Affairs Committee recommended its adoption. The Committee for Internal Affairs dealt with the bill on 27 May and unanimously recommended its adoption, subject to the Committee for Inner-German Relations doing likewise.[18] The Budgets Committee also endorsed the bill's adoption on 15 June, but its rapporteur, Dr Riedl (CSU) pointed out that election costs would arise.[19] The Bundestag then endorsed the recommendation of the Committee for Internal Affairs to accept the Ratification Bill in its original form on 17 June.[20]

During the second reading of the bill, there was general agreement that European unification should be stimulated; direction elections be held in 1979 if not 1978; the powers of the European Parliament increased; political co-operation promoted; and a high turnout encouraged. Simultaneously, the exchanges between the CDU/CSU and

SPD designed to show which was the more 'European' party, marked the start of the pre-election campaign.[21]

Following the Bundestag's adoption of the Ratification Bill, the Committee for EC Questions advised the Bundesrat against invoking Article 77(ii) of the Basic Law, which would have allowed it to call for the establishment of a mediation committee to reconcile any differences between it and the Bundestag. The Bundesrat accepted the Committee's recommendation.[22] Having secured the assent of both Houses the Act and bill were published in the *Bundesgesetzblatt* on 11 August, 1977.[23]

The fact that the Bundesrat did not invoke its rights under the Basic Law either to object to or to seek the amendment of the Government's Ratification Bill did not imply that the Bundesrat was satisfied with Government plans for holding direct elections to the European Parliaemtn. On 8 May 1977, a number of members expressed anxiety in respect of several matters, and these were articulated more forcefully when the Bundesrat considered the two pieces of parallel legislation which the Government introduced to implement the direct elections. In an appendix to the Ratification Bill the Government had anticipated a number of questions that proved to be of concern to the Bundesrat. Whereas in some other EC Member States it was insisted that direct elections should not lead to the accretion of the European Parliament's powers, the opposite view was held generally in the FRG. The Government's appendix noted as much; and the Bundesrat affirmed that it had endorsed the 1972 and 1974 recommendations of its Committee for EC Questions supporting the directly elected European Parliament's acquisition of genuine legislative powers.[24] The principle was therefore not controversial. However, the nature of the electoral system and the question of exactly whom the MEPs represented proved contentious, even though the Government appendix to the Ratification Bill stressed that both Article 137 of the Rome Treaty and Article 2 of the Act made it clear that MEPs represented the people, not the Member States.[25] Some of the Lander representatives, notably those from Saarland and Bremen, were to argue that this did not mean that MEPs elected from the Federal Republic should not also be representatives of the people in the Länder.

The Ratification Bill also passed through the Bundestag smoothly. However, the first reading of the three bills in the Bundestag revealed that the passage of the Election and Legal Status Bills would cause problems. It was hoped that these would not prove insuperable since there was general agreement that the three bills should be passed as expeditiously as possible, not only so that practical details could be completed promptly to allow the parties time to select their candidates but also so that the 1978 election date could be maintained.[26] It was also hoped that the FRG would set a good example to some of the less diligent Member States. Foreign Minister Genscher expressed the convictions that the direct elections would give new impetus to the EC, realise a citizens' Europe, promote democracy; realise the democratic expectations of Greece, Spain and Portugal; and prompt the European Parliament to acquire real powers. He noted that the Council of Ministers and the Commission should deal with all major and pressing problems confronting the EC and be accountable to the directly elected European Parliament: a view shared by both Government and Opposition.[27]

The Government hoped that the FRG would, as 'Modell Deutschland',[28] set an example to other EC states in the legislating of direct elections. This hope was thwarted as it became clear that disagreement over aspects of the Election and Legal Status Bills would hold up the process. Moreover, as other Member States seemed both unwilling and unable to complete the necessary procedures expeditiously, more time was spent scrutinising problematic issues than had originally been intended.

The passage of the Legal Status Bill in the Bundesrat

On 1 April 1977, the Federal Chancellor transmitted the Legal Status Bill to the Bundesrat.[29] This bill covered measures to ensure the free acquisition and exercise of a mandate in the European Parliament, MEPs' indemnities, immunities, rights to free travel in the FRG, and incompatibilities. The proposals were largely based on provisions of the Representatives Bill of 18 February 1977,[30] and so afforded German MEPs essentially the same legal position as Members of the Bundestag. Initially, no provisions were proposed concerning MEPs' remuneration on the grounds that appropriate common provisions were to be decided at the supranational level. The failure of the Nine to settle this issue meant that key provisions of the bill could neither be discussed nor passed until shortly before the elections.

The Bundesrat was required to make its position known on 13 May 1977, and considered the bill on 6 May. At the first reading of the bill, neither the Committee for Internal Affairs nor that for EC Questions raised objections. However, the Legal Affairs Committee successfully called on the Bundesrat to recommend a minor re-formulation of Article 5(i) and the deletion of Article 5(ii) which regulated MEPs indemnities and immunities.[31] The Bundesrat was primarily concerned with clarifying the position of dual mandated MEPs. The Government immediately referred the bill to the Bundestag with its view that the Bundesrat's recommendation regarding Article 5(i) and 5(ii) should be rejected. While dismissing the Bundesrat's suggestion that Article 5(ii) was superfluous, the Government proposed re-formulating the offending phrase in Article 5(i) regarding MEPs' immunities to stress that immunity should be regulated in accordance with the Basic Law.[32] The Bundestag accepted this after its Internal Affairs Committee had unanimously recommended a re-formulation of Article 5(ii) clarifying the question of dual mandated MEPs' immunity.[33] The Committee rejected its CDU/CSU members' contention that the legal position of MEPs should be definitively regulated in the Election Bill rather than in a special bill. This meant that although the Bundesrat endorsed the bill, certain matters remained outstanding pending decisions on MEPs' legal position, amd MEPs' remuneration.

Even so, there was a considerable delay between the Bundestag's Internal Affairs Committee approving the bill and its adoption. Concern at this delay led the Committee's Chairman to write twice to the President of the Bundestag urging the need to complete the legislative process promptly in view of the provision that those contesting the direct elections be entitled to up to two months' leave to prepare for them.

Further complications arising from the Member Governments' inability to fix a common salary for MEPs led the Bundestag to call for a national ruling on this. On 20 January 1979, it referred the bill back to the Committees for Internal Affairs, Legal and Budgetary Affairs. On 7 February, the Legal Affairs Committee recommended the adoption of a transitional arrangement, but on a majority vote rejected the CDU/CSU's view that in the interim MEPs' salaries should be based on the salaries of Bundestag Members and take account of special allowances. It was also suggested that the question of amending the Bundestag's rules of procedure to permit two German MEPs to sit and speak in each of the Bundestag's Committees be considered.

The Committee for Internal Affairs discussed the bill at five sessions and recommended that MEPs' pay should be related to that of Bundestag Members. The view of the European Parliament's enlarged Bureau was that MEPs should receive a basic salary equal to 40 per cent of the salary of a Member of the EC Commission; for German MEPs this would have meant a monthly salary of DM 6,900. The SPD subsequently advocated MEPs receiving DM 6,500 per month; and the FDP and CDU/CSU called for a monthly salary of DM 7,500. Accepting this, the Committee recommended that MEPs should receive the same salary as Bundestag Members (DM 7,500 per month); and that dual mandated MEPs be remunerated only once. This provision was to remain effective only until the adoption of a common salary scale for MEPs, and in any case no longer than the European Parliament's first term of office. Additional amendments were made to other clauses, and included provisions for free domestic air and rail travel. More importantly, the term 'representative of the European Parliament' was altered to 'Member'.[34]

The Budgets Committee calculated that the cost of the financial arrangements governing MEPs' salaries and travel allowances would amount to DM 4,500,000 in 1979; and DM 8,500,000 for each of 1980, 1981 and 1982. A special vote was necessary to add this to the 1979 budget; thereafter, the amount was to be automatically incorporated into the budgets.[35] On 29 March 1979, the Bundestag approved the Internal Affairs Committee's recommendations, and stipulated that it would reconsider the financial provisions if the European Parliament failed to produce common rules for MEPs by 31 December 1981.[36] The bill was then transmitted to the Bundesrat which had until 20 April to consider it.

On 6 April 1979, the Bundesrat unanimously adopted the Legal Status Act on the recommendation of the Internal Affairs Committee.[37] This effectively completed the process of implementing legislation to facilitate the holding of direct elections. Despite sharp differences of opinions between the major parties, obstructionism was not rife. Overall, a constructive attitude was adopted, and delay in securing the passage of the Legal Status Law was due as much to external forces — the desire to await common European provisions on salaries, for example — as to inter-party disagreement.

The Election Bill in the Bundesrat

The passage of the Election Bill was a good deal more complicated than the passage of the Ratification and Legal Status Laws. The detailed provisions regarding the nature of the proposed electoral system based on federal lists proved so controversial that the Saarland's Bundesrat representatives called upon the Bundesrat to establish an Arbitration Committee between the two houses of Parliament. However, the Bundesrat could not act to establish this Committee until the Bundestag had passed the bill and transmitted it to the Bundesrat on 31 March 1978. It then had twenty-one days in which to call for the arbitration procedure. However, in the interim, objections to the Government's proposals had been rehearsed in both the Bundestag and the Committees of the Bundesrat. The Election Bill was to prove the most controversial of the three bills. It was the bill over which Government and opposition views clashed and crystallised; and the one where the basic argument over the electoral system — on federal or Land lists — led to interminable wrangling. In the CDU's case, the advocacy of a Land list system was largely inspired by fears concerning the CSU's aspirations as a fourth party; whereas the SPD was intent upon avoiding the adoption of a system likely to accentuate regional and Land issues in a supranational campaign. The FDP, by contrast, unable to present attractive candidates for all Länder, and with organisational and staffing problems, inclined towards the federal list system. The arguments advanced in the Bundestag mirrored those in the Bundesrat, where the CDU/CSU was in a majority and began by contesting the status of the bill — insisting that it required Bundesrat approval.

The bill was divided into three sections. The first dealt with the election of MEPs (Articles 1-20); the second with the acquisition and loss of membership of the European Parliament (Articles 21-24); and the third with the conduct and financing of the elections (Articles 25, 26 and 28), amendment of the Penal Code (Article 27), provisions for Berlin (Articles 29 and 30) and the entry into force of the bill (Article 31).

Although the first part stipulated that the elections be conducted according to the d'Hondt system of proportional representation on the basis of federal lists, the preamble to the bill setting out its objectives pointed out that an alternative would be a system of linked Land lists or the usual Bundestag electoral system.[38] As with Bundestag elections, parties failing to obtain at least five per cent of the total valid votes cast throughout the constituency would not qualify for participating in the allocation of seats.[39] The five per cent clause was not meant to discriminate against transnational groupings but was intended — as in Bundestag elections — to prevent a multitude of tiny parties gaining seats.

The bill also deviated from the usual provisions governing the eligibility to vote in Federal elections, and provided for Germans resident for at least three months in other EC states to vote in direct elections either by presenting themselves personally at the polling station or by postal vote. Normally, the 170,000 Germans of voting age resident in other EC Member States cannot vote.

Political parties and organisations organised on a membership basis in the EC could contest the elections on the basis of federal lists. The bill specified regulations governing the content and form of the federal lists, nomination procedures, voting, electoral machines, and verification and announcement of the results. The Bundestag's President was to be responsible for immediately informing the European Parliament's President of the results; but neither verification nor counting could proceed before voting had been completed in all other EC Member States.

The second part of the bill dealt with the acquisition and loss of membership of the European Parliament. The Council's Act specified that membership of the European Parliament was to be incompatible with that of a national government or any EC institution. The Election Bill specified further incompatibilities: the Federal President, membership of a Land government, being a judge of the Federal Constitutional Court, a Parliamentary State Secretary, a civil military official of the Bundestag and an official for data collection. It was also ruled that MEPs would lose their seats if their party were declared unconstitutional under the Basic Law.

In accordance with existing practice the bill accepted the need for some state financing of the direct elections campaign.[40] The preamble explained that the 1978 federal budget proposed provision of approximately DM 37.6 million to cover postal costs and expenditure incurred in preparing and holding the elections. However, the extent to which the parties were to be reimbursed was left open to discussion in the course of the legislative process. In the event, suggestions that parties receive no more than DM 1.50 per voter were rejected on the grounds that parties contesting Landtag elections would have depleted coffers; that, more importantly, the European elections were at least as important as Bundestag elections; and that the parties should engage in wide-scale campaigns to generate public awareness and interest in turning out to vote. This resulted in an allocation of DM 3.50 per voter for the FRG's 42 million eligible voters for parties polling at least five per cent of the vote. Either 20 per cent or 40 per cent of the amount to be reimbursed would be advanced in the fourth year of the European Parliament's term, or in the election year, in accordance with the dues payable at the preceding election, respectively.

Few fundamental constitutional issues were raised by the principle of direct elections: Article 22 of the Basic Law provides for powers to be transferred to supranational bodies and so reduced the likelihood of strife over questions of sovereignty as in Britain and France. However, the Bundesrat's insistence that the bill required its consent was to prove problematic and delay its adoption. When the Bundesrat considered the bill on 6 May 1977, it became apparent that the Government would be hard-pressed to secure its passage by the target date of November 1977.

Following the Bundesrat Committee's scrutiny of the Election Bill, the Committee for Internal Affairs, EC Questions and Legal Affairs made several recommendations to the Bundesrat calling for modifications to a number of articles. It was argued that because the bill affected the jurisdiction of the Länder, it required the Bundesrat's approval and so the introductory words of the bill were amended to make this clear. The Government and Opposition were divided on this issue. Not surprisingly, the CDU/CSU, having a majority in the Bundesrat, argued that it required the Bundesrat's assent. The view of the SPD and FDP was that direct elections were not a State-administered activity as under Article 80 of the Basic Law. According to Bangemann, 'holding these elections is not the execution of a normative decision of the Federal legislator, but rather the articulation of the act of a State organ'. The Bundesrat's argument was rejected by the Government.[41]

The Bundesrat also contested the desirability of the federal list system.[42] On 6 May 1977, the Chairman of the Bundesrat Committee for Internal Affairs, Minister Titzck (Schleswig-Holstein) noted that his Committee questioned the acceptability of the Government's proposals for the holding of direct elections, according to the normal d'Hondt proportional representation system based on federal lists. At the initiative of the Saarland Parliament, whose members felt that such a system would result in the under-representation of smaller Länder in the European Parliament, the Bundesrat expressed reservations against the federal lists. It adopted a recommendation asking the Government to examine whether federal lists could be replaced by Land lists. Whereas the Minister for North Rhine Westphalia Dr Hirsch, recalled that direct elections were to represent the people not the Länder, Dr Vogel (Rhineland Palatinate) argued that since the EC should logically become a federal union, a system of linked Länder lists would better reflect federal principles. The federal list system was also criticised as being too distant from the people.[43] The Bundesrat voted to reject the federal lists, and asked the Government to examine whether Land lists would not be more appropriate, arguing that if federal lists were to be retained, then certain amendments to the bill were necessary both for clarity and in order to satisfy the Bundesrat's interests.

In addition, the Bundesrat recommended deleting the requirement that the first ten candidates give their profession or status on the ballot paper lest this prejudice the equality of opportunity of all candidates; and objected to membership of a Land government being incompatible with membership of the European Parliament on the grounds that the Länder were not directly EC Member States.[44] The Legal Affairs' Committee requested the Government to try and avoid creating the idea that there would be special Berlin MEPs; and the Internal Affairs' Committee asked the Government to present a proposal on the financing of the elections and the reimbursement of electoral expenses during the course of the legislative process.[45] The Finance Committee raised no objections against the bill.

At the plenary reading of the bill on 6 May 1977, the recommendation to invoke the Bundesrat's rights under Article 76(2) of the Basic Law was approved, as were the Committees' recommended modifications. A minor charge emphasised that political organisations as well as parties should be eligible to contest the elections.[46]

The Government accepted some minor alterations suggested by the

Bundesrat, and made concessions on others — notably the federal versus Land lists controversy where it conceded that if a more acceptable solution could be found in the course of the legislative process, it would not object to its being considered. This left the door open for a compromise formula allowing parties to submit either federal or Land lists. However, when the Government passed the bill onto the Bundestag with its views on the Bundesrat's opinions and recommendations, apart from rejecting the argument that the bill had Bundesrat approval, it repudiated the Bundesrat's recommendations that candidates should not be required to state their profession on the ballot paper, and that membership of a Land government be compatible with membership of the European Parliament.[47]

Resolution in the Bundestag

At the first reading of the three bills in the Bundestag, in reply to Foreign Minister Genscher, Dr Lenz (CDU/CSU) welcomed direct elections but immediately alluded to features of the Council Act which he felt were not only unfair but also likely to be exploited by those hostile to supranationalism in subsequent efforts to draft a common electoral law. He was particularly concerned by the fact that not only had Luxembourg six seats for 300,000 inhabitants, but that the small members of the EC together had 86 seats for only 31 million inhabitants against the FRG's 81 seats for a population of almost 62 million.[48] He also objected to the provision for Berlin where not only were members to be elected on the basis of a Land list but also were to be called 'Berlin representatives', thereby possibly undermining the fact that it was an integral part of the EC. Lenz also wondered why the Government had changed its mind since 8 September 1975 when the Ministry for Internal Affairs had recommended the adoption of Land lists which would not discriminate against Berlin. Refuting this, Dr Bangemann (FDP) pointed out that Berlin's representatives were being elected by the Chamber of Deputies for appointment to the European Parliament in the same manner as used for the Bundestag.

Dr Lenz feared that the federal list system would result in MEPs being too distant from EC citizens. However, Dr Bangemann argued that to the contrary the ratio of candidates to voters or party members would remain approximately the same in either case.[49] More importantly, Dr Lenz felt that MEPs elected on the basis of federal lists would be too dependent on the body — be it the party leadership, or possibly the parliamentary party — that had approved their candidature, and position on the federal list. This in turn, he argued, might make MEPs from governing parties dependent on the Government, and lead to their not having the independence that the CDU/CSU hoped they would have. To prevent this, he called for appropriate reforms to be made to party ordinances (these were, in fact, made). The CDU/CSU, sharing Dr Lenz's reservations, advocated the adoption of the usual Land-based practices used in federal elections for direct elections. The CDU felt that the advantages of such a system outweighed any speculative gains the CDU might enjoy under a federal list system which was seen as the rational system for both the SPD and the FDP.

Dr Lenz argued that a Land-based system had the following merits: it would circumvent certain technical difficulties; ensure the representation of all the Länder (thereby meeting the acute fears of small parties in Bremen and the Saar that the federal list system would result in candidates from their regions failing to gain election to the European Parliament); better reflect the FRG's federal structure; provide for dual candidatures to enable a candidate to stand in several Länder; permit the combination of Land lists — especially in the smaller Länder; and would provide a means of including West Berlin MEPs on a list. In addition, Dr Lenz argued that not only was a Land system a system envied by the FRG's neighbours, but it could be expeditiously introduced and was especially appropriate since the first direct elections were being conducted according to temporary, transitional systems pending the adoption of a common electoral procedure.[50]

Against this, it must be remembered that internal inter-party problems militated against the CDU accepting a federal list system. Until the autumn of 1977, the CDU/CSU had discussed and favoured the adoption of a system of proportional representation with combined Land lists wherein all votes for each list would be added together to produce a federal total, the number of seats for each party would be calculated according to the d'Hondt procedure at the federal level and distributed in proportion to the number of Land list votes received by the parties in each Land.[51] The CDU/CSU had subsequently modified this proposal to align it with the usual election procedures by suggesting that half the MEPs be elected on the basis of direct election from forty constituencies (six to seven times the size of Bundestag constituencies), and the rest on the basis of combined lists. This was rejected because it was argued that constituencies with 1.5 million inhabitants apiece would be unwieldy and impersonal.

There can be little doubt that one of the main reasons inclining the CDU in favour of Land lists lay with the prospect of the CSU 'going federal' and competing against the CDU for votes. Not only had this been one of the most potent threats by the CSU leader, Strauss, to the CDU — which feared losses of support if Strauss presented himself as Chancellor candidate in federal elections — but the CSU spokesman on European policy, Aigner, came out in favour of the federal list system, and some members of the CSU saw European elections as a golden opportunity for testing the CSU's chances as a fourth federal party in subsequent domestic elections. Moreover, the importance of this had to be viewed in the perspective of the expectation that direct elections if held in 1978 or 1979 would result in European and federal elections coinciding in 1988 or 1984 respectively. The CDU feared that their position would be threatened under the federal list system over the long term, especially if this system became a feature of the common electoral law.

Defending the Government's proposal for federal lists, Dr Schäfer (SPD) argued that the FRG was the only federal member state, and federal (*qua* national) lists seemed logical: the aim was for direct elections to represent *EC citizens*, not the citizens of the EC's member states.[52] This led him to query the CDU/CSU's view that MEPs should be allowed to hold a simultaneous mandate as Ministerpräsidents, whose tasks were to represent the interests of their Länder, and whose role was therefore logically incompatible with promoting the interests of the EC and the European Parliament. Similarly, the SPD/FDP argued that federal lists would prevent Land and regional issues dominating the European elections' debate and creating unrealistic expectations among the public of MEPs' ability to realise Land interests via the European Parliament.

Despite differences between the parties over the question of incompatibility, all were agreed that prominent politicians should seek election to the European Parliament. Although it was argued that Länder lists might encourage regionalism, it did not follow that candidates from smaller Länder would fail to gain selection since the parties could opt to put them at or near the top of the lists. The CDU/CSU's argument in favour of using normal federal election procedures was rejected on the grounds that it would mean electing forty MEPs in specially drafted constituencies some of which — in Lower Saxony, Baden-Württemburg or Bavaria — would be so heterogeneous that a single MEP could not claim to represent their constituents adequately. Moreover, Dr Bangemann rejected any system likely to lead to a 'Europe of minorities'.

Like the CDU/CSU, the FDP's attitude towards the question of Land or federal lists was conditioned by electoral considerations. The FDP certainly feared that it might fail to muster the five per cent minimum of the votes, and so not be eligible to participate in the distribution of seats to the FRG's seventy-eight MEPs under the Land list system; and that it would fare better under federal lists. Even so, the Federal Ministry of the Interior originally opted for a Land-based system.

Denying that the FDP's support for the federal list was determined by electoral considerations, and rejecting Dr Lenz's suggestion that the distribution of seats in the European Parliament should match the distribution of the population on the grounds that were this principle realised it would result in a parliament of 850 members — too large to be effective — Dr Bangemann stressed the functions of the proposed electoral law. It was an interim and simple law designed to facilitate the greatest possible participation.

The Bundestag's Internal Affairs Committee scrutinised the bill and recommended acceptance of most of its Articles without amendment. It proposed modifications (often by way of refinement and clarification) that often reflected those of the Bundesrat. It drafted an additional paragraph specifying the applicability of the federal electoral law; adopted and refined the Bundesrat's reformulation of Articles concerning the nomination of MEPs. The Bundestag also adopted the recommendation that substitutes could appear on the ballot paper alongside the candidate; and a corresponding reformulation of other Articles. The stipulation that candidates should not be selected more than six months before the direct elections was altered to nine months in view of the expected postponement of direct elections, and given that parties had already initiated preparations for them. A third paragraph was added to Article 12 to provide for substitutes to replace any candidates who died before the elections.

The CDU/CSU's proposal to delete the Government's ruling that membership of the European Parliament be incompatible with appointment to, or membership of a Land government, was rejected by both the Legal and Internal Affairs Committees. Instead, a further incompatibility was inserted making the post of parliamentary state secretary incompatible with being an MEP. Although the CDU/CSU's proposal to insert the word 'German' before 'Bundestag' was accepted, its proposals to the Internal and Legal Affairs Committees to alter the federal list system in favour of Land and constituency systems, and to give each Land at least one seat in the European Parliament was rejected: the SPD/FDP argued that the latter simply benefited the strongest party in a given Land. Similarly, both Committees rejected the CDU/CSU's proposal to remove any qualifications regarding residence requirements for the enfranchisement of Germans in other EC Member States, and to extend the vote to all Germans abroad who had left the FRG within a five year period.[53] Dissatisfied with the rejection, the CDU/CSU was to table amendments during the bill's second reading in the Bundestag on 16 March, 1978.[54]

While many of the Bundestag's Committees recommendations were subsequently incorporated into the bill, this could not be passed because of continuing disagreement over the electoral system. Even though the outstanding issues were re-scrutinised by the Committees after the summer recess, it proved impossible to find an acceptable solution in 1977. Although the bill was placed on the Bundestag's agenda on 5 October, 1977, the CDU/CSU, FDP and SPD agreed to postpone it. On 17 February 1978, the bill was referred back to the Legal and Internal Affairs Committees.

In the meantime, intensive consultations were conducted between the parties and the Minister of Internal Affairs. These resulted in a series of compromises being reached; the adoption of a new Article 28 providing for parties to receive DM 3.50 per eligible voter; and a number of technical and editorial amendments to the bill. The financial arrangements were examined and accepted by the Budgets Committee which estimated that expenditure would reach DM 147,204,000 and necessitate additions to the 1978 allocation.[55]

On 8 March 1978, the Bundestag's Internal Affairs Committee unanimously approved (with one abstention) compromises proposed for the bill's second reading in the Bundestag. The compromise on the electoral formula advanced was simple insofar as it avoided either a federal or Land list system. Instead, it stipulated that the elections be conducted according to a list-based system whereby voters would have one vote, and lists could be established for either a single or several Länder together. This meant that a party could combine all its Länder lists, so effectively having a federal list, or just have one or several separate Land lists. This met the CDU's anxieties and meant that, as with federal elections, it was for the CDU and CSU to agree to desist from contesting seats in each other's areas. The European elections were not to become a test of the CSU's ability to become a fourth federal party.[56] Consonant with the agreement to permit Land lists, the Bundestag's Legal and Internal Affairs Committees accepted the Bundesrat's view rejecting the Government's argument against each Land having an electoral committee.

The Bundestag passed the Election Bill on 16 March 1978. When considered by the Bundesrat on 21 April 1978,[57] the Saar still concerned that it would fail to secure one seat in the European Parliament, unsuccessfully requested the Bundesrat to call for the establishment of an Arbitration Committee in the hope of securing acceptance of a provision assuring each Land at least one seat.[58] The Saar's request for invoking the Arbitration Committee was defeated. The Bundesrat then voted in support of the opinion of its Legal and Internal Affairs Committees that the bill required Bundesrat approval. The Bundesrat Vice-President Dr Albrecht asked the Bundesrat whether the bill should be passed. A majority for this having been obtained, he declared that it had approved the bill in conformity with the Basic Law.

The legislative process to facilitate the holding of direct elections to the European Parliament was finally completed in April 1979, when provisions governing the status of MEPs were finalised under the Legal Status Bill.

Conclusion

The legislative process initiated to facilitate the holding of direct elections followed normal practices and procedures. Delays were due as much to the all-party desire to adhere to common EC-rulings — on topics like MEPs' salaries, for instance — as to wrangling over the electoral system.

Throughout the debate over the electoral system, national political considerations conditioned party reaction to the proposed Land or federal list systems. This led to CDU anxiety lest the CSU 'go-federal' for the European elections, and use them as a test run for the 1980 federal elections and Strauss' Chancellorship aspirations. All Bundestag parties are committed to intensifying integration, the EC's enlargement, expanding the scope of the European Parliament's influence and competence — especially in regard to areas where national parliaments lack authority, and to promoting increased co-operation. Some of the issues regarding the representation of the Länder and the FRG in the directly elected European Parliament are likely to be rehearsed again if a common electoral law or procedure is discussed. The FRG is keen to adopt and adhere to supranational provisions and it is possible that the compromise formula regarding the electoral system will provide a useful example that could be adapted for a common electoral law. In addition, the FRG respects the status of MEPs, regarding them of equal stature to Members of the Bundestag and entitled to enjoy similar privileges.

Notes

1 Thanks are due to Dr Reuter of the Bundesrat Pressestelle for answering questions and providing documentation.
2 See J. Lodge and V. Herman, *Direct Elections to the European Parliament: A Community Perspective*, (Macmillan, London, 1980).
3 See the bibliography on the Parliament of the Federal Republic.
4 K. Adenauer, *Memoirs 1945-1953* (DVA, Stuttgart, 1965). Also see A. Baring, *Aussenpolitik in Adenauer's Kanzlerdemokratie* (Oldenbourg, Munich, 1969).
5 See R. Hrbek, *Die SPD, Deutschland und Europa* (Europa Union, Bonn, 1972); J. Lodge, *The European Policy of the SPD* (Sage, London, 1976); and H. Speier and W.P. Davison (eds) *West German Leadership and Foreign Policy* (Row and Peterson, Illinois, 1957).
6 Although the Germans supported the direct election of all MEPs of an expanded European Parliament, they suggested that for a transitional period, only half of them should be directly elected. For details, see *Europa-Politik der SPD*, Reihe Aussenpolitik, no.3, SPD Vorstand, Bonn, 1971, p.24.
7 J. Lodge, op.cit., pp 5-20.

8 See *Bulletin*, 7 March, 1973 and 5 February, 1974; Brandt's speech to the Hague Summit in *Parlament*, vol.19, no.50, 13 December 1969, and his speech to the Ständiger Ausschuss of the Bundestag on 30 October 1972 in *Reden und Interviews*, vol.II, Presse und Informationsamt der Bundesregierung, Bonn, 1973, p.478; and W. Scheel, *Bundestagsreden* (AZ Studio, Bonn, 1972), p.196.
9 *CDU: Das Berliner Programm mit Beschlüssen des Hamburger Parteitages 1973* (Union Betrieb, Bonn, 1973), p.10.
10 On 11 December 1973, the CDU/CSU Opposition proposed electing German MEPs via a third column included on the usual ballot paper alongside that for direct candidates to the Bundestag and the Land lists.
11 See J. Lodge, 'Britain and the EEC: Exit, Voice or Loyalty?', *Co-operation and Conflict*, vol.10, 1975, pp 199-216.
12 See CDU *Resolution for Europe* of 13 June 1977; *Beschlüsse zur Aussen, Friedens- und Sicherheitspolitik, Europapolitik, Nord-Süd-Politik* (Vorstand der SPD, Bonn, 1977) pp 24-27; *Leitlinien liberaler Europa-politik* (FPD, Bonn, 1975) pp 17, 20-21, 30-32; *Programm der SPD für die erste europäische Direktwahl 1979* (Vorstand der SPD, Bonn, 1978); CSU, *Erlanger Manifest Thesen für Europa* (CSU Landesteigung, Munich, 1979) and *Vörwarts Dokumentation*, 14 June 1977, p.2.
13 The bill referred to 'Land Berlin', not *West* Berlin. No reference was made either to the Four Powers responsibilities over all Berlin. Instead, reference was made only to the Western powers. The USSR's objections have been repeatedly rejected by the FRG, and the Western powers who on 20 September 1976 referred to the fact that the Rome Treaty applied to West Berlin. West Berlin received aid from the EC's Regional Fund. The fact that Berlin's MEPs were in fact, to be appointed to the European Parliament, rather than directly elected, did not, contrary to Soviet allegations, constitute a breach of the Four Power Agreement of 1971 over Berlin, since Berlin's delegates to the Bundestag are similarly designated rather than directly elected.
14 *Drucksache*, 8/360.
15 Bundesrat, *Drucksache*, 169/77.
16 Bundesrat, *Drucksache*, 167/77.
17 Bundesrat, *Drucksache*, 168/77.
18 Bundestag, *Drucksache*, 8/561, p.2.
19 Bundestag, *Drucksache*, 8/596.
20 Bundesrat, *Drucksache*, 283/77.
21 Bundestag, *Stenographischer Bericht*, Plenar protokoll 8/32, pp 2431 (D)–2438(B).
22 Bundesrat, *Stenographischer Bericht*, 447 Sitzung, 24 June 1977, p.163 (B).
23 *Bundesgesetzblatt*, Teil II, Z1998A.
24 Bundesrat, *Stenographischer Bericht*, 445 Sitzung, 6 May 1977, p.68C.
25 Bundesrat, *Drucksache*, 169/77, 01.04.77, p.11.
26 See Foreign Minister Genscher's (FDP) statement to the Bundestag on 26 May 1977; Bundestag, *Stenographischer Bericht*, Plenarprotokoll 8/29, pp 2036 (B) (C) ff.
27 Ibid.
28 The phrase 'Modell Deutschland' was an SPD election slogan in the 1976 General Election campaign.
29 Bundesrat, *Drucksache*, 168/77, 01.04.77, p.2.
30 *Bundesgesetzblatt*, IS, 297.
31 Bundesrat, *Drucksache*, 168/1/77, 25.04.77 and *Drucksache*, 168/77 (Beschluss, 06.05.77).
32 Deutscher Bundestag, 8. Wahlperiode, *Drucksache* 8/362, 06.05.77.
33 Deutscher Bundestag, 8. Wahlperiode, *Drucksache* 8/918, 20.09.77, p.5.
34 See Bundestag, *Drucksache* 8/2707.
35 Bundestag, *Drucksache*, 8/2708.
36 Bundesrat, *Drucksache*, 148/79; Gesetzesbeschluss des Deutschen Bundestages, 30.03.79; and Bundesrat, Zu *Drucksache* 148/79; Beschluss des Deutschen Bundestages, 30.03.79. See Bundesrat, *Plenarprotokoll 471*, 70A; and Bundesrat *Drucksache*, 148/79 (Beschluss), 6.04.79.
37 Bundesrat, *Drucksache*, 167/77, 1.04.77.
38 Ibid., p.2.
39 This is examined in detail by O. Grabitz, *Europa-Wahlrecht: Die deutschen gesetzlichen Bestimmungen fur die erste Direktwahl des Europäischen Parlaments* (Institut für Europäischen Politik, Berlin, 1977), pp 80 ff.
40 Bundesrat, *Drucksache*, 167/77 paras 3.6 and 3.7, p.13.
41 M. Bangemann, 'Preparations for Direct Elections in the Federal Republic of Germany', *Common Market Law Review*, vol.15, 1978, pp 321-35, at. p.329.
42 Deutscher Bundestag, *Drucksache*, 8/361, Anlage 3, pp 24-25.
43 Bundesrat, *Stenographischer Bericht*, 445 Sitzung, 06.06.77, pp 72 (C)–73 (B).
44 One of the targets of this provision was CSU-leader Strauss.

45 Different recommendations emanated from different committees, although there were no major disagreements between them.

46 See *Stellungnahme des Bundesrates, Drucksache*, 167/77 (Beschluss) 6.05.77; and *Antrag des Landes Nordrhein-Westfalen, Drucksache*, 167/2/77, 4.05.77.

47 Deutscher Bundestag, *Drucksache*, 8/361, Anlage 3, p.25.

48 Deutscher Bundestag, *Stenographischer Bericht*, Plenarprotokoll, 8/29, p.2037 (C).

49 Bangemann, op.cit., p.325.

50 Deutscher Bundestag, *Stenographischer Bericht*, Plenarprotokoll 8/29, pp 2038-40.

51 Bangemann, op.cit., p.323.

52 Deutscher Bundestag, *Stenographischer Bericht*, Plenarprotokoll 8/29.

53 Deutscher Bundestag, *Drucksache*, 8/917.

54 Deutscher Bundestag, *Drucksache*, 8/1632.

55 Deutscher Bundestag, *Drucksache*, 8/1609.

56 See the Krey, Wittman, Wolframm report in Deutscher Bundestag, *Drucksache*, 8/1602, pp 13-15.

57 Bundesrat, *Drucksache*, 156/1/78 and Bundesrat, *Bericht über die 457 Sitzung*, 21.04.78.

58 Both Bremen and the Saarland felt disadvantaged. The problem lies in the fact that the Länder differ widely in size and population. Bremen is the smallest with a population of 700,000; Nordrhein-Westfalen is the largest with a population of 17 million. In the Bundesrat no Land has fewer than three votes, and none has more than five votes. Strictly proportional representation based on three votes for Bremen would give Nordrhein-Westfalen 70 votes.

The Parliament of the Federal Republic: some readings

K. von Beyme, *Die parlamentarischen Regierungssysteme in Europa* (Pieper, Munich, 1972). An exhaustive historical analysis of parliamentarism.

G. Loewenberg, *Parlamentarismus im politischen System der BRD* (Rainer Wunderlich, Tubingen, 1979); *Parliament in the German political system* (Cornell U.P., Ithaca, 1967). A behavioural and procedural analysis of the parliament in its first two decades.

U. Thaysen, *Parlamentarisches Regierungssystem in der BRD* (UTB, Oplanden, 1976). A short introductory study of functions and problems focussing on: governmental control, representation, legislation.

W. Steffani, *Parlamentarische und präsidentielle Demokratie* (Westdeutscher Verlag, Oplanden, 1979). A comparative analysis of the different constitutional and organisational structures and of political behaviour in the FRG, UK, USA.

G. Lehmbruch, *Parteienwettbewerb im Bundesstaat* (Urban, Stuttgart, 1975). An historical analysis of the development of party and government competition in a federal political culture.

W. Euchner, 'Zur Lage des Parlamentarismus' in G. Schafer and C. Nedelmann, *Der CDU Staat* (Kümmerle, Frankfurt a.M., 1969), vol.I. A critique of the ideology of parliamentarism and its decline.

P. Schäfer, *Der Bundestag* (Westdeutscher Verlag, Oplanden, 1975), 2nd ed. A useful general work.

6 France: The Impossible Compromise or the End of Majority Parliamentarism?

Dominique Remy with Karl-Hermann Buck

Any process of codifying social or political issues in Parliament is structured by two elements: on the one hand, parliamentary customs and constitutional procedures constrain the process; on the other it is conditioned by the political history of the text submitted for approval. In the case of the French law on direct elections the two aspects are of equal importance, since the issue brought into focus established conflicts between the factions of the governmental majority. The issue thus threatened the functioning of the majoritarian parliamentary system that was established in the period 1958-1962.[1]

The normal legislative process

The passage of a bill, both in the pre-legislative preparatory stages and in its parliamentary scrutiny, depends essentially on its origins. Opportunities exist for social groups to participate in the process, either through their political connections, or as representatives of economic or professional interests. If the text is of parliamentary origin, it may even have been elaborated in collaboration with representatives of regional or professional interests whose clienteles are closely associated with a party or Deputy. For Government Bills, the administration itself may establish consultation with those interests affected, even before the parliamentary phase has begun, as was the case for the legislation on abortion. Alternatively, the Government Bill may reflect a compromise already agreed between social groups, as occurred in the legislation on monthly salaries.

After formal presentation to the National Assembly or Senate, a bill is sent to one of six permanent Committees — unless, in exceptional circumstances, a special committee is created.[2] In the Committee, composed of deputies designated by the party groups proportional to their strength, the text is examined collectively but under the guidance of a rapporteur. The discussions are not public, and votes are by show of hands.

The bill then passes to the plenary, when and if it is selected by the

99

Committee of Presidents.[3] The debate comprises three elements:

a) presentation by the Committee rapporteur of the original text together with amendments;

b) general discussion in which any Deputy may intervene and present amendments, subject to the constraints of the Constitution;[4]

c) formal approval of the text and of modifications to it, either by a formal vote, or by a show of hands.

The bill then passes to the other chamber in its modified form. If accepted, it must be promulgated within a fortnight. If it is further modified, then the *navette* procedure ensures: the Government may establish a Conciliation Committee (*commission mixte paritaire*) to propose a compromise to the two assembles; but if the compromise is not accepted, then the Government may decide in favour of the last vote of the National Assembly.

The preponderance of the Government *vis-a-vis* the Parliament is the primary characteristic of this legislative process. Support for the Government by the Senate is a second characteristic that is important when conflict emerges between the Government and the National Assembly. The source of governmental dominance lies in the procedure for selecting the agenda: the majority controls the Conference of Presidents, and Government Bills always obtain priority, even when no urgency procedure has been called for. Subsequently, the Government has a variety of weapons with which it may discipline its majority, limit debate and resist amendments.[5]

Any conflict between Deputies, or between Parliament and Government, may be brought before the Constitutional Council at any time prior to promulgation. Recruitment to this body favours the Government's majority, and its jurisdiction is limited;[6] it therefore represents a further means for Government to enhance the legitimacy of its proposal before Parliament.

In consequence, bills opposed by the Government can only be passed as a result of a split in the majority and a coalition with a part of the opposition. The significance of the Government's weapons to coerce the majority has been apparent both during the period when the majority parliamentary system was being established (1958-1962), and since the time when the Gaullist movement ceased to control the Government (1974). At other times, party discipline has been sufficient to ensure cohesion, and it is extremely rare for bills or amendments derived from the opposition even to emerge successfully from the committee stage.

The Senate may exert influence at three levels. Since it has a different political composition from the Assembly, its Conference of Presidents may decide, for example, not to place on the agenda a text which the National Assembly has accepted against the wishes of the Government. When the Government makes a bill an issue of confidence, and assuming that no majority can be found in the Assembly to overthrow it, then the Senate alone provides sanction for the legislation. Finally, the traditional expertise of the upper chamber may enhance its negotiating position in a Conciliation Committee, and thus help it to support the Government's position.

In principle all texts relating to international affairs follow the normal legislative path. The majority of such texts comprises a single article ratifying an international agreement, and these rapidly pass through the procedures described above. However treaties, presented as Government Bills defining an agreement already effectively determined, undergo a special parliamentary procedure insofar as they are not subject to amendment. The opportunity for deputies to intervene is thus still further reduced.[7]

The General's Europe

Whilst the history of attempts to strengthen European solidarity antedates World War II, it is essentially the evolution since the signing of the Treaty of Rome that marks the conflict over direct elections. The attitude of government and the majority underwent significant change in the intervening period, and we have therefore distinguished three sections for analysis: the Government and majority attitudes during the Gaullist period, 1958-74; their attitudes in the Liberal period beginning with the election of Giscard d'Estaing to the Presidency in 1974; and the evolution of the opposition parties.

Nevertheless, the earlier history of the Community has some bearing on this issue. Three contradictions emerge from the pre-Gaullist era, and they bring about the complex political cleavages in the 1970s. Firstly the Common Market was the product of long negotiations that occurred in the Fourth Republic, conducted by politicians who were excluded from power in the Gaullist era. Fifth Republic leaders thus associated moves towards direct elections with the preceding regime, and were reluctant to press the issue forward.

Secondly, it is clear that the goal of the first generation of Europeans — people such as R. Schuman, G. Monnet and P. Reynard — had been to maintain Europe as defined at the Yalta Conference within the Western alliance, to consolidate it through agreements and institutions, and to link it more closely to the United States. This voluntarist approach was adopted by most of the groups supportive of European integration, but it contrasts with the *dirigiste* approach of Gaullist foreign policy, whose central elements are national independence and *ouverture* to the East.[8]

A third contradiction arises from the antagonism of the founders of the Fifth Republic to the system of 'Assembly Government' that had dominated the preceding regime. They agreed that a strong executive was essential to contain the 'natural' tendency of an assembly to expand its powers. Thus successive governments in the period 1958-1974 placed priority on the establishment of a Council of Government leaders, rather than on a directly elected assembly.

The earliest proposals for European Union put forward by the Gaullists (RPF) in 1949 envisaged rule by intergovernmental council as a first phase in the development of a European confederation.[9] The Parliament was not to emerge until the second phase — and even then its definition was somewhat ambiguous. At the same time, the Gaullists proposed the use of 'a solemn referendum on Europe'. This device would provide for the mobilisation of mass support for the European institutions — both in a referendum authorising the election of a constituent assembly, and in a referendum to ratify the constitutional proposal. On this basis the Gaullists could deny any hostility to voting, even if the measures that they proposed seemed to their political and European partners to be dilatory excesses. Thus General de Gaulle and the French representatives in the European Parliament, were able to oppose the text of the Dehousse Convention in 1960, and to promote the idea of a referendum.[10] The Independents rallied to this policy in 1960, and the Moderates gave their support later.[11] But the MRP ministers did not believe the European commitment of the Government, and they resigned in 1962 after making a solemn protest in the National Assembly — an incident hitherto without precedent in the Fifth Republic.[12]

Throughout the numerous debates on ratification, budget, general policy statements, foreign policy declarations, and parliamentary questions, the position of the Government varied little between 1958 and 1974. However the development of the Economic Community and the ratification of successive complementary treaties undermined the *waiting game* of the Government. Each ratification was, in effect, a further step in the institutional development of the Community. The method of recruitment of members of the Assembly was, therefore, thrown into the limelight at each stage.

After the failure of the Dehousse Convention, France took the initiative and put forward the proposals known as the 'Fouchet Plan' — which eventually collapsed in April 1962. Although this scheme enabled the Foreign Minister to present a respectable image before the National Assembly,[13] the measures did not represent any real commitment to direct elections. During the debate ratifying the treaty providing for a unified assembly in 1965, the rapporteur supported the technical amelioration arising from this rationalisation, but rejected any political implications. The Government supported the essentially technical nature of the proposals, and the National Assembly gave its consent, with only the Communist Party voting against.

In 1969, during the debate in the European Parliament that threatened to bring the Council of Ministers before the Court of Justice, the Gaullist spokesman criticised the unrepresentativeness of the Assembly. M. Habib Deloncle (UDR) tabled an amendment to establish the principle of 'one vote, one value' without which the Assembly would lack the legitimacy necessary for legislating. Similarly, the President of the Republic, G. Pompidou, expressed reservations about direct elections at the Paris summit in 1972.[14]

During the ratification of the Budget Treaty in 1970, the Government suggested that the achievement of the Economic Community now justified a step forward in political integration. The PCF hardened its opposition; and numerous Gaullists suggested that a system of assembly government would relegate the Council of Ministers to a back seat.[15] The absence of enthusiasm for this bill — voted under the 'urgent motion' procedure, and after referral to the Constitutional Council — was merely a parliamentary reflection of the lack of concern by the Government for the implementation of direct elections.

Having warned of the dangers of assembly government which would result from direct elections; and after insisting subsequently that the precise representation of population was a necessary requirement, the Gaullist group added an opportunist argument against the Patijn proposals in 1975. To rush into such an important change in the powers of the Assembly, without full agreement between all the Member States, was to retreat into institutional change without considering the inconsistencies of the proposal. In the European Parliament, the Gaullists abstained and launched a national campaign against the Patijn proposals, and then against the Act of 20 September, 1976.[16] The vigour of the campaign reflected the constitutional significance of the issue as perceived by Gaullists, and its strategic importance in the context of the decline of Gaullist influence in the Government.

The Liberal Europe

The 1974 presidential elections marked an important turning point in French politics. For the first time since 1958, the Head of State was not a Gaullist; and after Chirac's resignation in 1976, the Prime Minister was no longer Gaullist either. The new President was a member of the liberal wing of the majority, and had defeated the Gaullist candidate at the first ballot of the election. He had always been open about his pro-European sympathies, and the inclusion of centrist political and parliamentary forces within his majority coalition reinforced his attitude. The centrist politicians had always provided the backbone of European action: P.H. Teitgen (MRP) had argued strongly for a single assembly and direct elections in 1957;[17] Jean Lecanuet's Presidential election campaign in 1965 was based essentially on its European policy; centrist leaders, together with certain Socialists,[18] have provided the main thrust of most pro-European parliamentary activity, and have played leading roles in the principal European movements.

Table 6.1
Parties in the National Assembly, March 1973

	Party	Abbreviation	Vote(%)*	Seats†
	Communist Party (Parti Communiste Francais)	PCF	20.8	73 (+1)
	Socialist Party (Parti Socialiste)	PS	} 23.7	89 (+1)
	Left-Radicals (Mouvement des Radicaux de Gauche)	MRG		13
G	Reformists (Reformateurs Democrates Sociaux)	RDS	6.9	34 (−13)
G	Centrists (Union Centriste)	UC		30
G	Independent Republicans (Republicains Independants)	UDF≠ { RI	} 45.5	55 (+6)
G	Gaullists (Union Democratique pour la Republique)	RPR≠ - UDR		183 (−14)
	Independents (Non Inscrits) and others	NI	3.1	13 (+4)
Total			100.0	490 (−15)
Turnout			81.0	

* Share of valid votes cast in the Second Ballot of the Legislative Election, March 1973.
† Seats in National Assembly, March 1973 (± changes at June 1977).

≠ UDF = Union pour la Democratie Francaise (Founded February 1978).
  RPR = Rassemblement pour la Republique (Founded December 1976).
G Party forming the Government from May 1974.

Prior to the 1974 election, Giscard d'Estaing's party, the Independent Republicans, had espoused the unusual idea of an *indirectly* elected European Senate, in the hope that by linking a more specific recruitment mechanism to a more clearly consultative chamber, they could increase legitimacy without threatening any increase in powers.[19] This idea did not gain ground, and after his election the new President made a number of initiatives in his first two years of office towards a solution to the impasse at the Council level. Nevertheless his Government's policy oscillated between demands for representation in proportion to population,[20] and opposition to any increase in power. The ambiguity of the French stance thus reflected the contradictory demands of the political forces within the majority.

Since the European Council[21] had brought together European Heads of State on a regular basis; and given the relaxation of international tensions as well as a growing international pressure for a decision on this issue; it was important for a solution to be reached and for the legislation to be enacted prior to the legislative elections of March 1978 — lest a left-wing victory might give the whip hand to the Communists instead of the Gaullists. Thus from the end of 1975, government strategy changed from restraining the Centrist demands to fighting off the Gaullists, who were hostile to direct elections.

Two explanations can be offered for this pattern of institutionalisation of conflict. The first relates to the perception of the issue within the governmental majority. Whilst previous reforms had been presented as administrative changes or a minor improvements in the efficacy of the European Parliament, this reform affected the legitimacy of the institution itself; and furthermore it took the recruitment process away from national political institutions. It is also important that previous roles as governmental actors, or as government supporters, were no longer effective in ensuring a disciplined majority — for Gaullists now had a more tenuous relationship to government. So postures hardened; and when the reform of the EP budgetary system came up for debate in 1976, just before the direct election debate, the RPR was no longer reserved — it had become hostile. Despite appearances, the debate was therefore based on more than dogma.

The second explanation relates to the electoral situation in which the parties were involved. In the municipal elections in March 1977, the left won a number of victories over a majority which was often divided. The parliamentary elections due in March 1978 were sufficiently close as to induce competition between the parties of the majority and consensus between the parties of opposition.

The united opposition

After World War II the French Socialists' European policy showed federalist sympathies, yet had more anti-Communist than genuinely socialist intentions: Western Europe, originally conceived as a Third

Force, should contribute to rapid industrial development in France, should open new markets and keep the German revival under control.[22] Torn between opposition to German rearmament and the criticism of its lack of supranationalism, the Socialists divided and thus helped to reject the idea of a European Defence Community in 1954.[23]

In the Fifth Republic, and particularly after the foundation of the new Socialist Party (Parti Socialiste, PS) in 1969, the Socialists became more critical of 'atlanticist' ideas — the recruitment of new, younger and more militant voters and members is one explanation for this. But they also rejected the Gaullist conception as a 'ridiculous independence', implying the dangers of French isolation. Some members of the traditional right of the party saw Europe as a means of attaining Socialism, and as a bulwark to economic stagnation and the resurgence of the right: 'Without Europe, Socialism is impossible'.[24] However the left wing CERES faction argued the 'préalable socialiste', insisting that a Socialist government should have sufficient margin to implement Socialist policy, without threatening French membership of the EC.[25] Whilst the 1972 party programme was not opposed to development of the Community, it was clear that no strong initiative would come from the PS. The Common Programme signed with the Communists in June of that year studiously avoided the issue of direct elections, referring only to the need for a proportional designation of representatives.[26]

At the Bagnolet Congress on Europe in December 1973, it was clear that the party was still divided. The right, including ex-Socialist leader Guy Mollet, argued for a rapid development of supranational institutions and for direct elections. The left withdrew its motion on the 'préalable socialiste' for internal coalition considerations,[27] though its report was highly critical of the general orientations of the EC. The majority report sought an extension of the European Parliament's 'role, mission and powers' — control, budgetary and legislative powers, with the right of initiation and codecision in certain fields — but pleaded only for the 'progressive democratisation of designation procedures'.[28] The compromise of the party leader, Mitterand, called for 'new policies before new structures', and unanimity was subsequently achieved on a motion calling for direct elections to be held on a proportional basis — on the method for direct elections, if not on the policy itself.

The internal divisions re-emerged in 1976, in the wake of the Council decisions, the European Parliament's adoption of the Patijn Report (supported by the PS, with the PCF abstaining), and the Tindemans' report (poorly received even by close collaborators of Mitterand). According to M. Sarre, member of the party executive and of CERES,

106

direct elections would 'help to mask Giscard's anti-socialist politics' and split the Union of the Left. On the other wing Pierre Mauroy, seen by many as a serious rival to the Socialist Party leader, Mitterand, was calling for a strong European Parliament with real powers. Eventually the Party gave its support for direct elections — provided that they were held on a proportional basis — and opposed any extension of its powers.[29]

At the same time, an intensive consultation was being conducted behind the scenes by senior officials of the French administration, pro-European politicians and experts, with Georges Spenale, the French Socialist President of the European Parliament. The matters in dispute bore on technicalities of French Law in regard to direct elections, but they provided a mechanism for direct influence by a man with impeccable connections with both the European Parliament and the Socialist Party.

The Communist Party had been excluded from membership of the European Parliament by the Gaullists until 1973; prior to this it had argued for a more proportional system of representation in the European Parliament, whilst criticising the existing general orientation of the EC. It expressed hostility towards any enlargement of the European Parliament's powers and competences, lest national sovereignty should be lost. But towards the issue of direct elections, it showed a certain amount of 'tactical flexibility'.[30]

Prior to 1974 the Party had not fully and formally rejected the idea of direct elections. After the Paris Council of December 1974, it became more hostile to the issue. But the Party was primarily concerned with ensuring (like CERES) that the national Common Programme took priority over EC matters, as was made clear in the debates with the PS on the Common Programme between 1975 and 1977. In opposing the 'subjection of France to imperialist powers', the Party was adopting a nationalist stance that was similar to that of the Gaullists.

Thus in July 1976, the Political Bureau issued a statement that:

> The PCF is, as a matter of principle, in favour of direct elections, with a proportional representation electoral system. But there is a different problem. Through direct elections to the European Assembly, they want to give it more powers . . . to use it as a democratic alibi to conceal the bankruptcy of the common market and to try to impose common austerity policies.
>
> . . . the PCF will fight against any threat to national sovereignty through extension of the powers of the European Parliament.
>
> . . . and will use any means to further the cause of a Europe for workers . . . .[31]

This statement reflected the conclusions of the important XXII Party Congress in February 1976, which expressed no hostility to direct elections held on a proportional basis. There is no doubt that the PCF would have preferred not to have direct elections, but after the Council had taken the decision, its primary concern was to take steps to contain the supranationalist consequences. The defence of national sovereignty, which became the second stage of the Party's strategy, had two political consequences which were important to the PCF: it disturbed the stability of the governing majority, and it attracted the attention of the Gaullist electorate.

Thus on 4 April 1977, Marchais, leader of the PCF, announced that:

> Direct elections to the EP is not a problem as a system of designating a national representation. If it was only that, we would be in agreement . . . .
>
> But the problem posed by direct elections . . . is the serious threat to our independence and our sovereignty, completely inconsistent with the Treaty of Rome.[32]

Whilst this has been frequently interpreted as a volte-face in the Communist Party's policy, it is clear that the PCF leader was merely playing different chords of the strategy-and-tactics piano, and was in no way inconsistent with previous policy statements.

The articulation of the issue in Parliament

Before considering the bills on direct elections and the manner in which they evolved and were passed, it is necessary to examine the prior behaviour of the parliamentary actors. The different usage of parliamentary tactics helps to expose the strategies of the parties, and their attitudes in June 1977.

The previous ratification debates on EC agreements (June 1965, June 1970 and December 1976) define an evolving scenario, but the events of 1977 do not fit the same pattern. The reservations of the Gaullists and the Communists increased in this period: the former reluctantly voted the measures proposed by their own leaders on the first two occasions; the latter voted against all these bills, and thus comprised the sole opposition force. In 1970 the PCF also put down a 'question préalable', and in 1976 they proposed merely a redrafting ('motion de renvoi'). In 1977, their attitude moderated as the prospect of coming to power came closer. In 1976 the Gaullists, virtually free of participation in government, threatened to call for an adjournment, thus indicating a hardening of their ideological position.

As an evaluation of the spontaneous attitudes of Deputies and groups towards direct elections, analysis of the patterns of submission of Private Members' Bills (propositions de loi) and parliamentary questions indicates the development of the issue. For the former, a low mean rate of one every other year is evidenced (see table 6.2), with an emphasis on three peak periods: 1963(2), 1968(2) and 1973(3). Oral questions were more frequently posed, but their rhythm is more pronounced in the 1974-77 period, and written questions confirm this later interest. It is notable that the Senate demonstrated a more active interest, at least in the use of parliamentary questions.

Table 6.2
Private Members Activity on Direct Elections, 1957-77

	1957-1969		1970-1973		1974-1977	
	Nat. Assy.	Senate	Nat. Assy.	Senate	Nat. Assy.	Senate
Private Members' Bills	3	1	5	1	—	—
Oral Questions	2	2	2	2	3	8
Written Questions	—	—	—	—	3	7

Source: analysed from *Journal Officiel*

The origins of this activity lay predominantly with the pro-Europeanists — six of the ten Private Members' Bills come from Centrist and Socialist groups — though the groups hostile to the EC were also important sources. These six pro-European bills were virtually identical in form — proposing a date for direct elections and asking for the Government to propose the details — and they never reached the agenda. The three Communist bills were also duplications of each other.[33] The exception was a Bill by de Broglie (UDR) proposing indirect election on the same electoral college system as used for the Senate.

Of the oral questions, only the three latest questions in the National Assembly dealt directly with direct elections. One asked about the implication of delays in Britain for the European elections. The other two were from Michel Debré (RPR), the strictly orthodox Gaullist and former Prime Minister, who queried the constitutional compatibility of the direct elections proposal in December 1975, just after the European Parliament had passed the Patijn proposal; and secondly, he raised the question of controls over finance for the election campaigns (6 May 1977). (Perhaps one should also note his earlier question in 1957, when he expressed concern about the haste with which preparations for direct elections were proceeding!) The other oral questions were of a more general character about how the Government proposed to push forward the institutional development of Europe, and how it would stimulate and inform public opinion about the future elections.

In the National Assembly, the three written questions also derived from Debré: in December 1975 he again raised the question of constitutional incompatibility by this means, and called for a debate on the issue. Then he asked about the President's statements on a confederal Europe. Finally he proposed that incompatibility of elected mandates to the EP could only be determined by the national Parliaments — an attempt to retain control by the latter body. On the other hand, the questions in the Senate all derived from Centrist members — five of the seven written questions came from M. Jung (Republicain Populaire) — and they provided the only precise expression of demand for political and legal union in Europe.

Finally, we come to the report of Senator Nuninger dated 11 June 1975, which was organised by the Legal Affairs Committee in response to a petition with 3,084 signatures of municipal and departmental councillors, Deputies and former Deputies. The petition sought both to publicise the idea of direct elections, and to initiate debate on a Constitution for Europe. Whilst the report was not debated in the Senate, its preparation symbolises yet again the practical concern of the upper chamber for the European idea.

The contents of the two bills

In France, two bills were necessary to put the direct election policy into effect. The first provided ratification of the Act arising from the European Council's Decision in September 1976, and thus established the principle of direct elections; the method of implementation was defined in the second bill. The content of these two bills reflect the contradictions which the Government was obliged to face in order to mobilise the maximum support. These constraints also explain the ambiguities that are in the text.

The Constitution and the Standing Orders (Réglement) of the National Assembly prescribe specific procedures for the ratification of treaties.[34] Since these procedures could not be applied to the electoral law itself, there had to be two laws. Initially the Government expected to pass the Ratification Bill in the spring session of 1977, and to deal with the Implementation Bill that autumn. However, in response to the collective pressure of the PCF and the RPR, the Government agreed to present the bills together. Nevertheless logic required that they be taken in succession.

The Ratification Bill consisted of six pages of explanatory preamble, followed by the two Articles of the bill itself, together with the text of the Act agreed by the Council. The preamble began with an assurance and a justification of the Government's policy. The guarantee was provided by the decision of the Constitutional Council of 30 December 1976, which was also referred to in the two Articles of the bill itself. The justification arose from the interpretation of past decisions in regard to this issue: no government had renounced Article 138 of the Treaty of Rome, indeed it had always been argued that 'implementation was dependent on the evolution of the Community'. The evolution was marked by two steps: the decision of the Hague European summit in 1969 to re-examine the direct elections issue in Council; the acquisition by the EC of its own resources in 1974, together with the reform of the European Parliament's budgetary process. Thus the Government sought to link its direct elections proposal to previous commitments made under Giscard d'Estaing's first Prime Minister — and Gaullist leader — Jacques Chirac.

The preamble concluded with the assertion that 'the Government does not support any extension to the powers of the parliamentary Assembly'. This declaration introduced the second Article of the bill, which stipulated that any change in powers, that had not been authorised or ratified in accordance with the procedures laid down in the Treaty of Rome, and that had not satisfied the necessary constitutional procedures, 'would be null and void in respect of France'.[35] This text resulted from negotiations between the Government and M. Couve de Murville for the RPR; but some Gaullists, represented in debate by Michel Debré (RPR), were not satisfied with the legal value of this clause: it did not constrain the other nations. Nevertheless, the incorporation of the second Article differentiates this bill from the normal single article treaty ratification.

The other bill had a mere two pages of preamble, but was followed by twenty-five Articles set out in nine chapters. The key provision in Article 2 provided for proportional representation on the basis of closed party lists. This innovation had been demanded for many years by the parties of the left and of the centre — at least when the latter were not in the governmental majority — but it was modified by two provisions favouring the larger parties: first, remainders distributed on the highest average principle; second, a threshold to eliminate those lists obtaining less than 5 per cent of the vote. The third Article declared simply that 'The territory of the Republic forms a single constituency'. In these two clauses lay the whole of the Government's strategy to maximise parliamentary support for the text. On the one hand the electoral system satisfied the traditional demands of the left, as well as appealing to the smaller parties of centre and right which could now compete alone and achieve fair representation without having to form electoral alliances. On the other hand Gaullist fears of a breakthrough by regional parties would be minimised by the use of a national constituency.

The other feature of the bill was that it favoured the large parties already represented in Parliament. The deposit of 100,000 Francs was returnable to those exceeding the 5 per cent threshold; the same criterion was used for the state contribution to campaign expenses. The majority of the radio and TV campaigns was shared between the lists of parties already forming parliamentary groups in the national Parliament.[36]

The constitutional wrangle

At the very beginning of the process, when the EP adopted the Patijn Report at the end of 1975, M. Debré led a preliminary campaign regarding the constitutional restrictions on the use of elections: revision of the Constitution was the precondition he insisted upon, even before the interconnected issues of 'transfer of sovereignty' and 'future powers' came into focus. The latter issue was first articulated by the RPR in November 1976, and a 'Committee of French Unity and Independence' was set up shortly afterwards.[37] The problem of sovereignty raised two questions: a legitimacy question — 'can a non-national democracy be legitimate?' — and a legality question — 'will the future Assembly respect the powers granted by the Treaty of Rome?'[38]

The first question arose from a specific ideological approach to the EC itself, and could never be satisfactorily answered. The Government, the Prime Minister and the President all gave assurances in regard to the second question — that the French Government was opposed to any extension of the competences of the directly elected Assembly. But the pro-Europeans within the majority had never concealed their ambitions, and from time to time public statements by political leaders re-opened the issue. Neither the decision of the Constitutional Council nor the passing of the bill were effective in closing this debate.

The referral of the issue to the Constitutional Council by the President of the Republic marked the third phase in the dispute. Jurists had argued not only about the Council's sphere of decision: 'could it determine merely the conformity of the September agreement to the Treat of Rome, or could it also define its conformity to the French Constitution?' but also as to the legality of the Council making a decision after the signing of the agreement and without a revision of the Constitution.[39] It was agreed that the Council's judgement of 1970, in regard to the ratification of the new budgetary powers of the Assembly, could not be used as a precedent since it concerned an 'administrative' measure, and not an 'executive' measure as was the case in 1977. But M. Debré's case on behalf of the diehard Gaullist faction was different: he claimed that the introduction of judicial review into the 1958 Constitution was precisely in order to control situations like Article 138 of the Treaty of Rome. The decision of the Council, though secret, can only have been achieved by a majority of one, given the sympathies of some of its members for the former Gaullist leader's argument: in the decision given on 30 December 1976, the constitutionality of the Act was accepted.[40]

In its decision, the Council tried to respond to the legitimacy question by assuring that an international election threatened neither the sovereignty nor the indivisibility of the Republic. It failed to respond to the legality question — merely asserting again that renegotiation of the treaties and constitutional revision would be necessary prior to any increase in powers. M. Debré and the Committee for Unity called for a treaty negotiation specifically to limit the future powers of the Assembly, and from early 1977 he advocated the signature by the Nine of an additional protocol containing measures designed to limit Assembly powers: notably limited sessions, agenda agreed unanimously by the European Council, and no responsibility of the Commission before the Assembly.[41]

The Gaullist movement divided at this juncture. The Movement for the Independence of Europe, led by M. Guichard, sought to distinguish between direct elections — which it supported — and the question of Assembly powers. M. Couve de Murville, posing as a moderate and a mediator, suggested that the protocol would probably not be agreed by the Nine, given the unconditional nature of the existing agreement. Moreover a law would be a more substantial form than a protocol, which would not bind subsequent governments. In April 1977, the President of the Republic rejected the idea of renegotiating a protocol — but agreed to the idea of an additional article, with a view to further enlarging the ultimate vote.

The two bills in Parliament

Three central characteristics define the legislative procedure adopted:

a) the Ratification Bill was not voted, but the Implementation Bill was passed with virtually the entirety of both chambers in support.

b) the Senate played a very special role in the parliamentary process, both in terms of procedure and in its political contribution.

113

c) Once the principle had been won, the doctrinal conflicts subsided and the debate on the electoral method was relatively brief.

In order to escape from the impasse created by the obstinacy of the Gaullist-Communist opposition, the Government adopted an exceptional parliamentary procedure, that released it from its political mortgage. On the 7 June, 1977, the Communist Party tabled a *motion de renvoi*; two days later, the RPR tabled a motion for the adjournment (and M. Debré withdrew his *question préalable* of 25 May); the next day the Foreign Affairs Committee duplicated this demand. The refusal of the RPR to withdraw its motion, strengthened by the vote in Committee (13 for the adjournment: PC and RPR; 5 against: UDF; 6 not voting: PS and MRG), forced the Government to employ — for only the eleventh time since 1958 — the procedure by which the Government makes the bill an issue of confidence (Constitution, Article 49iii). The bill then automatically becomes law after twenty-four hours unless a censure motion is tabled. By this means the Government could override the various motions, and pass the bill without the positive support of the opposition and without creating a serious crisis within the majority.

The use of this strategy engendered the hostility of both the PCF and the Gaullists. The former were aggrieved at being deprived of the right to sanction a law. The latter were concerned at the irreversibility of the process — whereas on previous occasions there was an opportunity to subsequently reconsider the texts. The Socialists did not openly criticise the procedure — indeed they appreciated the opportunity of avoiding a public demonstration of the fundamental differences with their partner, the Communist Party. The Prime Minister, M. Barre, and the spokesman for the Republican Party, M. Chinaud, rejected these criticisms and justified the strategy on the grounds that the reform was a part of Government policy, and this warranted the use of such procedures as were necessary for its successful passage.

The debate on the constitutional device, which was being used for the first time against the principal author of that Constitution, M. Debré, was coupled with a dispute about the Standing Orders. Unlike the Senate, the Standing Orders of the National Assembly do not allow amendments to be tabled for international agreements. The Government had included in the Ratification Bill, as a result of the negotiations with the RPR described above, a second Article which took the sense of the bill beyond the scope of a mere ratification.[42] So a new controversy developed, involving the Gaullists and the left-wing opposition, including the Socialists on this occasion. Only the President of the Assembly was in a position to resolve the conflict: President E. Faure, a member of that wing of the RPR which supported direct elections, decided in favour of the Government — that the second Article merely reinforced the first; it therefore concerned international relations, and could not be the subject of amendment. Nevertheless, the Communists tried to vote an amendment in the Senate, which was declared out of order.[43]

Other procedural devices were also employed to facilitate the passage of the two bills. In particular, the declaration of urgency (Constitution, Article 45ii) gave priority so that both bills were voted within a month, even though the action of the Senate necessitated a Conciliation Committee and a Second Reading. One consequence of this was that the National Assembly began to debate the second bill before the Senate had dealt with the principle.

The probability of rejection was much lower in the Upper Chamber, given the pro-European senatorial activity discussed previously, the crucial role of Centrist groups in this assembly, and the relative weakness of the Gaullist and Communist groups. Since the Government is not responsible to the Senate, it did not need to shield itself from the impact of a vote. In the event this was won, by 220 votes in support of the Ratification Bill and none against: the Communists abstained, whilst almost the whole of the Gaullist group did not vote (see table 6.3). On the other hand the Government had to find a means of

Table 6.3
Party behaviour in the five Parliamentary votes

	a. The anti-European coalition				b. Dissent within parties
	Comm. PCF	Soc. PS + MRG	Libs. RCDS + RI	Gaull. RPR	(nos. of Deputies/Senators *not* voting with party group)
Senate: Ratification Bill	B	A	A	B	2 Gaull, 5 Libs 1 Soc, 5 Centrists
Senate: Implementation Bill	B	A	A	A	3 Centrists
National Assembly: Committee Amendt.	C	C	A	C	37 Gaull, 5 Libs
National Assembly: PCF Amendment	C	C	A	C	11 Gaull, 5 Libs 7 Soc, 3 Comm
National Assembly: Implementation Bill	A	A	A	A	8 Gaull 1 Soc

Key: A = Party Group supports Government
      B = Party Group abstention/no vote
      C = Party Group votes against Government

115

avoiding amendment, and it used Articles 41, 53 and 54 of the Constitution: the former rejects any bill or amendment that is outside the domain of the law; the latter two Articles entrust the responsibility for the signing of treaties to the Executive.

The debate in the Senate was very lively and relatively long (see tables 6.4 and 6.5). Though they had no real sanction, the Senators felt obliged to give some sort of political control to the bill, and to inject into the debate the 'real dimensions of the issue', above and 'beyond the quarrels of parties and the plots of politicians'.[44] Whilst they were constrained in performing this role during the debate on ratification, they were able to fulfil it during the debate on implementation.

Table 6.4

Interventions in the debates on Direct Election Bills
(nos. of interventions)

BILL	Independents NI		Gaullists RPR		Liberals UDF		Socialists PS+MRG		Communists PCF	
	Nat. Ass.	Sen.	Nat. Ass.	Sen.	Nat. Ass.	Sen.	Nat. Ass.	Sen.	Nat. Ass.	Sen.
Ratification	2	2	9	2	10	7	5	9	4	2
Implementation	—	1	1	1	1	6	1	3	1	1

For the second bill, the Committee in the National Assembly had adopted only one additional amendment, which was voted in plenary session (see table 6.3) by a majority including the Gaullists and the whole of the Left,[45] in spite of the Government's opposition. The Committee amendment — signed by the rapporteur, 1 RPR, 1 PCF and 1 Socialist (with CERES, left-wing sympathies) sought to retain exclusive control over direct elections in the hands of the French Parliament. The Government suspended the session and tried with the President of the Committee on Laws to rule the amendment out of order — without success. The amendment was carried by 325 votes to 145. The second modification, only partly accepted by the Committee, was proposed by Michel Debré: he sought the application to MEPs of the same tax principles as obtained for Senators and Deputies. Whilst the Government argued that this was the proper concern of the EP, the proposal was accepted by the Assembly without a public vote. The third contribution of the Assembly was introduced by a Gaullist deputy with the prior and explicit agreement of the Government, but against the recommendation of the Committee. It restricted the state-sponsored election campaign to the national political parties. Paradoxically, the latter Article was later completely changed by the Senate.[46] However the treatment of the bill at First Reading demonstrated the extreme fragility of the Government when faced with a coalition between its alliance partner and the opposition.

In the Senate, the Government had to face a different type of attack: from the Atlanticists and Europeanists who sought not only a return to the original text, but also some further modifications to its delicate equilibrium. On the recommendation of the rapporteur and the Senate Committee, the Senate adopted eleven amendments — six of which were of a technical or judicial nature, which demonstrated the serious workmanship of the upper house, but which did not relate to any real political conflict. The other five modified the text to such an extent that the PCF began to argue vigorously for the National Assembly's version, and then abstained on both First and Second Readings in the Senate (see table 6.3).

First of all the Senate Committee's rapporteur modified the additional Article giving parliamentary control over direct elections, arguing that there was a danger of conflict between the bill and the Treaty. It now read that the method of election 'can only be changed by new legislation'. This emphasised the National Assembly's point that Parliament should not be forced to accept new electoral arrangements presented as a package in an unamendable international agreement. Secondly, the Article concerning the tax status of MEPs was removed. Thirdly, the new Gaullist Article on election campaign expenses was turned on its head to open the election campaign to *all* the lists presented. The other two amendments were important changes, though they did not conflict with the National Assembly's text: the one ascribed to the State the costs of the official campaign on radio and TV, whilst the other extended these provisions to the overseas departments and territories (DOM—TOM). There were also a number of unsuccessful amendments proposed by the Europeanists which aimed at weakening the national characteristics of the election by regionalising it in some respects, and at lowering the threshold of representation in order to enlarge the opportunities for candidates.

Although the text contained twenty-five Articles, compared with the two Articles of the Ratification Bill, and despite extensive amendment by the Senate, the debate on the Implementation Bill lasted about half as long as the debate on the principle (see table 6.5). Similarly, only four Deputies spoke in the Implementation debate in the National Assembly (thirty in the Ratification debate); whilst in the Senate the ratio of interventions was about two to one.[47] Two factors explain the collapse of parliamentary interest which was particularly evident in the Gaullist camp: firstly, for the Gaullists the principal issue was the single national constituency for the election; once the concession had been

117

Table 6.5
Duration of Parliamentary debate on Direct Election Bills (hours)

	National Assembly	Senate
Ratification	11	8½
Implementation	6	5

made, subsequent disputes were no more than formal gestures. Secondly, the conflict was an essentially symbolic action, designed to depict the difference of opinion on the principle itself and its consequences; in this sense, the action goes on.

The opposition(s): papering over the cracks

The divisions within the opposition were clearly demonstrated by the differences between the policy positions of the parties, and they were reflected in the parliamentary votes (see table 6.3); dissent within the parliamentary groups was also evident. However, the split in the majority, together with some procedural juggling, enabled the opposition to conceal its division, at least in formal terms. At the same time, the efforts by some parties to lay the foundations for European electoral platforms may in the long term have some impact on national party alliances.

The Communist parliamentary group tabled some amendments, insisting that proportional representation with national lists be mandatory for all subsequent elections and that any extension of the Assembly's powers be banned, stipulating that if this was violated, such powers would be declared null and void within France. They also demanded that ratification be postponed until sufficient guarantees had been obtained from the other Member States.

Relations between Socialists and Communists worsened as a result of the debate on European integration and direct elections. On 6 June, 1977, the Bureau of the Union of Socialist Parties in the EEC, adopted a proposal for a common electoral programme. M. Rocard (PS) had been in charge of the part on Social Policy — it is rumoured that his German counterpart, Minister Ehrenberg, was astonished at the ease with which Rocard accepted more moderate SPD ideas. M. Pontillon made major contributions to the section on the EC's foreign policy.

Aware of the Communist criticism of the Socialist Party's tendency

118

to veer to the right, and conscious of the delicate state of relations with the PCF, the Socialist Party secretariat refused either to distribute this proposal officially, or to study it before December 1977. The Executive Bureau decided not to adopt the project in mid 1978, by an almost unanimous vote.

The Communists also wanted to hide their differences with the PS from the public, so that a complete break could be avoided and so that the PCF could exercise some influence in the PS, through its left-wing which gave priority to the Union of the Left.

During the debate in the National Assembly, socialist opinions were represented by A. Chandernagor on behalf of the traditional pro-European wing, and P. Cot on behalf of the official party-line. Cot criticised the refusal to take the amendments into account, since the Assembly would become a mere 'rubber stamp' for governmental decisions. However, he declared, the European Parliament might serve as a 'tribune for socialist and French interests, a place to strengthen solidarity, to spread the idea of democratic planning and nationalisation, and to fight for a Europe of the workers'.

For the Communist Party, M. Bordu declared that the PCF was in favour of 'an EEC of economic and social progress, a co-operation on the basis of voluntary association among our countries'. M. Ansart pointed out that the rejection of the amendments meant a disregard towards the national Assembly 'precisely at the moment when the EC was allegedly to be democratised'. A progressive and democratic EC would be better attained by stable economic development and social politics on a *national* level.

The political significance and parliamentary implications of the debate

Prior to 1957, traditional partisan cleavages had been shaken by the proposals for a European Defence Community, and several governments had been threatened.[48] The arena of European policy, symbolised here by the issue of direct elections, thus provides an important test of the operation of political institutions and the condition of political parties. More specifically, this debate has demonstrated the vulnerability of the executive when its majority is divided. On the other hand, it has shown the efficacy of the mechanisms introduced in 1958 to create a 'rationalised parliamentarism', and thus to strengthen the position of the Government.

The Government found itself torn between its own international commitments and the contradictory demands of its own majority. The smallness of the policy area within which it had to perform delicate manoeuvres was due essentially to the splits within the majority. But these divisions, and indeed those of the opposition parties, were not clearly evidenced in either the debates or the votes in Parliament – for the latter this was due to traditional acceptance of party discipline, whilst for the former the proximity of national elections encouraged subservience to the party organisation. Thus the only dimension evident from an analysis of parliamentary activity divides Gaullists and Communists from Socialists and Liberals, with sovereignty as the major issue. But in the five formal votes in Parliament, the RPR always adopted a position distinct from that of the PCF (see table 6.3).

It is also clear that the successful passage of the bills through Parliament did not close the debate. Immediately after the parliamentary elections, the Gaullists took up the offensive again, their strategic position within the majority giving them a powerful leverage on the Government. In the twelve months from the elections in March 1978, six Private Members Bills were tabled;[49] two of these were passed by the Assembly, one from the RPR and one from the PCF. The former made it illegal for lists to receive subsidies either from France or from abroad. The second warned of 'interference by a foreign institution (i.e. the EC) in the election of the French representatives'. The two measures were incorporated into a single bill and given a successful First Reading in the National Assembly in December 1978. The vote demonstrated the same party cleavages that had been evidenced in the earlier debates, with the PCF and RPR allied together (see table 6.3). The Government did not bother to oppose the bill in the National Assembly – it relied on its being swallowed up in the Senate. Indeed the bill was never put on the agenda of the Senate, despite the Communist's request (9 January, 1979) for an Extraordinary Session of Parliament to consider the text.

In other contexts, the Gaullist faction and other non-Communist nationalists have been reunited from time to time in response to various French ministerial declarations or foreign politician's speeches.[50] The Gaullists have renewed their call for an assurance or protocol from the Nine on future powers, threatening the unity of the majority, with the consequential distortion of EP representation, if their demands were not met. On 19 November, 1978, the President of the Republic formally rejected this stratagem as without consequence, given the second clause of the Ratification Bill and given the absence of juridical standing of such a protocol.

M. Chirac's response was the 'Cochin declaration', in which he gave a serious warning of the dangers of supranationalism in Europe. 'As always occurs when France's standing is threatened, the voice of those who speak for foreign interests can be heard, murmuring peaceful and reassuring sentiments. Pay no heed, my friends: they represent the torpor that precedes the stillness of death.' The statement marks a climax to the posture of resistance by the most important faction in the majority, a strategy that had begun with Chirac's resignation as Prime Minister in the summer of 1976. The resolution of this conflict within the majority undoubtedly also took place within the RPR itself, but the existence of this internal dispute helped to provide a system of party competition peculiar to the European issue.

The second aspect of this conclusion is an evaluation of the efficacy of the mechanisms of the 'rationalised parliamentary system' introduced in 1958. Five characteristics testify to the predominance of the Government in the adoption of legislation, even when it is in a vulnerable political position.

Firstly, the Government decided to refer the issue to the Constitutional Council, after some hesitation in regard both to the competency of this body and to the political consequences of an unfavourable decision. The goal was to disarm the constitutional critics of the bill, and the Council decision considerably strengthened the Government's position shortly before the debate began in Parliament.

Secondly, the Declaration of Urgency enabled the negotiations between the two Chambers to be abbreviated after a single reading in each House. Although this device has been used relatively frequently (twenty-three times in 1977), its use demonstrates the Government's desire to have the bill passed before the end of 1977, so that it could be ascribed as part of the achievements of the majority before the parliamentary elections. In consequence, the two bills both passed in a month — whereas the average duration for the passage of a governmental bill is 166 days.

Thirdly, the use of Article 49 of the Constitution to make the Ratification Bill an issue of confidence demonstrates a high level of Government coercion, the more notable given that the device had been used only eleven times in the whole of the Fifth Republic. The implication of the device was that it became the responsibility of the opposition to vote a motion of censure with an absolute majority of the chamber — failing which, the bill would automatically become law. When the addition of the supplementary Article in the Ratification Bill — in itself an exceptional feature — failed to satisfy the dissident faction within the majority, Article 49 had to be invoked in order to avoid a split in the majority on a major item of government policy, only a few months before an essentially bipolarised election. The first bill passed to the Senate in this way without the National Assembly making any decision. On the other hand, the role of the Senate could be correspondingly enhanced, given its more favourable attitude to both bills, and the fact that the Government was not responsible to the upper chamber. It voted the first bill; and given that the deputies accepted its

121

version of the Implementation Bill at Second Reading, after a governmental speech delineating the fundamentals of European policy, it may be said that the Senate also presided over the destiny of the second bill.

Fourthly, the use of the conciliation committee procedure to resolve the difference between the two Chambers is important, particularly given the Government's objective. The joint Committee's proposal, which ultimately obtained, was based entirely on the Senate proposals. Whereas one might assume, in the absence of any systematic analysis, that the norm would be for a compromise balancing equally the demands of the two Chambers, or even favouring the politically dominant National Assembly.

Finally, in quantitative terms, it is clear that the ratification debate differed significantly from other treaty ratifications. Only two or three Deputies would normally participate in a ratification debate, whereas in 1977 thirty Deputies and twenty-four Senators spoke in their respective Chambers. Conversely the Implementation Bill received a less extensive treatment, whereas one might have expected that a measure, dealing with an issue so close to the hearts of politicians as an election, would generate a considerable debate from a body composed entirely of experts in this matter.

Thus in France the legislation of an international agreement appeared more like the debating of a major policy bill; whilst the new electoral law did not generate any innovatory ideological discourse in Parliament. In part this was due to the resolution of the electoral system issue in the pre-legislative stages; in part to the irresolvability of the question of legitimacy, which remains an issue even after the first election.

The legislative process on direct elections marks a considerable accomplishment for the institutions of the Fifth Republic and for the majority parliamentary system. Although the pattern of the legislative process was unusual in various ways, it was possible in the end for the Government to carry the legislative proposal without fundamentally threatening the existing coalition structures. Moreover in order to achieve this goal, it had to use the most authoritarian device at its disposal against those who had created the constitutional provisions.

Notes

1 See J.L. Parodi, *Les Rapports entre l'Executif et le Legislatif sous la Cinquième Republique* (A. Colin, Paris, 1972).
2 In the 1973-1978 legislature, nine special Committees were established whilst 1,895 bills were examined. Apart from the main Committee, other Committees may ask, or be asked, to give an opinion (*avis*).
3 The Conference of Presidents consists of representatives of the Government, the Presidents of each Assembly and the Presidents of all party groups and Committees in the Parliament.

4 Amendments may not increase public expenditure, and they must be consistent with the 'domain of the law' defined in the Constitution (Articles 34, 40, 41).

5 The package vote procedure (*vote bloquée*: Article 44iii), which provides for a single vote on the Government's text of a bill, was used 126 times in the 1973-78 legislature. The urgency procedure (*'declaration d'urgence'*: Article 49iii) makes the bill an issue of confidence, and was used twice in the 1973-78 legislature: once for the Direct Elections Bill, and once for a Supplementary Finance Bill.

6 The Constitutional Council consists of nine Councillors, three named by the President of the Senate, three by the President of the National Assembly and three by the President of the Republic, who also names the President of the Council. These three Presidents shared with the Prime Minister the exclusive right of referral, until 29 October, 1974, when sixty Senators or Deputies could also make a reference, except for international treaties.

7 See A. Brouillet, *Le Monde Diplomatique*, May 1979.

8 P. Dabezies and H. Portelli, 'Les Fondements de la Querelle Politique', *Pouvoirs*, 1977, pp 67-89.

9 P. Manin, *Le R.P.F. et les Problèmes Européens* (P.U.F., Paris, 1966).

10 Cf. the arguments of M. Vendroux during the debate on the draft convention in the European Assembly in May 1960.

11 Cf. the European themes of M. Lecanuet's presidential campaign against General de Gaulle in 1965.

12 On 13 June 1962 the Government rejected a demand by the Foreign Affairs Committee for a vote at the end of a debate on foreign policy. The Committee President then read a text signed by 293 Deputies (Socialist, Centrist, MRP, Independents, and others) supporting European integration. These Deputies then left the Chamber, leaving Communists and Gaullists facing each other.

13 M. Couve de Murville, Minister for Foreign Affairs, speaking prior to the 'Europeans motion' cited above. *J.O. D.P. A.N.*, 13 June 1962, p.1664.

14 See J.L. Burban, 'Les Gaullistes et l'Election du Parlement Européen au Suffrage Universel Direct', *Revue du Marché Commun*, no.193, January 1978, p.79.

15 'We had enough trouble in France getting rid of the assembly government. That was not all so that some new fairy godmother could give it to the new-born Europe as a christening present.' M. Habib Deloncle, *J.O. D.P. A.N.*, 28 April 1970, p.1337.

16 A. Sanguinetti, in the Gaullist journal *l'Appel*, 29 October 1976. Cf. C. Bourdet (PSU), 'Comme en 1940', *Le Monde*, 15 June 1977.

17 *J.O. D.P. A.N.*, 16 January 1957, p.12.

18 One of the Vice-Presidents of the European Movement is P. Jacquet, member of the National Executive of the Socialist Party.

19 The Giscardians supported the idea of a European Senate from November 1966 until 1974: J. Destremeau, *J.O. D.P. A.N.*, 19 June 1973, p.2259.

20 Speech by President V. Giscard d'Estaing, *Le Monde*, 21 October 1975.

21 The European Council — a regular meeting of the Heads of State of the European Community — was inaugurated in 1972 under President Pompidou, but regularised and institutionalised in December 1975 by his successor, Giscard d'Estaing.

22 See B. Criddle, *Socialists and European Integration* (Routledge, London, 1969); S. Charlton, *The French Left and European Integration*, (U. of Denver, Denver, 1972); various articles in J. Rideau (ed.), *La France et les Communautés Européennes*(L.G.D.J., Paris, 1975); for more details see K.H. Buck, *Die italienischen und französischen Sozialisten und Kommunisten und ihre Haltung zur Europäischen Integration* (unpublished thesis, Tubingen, 1977).

23 For anti-German ideas see also A. Savary, *Pour le nouveau parti socialiste* (Seuil, Paris, 1970) p.153; *Le Monde*, 1 December 1970, p.9; see also the selection of documents in the publication for the Bagnolet Congress, 1973: *Les Socialistes et l'Europe*.

24 *Democratie Socialiste*, May 1970; A Ferrat, 'L'Europe et le socialisme', *Revue du Socialisme*, vol.216, 1968, pp 785-807.

25 See contributions in: *Les socialistes et l'Europe*, op.cit.

26 Ibid., p.26ff.

27 Ibid., p.26ff., p.63.

28 Ibid., p.19-21.

29 *Le Monde*, 24 January 1976 and 8-9 February 1976.

30 See J. Denis and J. Kanapa, *Pour ou contre l'Europe*,(Ed. Sociales, Paris, 1969); various studies by Timmermann, published by: Bundesinstitut fur ostwissenschaftliche und internationale Studien, Köln; P. Bordu in: *Cahiers du Communisme* no.2, 1974, pp 94-102; see also J.L. Burban, 'Les communistes et l'élection du PE au suffrage universel', *Revue du Marché Commun*, vol.199, 1976, pp 373-80.

31 For more party statements on these matters, see: 'Les Communistes Français et l'Europe', *Bulletin des Communistes Français à l'Assemblée des Communautés Européenes*, Luxembourg, nos.1-3, 1978/79.

32 Ibid.

33 In these texts it is argued that the representatives of the French Parliament to the European Parliament should be elected by proportional representation and not by majority vote. They do not therefore relate directly to direct elections. Nevertheless they indicate both the developing interest of the PCF in the EC and the fact that the party was seeking a more equitable representation of party groups, without any fundamental change in the method of recruitment.

34 The 1958 Constitution states that treaties and international agreements may only be ratified or approved by the passing of a law (Section 6, Article 53).

35 Article 2 of the Ratification Act states that: 'Any modification to the powers of the Assembly of the European Communities, as they stand at the date on which the Act providing for direct elections to the Assembly was signed, which have not been ratified or approved according to the procedures defined in the Treaties of Paris and Rome, and which have not given rise to a revision of the Constitution in accordance with the decision of the Constitutional Council of 30 December 1976, will be null and void in respect of France.'

36 Article 17. The reference to 'parliamentary groups' has important political implications. It excluded from the radio-TV campaign not only those parties not represented in Parliament, but also those parties which were too small to form a single group, e.g. the left-Radicals (MRG).

37 The 'Comité pour l'Unité et l'Indépendance de la France' was created on 20 January 1977. On the 8 May 1977, a committee 'contre une Europe capitaliste germano-americaine' was established, and on 15 June 1977 a declaration 'contre une Europe supranationale' was issued. These two movements brought together radical Gaullists such as General Binoche, the Young Gaullist movement (UJP), some leaders of the extreme right (NAF) and of the extreme left (such as J.P. Sartre and C. Bourdet).

38 Cf. G. Vedel, 'Les Racines de la Querelle Constitutionelle', *Pouvoirs*, op.cit., pp 23-37.

39 Several past or present members of the Constitutional Council debated whether the Council was competent to determine this issue in *Le Monde*: L. Philip, F. Luchaire, P. Boitreaud, J. Robert, *Le Monde*, 13, 24, 26 November 1976.

40 The Constitutional Council offered the following justifications:
- The sole object of the decision of 24 September 1976 was to create direct elections to the European Parliament.
- The preamble to the French Constitutions of 1946 and 1958 preclude any transfer of sovereignty.
- The text in question does not provide for any change from the existing powers of the European Parliament.
- Direct elections create neither new sovereignty, nor institutions incompatible with national sovereignty. Any change in the treaties must arise from their renegotiation.
- The agreement of 20 September 1976 does not threaten the indivisibility of the Republic.
- Sovereignty as in Article 3 of the Constitution can only be national.
- The EP cannot share in national sovereignty: the text cannot therefore be criticised as unconstitutional in terms of Articles 23 and 24 of the Constitution, which affect those institutions which do share in national sovereignty.

41 The other points in M. Debré's protocol were:
- that the regulation of the simultaneous holding of several elected offices, and of incompatibility with other offices, must be the responsibility of national parliaments.
- that on request by any Member State, the Court of Justice should adjudicate the conformity of actions of the European Parliament to the Treaty of Rome.

42 See note 35.

43 The Government had rejected M. Debré's amendment as out of order (Article 41: outside the domain of the law). M. Foyer, President of the Committee on Laws, disagreed with the Government's interpretation, even though his Committee had rejected the amendment. But the view of M. Edgar Faure, President of the Assembly, was that it was out of order.

44 J. Cluzel (Centrist: UDCP), *J.O. D.P. Sen* 1977, p.1661.

45 Proposed in Committee by the left-wing Socialists: the party was not united on this point.

46 The Minister of the Interior had specifically defended an amendment to restrict the state election campaign to 'national parties'. But he did not even speak for it in the Senate, where it was changed on the recommendation of the rapporteur.

47 The difference in duration of plenary debate between the two Chambers is in part a function of the different emphasis on committee work and plenary debate.

48 The proposed European Defence Community definitively failed when the French National Assembly refused to ratify the treaty in August 1954, during the government of P. Mendes-France.

49 The four unsuccessful propositions were:
> 2 forbidding the simultaneous holding of different elected offices (cumul des mandats/ dual mandate), by the RPR and some UDF members;
> 1 proposing that deputies may be represented at the EP by their *suppleant* (substitute), by the UDF;
> 1 proposing a parliamentary delegation to the EP, by M. Royer (RPR).

50 In December 1978, the Prime Minister addressed a meeting of the Club Perspectives at Réalités, whose president was the former Economics Minister, R. Fourcade. M. Barre commended the idea of a referendum on an increase in the powers of the EP, and thus reinforced a proposal initiated by M. Fourcade.

51 *Le Monde*, 7 December 1978.

The French Parliament: some readings

J.L. Parodi, *Les Rapports entre l'Executif et le Legislatif sous la Cinquième Republique* (A. Colin, Paris, 1972). An important study of the centre of power, the focus on the first legislature is followed by numerous observations on the period 1958-72.

P.M. Williams, *The French Parliament, 1958-67* (Allen and Unwin, London, 1968). An excellent study of the legal status and political working of the parliament in the Gaullist period.

J.C. Maout and R. Muzellac, *Le Parlement sous la Cinquième Republique*, (A. Colin, Paris, 1971). A brief student's guide to the central issues.

J. Gicquel, *Essai sur la Pratique de la Cinquieme Republique*, (L.G.D.J., Paris, 1968). An analytic approach to the functioning of the institutions.

J.M. Cotteret, *Le Pouvoir Legislatif en France*, (L.G.D.J., Paris, 1962). A thorough overview.

E. Guichard-Ayoub, C. Roig and J. Grangé, *Etudes sur le Parlement de la Cinquième Republique* (P. U.F., Paris, 1965). Studies of specific aspects of the parliament in the first two legislatures.

P. Avril, *Les Francais et leur Parlement*, (Castermann, Paris, 1976). An overview of relations between public and parliament.

7 Ireland: An Eager Consummation

Edward Moxon-Browne

Preliminaries

In the period leading up to the Act of 20 September 1976 in which the nine EC countries formalised their decision to hold direct elections to the European Parliament, Irish public opinion displayed increasing support for those elections. Indeed, support for the elections in Ireland was consistently higher than in the other two new members, the UK and Denmark. From a level of support of 45 per cent in September 1973, the Irish figure had risen to 63 per cent by the end of 1976. The comparable figures for the UK were a rise from 33 per cent in September 1973 to 57 per cent at the end of 1976 whereas Danish opinion remained relatively unchanged — 36 per cent in September 1973 rising to only 42 per cent three years later.[1] It should be noted, finally, that all three countries, even by 1976, remained the least supportive of the Nine regarding direct elections to the European Parliament.

This Irish attitude towards a step which is generally regarded as strengthening the EC is consistent with attitudes generally displayed in the Republic towards European affairs. The Referendum of 1972 which had been held to permit a change in the Constitution[2] yielded a 'yes' vote of 83 per cent. It is often suggested that the inevitability of British entry by the Spring of 1972 was largely responsible for this overwhelming endorsement of Government policy but, since that time, Irish reactions to British 'renegotiation' in 1975, and to Britain's attitude towards the Economic and Monetary System in 1978, suggest that neither Irish policy-makers nor public opinion are as subservient to British policy as is often asserted. On the other hand, it must be conceded, that the experience of EC membership has gone a long way towards stiffening Irish resistance to the slavish acceptance of policies made in Whitehall. Reaction to the Tindemans Report and to the Patijn Report which, in different ways, endorsed a stronger Community, suggested that Ireland could be counted among the best of 'Europeans' in the years of economic recession which followed in the wake of the 'oil crisis'.

The road which led from the Patijn Report to the Council Act of

20 September 1976 was one of almost continuous lobbying on the part of the Irish Government for a fair share of the seats in the enlarged Parliament. The original suggestion that Ireland should have thirteen seats was sternly resisted by the Minister for Foreign Affairs, Garrett Fitzgerald. The eventual decision that Ireland should get fifteen seats in a 410 seat Parliament came after lengthy discussions in the European Council of 12-13 July 1976. A critical element in the final figure of 410 had, apparently, been the Irish Taoseach's insistence that Northern Ireland should have three seats to ensure representation of the Catholic minority. This concession involved, in turn, expanding the allocations of the four large countries (UK, France, the Federal Republic and Italy) from seventy-eight to eighty-one and hence to a total of 410.[3]

Meanwhile, in Ireland itself, the background to the legislation for direct elections in Ireland had been prepared by the Seventh Report of the Joint Committee of the Oireachtas on EC Secondary Legislation. The Seventh Report was published in June 1975 — just over two years before the bill was introduced into the Dail by the new Fianna Fail Government. The Joint Committee had had some doubts about whether it was competent to express opinions on direct elections but it was decided that the phrase 'acts of the institutions' could be interpreted to cover a resolution from the European Parliament. Hence, the decision to consider direct elections.

The Seventh Report addressed itself to three themes connected with direct elections but acknowledged that there were other topics which might have to be dealt with at a later date. The three themes considered were: (a) Irish representation in the Parliament; (b) the method of election; and (c) the question of dual membership. Although the Committee should be commended for raising these issues three years before the elections were actually due to be held, it is easy to see in retrospect that their actual recommendations were abortive in the sense that they were either overtaken by events or simply ignored.

On Irish representation, the Joint Committee took the view that Ireland needed to maintain its relatively good ratio of seats to population in the enlarged Parliament, and that there should be adequate representation to ensure that Irish interests could be properly defended on the Committees of the Parliament. The suggestion that Ireland should receive thirteen seats in a Parliament of 355 (as was then being mooted) was grudgingly accepted but the Joint Committee urged that 'every effort be made to obtain at least 18 seats under the proposed Convention'.[4]

On the electoral system to be used for the direct elections, the Joint Committee took a number of general factors into account. There should be some attempt to ensure that Irish MEPs 'have and be seen to have a close relationship with the political structure in this country and that the system of election should facilitate the maintenance of the relationship'.[5] Another factor was that, after 1980, it was assumed that the EC would be adopting a common electoral system and that, therefore, some attempt should be made to approximate to a hypothetical European electoral system. Finally, it was considered important that the system should be reasonably simple to operate and not too unfamiliar to voters.

Three electoral systems were dismissed as unsuitable. The single transferable vote system in multi-member constituencies used in national elections was discarded because the 'inevitable huge size of any constituencies selected would . . . make it wholly impracticable for elections to the European Parliament'.[6] The 'first past the post' system was rejected because it had proved unacceptable to the Irish electorate when submitted to them in two referenda. The Joint Committee added that the system tended to produce results which did not accurately reflect voting patterns and that its claim to produce strong governments was not relevant to the European elections. The alternative vote system in single member constituencies was not recommended because the size of the constituencies would involve counts and transfers of huge numbers of votes. 'Unless there were a very restricted right of nomination of candidates these operations might well reach staggering proportions'.[7]

Concluding that these three systems (which are familiar to Irish voters) were not suitable for the direct elections, the Joint Committee then proceeded to recommend the 'list system' on the grounds that it would link MEPs with national political affairs and also approximate to the system most likely to be adopted for all nine countries. The Joint Committee pointed out that the list system could be used in regional constituencies or in one national constituency but came down in favour of the latter. Other recommendations pertinent to the adoption of the list system were that casual vacancies would be filled by the next name on the party list. Voters would have the opportunity to alter the list order in the election.

The third topic which the Report considered was the question of the dual mandate. In view of the Committee's feeling that links should be preserved between the directly-elected Parliament and the national political system, and its belief that the MEPs 'knowledge and experience of European affairs should continue to be available to the Houses of the Oireachtas',[8] it recommended that non dual mandated MEPs should have a 'right of audience in the Dail and Seanad and in appropriate Committees of both Houses'.[9]

The Coalition Government introduced its European Assembly Elections Bill 1977 in April 1977. Since its contents were substantially the same as those of the bill introduced subsequently by the Fianna Fail

Government, there is no need to discuss them here. The constituencies proposed in the bill by the Minister of Local Government, Mr Tully, provoked a great deal of controversy. The proposal was to have four constituencies: a 3-seater for the County Borough of Dublin; a 3-seater for Ireland East (Dublin County plus four adjoining Counties); a 4-seater for the North and West; and a 5-seater in the South. Fianna Fail attacked these plans on the grounds that they amounted to a 'gerrymander' designed to maximise Coalition successes in the direct elections. Mr Lynch pledged himself to an impartial boundary Commission if Fianna Fail was returned to power in the approaching general election.

Table 7.1
Parties in the Dail, June 1977

Party	Abbreviation	Vote %*	Seats†
Labour	Lab	11.6	17
Fine Gael	FG	30.5	43
G Fianna Fail	FF	50.6	84
Others		7.3	4
Total		100.0	148
Turnout		75.4%	

*Share of valid votes cast in General Elections, June 1977.
†Seats in Dail, June 1977.
G Party forming the Government.

Political foreplay

Following the general election of June 1977, the new Fianna Fail Government announced that it would be introducing a bill for direct elections to the European Assembly. Before this could be done, however, the Government set up a Commission to make recommendations for the constituencies to be used in the direct elections. The previous Government's plan for constituencies could always be tarred with the brush of 'Tullymandering'[10] whereas the new Commission was to be non-political and impartial. There was, however, a sense of urgency in the Government's instructions to the new Commission which was asked to report by mid-October and was given fairly stringent terms of reference:

129

to advise and report on the formation of the constituencies for elections to the Assembly of the European Communities. In making its report the Commission should have regard to the following guidelines —

1 The system of election to be the system of proportional representation by means of the single transferable vote,

2 the number of members to be elected for any constituency to be not less than three,

3 there should be reasonable equality of representation as between constituencies,

4 each constituency should be composed of contiguous areas, and

5 the desirability of avoiding the breaching of county boundaries;

6 in the application of these guidelines there should be regard to geographical considerations including the extent of the proposed constituencies.[11]

The Commission invited submissions but received only 19 by the closing date of 19 September. The Commission published its Report on 4 October. In its conclusions it stated that there was no 'perfect formula for the "best" or "ideal" formation of constituencies. The most that can be done is to devise a scheme which, in addition to meeting certain objective criteria, appears to provide a reasonable basis for the fair conduct of elections and has due regard to social and economic factors, the electorate and density of population as well as to total population'.[12]

The Report recommended four constituencies: Connacht-Ulster (three representatives); Dublin (four representatives); Leinster (three representatives); and Munster (five representatives). The fact that Dublin is the smallest constituency geographically but one of the largest in terms of population underlines the main problem which the Commission faced — namely, that of striking a balance between geographically compact areas, and ones of reasonably equal population. The imbalance in the density of population between the eastern and western seaboards is a problem that has not only electoral but also economic and social ramifications. However, in terms of electors per representative, the Commission succeeded in slightly favouring the western side of the country.

When the Report was published, it was widely acclaimed as being fair;[13] and it aroused no controversy in the debates on the bill in the Oireachtas. Once the Commission had reported, the Government was able to publish its European Assembly Elections (No.2) Bill which it did on 14 October 1977.

Table 7.2
Size of constituencies

Constituency	MEPs	Population (1971 census)	Population per MEP
Connacht-Ulster	3	598,106	199,369
Dublin	4	852,219	213,055
Leinster	3	645,921	215,307
Munster	5	882,002	176,400

The parties come together

The provisions of the bill were substantially the same as the bill which had been put forward by the Coalition Government earlier in the year. The voting system was to be the STV form of proportional representation as stipulated in the terms of reference which had been given to the Electoral Commission. In adopting this electoral system against the advice of the Joint Committee's Seventh Report, the Government was undoubtedly motivated by expediency — any other electoral system would have caused controversy and, hence, delay in the legislative process. The general conduct of the election was to follow that for Dail elections. The deposit for candidates was to be £1,000. Only those eligible for the Dail would be eligible for the European Parliament; and any mid-term vacancies which occurred would be filled by appointment by the Dail. The franchise was a generous one — both Irish citizens and other EEC citizens could be eligible for voting provided they were normally resident in the State. Finally, there were to be four constituencies, each returning between three and five members to the European Parliament.

Before considering the passage of the legislation on direct elections through the Houses of the Oireachtas, some time should be spent describing the Irish legislative system. In a strictly formal sense, bills pass through five stages in each House, and are then signed by the President to become law. The first stage is accomplished by the publication of a bill. It is a formal stage which involves no debate. A Government bill is introduced in the Dail by a member of the Government. The second stage debate centres on a motion 'That the bill be now read a second time'; and only general principles are raised at this point. If the second stage is agreed to, the bill is considered in Committee — usually a Committee of the whole House, but occasionally a special or select Committee. In the Committee stage, the bill is considered section by section. Amendments may be made, sections deleted and new sections inserted. Amendments must be confined to verbal alterations; they cannot negative the sense of a particular section. The fourth (Report) stage sees the bill being discussed *in toto* and further amendments may be made although these normally arise out of points raised at the Committee stage. Debate, at this stage, tends to be strictly related to the amendments being proposed. Before moving to the fifth stage, the motion 'That the bill (or the bill, as amended) be received for final consideration' is decided. At the fifth stage, further debate is possible but only verbal amendments can be made. The motion then put to the House is 'That the bill do now pass'. The bill is then sent to the other House (normally Dail to Seanad) where it repeats the five-stage process although a bill *coming from* the other House is deemed to have passed its first stage. Finally, the bill goes to the President for signature and this happens not earlier than five days but no later than seven days after the bill is presented to him. However, under Article 25.2 of the Constitution, the President can be requested by the Seanad to sign the bill earlier.

In more general terms, the legislative process of the Oireachtas is notoriously ill-adapted to the needs of the late 20th century. Based on the Westminster model but without even its modest innovations, the Oireachtas suffers from its 19th century origins. It is very pertinent for for the debates on the legislation for direct elections to note some of the observations of a leading writer on Irish Government.[14] He makes several points: that most TDs are ill-informed on current issues; that only Ministers well-briefed by civil servants can take command in debates; that debates are often set-piece affairs; that the speeches are often discursive; that TDs often use procedural pegs to hang speeches aimed at local interests in their constituencies. Chubb summarises the legislative process thus:

> The Government is committed, and the bill is sponsored and con-ducted during its passage through the Oireachtas by the minister. Backed by the Government majority, he expects to get it through relatively unscathed, though amendments may be accepted and, even at this late stage, proposed by himself to improve the bill.[15]

The Dail

The bill was introduced in the Dail on 18 October by the Minister for Defence (Mr Molloy) who suggested that the second stage be taken on 25 October. The suggestion was agreed to.

The second stage of the legislative process opened on the 26 October and concluded, after four hours of debate, on the following day. The

132

second stage debate was marked by a remarkable degree of consensus between the main parties since the bill so closely matched that of the previous Government. There was also a tendency among TDs to debate issues which were not relevant to the bill and this must be seen as symptomatic of the lack of opportunity for the Oireachtas to debate EC affairs.

Table 7.3

Proportion of time in second stage debate spent on principal topics

Topic	% time
The Constituency Commission	32
Issues not related to the bill (e.g. MEPs' salaries)	15
The Connacht-Ulster constituency	14
Local government elections	10
Miscellaneous issues related to the bill	10
Casual vacancies	7
Electoral deposit	7
The count	5
Total	100%

The topic most popular in the debate was the work of the Commission which had recommended the constituencies for the direct elections. In his opening speech, the Foreign Affairs Minister, Mr O'Kennedy, asserted that the work of the Commission had ensured that no suspicion of party political advantage could be cast on the conclusions it had reached; and he expressed his gratitude to the Commission for its work. This congratulatory theme was echoed in many other contributions to the debate — understandably in view of the fact that the constituency boundaries were the only substantially novel feature in the bill. The principal spokesman for Fine Gael in the debate, Mr T.J. Fitzpatrick, allowed a note of sarcasm to colour his own praise for the Commission's work:

> I hope I will not sound ungracious if I say nobody had a better right to introduce the Commission system than the Fianna Fail party because, over the past 50 years, the constituencies were revised a goodly number of times and they revised them in their own way, for their own benefit, and for their own purposes. . .[16]

The Labour Party spokesman, Mr Quinn, also welcomed the

Commission's work on the constituencies and looked forward to the extension of the principle to cover constituency boundaries for domestic elections.[17] This general approbation of the Commission's work was repeated in almost every contribution made during the second stage debate.

The only reservations expressed on the work of the Commission were related to the constituency of Connacht-Ulster in the north and west of Ireland. A pervasive fear was that the area was geographically too large, and too heterogeneous, to be represented by only three MEPs despite the fact that no more were warranted by its population. Mr Calleary's (FF) contention that the people of the constituency would not *know* the candidates, was expanded upon by Mr Lalor (FF) who depicted the heterogeneity of the Connacht-Ulster area:

> I think you will appreciate that from the point of view of affinity or the sharing of interests the people of Laois and the people of Donegal are not all that akin. We have the bogs. You have the mountains. I don't think the aspirations of the bogman in Laois, whom I represent, are exactly in line with the aspirations of the shrewd Donegal people.[19]

Mr Briscoe pointed out, later in the debate that a third of the Irish population lived in Dublin and, therefore, the West of Ireland should not feel that it had been treated unfairly.[20]

Another major concern raised during the debate was the possibility that the Government might decide to have the direct elections on the same day as local government elections. Although this matter was not pertinent to the bill being debated, it attracted a considerable amount of comment. Opinion in the debate was split evenly between those who favoured holding the two elections simultaneously because it would save money and increase the turnout, and those who were against the idea because it would cause confusion and detract from the importance of the European election. Mr Quinn (Lab) urged the Government not to 'resort to the tactic of holding the European elections on the same day in order to guarantee a high turnout. That would be a dishonest approach . . .'[21] Mr Moore did not think such a ploy would be necessary since 'The people will be very interested in these elections'.[22] But other speakers urged the Government to hold the elections simultaneously precisely because they feared a low turnout. Mr White (FG) argued that it would be a good idea 'particularly in country areas . . . it would ensure a full turnout of voters'.[23] The economic argument was advanced by Mr Briscoe (FF):

> If it was convenient to hold the two elections on the same day, I

would be in favour of it because the cost of mounting elections is fairly substantial . . . it would make sense to hold the elections together if the dates were in line.[24]

In his winding up speech, Mr O'Kennedy (Foreign Affairs Minister) would not commit himself one way or the other on the question of holding two elections on the same day.[25] Some time after the debate, of course, the Government decided to hold the local government elections and European elections simultaneously. In some polling stations, voters were faced with three ballot papers!

The next most urgent subject of concern in the debate was the level of salaries to be paid to MEPs after direct elections. This was also a topic outside the limits of the bill, as the Speaker pointed out more than once during the debate. Again, opinion was divided between those who believed the job was more important than work in the Oireachtas and should be rewarded accordingly, and those who felt that a gulf of envy might open up between MEPs and members of the Oireachtas. Mr White (FG) argued forcibly for the high salaries:

> When people talk about £30,000 salaries they do not realise that many sacrifices will have to be made by politicians if they are serious about the European elections. Many of them will be away from their homes for weeks, working 70 to 80 hours per week. It is only right that the salary should be high because it will encourage a better type of individual to stand for the European elections . . . . If you want the right kind of representation in Europe, you must pay the right salary and we should not be apologetic about it.[26]

The other side of the argument was put most fully by Mr Mitchell (FG). He argued that the European Parliament was not a very important assembly and that the salaries and expenses of Irish MEPs would cost about £1 million per annum after direct elections. 'The salaries are certainly an outrage in the Irish context . . . it will be difficult for Members of this House to survive the rush for nomination. It will get to the stage where membership of the Government will become a positive disadvantage because the financial loss involved will be so great'.[27] In his summing up speech, Mr O'Kennedy (FF) was evasive on the question of MEPs salaries arguing that the really important point was not the money but 'the currency, the value, they (MEPs) put on themselves'.[28]

Two other matters arose during the debate which deserve to be mentioned. One was the size of the deposit (£1,000) being proposed in the bill. On the whole this sum was supported as a guarantee against spurious candidates standing for election. Mr Lalor (FF) argued that there was a danger that £1,000 might not discourage someone who wanted to use the media to 'sell' a political viewpoint rather than campaign seriously for the European Parliament. On the other hand, a higher deposit would discourage some bona fide candidates.[29] Mr Enright (FG) argued, however, that £1,000 was too high:

> Individuals contest elections irrespective of what views they hold and they are entitled to put them before the people and see what the people think. The people very quickly give that answer if they are not satisfied with what such candidates represent . . . . The Irish people are shrewd enough to make a decision and I think it would be wrong to specify a deposit which would scare off would-be candidates.[30]

Due to the number of candidates standing in each constituency, concern was expressed in the debate on the alleged advantages of candidates whose names were early in the alphabet. Mr Creed (FG) argued that the shape of the ballot paper should be considered carefully since he was inclined to accept the view that names at the top or bottom of the list had an electoral advantage. This was a response to an earlier exchange on this topic:

> Mr Moore: We should have a look at our ballot paper as well as the European ballot paper which may be a different shape. I have often thought if we had a round ballot paper it would be the ideal thing.
>
> Mr D. Andrews: What would happen to the A's?
>
> Mr Moore: We would all be equal.[31]

The Foreign Affairs Minister, Mr O'Kennedy, dealt with the subject of ballot papers in his winding-up speech. He made the point that this problem, along with several others raised in the debate related to the conduct of elections generally and should, therefore, be dealt with in the context of reforming electoral law as a whole. He was sure that his colleague, the Minister for the Environment, would be dealing with all such points.[32] The next stage of the bill, the Committee stage, was ordered for 2 November.

During the Committee stage, a number of issues were raised in advance of the Report stage where the main changes to the bill were made. The principal concern was the way in which the votes were going to be counted. Both Mr Fitzpatrick and Mr Kavanagh expressed concern on this issue. One worry was that the long distances from polling booths to counting centres might expose ballot boxes to the dangers of either accidents or terrorist attacks. The other anxiety was that if two elections were held on the same day, the ballot papers might get mixed up.

The only other topic of importance raised at the Committee stage was the way in which casual vacancies might be filled during the life of the Parliament. What would happen if an MEP changed his political group in the Parliament? Would it be the new political affiliation or the former one which was responsible for appointing the successor? The response from the Minister was that it was the original political party which sponsored the candidate in the election.

It was during the Report stage that issues raised in the previous stage were expressed in the shape of twenty-four amendments. Almost all of these were minor textual alterations relating to the fact that the electoral law was somewhat out of date. Of the twenty-four amendments, 9 were introduced by the Government and all were passed. The remaining fifteen amendments came from the Opposition and of these, 2 were accepted, 3 were lost, 4 were withdrawn during debate, and 6 were not moved (because they hinged on other amendments that were defeated). There were only three TDs (Mr Fitzpatrick (FG), who put down 15 amendments; Mr Barrett (FF) 9 amendments; and Mr Kavanagh) who spoke during the whole of the Report stage which underlines the way in which European affairs are often handled by a tiny fraction of the whole Dail.

The Report stage was concluded on 30 November and the fifth stage was taken immediately and consisted solely of a speech from each of the two main spokesmen concerned with the bill: Messrs Fitzpatrick and Barrett. The bill then went to the Seanad.

The Seanad

Having cleared the Dail, the bill was dealt with in the Seanad on 7 and 8 December. The bill had to go through similar formal stages but the whole process was much more straightforward than in the Dail. The debate lasted four and a half hours *in toto*. The second stage debate was opened by Mr Barrett, Minister for the Environment, and he touched on the themes which had aroused most interest in the Dail. He was followed by seventeen Senators[33] all of whom kept to fairly general observations on the bill and on the desirability of holding direct elections. The work of the Constituency Commission drew praise from all political parties as it had in the Dail debates.

In the later stages, more detailed criticisms of the bill were made. Although a number of amendments to the bill were tabled (to allow their proposers to speak) none of these amendments was actually accepted. Throughout the debate, the Minister for the Environment answered questions from Senators and acted as a pilot for the bill until it reached its final stage in the early afternoon of 8 December.

Among the various aspects of the bill which Senators discussed, four are worth some more detailed attention: the size of the deposit for prospective candidates; the possibility for Irishmen abroad to have votes; the filling of casual vacancies; and the definition of the limits of a polling station. On the deposit,[34] it was suggested by Mrs Robinson that the sum of £1,000 might deter serious candidates of modest means to which the Environment Minister responded that the Euro-constituencies would be ten times the size of Dail constituencies and, therefore, a deposit ten times the Dail deposit did not seem excessive. Mrs Robinson wondered whether the British figure of £500 might not be adequate, to which Senator Yeats retorted:

> In fact, £1,000 is no way excessive. A better way of dealing with the English situation would be to ask why they are fixing a figure which is half ours rather than asking why we are fixing one double theirs.[35]

On the question of Irish citizens outside Ireland,[36] it was suggested that those working in the European institutions in Brussels and Luxembourg, should be allowed to have a postal vote and that their relatively small numbers would make this quite feasible. Mr Barrett replied that postal votes were restricted to the Army and the Garda and that to select the Irish working in EC institutions would be to discriminate unfairly against other Irish people working abroad in EC countries:[37] 'Why should we be selective for a few and exclude the others?'

As we have seen, the filling of casual vacancies[38] had stimulated some concern in the Dail. In the Seanad, the main focus of anxiety was that when a vacancy occurred it might be filled by someone from a different constituency since there was nothing in the bill to prevent this from happening. Mrs Robinson gave an example:

> Let us say it was a Fianna Fail representative in Connacht-Ulster who died — and then the Fianna Fail Party decided they wanted to give experience to a Dublin based Fianna Fail person, surely this would not represent the needs and desires of the regional constituency?[39]

Linked to the same issue was the problem of what to do about an MEP who changed his political allegiance while in the European Parliament or who had been elected by an interest group rather than a political party. In the latter case, the Minister replied, the Dail would act using its good sense. In the former eventuality, it was the party which had originally sponsored the candidate who would fill the vacancy.[40]

Finally, there was lengthy consideration as to what constituted being 'on the premises' since Rule 46 of the bill stipulated that anyone 'on the premises' by 9 p.m. would be entitled to vote. Did this mean in the polling *room* itself? In the *building*? or in the *grounds* of the building? These questions provoked a heated and extremely technical legal debate (there are enough lawyers in the Seanad to guarantee a high level of legal expertise). The Minister tried vainly to keep both feet on the ground with a touch of humour:

> Mr Cooney: Do we mean the building and the curtilage or the building only?
>
> Mr Barrett: 'Premises' has a very definite legal meaning. It has when one is caught in a pub, as I have been.[41]

And later he exclaimed in exasperation: 'How extreme are we going to be? I am at a loss to know how we ever conducted elections all these years'.[42]

At the conclusion of the Seanad debate, a motion for early signature was agreed to. This is a measure used to accelerate urgent bills since the President is normally given seven days to sign a bill which is presented to him. The need for haste on this occasion was the compilation of the electoral registers which was being carried out at the time.[43] The signature of the Irish President was the final process; and the bill became the European Assembly Elections Act 1977.

Postlude: reflections on the Act

What explanations can be given for the relatively smooth and uncontroversial passage of direct elections legislation through the Oireachtas? In the first place it has to be emphasised that the level of agreement between the three parties on this bill was fully in keeping with the normal consensus displayed towards EC issues. This consensus stems from the political culture which places a high premium on local politics and local personalities. Foreign affairs have never loomed large in the domestic scene[44] and, therefore, differing approaches to foreign policy issues are not widely appreciated among the electorate at large. Despite the divergent origins[45] of the two main parties, they find common cause in Community membership. To Fianna Fail it is the best arena in which to exert national independence and it carried with it the chance, at least, of national re-integration. To Fine Gael, it is the pragmatic course to follow; it is the path which minimises conflict with the United Kingdom and it involves tacit recognition of Northern Ireland's status without according that status undue significance. Indeed, in the Fine Gael party Dr Fitzgerald constantly alludes to the paradoxes which flow from Northern Ireland's position inside the United Kingdom and which are only silhouetted more sharply in the context of the EC. To both major parties, and latterly to the Labour Party, the result of the Referendum in 1972 gives any Government of the day a clear mandate to pursue policies in the EC which are both constructive and generally integrationist.

To these general considerations, which apply to the broad question of EC membership, this particular bill had the important added advantage of being virtually a replica of the bill introduced by the preceding Government. Ironically, the intervention of a General Election which might have been used, in some countries, as a pretext for delaying legislation served, in this case, as a catalyst for greater urgency. The only significant difference in the Fianna Fail Bill, the revised constituency boundaries, were (as we have seen) welcomed by all parties. Undoubtedly, this welcome can be attributed as much to the general precedent which had now been set as to the specific piece of work performed by the three-man Commission. Nevertheless, there was profound relief that the controversy stirred up by the Coalition's constituency proposals, and the concomitant cries of 'Tullymandering',[46] were not to be repeated on this occasion.

Another factor which certainly helps to explain the business-like passage of the bill, is the constant awareness, revealed throughout the debates, of problems encountered by the British Government in getting its direct elections legislation on to the statute book. As the bill passed through the Dail, it became increasingly unlikely that all the Nine would be prepared for elections in the Spring of 1978. But there was a general feeling, only rarely expressed, that Ireland should be ready for 1978 elections whether or not these were eventually held. This attitude was fully consonant with the welcome accorded the Patijn Report, and with the policy of the Government in trying to maximise both the status of the Parliament in the Community's decision-making system, and the size of the Irish delegation within the Parliament. All along it has been a source of tension within the European Progressive Democrat Group (largely Franco-Irish) that France and Ireland generally take opposite views when it comes to debating extra powers for the Parliament.

The road now lay open to direct elections. The question which faced the parties was what sort of relationship ought to exist between directly elected MEPs (especially non dual-mandated ones) and their national Parliament. The only official pronouncement on this subject up to that time had been the recommendation of the Joint Committee in its 7th Report (on Direct Elections) which appeared in 1975. In this Report the Joint Committee recommended that MEPs who were directly elected, and non dual mandated, should have a right of audience in each House of the Oireachtas.[47] There is no reason why this recommendation is any more likely to be accepted than other recommendations in the Joint Committee's 7th Report. The only political party to have made any decision (at the time of writing) is Fianna Fail which will require directly elected MEPs to report periodically to the parliamentary party in Dublin. Debate on this issue is likely to warm up as the direct elections get nearer. The Irish Council of the European Movement has commissioned a discussion paper on the subject which is intended to stimulate such a debate.

The links between the Oireachtas and the European Parliament will be more than a matter of mere convenience. They will reflect, in a real sense, the whole philosophy of EC membership. The degree to which it is considered desirable to *control* MEPs depends very much on one's attitude to national sovereignty being eroded by any extensions of the powers of the Commission or the Parliament. For this reason, if for no other, the model of a European Grand Committee, suggested by the House of Lords,[48] is not likely to find favour in Ireland, nor is any temporary membership of the Oireachtas along the lines of temporary Lords membership which has been mooted for British MEPs. This latter course would require a constitutional change and hence a referendum and no-one is in the mood for unnecessary referenda at the moment. What seems most likely in Ireland is that the Fianna Fail model will be copied, to varying degrees, by the other parties; and this may be supplemented by some arrangement whereby MEPs can gain access to Leinster House to speak in, or listen to, debates on EC matters. We have already noted that MEPs have the right to participate in, but not vote at, meetings of the Joint Committee in EC Secondary Legislation;[49] and there is no clear reason why greater involvement in national parliamentary politics should be either sought or granted. The main preoccupation of non dual mandated MEPs should be their constituency where they will enjoy a special relationship, possibly one of superiority, to their national colleagues who will, by definition, be representing much more particularistic interests. Generous travel allowances between Strasbourg/Luxembourg and the Euro-constituencies will make it nothing more than a matter of choice for MEPs to stop over in their national capitals.

Notes

1 See Appendix, chapter 2.
2 Article 46 of the Irish Constitution requires a referendum to be held whenever an amendment to the Constitution is contemplated. In this case, an addition to Article 29 was required so that EC legislation could take direct effect in Ireland.
3 For an account of this, see *84 Seanad Debates* 1338-9.
4 7th Report of the Joint Committee (Prl.4595) pp 9-10.
5 Ibid., p.11.
6 Ibid.
7 Ibid.
8 Ibid., p.15.
9 Ibid.
10 The previous Minister for Local Government (and hence responsible for elections) was Mr Tully.
11 See European Assembly Commission Report (Prl.6626) p.5.
12 Ibid., p.17.
13 Neither press nor politicians made any serious criticism of the Report.
14 B. Chubb, *The Government and Politics of Ireland* (Oxford U.P., London, 1974) pp 195-6. TD is an abbreviation for Teachta Data (i.e. MP).
15 Ibid., p.202.
16 *300 Dail Debates* 1271.
17 Ibid., 1281.
18 Ibid., 1314.
19 Ibid., 1384.
20 Ibid., 1443.
21 Ibid., 1283.
22 Ibid., 1291.
23 Ibid., 1295.
24 Ibid., 1443.
25 Ibid., 1458.
26 Ibid., 1294.
27 Ibid., 1396.
28 Ibid., 1461.
29 Ibid., 1386.
30 Ibid., 1312.
31 Ibid., 1288-9.
32 Ibid., 1457.
33 They were Senators Cooney, Brugha, Keating, Yeats, McDonald, Mulcahy, Murphy, Brennan, Robinson, Cranitch, Markey, Hyland, Howard, Herbert, McCartin, Ellis.
34 Section 10 of the bill.
35 *87 Seanad Debates* 811.
36 Section 1 of the bill.
37 *87 Seanad Debates* 807.
38 Section 15 of the bill.
39 *87 Seanad Debates* 816.
40 Ibid., 815.
41 Ibid., 846.
42 Ibid., 848.
43 Ibid., 856.
44 See P. Keatinge, *The Formulation of Irish Foreign Policy* (Institute for Public Administration, Dublin, 1973) especially chapter 6.
45 See M. Manning, *Irish Political Parties* (Gill and Macmillan, Dublin, 1972) pp 1-8.
46 See note 10.
47 7th Report of the Joint Committee (Prl.4595) p.15.
48 See 44th Report of the House of Lords Select Committee on the European Communities, HMSO, London 1978, pp 18-19.
49 See *301 Dail Debates* 956.

The Irish Parliament: some readings

B. Chubb, *The Government and Politics of Ireland* (OUP, London, 1974). The standard work on Irish politics.

Joint Committee on the Secondary legislation of the European Communities *Seventh Report* (Prl.4595). Deals with direct elections.

Joint Committee on the Secondary Legislation of the European Communities *Fifty-fifth Report* (Prl.6169). Deals with the functions of the Joint Committee.

P. Keatings, *The Formulation of Irish Foreign Policy* (IPA, Dublin, 1973). Describes how Irish foreign policy is made.

M. Manning, *Irish Political Parties* (Gill and Macmillan, Dublin, 1972). A succinct account of how the Irish parties originated and developed.

E. Moxon-Browne, 'Irish political parties and European Integration', *Administration*, vol.25, 1977, pp 519-32. Explores the way in which European issues are dealt with in the Irish Parliament.

E. Moxon-Browne, *Relations between the Oireachtas and Irish Members of the European Parliament after Direct Elections* (ICEM, Dublin, 1979). Sketches out the various links which might exist between Irish Euro-MPs and their national Parliament.

M. Robinson, 'Preparations for Direct Elections in Ireland', *Common Market Law Review*, vol.15, 1978, pp 187-98. Emphasises the legal aspects of direct elections.

8   Italy: How a Quick Start Became a Late Arrival

Maurizio Cotta

In a country like Italy with a multi-party system, the introduction of new electoral procedures is inevitably a sensitive task, particularly when there is a polarisation around large parties so that the existence of the smaller ones is threatened. The peculiar interdependence of large and small parties is a complex matrix that involves not merely the relationship between the major government party (Christian Democrats) and the other parties of the majority, but also the network of often hostile relations between Christian Democrats and the Communist Party.

The processing of the direct election legislation was further affected by its relation to the international system.. Firstly, insofar as the idea can be said to have been initiated from the European political arena, in the decision of the Council in 1976 and the pressure from the European Parliament in the preceding years, the legislation was unusual. Secondly, insofar as European decision centres exogenous to the Italian polity exerted constraints on the national process by determining certain 'common' aspects of the legislation — size, duration, incompatibilities of the supranational Parliament — and by defining a 'target' date, the policy-making process was somewhat different from other cases. Thirdly, the legislation itself involved two different aspects, the ratification of an international treaty and the construction of an electoral law (which were expressed as two separate laws); for these two types of laws the parliament normally accords different treatment, and the comparison between them provides a controlled means of evaluating the nature of the legislative process.[1]

As we shall see, all these factors made the direct election legislation peculiar — perhaps more so than for other countries. The small parties fought a forceful battle, as expected, on the maximisation of proportionality of the electoral system and were successful in gaining a form of veto power over the electoral bill. The international constraint affected the content of the Implementation Bill. The point that became relevant in this respect was that of the compatibility of the two parliamentary mandates. Since the Act of 1976 laid down that they were compatible, the proposals to forbid the double mandate put forward by certain parties or party factions had to be dropped.[2] As we shall see in more detail later, the time constraint also affected the Italian law-making process. Since the other major European countries were ready earlier with their legislation and were prepared to go to the elections in 1979, the Italian Parliament had to catch up so as not to be in breach of an international agreement. Thus the time element which is always one of the relevant parameters of the legislative process, was in this case determined from outside the national law-making system. All this should be kept in mind when we compare the direct election legislative process with the normal legislative one. This, of course, does not mean that the European legislation should be considered totally idiosyncratic. However, some general background knowledge of the Italian legislative process is necessary for a better understanding of the direct election process.

General characteristics of the Italian legislative process

The functioning of the Italian law-making process has been the subject of a considerable number of studies recently, focusing particularly on its parliamentary stages. Much less known is what happens outside Parliament, especially the role of the civil service and the impact of pressure groups.[3]

Our starting point is the institutional setting — i.e. that set of variables which forms the system within which political actors operate. This setting, resulting from constitutional provisions as well as from parliamentary Standing Orders (in particular the new Standing Orders of 1971),[4] reveals a number of features which correspond to a rather decentralised law-making process weakly controlled by the government. Among the most important features one should mention:

1 the bicameral system characterised by a perfect parity of powers of the two Chambers;

2 the strongly decentralised committee system;

3 the growth of the unanimity principle (or at least of very large majorities) for all decisions concerning the working of parliamentary processes, such as the planning of the parliamentary agenda.

Both the two Chambers (Chamber of Deputies and Senate) are popularly elected, through slightly different electoral systems which may produce minor differences in the strength of the parties in each.[5] Both Chambers have equal legislative powers. This means that a bill may be initiated in either Chamber and has to be approved by both Chambers in order to become a law. A bill approved by one of the two Chambers may be amended in the other Chamber; in this case it has to go back to the first so that the new text is discussed and approved again by that Chamber. The *navette* between the two Chambers goes on without limit, until both have approved the same version of a bill. It is clear that such a procedure gives the opposition (as well as factions within the majority) many opportunities to obstruct and criticise a bill during its passage.[6]

The second important feature of the institutional setting of the law-making process is the strong committee system. Within each Chamber there exists a number of permanent specialised committees (fourteen in the Chamber of Deputies, twelve in the Senate). Their powers extend to law-making: with the exception of certain types of bills explicitly mentioned by the Constitution (among them the ratification of international treaties and electoral bills) a bill may be enacted simply by being approved by a committee of each Chamber (this procedure is called *procedimento in sede deliberante*). Much of the less important legislation is thus passed without being debated at all by the plenaries of the two Chambers.[7] For more important pieces of legislation, the longer and more formal procedure is followed and the legislative committees perform only a preparatory role (this procedure is called *procedimento in sede referente*). Even in such cases the role of the committees is very important. It is particularly so whenever there is more than one legislative proposal concerning the same issue: the committee then has the function of bringing together the different proposals (a government bill and one or more parliamentary bills, or a number of parliamentary bills) and to draft a common text. Something similar happens when a government bill meets strong opposition in parliament, and the executive, for fear of not being able to push it through, accepts having its own bill 'improved' — to use the accepted political terminology. A bill may thus be thoroughly rewritten in order to incorporate some of the amendments moved by the opposition parties, or even by members of the government parties. This function is also performed by the legislative committees, as well as by *ad hoc* sub-committees set up within them.

If we also consider the planning of the parliamentary agenda, which requires the agreement of all the chairmen of the parliamentary groups (8-10 in recent legislatures), it becomes clear that for institutional reasons the legislative process is complex and requires a good deal of co-operation amongst all the political forces if it is to reach a positive conclusion. The vetoing opportunities available for even small parties are quite high.

We may now turn to the outcomes of this institutional setting. The quantitative and qualitative features of the legislative output of the

146

Table 8.1
Annual legislative output in some parliaments

	UK (1966-67)	Ireland (1965)	France (1966)	F.R.Germany (1949 – annual average)	Italy (1948-68 annual average)
Total bills passed	98	34	147	121	400
Private member bills passed	14	0	14	27	100
Per cent the latter are of total	14.3	–	9.5	22.3	25.0

Source: Adapted from G. Di Palma, *Surviving Without Governing*, (University of California Press, Berkeley, 1977), p.48.

Italian parliament have recently been explored in depth, notably by Alberto Predieri and Giuseppe Di Palma.[8] From a quantitative point of view, these findings reveal that, compared to other Parliaments, the Italian Parliament has a high level of legislative activity. The number of bills introduced by the Government and, especially, by MPs (from both majority and opposition parties) is extremely high. Of all bills introduced, a great number, especially of those proposed by MPs, never reach the discussion stage and disappear from sight. Nevertheless the number of bills that become law every year is still considerably higher than in most European parliaments (see table 8.1).

Can such outcomes be considered as proof of a high level of decisional efficacy? After making a detailed analysis of the content of legislative proposals Di Palma has answered this in the negative. The high number of laws enacted by the Italian Parliament (and the much higher number of bills introduced) is not a good test of decisional effectiveness, since the content of the majority of them is extremely particularistic and of limited importance, if compared to the legislative outputs of other parliaments (see table 8.2). The fact that most of the bills approved are of this type (known as *leggine*) is an important indicator of the weakness of the decision-making process which, far from being highly effective, as the quantitative data might suggest, is seriously hampered by the absence of a full consensus on the decisional rules.[9] In order to 'survive' as Di Palma puts it, in spite of this lack of consensus, the Parliament operates so as to reduce large issues into small microsectional measures, which meet the interests of clearly defined and numerically small clienteles without negatively affecting any other clearly defined group of electors. What cannot be disaggregated

Table 8.2
Importance of legislation in selected countries

	UK	Ireland	France	Italy
Number of bills	49	28	49	129
Average importance	3.2	3.1	1.3	0.99
Average number of Articles	19	35	7	5

Source: Adapted from G. Di Palma, *Surviving Without Governing*, p.69.

is deferred again and again, and quite often gets lost in the parliamentary maze until the dissolution of parliament kills the bill. By contrast, the highly disaggregated legislation can more easily achieve a consensus since it is less controversial; it is able, therefore, to bridge the severe ideological cleavages that still divide the Italian party system. Such qualitative peculiarities of the legislative output also explain why a very large part of the legislation is approved with the vote of opposition parties. This was clearly noticeable in the years before 1976 when the distinction at the governmental level between majority and opposition was unquestioned; it became less so in the period 1976-79 when all parties, except a few small ones of the left and of the right, joined the parliamentary majority (but without being admitted into the Government by the Christian Democratic party).[10]

We may now try to interpret such data alongside our findings on the institutional setting. The outputs of the legislative machinery, with the quantitative and qualitative aspects discussed above, are the product of a situation where institutional and political factors reinforce each other. We have seen that the institutional setting shows the features of a rather decentralised parliamentary model which makes tight control by the government of the law-making process difficult and, in the decisional process, favours the participation of all parliamentary actors, even those belonging to the opposition camp. To this one should add the type of party system that has existed in Italy since after the Second World War: 'a polarised multiparty system' as defined by Giovanni Sartori (table 8.3).[11] Such a party system has produced a situation where governmental coalitions have, most of the time, been extremely frail and have felt beleaguered, while at the same time the major opposition party (the Communist Party) has been highly cohesive. And when the majority-opposition dualism was overcome in 1976 and, more clearly in 1978, the result was an extremely hetero-

Table 8.3
Composition of Chamber of Deputies, June 1976

	Party	Abbreviation	% Vote*	Seats†
	Proletarian Democrats (Democrazia Proletaria)	DP	1.5	6
(G)	Communist Party (Partito Comunista Italiano)	PCI	34.4	227
	Radical Party (Partito Radicale)	PR	1.1	4
(G)	Socialist Party (Partito Socialista Italiano)	PSI	9.6	57
(G)	Social Democratic Party (Partito Socialista Democratico Italiano)	PSDI	3.4	15
(G)	Republican Party (Partito Repubblicano Italiano)	PRI	3.1	14
G	Christian Democrats (Democrazia Cristiana)	DC	38.7	263
(G)	South Tyrol People's Party (Sudtiroler Volkspartei)	SVP	0.5	3
	Liberal Party (Partito Liberale)	PLI	1.3	5
	National Democrats (Democrazia Nazionale)	DN	–	– (+18)
	Social Movement (Movimento Sociale Italiano)	MSI	6.1	34(−18)
	Others		0.3	2
Total			100.0	630
Turnout			93.4%	

*Share of valid votes cast in General Elections, June 1976.
†Seats in Chamber of Deputies (± changes at January 1979).

G   indicates party forming the Government.
(G) indicates party supporting the Government.

geneous 'grand coalition': after a very short honeymoon, this started to
fall apart on major issues. The political situation has thus reinforced
the institutional context. The absence of a coherent and cohesive
decisional centre at the executive level, has encouraged the already
existing institutional tendency for the disaggregation of legislative
outputs, as the easiest way to gain the parliamentary support — as well
as the support of the opposition — required to have legislation passed.

If this is the normal picture of the Italian law-making process, what might we expect for the passage of the direct election legislation? In Italy the legislation took the form of two separate government bills: one for the ratification of the international agreement; the other for its implementation, particularly for the specification of the electoral procedures. From our above discussion we might expect the Government bills which initiated direct election to have a clear advantage *vis-à-vis* Private Members legislation, both with regard to the probabilities of being approved (which was never in doubt) and to the chance of a speedier examination (which was more relevant). The other side of the coin is that this type of bill cannot be enacted directly by committee, but must be voted on the floor of both Chambers, which lengthens the legislative process. However, the mean time of approval for government bills voted in plenary is still shorter than that of the average Private Member's bill enacted directly by committee. The mean length of the law-making process for government bills voted in plenary is 239 days, while Private Members bills take an average of 778 days to be approved.[12] Finally, since the European elections legislation was not of a microsectional type but of national relevance, we may expect its time of approval to be somewhat longer than that of other government bills. The larger the relevance of a bill, the greater are its chances of being controversial and, therefore, its discussion being lengthier.

Another important question is that of the amending powers of the Parliament. As we have seen, a great number of bills have always been approved by large 'concurrent' majorities. This custom became even more frequent in the last legislature (1976-1979) when a coalition commanding a majority of more than 90 per cent of the parliament was established. The approval by large and heterogeneous majorities meant that a good number of amendments had to be granted to all the political forces so as to gain their approval to a measure. Indeed Di Palma has revealed that an average of 5.3 amendments are moved to all bills, and 2.1 are accepted. The number of amendments presented is a little lower for bills passed by the decentralised procedure, where a less formal working style allows easier agreement among the political actors. The number of amendments moved is higher for those bills passed on the floor of the Chamber where publicity stimulates a greater show of adversity. The number of amendments moved is particularly high for Government bills passed in plenary (an average of 18.3 amendments) but their rate of success is considerably lower than in other cases; only 10 per cent of such amendments are approved and this means that the real number of amendments passed for such bills is not greatly different from the general mean.[13] Since the legislation on direct elections falls in this category, we should expect a rather high number of amendments to be moved, but only a small number of them to be approved.

150

Our expectations in regard to the development of this specific law-making process have until now been extremely general and abstract as we have not focused on the specific issue under examination. As we have said, the European election legislation falls within a category of bills of national relevance which experience different legislative treatment than other bills. However, we must also take into account the particularities of the legislation. How are the issues underlying this legislation perceived by the relevant political actors, and how does this affect the decision-making process? In order to answer such questions a brief historical excursus is necessary. The European elections issue is not new; on the contrary, it has a background of almost thirty years which must be taken into account if we are to understand how the Italian parliament processed the direct election legislation.

The historical background of the direct election legislation

The background to the holding of direct elections in Italy was mainly favourable. Since the Second World War a large and growing majority of political opinions has been in favour of political integration and a directly elected supranational parliament. How can this be explained? First there is the question of national identity: Italy is not a country with such strong national feelings as, for example, France or the United Kingdom. This has to do with the historical processes of nation- and state-building, which in the Italian case are more recent than in many other European countries. The feelings of a common national identity, and loyalty to the central state, have therefore had less time to penetrate fully into the psyche of the people. To this one should add the negative experience with an authoritarian fascist regime that tried to build its fortunes upon nationalist rhetoric; the consequence was that after the ruinous fall of the fascist regime, all of the democratic parties have played down the nationalist appeal.

A second important point is that Italy had never been a first-class power like France, the United Kingdom or Germany. Thus Italy does not feel any risk of losing a privileged international status by merging with other countries; on the contrary, the chance of joining a united Europe was seen as an opportunity to become a potentially important political actor in the world. Besides, Italy, one of the losing countries in the Second World War, wished to escape from this unpleasant role, and become a full political partner of the other Western European countries. For this reason a European federation was viewed as a good passport.

Finally, after the Second World War some of the internal Italian problems were thought to be more easily solved within a larger European framework than in isolation. Among these were the problem of economic reconstruction and growth which could have profited from open frontiers and larger markets. And, on a strictly political level, it was important that there was a very large Communist Party whose loyalty to the regime was questionable and which had links with the Soviet Union, a country whose zone of influence extended near to the Italian border. The internal stability of the democratic regime appeared endangered, and the majority parties thought a larger, supranational guarantee was necessary in order to face such a difficult situation.

In the years immediately following the Second World War, such conditions led to a strong current of opinion in favour of the European project. An important role in this was played by the leader of the Christian Democratic party Alcide De Gasperi. It is worth remembering that De Gasperi — who for a long period until his death in 1953 was Prime Minister — had not had a purely national political background, for he had been a Member of the Parliament of the Austro-Hungarian Empire before the First World War, and was born in the boundary region of Trento which, before 1918, was under Austrian rule. Additionally other politicians who had been exiled during the fascist regime had established political ties with the other European countries, especially with France.

Support for the development of supranational unity has always been very strong in the centre parties (DC, PRI, PSDI, PLI) which have had a major role in forming Government coalitions. The Socialist Party, after the first years of the postwar period when it was closely allied to the Communist Party, soon sided with the pro-European parties. The only important dissenting opinion was that of the PCI (see table 8.3) which was against what it called the 'Europe of capitalists' for a long time. But since the early seventies, this party has changed its orientation and now supports European integration.[14]

Does this growing unanimity on the European issue mean that Italy has played a very active role in the promotion of the political and institutional unity of Europe in recent years, particularly in fostering the idea of a directly elected Parliament? The answer is that Italian politicians have generally adopted a favourable position in international meetings on the principles of political integration of the EC and direct elections. But their political action has not been very effective given the limited international weight of the country. When Community institutional developments became unrealistic — mainly because of French opposition to them — very little could be done by Italian politicians against such stubborn opposition. Consequently Italian politicians have only given limited attention to European questions. Public opinion has remained generally in favour of Europe[15] but the issue is of low interest compared to more immediate internal ones.

However, as evidence of the favourable attitude toward the principle of direct elections, we can recall a number of parliamentary initiatives that have been attempted in recent years to promote the elections either unilaterally or by joint action. Obviously, whenever a unilateral move was suggested, it was proposed to directly elect only Italian MEPs so as to stimulate the other countries to follow the move. The chronology of these initiatives is as follows:

February 1961	Motion presented by Deputies of the DC, PRI, PSDI and PSI seeking an international agreement on the subject;
October 1961	Motion presented in the Senate by the same parties in order to promote an international agreement;
September 1964	Parliamentary bill proposed by DC MPs for introducing unilateral direct elections of Italian representatives in the European parliament;
February 1965	Similar bill proposed by members of the centre parties in the Chamber of Deputies;
February 1965	Similar bill proposed by DC Deputies;
September 1966	Motion presented in the Chamber by the Chairman of the Liberal Party;
June 1968	Bill introduced by Deputies of the Socialist Party for the establishment of a study committee on this problem;
October 1968	Motion presented by DC Deputies;
June 1969	Popular initiative bill sponsored by the European Federalist Movement, calling for the unilateral elections of Italian MEPs;
May 1973	Bill introduced in the Senate by the Regional Assemblies of Piedmont and other regions calling for unilaterial elections.[16]

What was the fate of these initiatives? Most of them were purely symbolic acts and died very quickly. The bill that received the greatest attention was the one originated by popular initiative: this reached the Committee stage of consideration. It was discussed in the First and Third Committees of the Senate (the Committees for Constitutional Affairs and for Foreign Affairs) in February and April, 1971. A sub-committee with representatives of all the political groups was formed in order to more thoroughly discuss the proposal and report to the two Committees. The bill was again discussed in Parliament after the 1972 general elections by the same Committees, and deferred again to a sub-committee after a general two hour debate. It was discussed again in May and October, 1973, by the Committees, but no vote was taken on it and it then disappeared from sight.

We may thus conclude that the issue received some parliamentary attention, but that it never gained the political momentum required to

153

push it to a legislative outcome. The most probable explanation of this is that, on the one hand the national Parliament was reluctant to take a unilaterial decision in a field traditionally left to supranational, inter-governmental diplomacy and bargaining, i.e. an area typical of executive privilege; and on the other hand the Government knew how difficult it was to push ahead with the question at the supranational level and feared that a unilateral national decision might endanger, more than help, the solution of the matter.

Such previous parliamentary activity was, however, evidence that the Italian Parliament was ready to discuss the issue in a favourable atmosphere. And when an international agreement was reached in September, 1976, the legislative process could be set in motion without major objections. By that time the Communist Party had adopted a pro-European stance.

Given this political background, how do we then explain the somewhat surprising fact that Italy was the last country but one to approve the direct elections legislation? Can we conclude that there was some latent opposition to European integration that appeared during the law-making process? Or, was there perhaps a consensus on the principle of direct elections, but not on the contents of its implementation and, particularly, on the electoral system to be adopted?

The structure of the Italian direct election legislation offers a favourable opportunity for testing these hypotheses. The legislation was composed of two bills, the Ratification and the Implementation Bills. This meant that the political issue could be split into two separate sub-issues. The Ratification Bill would be more concerned with the general principle of the direct elections and their implication for the promotion of supranational institutions and the loss of national sovereignty. The Implementation Bill would be concerned only with the practical, but crucial, problems of the electoral system, and the questions of political representation that were raised. Thus by comparing the passage of the two measures we may examine what were the real issues at stake. Which of the two pieces of legislation received the greatest attention? On what was political conflict concentrated? Which of the two bills experienced greater difficulties in being approved? From what we have said about the general pro-European state of public opinion, we should expect the Ratification Bill to go through the law-making process experiencing neither great difficulties nor generating a heated political debate. We may hypothesise, therefore, that any problems will be concentrated in the Implementation Bill, where the choice of the electoral system will be more controversial and will also raise issues of internal politics.

From a superficial look at the two legislative processes this is exactly what happened. One has only to mention the fact that Italy was among

154

the first countries to enact the Ratification Bill (Act no.150; 6 April, 1977) and the last, bar Luxembourg, to adopt the Implementation Bill (Act no.18; 24 January 1979). It is well known that the length of time for approval of a legislative proposal is a rough, but rather reliable, indicator of the degree of conflict it raises.

It is necessary to examine the passage of the bills in greater detail. The international agreement between the Member States was reached on 20 September, 1976. The Italian Ratification Bill was presented to the Chamber of Deputies by the Government two months later (25 November) and was approved on 6 April, 1977. The legislative process lasted little more than four months (134 days). The Implementation Bill was introduced by the Government in the Senate on 28 July, 1978, and was enacted on 24 January, 1979, nearly six months (180 days) later.[17] The legislative process was, then, somewhat longer for the second bill.

Such data do not reveal the full picture about the difficulties that the second bill experienced in the legislative process. The point to be stressed is that when calculating the duration of the legislative process one should consider not only the parliamentary stage but also the period of time that precedes the presentation of the bill to the Parliament. The length of this period may also be an indicator of the conflict raised by a political issue. Inactivity or delay are typical answers to a conflict situation. However, it is difficult to identify and measure when the pre-parliamentary stage of an item of legislation begins: there is not always a clearly defined starting point. This is not our case. The first issue (ratification) had a clearly defined starting point: the Act of 20 September 1976. And also the second issue (electoral implementation) had one: the enactment of the Ratification Bill.[18] For the first issue we can then measure a very short pre-parliamentary stage (two months). Quite different was the case of the Implementation Bill which was presented by the Government sixteen months after the Ratification Bill had been enacted. This is a clear indication that the analysis of the passing of the direct elections legislation must take into account the pre-parliamentary as well as the parliamentary stage.

The legislative process

The pre-parliamentary stage

As already noted, the pre-parliamentary stage for the Ratification Bill was extremely short. This seemed to reflect a 'technical' period in which the Minister of Foreign Affairs drafted the bill, the Government discussed it, and introduced it to Parliament. The technical nature of the Ratification Bill and its pre-parliamentary stage allows us to concentrate on the fate of the Implementation Bill.

Before doing this, it is necessary to give brief consideration to the Italian political situation at that time. The general election of June 1976 produced a large increase (from 29 per cent to 35 per cent) in the PCI's share of the vote and the traditional distinction between majority and opposition began to fade. After the elections a minority Christian Democratic Government was formed: this owed its survival to the abstention of almost all the other parties with the exception of a few small extremist parties. In the summer of 1977, this Government obtained support for a common political programme agreed by five parties (DC, PCI, PSI, PRI, PSDI). In March 1978, a new Christian Democratic Government, with the parliamentary support of these same five parties, was formed. Thus, since 1976, governments had been able to rely on a majority of more than 90 per cent of the parliamentary seats. This large majority was also extremely heterogenous and major issues (i.e. those with a high conflict potential) were negotiated in private meetings of senior party representatives before reaching Parliament; otherwise the reaching of agreement in a larger and more public area might have been much more difficult.[19]

Given this political background how can the long delay before the implementation bill came up for discussion in the Parliament be explained? Why did the Government not present this bill soon after the ratification of the international agreement? Since the Government could not present an important bill, such as the direct election bill which potentially affected the numerical strength of parties, without having first reached an agreement with the major components of its parliamentary coalition, this delay showed that lengthy and difficult negotiations took place before the bill could be definitively drafted and submitted to Parliament.

The main issues that came to the surface were four, and for each the cleavage line ran between different parties. There was, firstly, the cleavage between large and small parties that is normal whenever a new electoral system is discussed, as small parties risk being heavily under-represented or even disappearing if the electoral system does not approach perfect proportionality. In the European election case, the general principle of proportional representation was accepted by all parties, as it was already adopted for national elections. The type of proportional system to be used was of considerable importance for the centre parties — notably the PSDI, PRI, PLI, which traditionally belong to the governmental arena — which might have been left without representation in the European Parliament. Discussion was therefore heated, and focused particularly on the size of the electoral constituencies and whether seats would be assigned at the constituency or at the national level. These factors affect the degree of proportionality of proportional representation systems.[20] The small parties, therefore, asked for the largest possible constituencies, preferring a single national constituency.

The second point was the question of preference votes: should the electors be allowed to give preference votes to some candidates on their preferred list (as in national elections) or not? Here the cleavage line was not so clear, and it did not run along strictly party lines. There was a more subtle division within parties, particularly strong within the Christian Democratic Party. The cleavage ran between the centre and the periphery of the party. In particular the central party apparatus was not very enthusiastic about preference voting, especially after the experience of the 1976 general elections, which were characterised by an unprecedented level of autonomous preference voting which upset the list orders proposed by central party offices.[21] On the other side, certain wings of the Christian Democratic Party, especially the more anti-communist wing, did not intend to lose this electoral instrument which could provide political leverage against those in the party leadership more favourable to the *compromesso storico* (i.e. alliance with the PCI).

Aside from such a political cleavage the issue of the preference vote raised other problems. The existence of the preference vote creates serious economic problems for the candidates since they have to campaign against each other on their own without the support of official party organisations and funds. Such problems would become even more serious in the European elections, since the size of the constituencies would in any case be larger than that of national elections, and the costs of campaigning therefore higher. A number of potential European candidates who were less financially endowed therefore opposed the preference vote, and favoured a fixed list, since the first solution would have deprived them of a fair chance to compete with richer party fellows. Among the opponents of the preference vote were some Christian Democrat MEPs. The other parties were, in general, less interested in the matter: the PCI because the preference vote is still strictly controlled by the party leadership with the result that there is not fierce competition among candidates; the minor parties because they expected to have only a few candidates elected and these would surely be the party leaders.

The third major issue concerned the vote of Italians living abroad, a question that had been frequently debated in Italy in recent years, for national as well as for European elections. The cleavage here was between the PCI — which was scarcely sympathetic with the idea of granting the right to vote to citizens abroad, whether by mail or through the Italian Consulates, and wanted to have it as limited as possible — and the other parties which were in favour of it.

Finally there were some problems concerning the representation of ethnic and linguistic minorities. This conflict put the linguistic parties in opposition to the other small parties, as the latter feared that by granting special rights to linguistic and ethnic minorities they risked losing some of the few seats they could otherwise be expected to win. Another point that raised some dissension was the proposal to forbid the dual mandate. Major politicians were generally against this, as it would have meant them being excluded from the European Parliament as none would have dreamed of leaving the national Parliament for the European one. In favour of the single mandate were lower level politicians hoping to get rid of the political primadonnas of their party.

This pattern of conflict explains why the take-off of the legislative process was so slow. As we have seen, the major conflicts did not run along majority—minority lines but cut across the majority itself in many different ways. The executive had then to come to terms with the conflicting requests of its large, but heterogeneous, majority.

Thus the pre-parliamentary stage, during which the government (and specifically the Minister of Internal Affairs and his staff) prepared the electoral bill, became extremely long and troubled. It was a period of intense negotiations between the specialists of parties and the government, and private negotiations about which the public knew something from time to time when a conflict came to the surface and reached the newspapers. Then the parties made public declarations of their positions, before the discussions went 'underground' again. Evidence of the great difficulties experienced at this stage lies in the fact that at least forty different drafts of the bill were prepared by the staff of the Minister.[22] Repeatedly it was reported that the bill was ready, and discussion of it by the Cabinet was announced, but then the Cabinet meeting would be cancelled and the bill would once again disappear, for it had to be renegotiated on certain points. In particular this happened in April 1978, when the Government proposal had to be rewritten because of strong opposition from the Christian Democratic parliamentary party (i.e. the party of the Prime Minister and all of the Cabinet). Many DC parliamentarians protested that the bill appeared to follow too closely the proposals of the Communist Party and some of the demands of the small parties. In particular it provided for a national constituency; no preference voting; the dual mandate; and made no clear provision for granting the vote to Italians living abroad — four points that many Christian Democratic MPs strongly resented.

Up to that time, negotiations had been mainly conducted at the level of top party officers and their experts; moreover the major coalition partner, the PCI, had received most of the attention. This had meant that less attention was paid to the feelings of the parties' peripheries. This was felt particularly in the Christian Democratic Party where large sectors of the periphery were not very satisfied with the parliamentary alliance with the Communist Party. The opposition of these Christian Democratic MPs was strongly supported by a national newspaper (*Il Giornale*) which had campaigned in the 1976 elections for anti-*compromesso storico* DC candidates.

In the same period the Movimento Federalista Europeo (a pro-European group) presented a legislative proposal which tried to find a compromise solution reconciling the interests of the DC and the smaller centre parties. Other opinion groups campaigned strongly in favour of preferential voting.[23]

The bill had thus to be discussed again. Only in July could a final project be approved by the Cabinet. In this version of the bill there were nine multi-regional constituencies instead of a national constituency; the preference vote had been reintroduced; the electoral system was very similar to that used for national elections (which meant that remaining votes which could not be counted at the constituency level would be added to a national pool); the incompatibility clause was still absent; and the right for Italian citizens to vote abroad was given only to those living in the EC countries who were still inscribed on the Italian electoral register (i.e. about 400,000 of at least one million and a half potential votes).

We can conclude this stage of the analysis with a number of observations. The pre-parliamentary stage is an extremely important and complex phase of the decisional process when an issue raises conflict. It is particularly important when a very large parliamentary majority brings together heterogeneous political viewpoints. The pattern of this decisional phase is characterised by secrecy: negotiations take place away from the eyes of the public among party elites and experts. Studies on consociational democracy have explained how and why this type of decisional procedure takes place.[24] The Italian case, in the years we have considered, shows some similarities to the consociational system, but at the same time it lacks other important features that are required by a coherent consociation. As the decisional process we are considering clearly shows, the consociational principle has some flaws, in particular concerning the control of elites over the lower strata of political movements and organisations, and the deferential attitude of rank and file members *vis-à-vis* party leaders.

In the Italian case, and particularly in certain parties, during the years of the grand coalition there has been an increase in the independence and autonomy of public opinion, as well as of middle-level political elites with regard to party leadership.[25] As we have already mentioned, since the 1976 elections preference votes have been supported by public opinion movements, with particular regard to Christian Democratic candidates. In our case this took the form of a rebellion of certain sectors of the Christian Democratic Party (mainly members of the parliamentary party) against the decision taken at the top of the party. The pre-parliamentary stage of law-making tends, therefore, to develop by a sort of pendular incrementalism. A first draft of the bill, produced by the ministerial bureaucracy according to the guidelines formulated by the Government, becomes the basis for top-level negotiations between the parties of the majority. The agreement reached may be contested by dissenting sections of one or more of the parties that have taken part in the negotiation; this happens particularly often within the largest and most factionalised party, the Christian Democrats. If the dissent becomes particularly vocal, and finds support in important sectors of public opinion (as happened concerning direct elections), the negotiations reopen. The Government and the top party leadership have to accommodate the requests of dissenters, but this in turn requires new negotiations with the other parties. At a certain point, however, when a fundamental agreement has been reached, some of the problems are put aside and left to be solved during the parliamentary stage of the process. It is to this stage that we now turn our attention.

The parliamentary stage

For this stage a comparison of the fate of the two legislative proposals will help to make clear the differences in the law-making process between non-conflictual and conflictual issues. The Ratification Bill was presented by the Government to the Chamber of Deputies on 25 November, 1976. Some time was required to have the bill put on the agenda of the Foreign Affairs Committee (in part because of Christmas holidays), but then the Committee disposed of it in one meeting of about one hour's length. After the Committee stage the process ran at the maximum speed of the slow-moving Parliament. Ten days later the bill was sent to the plenary, where, after a fortnight and in three short meetings, it was approved on 17 January, 1977, with the unanimous support of all but sixteen Deputies (6 from the small leftist splinter party Proletarian Democracy). The bill was then sent to the Senate, where the legislative process developed with the same speed. Three weeks after receiving the bill, the Senate had completed its Committee stage with the consideration of the bill lasting less than one hour. Ten days later the bill reached the plenary where it was approved unanimously after being discussed for seven hours.[26] Promulgation followed ten days later.

As the chronology has shown the legislative process developed with smoothness and regularity. The length of the law-making process was mainly caused by the crowded parliamentary agenda; and the greatest part of the time taken to approve the bill was taken by its waiting for consideration. Can we say the same for the Election Bill? A negative answer will soon be apparent from what follows. After a lengthy preparatory stage the Election Bill was ready to be discussed by Parliament at the end of July, 1978. The bill had by then become acceptable to dissenters of the Christian Democratic parliamentary party, but it still stirred some opposition, mainly from small parties fearing that they would be under-represented under a multi-constituency electoral system, as well as from the Communist Party which was not fully satisfied with certain aspects of the vote granted to Italian citizens abroad. Moreover, the proposal of abolishing the preference vote still lingered in the air arousing suspicions. The Government report with which the bill was introduced acknowledged the compromise reached between the request for the preference vote (which in order to be practical required small constituencies) and the request of the smaller parties to have the fullest proportionality (which required large constituencies). It left Parliament the possibility of further improving this compromise. It is worth noticing that the Government report referred explicitly to the legislative proposal drafted by the European Federalist Movement as having inspired the solutions adopted.

One difference between the Ratification Bill and the Election Bill is that the latter was presented by the Government to the Senate, while the former was submitted to the Chamber of Deputies. In the Italian bicameral system the two chambers have equal powers, and the Government has the choice as to where it presents its legislative proposals. This is generally determined by time-tabling considerations, but some political factors may also intrude. Because the chambers are elected by different electoral systems the strength of the parties may be slightly different in each; in the smaller Senate (315 members in comparison to 630 in the Chamber), larger parties tend to be over-represented and smaller parties under-represented. This may mean that certain types of coalition that do not make up a majority in the Chamber of Deputies may do so in the Senate (as happened during the passage of the abortion law). This was not relevant to the decision on the Election Bill, as it was expected that each chamber would pass it by a very large majority. What was probably behind the Government's decision to introduce the bill into the Senate was the fact that the small left-wing Radical Party was not represented there: in the Chamber, its four deputies often effectively adopted filibustering tactics. Since one of the most disputed issues was that of the representation of small parties in the European Parliament, the Government may have preferred to start the discussion of the bill in the Senate where it would not run the risk of such obstructionism (since the Radicals would be absent, and the other small parties more amenable to negotiation). And when the bill eventually arrived in the Chamber of Deputies, lack of time would prevent the Radical Party from adopting such obstructionist behaviour, as this could have imperilled the holding of the direct elections — which is not what the Radical Party wanted. Another reason for the Government's choice, was that the Senate provided a smaller and quieter environment which facilitated negotiations. Obviously such problems did not arise for the Ratification Bill.

The bill submitted to the Senate at the end of July did not appear for discussion in Committee before the end of September. This had to do mainly with the summer recess, since the Parliament does not meet between the beginning of August and mid-September. When the discussion of the bill started in the joint session of the Committees for Foreign Affairs and Constitutional Matters it was soon evident that it still raised a number of doubts and fears in many quarters. The small parties feared being under-represented by the multi-constituency system and requested a national constituency; representatives of the linguistic minorities (a tiny French minority in the Aosta Valley and a somewhat larger German minority in South Tirol) wanted to be able to elect at least one MEP; the Communist Party was not satisfied with the right granted to Italians living abroad to vote in Italian consulates — a principle against which it had also fought a lengthy, and discreet, battle with regard to national elections for fear of being openly or implicitly discriminated in its political appeal in countries where a Communist Party does not exist, has little weight, or is even legally forbidden.

The Government Bill had, then, to undergo some changes if it had to be approved; but this could raise the opposition of many Christian Democratic MPs in case the preference vote was abolished or made extremely costly by the introduction of the national constituency. Moreover, the DC and other centre and right parties would also fight against further limitations of the vote of Italians abroad. These two points also stirred the attention of active sections of public opinion. In particular *Il Giornale*, a newspaper that had strongly campaigned in the 1976 elections against a DC-PCI alliance, and had favoured the use of the preference vote as an instrument for choosing Christian Democratic candidates that were against that line, wanted the preference vote to be maintained as well as the right to vote abroad. The same position was held by the MILLE (Movement for a Free Italy in a Free Europe) public opinion group, a sort of voters' syndicate that had pursued the same strategy at national elections.[27] Such pressures were felt particularly by DC MPs.

After three meetings of the Joint Committees (on 27 September, 5 and 11 October, 1978) the different political orientations were clear, as was the fact that the bill had to be thoroughly rewritten if all the

162

requests were to be accommodated. The joint session of the two Committees (involving 55 Senators) was clearly not the right environment for such complex and delicate work. It was agreed, as normally happens in such situations, to create a small subcommittee, and the full meeting of the Committees was adjourned. The subcommittee was formed by the rapporteur of the bill (a DC Senator) and seven more Senators representing DC, PCI, PSI, PSDI, PRI and PLI (only the right-wing MSI and DN parties were not represented on it). The subcommittee had to redraft the bill, and then report again to the joint committee for a formal decision on it. The subcommittee worked in close contact (if not formally, nevertheless, substantially) with top party leaders and party experts on electoral questions.

The proceedings of such subcommittees are almost secret, and the public knows very little of what happens in them. That the task of the subcommittee was difficult became apparent by the long time it took to present a new draft — the end of November. As we shall see the Government Bill was considerably changed. The pendulum had swung again: the compromise now moved in the direction of the small parties without, however, completely reversing what had been obtained by the Christian Democratic parliamentary party. The small parties obtained the fullest proportionality, since a national constituency was established for assigning seats *among* the parties. The method adopted was that of natural quotients. However, the regional constituencies were kept but only for assigning seats *within* each party; thus the preference vote was maintained. However, the constituencies became larger and fewer (five instead of nine) and each grouped together more than one region. The electoral system was thus characterised by a threshold of representation which was proportionally lower than that for national elections for the Chamber of Deputies (despite the handicap of the lower number of seats at stake). With regards to the vote abroad, the PCI obtained from the subcommittee detailed guarantees for the equal rights of political propaganda of all parties in foreign countries: if in one country it was not possible to have such guarantees secured by an international agreement, Italians living in that country would not be allowed to vote there (they would only have the possibility of voting in the elections by returning to Italy).

The agreement reached in the subcommittee almost gave the bill its final shape. The following stages of the legislative process brought only minor changes. At this juncture international constraints were becoming clear: most of the other countries had already approved the direct elections legislation, or at least were at the final stages of the law-making process. The risk of Italy being the only country (together with Luxembourg) not ready for the first European elections was becoming apparent. The legislative process had then to gain speed, and this heavily influenced the next stages of the legislative process.

The draft proposed by the subcommittee was accepted almost without changes by the joint session of the two legislative Committees (on 23 November, 1978). The discussion and vote on the bill lasted only three hours; all but one of the amendments (concerning the rights of linguistic minority parties) were withdrawn or their consideration postponed for the plenary. The delicate agreement reached after long negotiations in the private meetings could not be reversed by the Committees.

The legislative process was then accelerated and the bill soon discussed in the plenary meeting of the Senate (on 2 December). From the general discussion in the plenary, it was clear that all the parties of the majority (DC, PCI, PSI, PSDI, PRI) plus one of the linguistic parties (the South Tyrol People's Party) and a small right-wing splinter party (National Democracy) would support the bill, while the Liberal Party would abstain and the Neo-Fascist Party (MSI) plus another small linguistic party (the Aosta Valley Union) would vote against it.

After the general discussion in the plenary, some amendments were moved. The most important concerned ethnic minorities and the compatibility clause between the national and European mandates. The President of the Senate refused to accept an amendment introducing the incompatibility between the two mandates on the grounds that it would be against an international treaty; and all the national parties voted against the amendment enlarging the representation of ethnic minorities. The Senate accepted only minor amendments and made no important changes to the bill which was thus approved rapidly.

It was then sent to the Chamber of Deputies (6 December, 1978) where two weeks later it was discussed in the Constitutional Affairs Committee. Given the time constraint, the Committee chairman (Mrs Nilde Iotti, PCI, MEP) suggested that no amendments be accepted to the Senate version. After a short debate (the whole meeting took approximately two hours) the proposal was accepted and the bill approved without changes. Only the extreme right-wing party representative (Mr Pazzaglia, MSI) voted against this. If everything went smoothly in the Committee, things were not to be so easy in the plenary. But this was to be expected. In the Chamber, the Radical Party applied limited filibustering techniques by tabling numerous amendments (53, while 3 more were presented by the MSI and 1 by the DP) on almost every Article. Of these, seven were withdrawn and the rest voted down. Only one amendment moved had limited success; the MSI amendment seeking to make the national and European mandates incompatible, was defeated (in a secret vote) by 300 to 94, the latter figure being more than the MPs of the MSI. The content of the other amendments does not warrant consideration as they were proposed as a protest against the fact that the Chamber was not allowed to freely discuss the bill. After three meetings and more than thirteen hours of debate, the bill was passed by 390—17 votes (with 18 abstentions). On 24 January, 1979, the bill was promulgated just before the Government crisis brought about the dissolution of Parliament.

Conclusion

In what ways did the European elections legislation differ from normal legislative processes? As we have observed several times, the time dimension is what most affected the law-making process. The time constraints that Parliament had to respect in order to comply with the international agreement, meant that the bill received a shorter examination than comparable legislation.[28]

The process was particularly short in the Chamber of Deputies, concerning the Implementation Bill where there was no opportunity to introduce any modifications to the legislation. It may even be suggested that the Government explicitly exploited these constraints in order to sidestep certain obstacles (such as the risk of more intense filibustering by the Radical Party). Perhaps the specific issue made the search for a compromise satisfying the interests of the smaller parties more intense than would have been for other issues. Apparently all parties shared the opinion that an electoral bill has to have the consent of all *constitutional* parties, even the minor ones.[29] This brought about a much more thorough redrafting of the Government Bill than normally happens. However, the formal number of amendments submitted and approved does not reveal the full story of Parliament's effectiveness as most of this work was done in the subcommittee of the Senate.

Beside these specific features, the legislative process developed along lines typical of law-making when controversial issues are at stake. This we have defined as pendular incrementalism. Such a process develops both in its pre-parliamentary and parliamentary stages through an alternation of secret and public steps: the secret ones are for negotiation, the public ones for appeals to public opinion, or to those parties or party factions that feel unsatisfied with the results of the negotiations. Each step normally produces a narrowing of the conflicing positions until the final compromise is reached. Such a process is particularly time-consuming, and because of the many steps and re-draftings of the bill the quality of legislation often leaves much to be desired (in particular, its interpretation tends to be difficult and to leave space for double meanings). Moreover, the chances of such a highly complicated and delicate law-making mechanism coming to a standstill are considerable: an issue may get out of hand and the pendulum work in the opposite way, thus magnifying disagreements instead of resolving conflicting positions. In such cases it will be very difficult for a legislative outcome to be produced. This, however, could not have happened to the European legislation, as the very large agreement on the fundamental principles involved created a sort of protective buffer around the law-making process.

Notes

1 See A. Lijphart, 'Il metodo della comparazione', *Rivista Italiana di Scienza Politica*, vol.1, 1971, pp 67-92, especially pp 79 ff; and his *Democracy in Plural Societies: a Comparative Exploration* (Yale U.P., New Haven, 1977), chapter 1.

2 For a more detailed analysis of the Act of 20 September, see M. Capurso, 'La decisione del Consiglio della Comunità europea per l'elezione dei componeneti dell 'Assemblea a suffragio universale diretto', *Rivista trimestrale di Diritto Pubblico,* vol.18, 1977, pp 1079-1094 and G. Troccoli, 'L'elezione a suffragio universale diretto del Parlamento europeo', *Rivista trimestrale di Diritto pubblico,* vol.18, 1977, pp 1577-1603. With regard to the compatibility clause, Troccoli rightly says, on juridical grounds, that the international agreement left a free choice to national legislation. In fact this clause was the result of a compromise between countries (such as Denmark) that wanted the double mandate to be made mandatory, and other countries who wanted it to be forbidden. The political interpretation of the clause was such that it would not permit national parliaments to make the national and European mandates incompatible.

3 For one of the few studies in this area see S. Tozzi, *Pressioni e veicoli. Storia di due leggi: il codice della strada e l'assicurazione obbligatoria,*(Giuffrè, Milano, 1975).

4 For a detailed analysis of the new Standing Orders see A. Manzella, *Il Parlamento*, (Il Mulino, Bologna, 1977).

5 The main differences between the two electoral systems is that in Senate elections no preference voting is permitted and, for the allocation of seats the remainders are calculated at the regional level, while they are calculated nationally for the Chamber of Deputies. The electoral system of the Chamber is, therefore, slightly more proportional.

6 M. Cotta, 'A Structural-functional Framework for the Analysis of Unicameral and Bicameral Parliaments', *European Journal of Political Research*, vol.2, 1974, pp 201-24; see especially p.221.

7 F. Cantelli, V. Mortara and G. Movia, *Come lavora il Parlamento*, (Giuffrè, Milano, 1974), pp 164 ff.

8 See F. Cantelli, V. Mortara and G. Movia, op.cit; F. Cazzola, *Governo e opposizione nel Parlamento italiano*, (Giuffre, Milano, 1974); S. Tozzi, op.cit; F. Cazzola, G. Priulla and A. Predieri, *Il decreto-legge tra Governo e Parlamento* (Giuffrè, Milano, 1976); A. Predieri (ed.), *Il Parlamento nel Sistema politico italiano* (Comunithà, Milano, 1975) and G. Di Palma, *Surviving without Governing*, (University of California Press, Berkeley, 1977).

9 Di Palma, op.cit., ch.III, pp 95-131.

10 After the elections of 1976 a Government with only Christian Democrat Ministers was formed, under the premiership of Mr Andreotti, and with the abstention of almost all of the other parties (PCI, PSI, PRI, PSDI, SVP). In June 1977, a common programme was discussed between the DC and the other abstaining parties. In March 1978 a new government led by Mr Andreotti was formed which received a favourable vote by the previously abstaining parties; the new Cabinet was also exclusively formed of Christian Democrat Ministers.

11 G. Sartori, 'European Political Parties: The Case of Polarized Pluralism' in J. LaPalombara and M. Weiner (eds), *Political Parties and Political Development*, (Princeton University Press, Princeton, 1966), pp 137-66.

12 Di Palma, op.cit., table 51, p.210.

13 Ibid., pp 59-64.

14 See for instance the main report to the XIIIth National Congress of the Communist Party (Milano, 13 March, 1972) by the Chairman, Enrico Berlinguer, published as E. Berlinguer, *Per un governo di svolta democratica* (Editori Riuniti, Roma, 1977), p.30.

15 See Appendix to chapter 2.

16 For a more detailed analysis of the legislative proposals before 1971, see V. Guizzi, 'L'azione del Parlamento italiano in favore dell'elezione a suffragio universale del Parlamento europeo', *Il Politico*, vol.36, 1971, pp 782-91.

17 The length of approval is therefore considerably lower than the mean for such type of bill as calculated by Di Palma (see note 12).

18 According to a declaration of the Minister for Foreign Affairs, during the final debate on the Ratification Bill, a technical committee was already at work studying the new electoral system before the first bill had been approved (*Acti Parlamentari Senato, Resoconto stenografico seguta* 24 marzo, 1977, 4349), quoted by S. Traversa, 'L'elezione del Parlamento europeo a suffragio universale e la legge elettorale italiane' *Rivista trimestrale di Diritto pubblico* vol.18, 1977, pp 1577-1603, p.1589.

19 For a recent and insightful evaluation of such aspects in the Italian political situation see A. Pappalardo, *Partiti e governi di coalizione in Europa* (Angeli, Milano, 1978), pp 98-114.

20 This point is emphasised by D. Fisichella, *Sviluppo democratico e sistemi elettorali* (Sansoni, Firenze, 1970), pp 121-30, 189 ff.

21 For the analysis of the role of preference voting in the Italian political context in recent elections see M. Cotta, 'Il rinnovamento del personale parlamentare democristiano', *Il Mulino*, vol.27, 1978, pp 723-42; and R.S. Katz and L. Bardi, 'Voto di preferenza e ricambio del personale parlamentare in Italia (1963-1976)', *Rivista Italiana di Scienza Politica*, vol.9, 1979, pp 71-96, especially pp 88 ff.

22 For the content of the four main schemes drafted see S. Traversa, op.cit., pp 1597-1603, who gives also the text of the proposals of the Movimento Federalista Europeo.

23 Among them especially the MILLE (Movement for a Free Italy in a Free Europe), a movement born on the eve of the 1976 general elections and strongly opposing any alliance of the DC with the PCI. This movement had proved particularly successful in supporting Christian Democratic candidates opposed to such an alliance through the preference vote; see M. Cotta, 'Il rinnovamento del personale parlamentare democristiano', op.cit., pp 723 ff.

24 See in particular what A. Lijphart, *The Politics of Accommodation*, (University of California Press, Berkeley, 1968), pp 126-31, says about 'summit diplomacy' and 'secrecy'.

25 A. Pappalardo, op.cit., pp 98 ff., underlines these aspects, to which one should add the absence of a deep rooted consensus on fundamentals, and acute ideological polarisation.

26 For a larger account of this debate see G. Troccoli, op.cit., pp 1558 ff.

27 See note 23.

28 See note 12.

29 In common political language all parties are considered *constitutional*, except the extreme right-wing MSI and some new extreme left-wing parties such as DP and PR. Obviously this is a purely political convention with no juridical ground. The political consequence of this distinction is that only the *constitutional* parties are allowed to take part in certain common consultations concerning the fundamental rules of the political game.

The Italian Parliament: some readings

F. Cantelli, V. Mortara and G. Movia, *Come lavora il Parlamento* (Giuffrè, Milano, 1974). A systematic analysis of the law-making processes and guide to how the Italian Parliament works.

F. Cazzola, *Governo e opposizione nel Parlamento italiano* (Giuffrè, Milano, 1974). A short essay dealing with the role of opposition parties in law-making.

M. Cotta, *Classe politica e parlamento in Italia; 1946-1976* (Il Mulino, Bologna, 1979). Examines the relationship between the characteristics of the political elites and the consolidation of the parliamentary institution.

G. Di Palma, *Surviving without Governing*, (University of California Press, Berkeley, 1977). An insightful interpretation of the legislative process.

A. Manzella, *Il Parlamento* (Il Mulino, Bologna, 1977). The most recent juridical book concerning the structure and functioning of the Italian Parliament.

A. Predieri (ed.), *Il Parlamento nel sistema politico italiano* (Comunità, Milano, 1975). Discusses recent developments in the role of the parliamentary institution.

G. Sartori (ed.), *Il Parlamento italiano 1946-1963*, (Edizioni Scientifiche Italiane, Napoli, 1963). The first analytic study of the Italian Parliament.

9 Luxembourg: a Big Issue in a Small State

Martin A. Wing

The institutions of State and the legislative process

As a constitutional monarchy with a unicameral parliament Luxembourg has developed an institutional balance which is as successful as it is unique in Western Europe. In legislative matters, four bodies play a role; the Grand-Duke, the government, the Chamber of Deputies and the Council of State. Each has a particular function which taken together ensure as smooth, stable and representative a system as is possible.

Constitutionally, the legislative initiative lies with the government and the Chamber, the Grand-Duke being responsible for sanctioning and promulgating laws. However, as in most states in Western Europe, government bills (projets de loi) have come to dominate the legislative timetable securing not only a larger percentage of enactments but also, in numerical terms, a lower mortality rate than bills sponsored by private members (propositions de loi).

The division between bills tabled by the government and those emanating from the Chamber is further institutionalised through the different paths they take before enactment. With government legislation, a draft is sent first to the Council of State, prefaced by an 'exposé des motifs' or explanatory statement, setting out its basic provisions. The Council, an appointed body, to a limited extent performs the role of a second Chamber although the opinion that it is required to produce on all bills and amendments proposed by both the government or Chamber, are only advisory and so, strictly speaking, it does not have the formal power to amend bills. However, no bill may become law until the Council has considered it, and frequently changes either in the overall approach or the details of a bill may be made as a result of its written opinion.

When the Council has completed its deliberations a bill then passes, along with the written opinion of the Council, to the Chamber of Deputies. There it is sent either to a standing committee or, in the event of there being no competent committee, a special committee is set up and then disbanded once it has completed its task.[1] It is at this juncture that effective scrutiny occurs; the committee studies the bill in detail along with any amendments the government and/or Council wish incorporated.[2]

A rapporteur is appointed to produce a report reflecting the committee's views, which he then presents to the Chamber at the beginning of the plenary debate. The report outlines the history of the subject of the bill, the committee's deliberations and explains any contentious issues. The final section comprises the amended bill as the committee would like to see it although future action on related issues may also be proposed.

In the plenary debate it is the text sponsored by the committee and not the original government bill that is debated. If the government or any deputy wishes to see further changes then they may be proposed and debated during this stage.[3] Similarly, motions may be proposed on the topic of the bill or related issues expressing a point which any individual or group of deputies wish to have adopted as the Chamber's policy.

Before the bill is finally passed, four votes must in theory be taken: article by article; each amendment; the bill as a whole; and a second constitutional vote after a delay of at least three months. In practice, however, the second constitutional vote is usually dispensed with (see table 9.1) if both the Chamber and the Council agree to this. In general, the vote is only forced if the principle of the bill is strongly opposed by the Council. Individual articles are frequently opposed, but taken as a whole the bill is considered necessary and so it is not delayed.

Table 9.1
The flow of bills through the Chamber of Deputies, 1976-78

Session	Number of plenary meetings	Bills presented			Laws passed		
		A	B	C	A	B	C
1976-77	76	75	4	4	82	2	7
1977-78	82	72	6	7	72*	1	6
	Total	147	10	11	154	3	13

Key

A 'Projets de loi'; bills presented by the Government.
B 'Propositions de loi'; bills presented by Deputies.
C 'Projets de reglements grand-ducaux'; implementing legislation presented in the name of the Grand-Duke.

*This figure includes two 'projets de loi' that had to undergo the second constitutional vote after three months and eight others that were passed at first reading.

In the case of a private member's bill, a text is tabled in the Chamber and then forwarded to a committee which decides whether to proceed with it or allow it to lapse. In the former case, copies are distributed to Deputies and the bill timetabled on the parliamentary agenda. On the set day, if five or more Deputies support it, the bill is discussed and a decision taken as to whether the Chamber shall pursue it. If a bill successfully negotiates this stage, it passes to the Council of State for its opinion. As with government legislation, a private member's bill is then transmitted to a legislative committee of the Chamber which discusses it before presenting a report to the plenary for a final debate and decision.

To process the workload the Chamber meets in plenary three afternoons per week and in committees every week-day morning. The parliamentary year commences in early October and continues until the following July with short breaks at Christmas, Easter and Whitsun. Within this timetable the workload of the Chamber is fairly heavy. Table 9.1 shows that on average, roughly one bill is presented and another passed at each meeting of the plenary. Whilst many of these bills will go through after only minimal formal debate, many others will give rise to amendments and wrangling between Deputies. In 1976-77 the average length of a plenary meeting was 3.77 hours and in 1977-78 4.01 hours which, when considered with the fact that committee meetings are held daily, represents a fairly high level of parliamentary activity in terms of the time spent processing bills. The reason why the Chamber is able to proceed at such a pace is the absence of major disagreement between the parties — with the exception of the Communist Party — differences being mainly questions of nuance or degree. As Flesch remarks, 'The business is transacted at a regular pace with astonishingly little drama'.[4] This reflects the high level of consensus in the country, which is a result of economic and social stability, despite a high level of immigration, and also a result of the recognition that major issues are determined beyond the Luxembourg borders.

Political environment

During the period of the passage of direct elections legislation, the government of Luxembourg was formed by a coalition of Liberals (Demokratesch Partei, DP) and Socialists (Letzeburger Sozialistisch Arbechterpartei, LSAP) (see table 9.2).

The five parties represented in the Chamber represent a broad spread of opinion. On the right, the largest party in terms of parliamentary seats is the Christian Social Party (Chreschtlech Sozial Voltekspartei, CSV). This is the only party to draw its support evenly from all four

Table 9.2
Parties in the Chamber of Deputies, May 1974

	Abbreviation	Vote %*	Seats (N)†
Communist Party (Kommunistesch Partei)	KPL	10.5	5
G Socialists Workers' Party (Letzeburger Socialistisch Arbechterpartei)	LSAP	29.1	17
Social Democratic Party (Sozial Demokratesch Partei)	SDP	9.2	5
G Democratic Party (Demokratesch Partei)	DP	22.2	14
Christian Social Party (Chreschtlech sozial Voltekspartei)	CSV	27.9	18
Others		1.1	—
Total		100.0	59
Turnout		85.2%	

*Share of valid votes cast in General Election, May 1974.
†Seats in Chamber of Deputies, May 1974.

G Party forming the Government.

electoral districts. It is a conservative and strongly confessional party with close ties with the Christian trade unions.

In the centre and centre-left are the Liberals who have had an erratic performance at elections since 1959, and the Social Democrats (Sozial Demokratesch Partei, SDP) a relatively new party formed after a breach within the LSAP in 1971. On the left are found two parties: the Socialists actively supporting the system, and attempting to effect change through co-operation with other parties; whilst the Communists remain isolated as a party of constant opposition owing to their strong pro-Moscow attachments.[5]

The small size of the country and the desire to make the Chamber as representative of electoral support as possible had led to adoption of the Hagenbach-Bischoff variation of the d'Hondt system for national elections. The country is divided into four districts each of which elects one deputy for every 5,500 inhabitants.

The parties publish lists of candidates (to a maximum of the number of seats) in each electoral district and seats are allocated to these lists according to the number of votes each receives — a figure arrived at by adding votes for lists as a whole to votes given to individual candidates — and the principle of the smallest electoral quotient.

Whilst Luxembourg may be viewed as the end-product of a series of historical accidents and international accommodations, its continued viability as a sovereign state has been considerably strengthened through economic progress and political stability, if not brought about then considerably enhanced by membership of the European Communities (EC). Consequently, Luxembourg remains one of the prime supporters of further integration as a rational response not only to these issues but also to the more immediate problems of its economic dependency on its trading partners and its inability to exert by itself, any real influence, at the international level, on the economic forces governing the economy.

The greater democratisation of the Communities' institutions, in particular the election of the Members of the European Parliament has for some time been viewed as one of the main avenues towards strengthening ties between the nine.[6] This viewpoint was shared for a considerable time by all shades of opinion represented in the Chamber of Deputies and found a ready echo in the government. This was effectively manifested in parliamentary documents. For example, in the report of the Foreign Affairs Committee of the Chamber of Deputies on the question of direct elections it states:

> Successive Luxembourg governments have always favoured the election of Members of the European Parliament by universal suffrage. This belief has been demonstrated both at the international and national levels by the attitude adopted in negotiations on European matters and by the pronouncements of the Chamber of Deputies.[7]

This attitude is overwhelmingly reflected in the Chamber where, prior to the October 1976 agreement of the Council of Ministers, several attempts were made both to introduce legislation for directly elected Luxembourg MEPs and to encourage the government to present its own proposals.[8] Whilst the motions have been successful in the Chamber, the government has consistently failed to act on the matter despite its avowed support. This prompted the introduction of a private member's bill in 1971. This, however, was thought to be too simplistic and as a result it was allowed to lapse by the Committee which decides whether to proceed with private members' bills. Despite its brevity it did attempt to tackle the major issues and embodied the major points of the proposals submitted by the government seven years later.

Outside the Chamber public opinion has, on the whole, also supported both EC membership and holding direct elections.[9] Whilst the level of opposition to the elections was never particularly great, its persistence did indicate a solid block of anti-election feeling. After 1976, it was reflected in the Chamber by the only party of consistent opposition, the KPL, which switched to this position from a previous policy of support. Indeed the first motion tabled in the Chamber in 1969 calling on the government to present a bill on electing Luxembourg's delegation to the European Parliament was put down by Herr Dominique Urbany on behalf of the parliamentary Communist Party. The following year a similar motion[10] was passed unanimously in the Chamber, again with KPL support. One explanation for this apparent volte-face stems from the KPL's traditional role as the party of opposition provoking one respected commentator — who is also a deputy in the Chamber and an MEP — to note '. . . it is as much an opposition *of* principle as *on* principle'.[11]

The legislation

As noted above, the issue of directly elected MEPs had been raised several times in the Chamber with four motions and one bill tabled in the period 1969-1975. With these indications of support in Parliament, one might have expected a speedy passage for any bill proposed by the Government. However, this did not prove to be the case. Following the Council of Ministers' decision in September 1976 to hold direct elections, two bills were presented to the Chamber; one to ratify the decision — presented on 7 June, 1977 — and another to govern how the elections should be conducted — presented on 9 February, 1978. Whilst the target of May/June 1978 was still, at least publicly, being aimed at, the decision to delay the elections for a further year ensured adequate time to resolve the contentious sections of the proposals. However, with national legislative elections due on 27 May, 1979 and European elections due on 10 June, 1979, pressure began to mount within both the Government and the Chamber to hold the two elections on the same day, i.e. 10 June. Whilst provision had been made in the bill for simultaneous national and European elections[12] certain changes had to be made to the existing electoral law. In October 1978 a further bill was presented to the Chamber designed to surmount these obstacles.

The Ratification Bill had a smooth passage through the legislative process. No changes were proposed by either the Council of State or the Chamber. Opposition among Deputies emanated solely from the parliamentary Communist Party, whose spokesman was the only speaker to attack the principle during the debate. Arguments advanced by Herr René Urbany, the KPL chairman, centred on the elections as a

173

vehicle to promote further integration amongst the Member States. Quoting from the Luxembourg Constitution, Herr Urbany noted that Articles 1, 32 and 50 state that Luxembourg is a free, independent and indivisible state whose sovereign power is exercised by the Grand-Duke though residing with the nation, with the Chamber of Deputies representing the country. Further integration of Member States and the provision of a directly elected European Parliament provided, according to Herr Urbany, a permanent and irreversible rejection of these constitutional safeguards, ensuring a progressive abolition of national rights. National independence and sovereignty were bound to disappear and with them all social and democratic progress. Laws would be passed in which Luxembourgers had had very little say, with only six seats in an assembly of 410. It was also true that 324 of the seats would go to the bigger states allowing their interests to dominate the business of the Parliament. Finally, the 'island of well-being in Europe' created twenty years previously had become a Europe of big multi-national concerns and finance groups showing little regard for national interests in their pursuit of profit.

The counter arguments advanced by the proponents of direct elections fell into three categories. Firstly, there were those deputies who saw the elections providing the Community with a shot in the arm and so helping further integration. Secondly, there were a large number of speakers who supported the elections because of the effect they would have both on the functioning of the Parliament and, through that, on the Community as a whole. Into this category fell those who viewed the elections as a means of democratising the European Parliament and thereby making it more legitimate. Through this, speakers saw it gaining powers and authority and thus being able to control the technocracy.

The final group of issues discussed was the technical considerations such as the number of constituencies that would be desirable; the retention of the dual-mandate; the number of seats allocated to Luxembourg and the matter of sovereignty raised by the Communists. None of these issues was decided as the debate dealt solely with the principle of holding the elections. However, the whole tone favoured the holding of elections and rejected the worries raised by the Communist Party. When the vote was finally taken after discussion in three plenary meetings, the Chamber supported the principle by 54 votes to 5 with no abstentions.

Before this, however, the Chamber and the Government had set up an *ad hoc* committee comprising Deputies and representatives from the Foreign Affairs, Justice and Interior Ministries with the aim of finding solutions to the problems engendered by direct elections. After having discussed the issues involved, it put its findings to the Government, in order to encourage the publication of draft proposals.[13]

A Government Bill was finally brought before the Chamber of Deputies on 9 February 1978,[14] seven months after the Decision and the Act concerning direct elections had been passed. Its general provisions varied only slightly from those which regulate legislative elections. Indeed, it proposed articles 1-84, 88-91, 93, 95, 98-145 and 235-266 of the existing electoral law should be retained for direct elections with only minor alterations. The bill, having been presented to the Chamber, was immediately despatched to the Council of State for its opinion. This was the first step in a series of proposals and counter-proposals involving the Government, the Council of State and the special committee of the Chamber.

With the appearance in October 1978 of the third bill designed to regulate simultaneous national and European elections it was decided that the two outstanding bills pertaining to direct elections, Projets de loi 2163 and 2231, should be considered together. Thereafter there followed parallel discussion and consideration by the Chamber, the Council and the Government of each others' suggestions and amendments, many of which were acceptable to all three. This is not to suggest that each acted without internal dissension and with disagreements arising only between the three institutions; on several occasions the legislative committee, which is where the solutions to the major problems are arrived at, was obliged to move to a formal vote on amendments. Not all proposed amendments were acceptable to the committee as a whole and were therefore either rejected or accepted on a majority vote.

One issue that had been skirted in the original proposals concerned enfranchisement of Luxembourg citizens resident in other EC states. In proposing the use of the same system for European and national elections, the possibility of voting other than by presenting oneself at the polling station was deliberately excluded. Although the matter of introducing postal voting for those unable to vote in person had been mooted in 1969, and the Council of State had approved it, the Legal Affairs Committee of the Chamber had voiced certain reservations and the Chamber had taken the committee's advice and rejected the bill. This issue was once again raised by the Council of State for the European elections. However, the committee felt that it would not be possible to overcome all the difficulties such a scheme would produce. In its place, it proposed that the Government should study this matter in relation to elections at all levels of government and submit a bill in due course. In the meantime, it suggested that Luxembourg citizens living in other EC states could return to Luxembourg and register on a special electoral roll set up specifically to resolve the problem. The Council's response was to reaffirm its preference for postal voting and to point out the major drawbacks to the committee's proposals. As a compromise it suggested that citizens living in other EC states should be able to register on a special electoral roll, providing they sign a declaration stating that they would not vote in their country of residence, and then return to vote in special polling stations in Luxembourg. This amendment was accepted by the committee and was included in the proposed final text discussed in the plenary.

The final issue of contention concerned the number of constituencies. In legislative elections the parties contest fifty-nine seats distributed amongst four constituencies. However, with only six seats reserved for Luxembourg in the European Parliament, the allocation between the constituencies might well have meant that certain parties would be over- or under-represented because of regional or geographically dispersed support. The solution proposed was the Hagenbach-Bischoff variation of the d'Hondt system as used in national elections, within a single national constituency.

Constitutional matters

The constitutional position concerning direct elections was raised by the KPL. The issue was solved at an early stage; it was decided that no changes would be necessary with the present institutional balance in the EC. The main question centred on whether the usual procedure for voting through legislation was appropriate for the bills concerned with direct elections. It had been suggested that European elections posited, in effect, a transfer of powers from the Chamber to the European Parliament — a move that called for three-quarters of Deputies to be present when the vote was taken and a two-thirds majority to pass the proposals. Eventually, it was agreed that since the Treaty of Rome had been signed and ratified by Luxembourg, and as this itself envisaged direct elections, there was no need to employ the special procedure. The matter was seen simply as the implementation of a prior agreement. Insofar as it was assumed the second elections will take place under a uniform procedure laid down by the European Parliament itself, however, it was agreed that this will involve a transfer of sovereignty.[15]

A further constitutional issue concerned the number of constituencies. Both the Foreign Affairs Committee and the working party had raised the issue of whether reducing the number of constituencies was a constitutional matter. It was agreed that as the relevant article of the Constitution dealt with national elections and that since no mention was made whatsoever of European elections, no problem existed.

The final debate and vote

When the two bills were finally brought before the Chamber they were once again taken together in debate but voted on separately. The debate was in three parts; firstly Deputies and Ministers spoke on the issue either as individuals, or as representatives of the Government or their party; secondly, amendments proposed in the first part of the debate were voted on before proceeding to a formal vote on the bills; finally, motions that had been proposed during the debate were discussed and voted on. Excluding the contributions made by the rapporteuse, who introduced the debate and answered points made by other speakers towards the end, nine speeches were made by Deputies and three by Ministers, two by the Prime Minister at the beginning and end of the debate.

In the first part of the debate, the parties outlined their positions. There were criticisms as to how the main issues — the number of constituencies, the number of votes that could be given to each candidate, holding simultaneous elections, enfranchisement of Luxembourgers in other EC states — had been dealt with though apart from the single amendment tabled by Herr Margue (CSV) the only major attack was made by Herr Urbany (KPL). He again raised several questions regarding the sovereignty of Luxembourg and the expansion of the powers of the European Parliament. Additionally, he proposed three amendments of which only one was of any consequence, the others not affecting the main proposals contained in the bills.

Table 9.3
Amendments proposed during plenary debate

Sponsor and Party		Subject of Amendment	Successful = 1 Unsuccessful = 2	Method of voting and result
Urbany	KPL	Replacing 'European Parliament' by 'Assembly of the European Communities'	2	Show of hands
Urbany	KPL	Deleting proposals for enfranchisement of Luxembourg nationals resident in other EC states	2	Show of hands
Urbany	KPL	Retaining same electoral system for future direct elections	2	Vote 50–6
Margue	CSV	Introducing postal vote	2	Show of hands

Most criticisms were matters of detail rather than opposition to the bill *in toto*. Even the attitude of the KPL seemed to be one of grudging acceptance to the provisions of the bills in general, the main battle against the principle of direct elections having been lost at an earlier date.

After the rapporteuse, Mme Flesch, and the Prime Minister had responded to the issues raised by the other speakers, the discussion moved on to the amendments proposed earlier in the debate. None of the amendments was acceptable to the Chamber — indeed only one went to a formal vote, the others being rejected on a show of hands. The three amendments proposed by Herr Urbany found minimal support amongst Deputies and never seriously stood much chance of acceptance. The other amendment, calling for provision to be made for postal voting, was greeted with greater sympathy since it was an issue that had been widely discussed for several years. However, at such a late stage problems involved in implementing such a system were considered too great, and hence the proposal was unsuccessful. The two bills then received their final reading and were approved Article by Article; then, each bill was voted as a whole, and both were carried by fifty votes to none with four abstentions. At the same time both were excused the second constitutional vote.

The final part of the debate concentrated on parliamentary motions proposed earlier, regarding issues marginally related to direct elections. The proposal to limit the number of Deputies in the Chamber to sixty reflected the constitutional provision whereby the number of Deputies increases periodically as the population grows. In discussing the electoral system for direct elections, Herr Wolter moved on to the deficiencies of the national electoral law. Secondly, several speakers from parties not represented in the European Parliament complained about the provision of financial assistance to parties which did number MEPs in their ranks. Consequently, Mme Lulling's motion was a protest at what she considered the unfair assistance given only to some parties. Finally, Herr Urbany protested about the reported agreement between the German Chancellor and the French President to site the European Parliament solely in Strasbourg. This matter had also been raised by other speakers who feared the Assembly would be lost to France and, once the strength of the condemnation had been diluted, the motion was passed by a convincing majority.

Table 9.4
Motions proposed during plenary debate

Sponsor and Party		Subject of Motion	Successful = 1 Unsuccessful = 2	Method of voting and result
Wolter	CSV	Fixing the number of Deputies in the Chamber at 60	2	Show of hands
Lulling	SDP	Condemnation of allocation of funds by EC to only certain parties	2	Vote 30–10 7 abstained
Urbany	KPL	Protest about the declaration of the German Chancellor regarding the future siting of the EP	1*	Vote 38–4 4 abstained

*This motion was amended by Mme Lulling, then again by Mme Flesch.

Overview

Although it is true that the bill concerned with the principle of holding direct elections had a smooth and relatively rapid passage to enactment, the same cannot be said of the bills stipulating the details of how the election should be conducted, for which complex extra-parliamentary negotiations were necessary. The postponement of the elections to 1979 created a further problem as to whether to hold national and European elections simultaneously. The Chamber and the Government had repeatedly expressed support for direct elections and it seems strange that the most overtly favourable parliament was the last to pass the requisite legislation. A further question is raised by the Government's failure to present a bill before the elections were postponed as had been done elsewhere.

This contradiction between the public statements and failure to act was explained during the plenary debates on the final two bills. The Government knew that it could get a majority on a vote agreeing to the principle of direct elections but would meet greater opposition to the details of how this principle should be realised. As a result the legislation was split, allowing the Government to obtain the Chamber's commitment to holding the elections before publishing the details of how they would operate. Whilst the issue of whether to hold simultaneous elections did cause some delay, this strengthened the Government's position in getting its preferred form of legislation adopted; by delaying until relatively late the Chamber's scrutiny of the second and third bills, the Government was able to push through its own solutions to the problems. Since the elections were imminent and there was general agreement as to their necessity — with the exception of the KPL — the Government had only to ensure that its proposals did not alienate too many Deputies too much. This it succeeded in doing and as a result headed off any major challenge.

Nevertheless, certain changes were made to the bill during the committee examination. Most were alterations to the wording or technical changes. However, one major alteration was successful, namely extending the franchise to Luxembourgers living abroad. In one sense this represented a major change in the electoral law but against this it must be noted that those who wished to take advantage of this had to return to Luxembourg to exercise their new-found right, hence greatly reducing the revolutionary aspect of the change. A further point worth noting is the role the Council of State played in extending the vote. Against the Government's wishes, the Council and the Chamber acted together and finally arrived at a compromise solution which was successfully included in the final Act. Thus, although the Council has no formal right to enforce change, its advisory role is a real one which it can, and does, wield effectively. Similarly, the committee undertook real scrutiny on behalf of the Chamber and spent four mornings going through the proposals. The fact that certain issues went to a formal vote indicates that the proposals met opposition at this stage and one can only conclude that greater changes were prevented by the coalition Government's majority amongst committee members.

Conclusion

The activity in the Chamber prior to the introduction of the Government Bills was overly supportive of directly electing Luxembourg's MEPs, irrespective of how other countries went about composing their delegations. This sentiment reached a peak in the late sixties and early seventies; although it did not disappear, the frustration of the Chamber's wishes caused the matter to be less conspicuous thereafter.[16] The resurrection of the issue at the European level stimulated further action at the national level which satisfied the demands of the Chamber. The main lesson that can be drawn from this is the supremacy of the Government on the principle — which may be classified as 'external relations', traditionally a concern of governments more than parliaments — with the Chamber playing the role of a pressure group. This conclusion is reinforced by the abject failure of the Chamber to successfully pass its own legislation on the matter: the only attempt to assert its constitutional right in this field was the 1971 bill, which was far too simplistic and consequently did not gain adequate support. It is true that Government Bills enjoy advantages which facilitate their passage — a factor demonstrated by the different fates suffered by the Government's and private members' legislation on this issue — but some private members' bills do succeed and in this light one is tempted to query the real legislative initiative powers, and hence decision-making capabilities, of the Chamber.

The different natures of the bills appear to have had an effect on their ease of passage through parliament. The Ratification Bill, being basically procedural, was uncomplicated and even its political aspects presented a straightforward choice of either support or opposition. As the other two bills were concerned with matters of regulation, both parliamentary debates and committee deliberations centred more on details. Since these provoked issues of partisan advantage, there was more dissension and disagreement, even though the principle was generally accepted. Through adopting a strategy of splitting the legislative scrutiny into two sets of bills — principle and details — and by careful timing, the Government was able to considerably depoliticise the second phase and so maximise support for the measures it was proposing.

Notes

1 In the event of a bill straddling the competence of more than one committee, the relevant committees meet together to discuss the bill.
2 Any amendment proposed to a bill must be considered by the Council before it is incorporated into the text. This is true even though it may mean that the legislative process is considerably drawn out. For example, the law on the organisation of the judiciary was presented in May 1977 but was not reported on until March 1979 and the Council expressed its opinion in writing nine times during this period.
3 It is usual for amendments at this stage to come from Deputies although occasionally the Government may also move an amendment in plenary sessions.
4 C. Flesch and M. Delvaux, 'The Luxembourg Chamber of Deputies: A Micro-cosmic Image of a Small Country' in European Parliament (ed.) *European Integration and the Future of Parliaments in Europe*, (European Parliament, Luxembourg 1975), pp 114-32.
5 For a more detailed description of the parties, see M. Hirsch, 'Luxembourg' in S. Henig (ed.), *Political Parties in the European Community*, (George Allen and Unwin, London, 1979).
6 See J. Santer, 'Des perspectives politiques nouvelles?', *Le Féderaliste Européen*, no.3, 1976, pp 30-2, and A. Lulling 'L'élection du Parlement Européen au suffrage universel: ses aspects positifs, ses problèmes, son defi', *Le Féderaliste Européen*, no.3, 1976, pp 26-9.
7 Report of the Committee on Foreign Affairs, no.2062[2], p.3.
8 Four motions have been tabled in the Chamber of Deputies:
    i   12.3.69 'The Chamber invites the Government to present a bill concerning the election of representatives of our country in supranational institutions by the people according to the procedures laid down in our laws governing legislative elections'.
    ii 24.4.69 'With a view to contributing towards the democratisation of the institutions of the European Communities, the Chamber invites the Government to present a bill on the procedures for direct election by universal suffrage of the Luxembourg representatives at the European Parliament as soon as is practically possible'.
    iii 3.12.70 'After protracted examination, the Chamber . . . restates with concern its motion of 24 April, 1969, in which the Government was invited to present a bill on the procedures for the direct election by universal suffrage of the Luxembourg representatives at the European Parliament as soon as is practically possible.'

iv 22.1.75 'If the proposals of the European Parliament are not accepted within the near future the Chamber begs the Government to lay before it concrete proposals as soon as is feasible with the aim of electing the Luxembourg representatives at the European Parliament by universal suffrage'.

9 See Appendix, chapter 2.
10 See note 8 above; motion presented 24.4.69.
11 Flesch and Delvaux, op.cit., p.119.
12 Article 83, Projet de loi no.2163.
13 The deliberations and recommendations of the committee were never made public. However, the principal proposals made formed the basis of the Government legislation.
14 The main provisions of the 1978 bill were as follows:

1 Compatibility of national and European Parliamentary membership, though it would cease to be obligatory.
2 Six Luxembourg seats to be held for five years.
3 Retention of majority of existing national legislative law for European elections.
4 Single national constituency.
5 Same electoral system to be used in European elections – with minor alterations – as in national elections.
6 Each electoral list should contain 12 names to remove the necessity for by-elections in the case of MEPs leaving the EP.

15 Report of the Committee on Foreign Affairs, op.cit., p.6.
16 It should be remembered that around this time economic problems and the oil crisis assumed great importance and tended to push other issues aside.

The Luxembourg Chamber of Deputies: some readings

M. Delvaux and M. Hirsch, 'Le Grand-Duché de Luxembourg: aspects de sociologie politique', *Res Publica*, vol.18, 1976, pp 101-13. A general socio-political review.

C. Flesch and M. Delvaux, 'The Luxembourg Chamber of Deputies: a Micro-cosmic Image of a Small Country' in European Parliament, *Symposium on European Integration and the Future of Parliaments in Europe*, (European Parliament, Luxembourg, 1975), pp 114-32. A short interpretation of the role of the Chamber.

R. Fusilier, *Les Monarchies Parlementaires*, (Ed. Ouvrieres, Paris, 1960), pp 555-602. An institutional interpretation.

M. Hirsch, 'Luxembourg' in S. Henig (ed.), *Political Parties in the European Community*, (Allen and Unwin, London, 1979), pp 170-4.

P. Majerus, *L'Etat Luxembourgeois*, (St Paul, Luxembourg, 1970), pp 173-208. A comprehensive review of the structures of government in Luxembourg.

G.L. Weil, *The Benelux Nations*, (Holt Rhinehart and Winston, New York, 1970).

10   The Netherlands: Last but not Least

Rinus van Schendelen

This chapter is concerned with a description and analysis of the direct election legislation in the Netherlands. The focus is on the Ratification and Implementation Bills, which were passed for the elections. This is included in a broader description of Dutch political events relating to the direct elections from 1970 onwards. Before we present our case-study, we shall first summarise the main characteristics of the Dutch legislative process so that the direct election legislation can be seen in comparative perspective.

The normal legislative process[1]

In order for a bill to become law both the Government and Parliament must agree on the text. In political terms, the Government is identical to the Cabinet, which has to reach internal consensus about the bill, proposed by the responsible minister, before it is sent to Parliament. The minister's proposal is preceded by a departmental process of preparation in which various advisory committees, interdepartmental co-ordination committees and pressure groups normally participate. At this preparation stage, parliamentary demands, as articulated in the formal debates within Parliament or in the more informal and private interactions with members of the Cabinet or civil servants, can also be taken into consideration.

After this process of preparation, when the responsible minister has proposed his bill to the Cabinet, the Council of State gives an opinion. Once the Cabinet, taking into consideration this advice, has reached agreement on the text of the bill, the parliamentary process can begin.

The Parliament consists of two chambers of which the Second Chamber (Tweede Kamer) is the more important. This is because it is entitled to initiate and to amend legislation, whereas the First Chamber (Eerste Kamer) can only reject, pass or delay proposed legislation. The parliamentary legislative process starts in the Second Chamber. Once a bill has been passed in both Chambers it is sent back to the Cabinet for confirmation and, through the Minister of Law, for publication and implementation.[2]

In addition to the legislative relationship between Cabinet and Parliament, there is a political relationship on which the Cabinet's political stability is based. To ensure its survival, a Cabinet needs the support of a majority in the two Chambers. In fact, the support it receives from the directly elected Second Chamber, which possesses the more important legislative powers, is decisive. When such a supportive majority does not exist then constitutional principles require that the Cabinet or the Parliament be dissolved.

Because the Netherlands has a multi-party system where usually between ten and fifteen parties are represented in Parliament, Cabinets are formed of coalitions between the parties. The formation of a Cabinet is usually a lengthy process, especially when there are several possible coalitions or, in the opposite case, when there is no apparent possibility of a coalition at all due to the state of relations between parties. This has increasingly been the position since 1970, the period relevant to this study. Some indicators of this are: the formation of the three successive Cabinets of 1971, 1973 and 1977, which took 69, 163 and 207 days, respectively, from the election day to the formation of the Cabinet; not one Cabinet between 1971 and 1977 completed its full four-year term of office; and an extra parliamentary election was held in 1972.[3]

The political relationship between Cabinet and Parliament, and particularly its increasingly fragile nature, affects the legislative relationship. In order to increase the probability of Cabinet stability, the parties forming the majority coalition set out the principles of their coalition in a pact. In addition, once the Cabinet is formed, regular meetings have to be held in which the leaders of the coalition parties, parliamentary party specialists, and the responsible members of the Cabinet come together in order to settle new political disagreements. Both in the original pact, and in these subsequent meetings, many legislative issues acquire their basic formulation. The formal process of legislation is then only a ratification of the more informal agreements made earlier. The Cabinet's proposals are already adapted to the demands of its majority coalition and, because of this, are ensured success in the parliamentary process of legislation; the opposition parties are hardly effective.

Against this background it becomes understandable that nearly all legislation is formally initiated by the Cabinet and not by Parliament: it is rare for members of the majority to initiate laws, for the pact and the regular meetings of the Cabinet provide sufficient opportunities for this function to be performed. For the opposition parties, such initiatives seldom meet with any success.[4]

The same complex political situation also explains why nearly all the Cabinet's legislative proposals are adopted by Parliament; less than 1 per cent is rejected or withdrawn. The use made of the right to amend the Cabinet's legislative proposals is also modest: the number of successful amendments almost equals the number of bills passed, which implies a mean of about one amendment per bill. The most important political variable in the process of legislation is its tempo or pace. There is no deadline set for the passage of a legislative proposal once it is introduced into Parliament. When some members of the majority-coalition in Parliament have objections to a proposal, which they have not been able to get accepted as amendments, they prefer a slowing-down of the legislative process to the passing of the bill: their colleagues in the coalition may also prefer this to an open exhibition of dissension within the coalition and with the Cabinet. The members of the opposition are, in principle, always prepared to slow down the processing of the Government's bills.[5] In fact, about half of the number of bills introduced by the Cabinet in a parliamentary year, is still undecided at the end of that year. Of the bills accepted by Parliament, the mean duration of the parliamentary process is almost four hundred days (thirteen months) with a range around the mean of between one week and fifteen years.[6]

Within Parliament, especially in the Second Chamber, the principal characteristic of the legislative process is a division of labour.[7] Each bill is assigned to either a permanent or a special committee. In each committee, all parliamentary parties are in principle represented by at least one member. These members act as party-specialists for their party, they are more informed about the bill(s) in committee than are their party colleagues, to whom they provide voting cues. In the larger parties there is, for each bill, normally, more than one specialist; they come together in a party committee, which gives cues to other party members. The specialists of the parties in coalition also meet, if necessary, in order to arrange a common strategy against the opposition parties. The more detailed the pact and agreements are between the Cabinet and its majority, the smaller is the necessity in specific cases for such meetings. The specialists, united in the parliamentary committee, determine the legislative tempo, and in most cases they orchestrate the voting behaviour of their party colleagues.

In order to summarise the general outlines of the legislative process, we may formulate the following expectations for the case-study:

a) legislation is initiated by the Government;

b) the mean legislative tempo is approximately one year, but the range is wide;

c) only a single amendment is made;

185

d)   the few party-specialists determine both the nature of the legislative process and the pattern of voting behaviour in the plenary session.

Direct elections in an active Dutch Parliament: 1970-1974

In their 1971 general election programmes, all of the main parties promised to strive for direct elections to the European Parliament.[8] After the election, these parties occupied 83 per cent of the seats in the Second Chamber. Of the five parties forming the Government coalition, four belonged to the large majority and controlled 49 per cent of the Second Chamber. A few opposition parties explicitly demanded early election of the Dutch members of the European Parliament, even if their country was to be the first and only one with directly elected MEPs. In such a favourable political atmosphere, one might have expected quick and positive legislative action by both the Cabinet and the Parliament.

The new Cabinet, like its predecessor, declared its interest in 'democratic parliamentary control within the EEC' but, again following the example of its predecessor, did not take any legislative initiative.[9] In the summer of 1970, such an initiative was taken by the MP (and MEP), Mr Westerterp, who belonged to the large Catholic Party which has been a Government party since 1946.[10] The bill proposed a preliminary scheme for the direct election of the Dutch MEPs. Within a few months, the Suffrage Council (the official advisory organ of the State) commented on the bill: 'The technical implementation of the bill would create such problems that, in order to reach some balance, substantial gains from the proposal would be necessary . . . the positive elements of the proposal seem to be of very low value . . . .'.[11]

A Committee of the Second Chamber was formed specifically to process the bill. It made a first report at the end of 1970, which praised the initiative, but posed many questions concerning the Suffrage Council's comments. A few weeks later, at the end of January 1971, Mr Westerterp replied to the questions and adapted his proposal to some of the Suffrage Council's criticisms. In April the Special Committee of the Second Chamber made its final report and declared the proposal ready for the floor.

Thus far the legislative initiative of Mr Westerterp seemed to have had an average parliamentary speed and positive result. The proposal, however, never reached the floor. In December 1977, it was withdrawn, and the Special Committee was dissolved.

A more or less similar history applied to a second legislative initiative by Mr Westerterp in March, 1973.[12] In this proposal, he asked for a change of the Constitution so that it would be possible to have 'special' members of the Dutch Parliament. These would be MEPs who would have to be directly elected and who would then have an advisory status in the national Parliament. In July 1974, more than one year later, the Suffrage Council commented on this second initiative and declared the proposed change of the Constitution to be 'a curious construction'.[13]

The same Special Committee which handled the first initiative, also had to process the second, but it never reported on the proposal. In December 1977, this proposal was withdrawn together with the first bill and the Special Committee was dissolved.

The following reasons seem to explain the failure of these initiatives. Firstly, support for the idea of direct elections to the European Parliament was much larger in Parliament than in Cabinet. In fact, the Government did not take any legislative initiative; it only transmitted the Suffrage Council's two very negative advisory reports. One explanation for this difference in support is that the issue of direct elections was rather popular but, at the same time, somewhat delicate to promote at the level of the European Community. A large and active part of the public very much liked the idea of more democratic control of the EC and of more public control of MEPs. On the other hand, the issue was rather delicate for the Government because it could irritate some other Member States, such as France, where the issue of the direct elections was not seen in terms of democratisation, but in terms of loss of sovereignty. This could well have tempered the Dutch Cabinet's willingness to take over Parliament's initiative. Besides, the initiative was highly convenient for the Cabinet: it partially satisfied public demand, symbolised the democratic attitude of the Government coalition, and yet it was fully under the control of the coalition and did not create formal obligations for the Dutch Cabinet.

A second reason for the legislative failures of the two initiatives seems to be that the issue was soon surpassed by two other political issues of a more startling character. The first type can be described as the increasing instability of the Dutch political system.[14] The 1971 Cabinet lasted only one year, after which new elections were held. The outcome of these elections was rather dramatic: many parties either lost or gained seats, there was an electoral gain for the smallest parties (whose share of seats increased from 17 per cent to 29 per cent); more than 30 per cent of the MPs were brand-new; and, related to such changes, the formation of a new cabinet took nearly half a year.

The second type of issue concerned policy crises. First of all, there was the stagnation of the economy and the more strained relationship between the groups most closely involved in the social and economic

187

policy of the governments, employers and employees. In addition, the Middle East oil crisis occurred, and the consequential crisis in Dutch international relations arose because the country, together with the United States, was explicitly boycotted by the oil-producing countries, and was not clearly supported by the other EC Member States.

The two types of crises were partly related to each other.[15] The policy crises were a problem for the Cabinet, but they also were an aid to it because they provided the opportunity to demand, and get, from Parliament the Delegation Act through which powers in many policy fields were transferred from the Parliament to the Cabinet in 1974. In consequence the Cabinet did not need to worry about obstruction by the Second Chamber. The crisis atmosphere meant that in other policy fields, the Government coalition in Parliament acted in a much more united manner and was more willing to comply with the Cabinet's demands. But what is more important here, is that these developments precluded consideration of the direct elections.

A third and last reason for Mr Westerterp's failures seems to be that Mr Westerterp himself changed his status. Shortly after the Special Committee of the Second Chamber had published its final report on his first initiative and declared it ready for the floor, he joined the new Cabinet as Under Secretary for Foreign Affairs. According to the Constitution, he had to leave Parliament and, therefore, had to transfer all his personal enthusiasm for the bill to colleagues. In fact, all impetus concerning his initiatives was lost. Some proof of this is that during the short time that Mr Westerterp returned to the Parliament after the fall of the Cabinet in 1972, he initiated his second proposal concerning the special status for MEPs in the Dutch Parliament. As pointed out previously, his initiative failed completely, but it must be noted that two months after its introduction, Mr Westerterp had to leave the Parliament again because he was appointed Minister of Public Works.

In evaluating the direct election legislation between 1970-1974, we have to conclude that it differs from the normal process of legislation. The initiative for the legislation came not from the Cabinet, but from Parliament. Besides, the legislative tempo became extremely slow after a normal start; amendments were not brought forward, not because of the normality of this legislative process but because of its failure to reach the floor at all; and for the same reason, cue-giving specialists did not come into operation.

The years 1975—1976: back to normalcy

In the following two years, the issue of direct elections to the European Parliament appeared to lose the high intensity of interest of the early seventies. But, nevertheless, on several occasions the issue came up in debate in the Second Chamber:

a)   during the yearly processing of the Budget Bill for the Ministry of Foreign Affairs;

b)   during the periodic reviews by the Standing Committee for Foreign Affairs regarding the Minister's yearly report on the EC;

c)   during the processing of other bills relating to the EC, and

d)   during question time and other debates.

We shall give a short description and analysis of these.

(a)   *Budget debates*

In the explanatory memorandum on the Foreign Affairs' Ministry of 1975, one theme dominated all others: European co-operation was in crisis.[16] The decision-making system within the EC was performing badly; there was a regretted development from a community way of solving problems towards an intergovernmental way; and deadlock was reached over the Regional Fund, monetary, fishery and other policies. Nothing was said about direct elections in the memorandum, but the issue was raised incidentally by some MPs and the Foreign Minister, Mr van der Stoel, during the debate.[17] Several times the Minister praised the Dutch efforts ('fifteen years long') to have direct elections to the European Parliament, the measure for which the European Parliament itself had voted one month before. Not one MP objected to the praise; indeed, the Minister was asked to push the issue further in the Council of Ministers.

The 1976 budget memorandum failed to mention direct elections.[18] Again the crisis theme dominated all others and, again, the issue was raised incidentally from the floor.[19] The Minister repeated that he was satisfied with the Dutch efforts and stated his ambition to push it further because some aspects (such as a common date, the number and distribution of seats, and the question of the double mandate) had still to be settled.

The 1977 budget memorandum was different from the two foregoing ones.[20] As in the early seventies, the Cabinet declared its intention to consider the direct elections as 'having, of course, the first priority in striving for a more democratic Community'.[21] A few months earlier the Council of Ministers had agreed to hold direct elections in 1978. During the 1977 Budget debates, both MPs and the Minister considered these to be a certainty and mainly discussed aspects of their implementation. A motion brought forward by a group of MPs was passed extending the franchise to Dutch citizens throughout the Community.[22] Another group of MPs proposed an amendment to the Budget, setting aside money to subsidise the national promotion of direct elections; this amendment was adopted by the Minister.[23]

During the debates several MPs asked for an early ratification of the European Act on direct elections and for implementing legislation; more specific questions were also asked relating to the single or double mandate issue, the location of the European Parliament, and the franchise.[24] Some MPs and the Minister praised each other for their efforts and success in getting direct elections accepted at the Community level.

(b) *Periodic reviews*

The Minister of Foreign Affairs' 1973 report,[25] presented at the end of 1974, was debated in the winter of 1975: direct elections were not mentioned in it. In the debates, which occurred at a public sitting of the Standing Committee for Foreign Affairs, only a few MPs and the Under-Secretary devoted any remarks to the direct elections and concluded that the missing variable was political will at the Community level.[26]

In his report on 1974, a few months later, the Foreign Minister expressed his satisfaction with the decision, taken by the European Council in Paris, 1974, to strive for direct elections in 1978.[27] In the public meeting of the Foreign Affairs Committee, some MPs also expressed their satisfaction, but most attention was devoted to the apparently attractive theme of crises in Europe. The Minister, Mr van der Stoel, repeated that 'the Netherlands are famous in Brussels for their support of more European integration. If the other countries followed suit, the process of integration would certainly have proceeded much further'.[28]

In the 1975 report, direct elections were hardly mentioned.[29] There were no new developments at the Community level to report on. The Committee debated this report one year later, in August 1977, at a time when new developments were indeed taking place.

(c) *Other legislation*

On two occasions, when other bills related to the EC were debated in Parliament, direct elections came under discussion. The first at the end of 1975, was the ratification of the Lomé Treaty, concerning the relationship between the EC and the developing countries.[30] In that discussion some MPs, notably Socialists, said that the role of the European Parliament must be kept limited as long as the Parliament was not directly elected 'and, because of that, was not legitimised by the electors'.[31]

The second occasion related to the ratification of the change of the Treat of Rome, which granted the European Parliament larger budgetary powers.[32] In the explanatory memorandum, this change was placed in the context of the more comprehensive reappraisal of the role of the European Parliament within the EC at that time, as was also apparent from the then recent decision of the European Parliament to strive for early direct elections. The responsible Ministers stressed how important the Dutch role was in pushing the issue so far.

The parliamentary debates on this ratification were combined with those on the Government's paper on European Union, which was a commentary on several reports including those of Marjolin, Spierenburg and Tindemans.[33] As a matter of common sense, the Government repeated its opinion that the European Parliament had to be directly elected. In the debates, in September 1976, two weeks before the decision to have direct elections was taken by the Council of Ministers, many MPs expressed their impatience with the Council decision-making process and, assuming some positive outcome, also with the national implementation process. The issue of the double mandate, the special status for MEPs in the national Parliament, the national election system, and the distribution and number of seats were also raised.

(d) *Miscellaneous*

In the Spring of 1976, the Minister of Home Affairs sent to the Second Chamber a report of the Suffrage Council, which had been requested by the Government to prepare a report for the time when the decision to hold direct elections was taken at the EC level. The Council preferred the introduction of a special Implementation Bill to a change of the existing election law. In this bill there would be more room for special demands and regulations. A Special Committee, drawn from the Second Chamber, discussed the report. Two MEPs, Mr Patijn (PvdA) and Mr de Koning (CDA), proposed that a special advisory status in the national Parliament be granted to directly elected MEPs. Such an arrangement would give to both parliaments, the benefits of some linkage.[35] The proposers, the Suffrage Council and the Minister all agreed that such an arrangement would require a change of the Dutch Constitution. The proposed advisory status for MEPs was not considered useful either by the Suffrage Council or by the Minister.

Another short debate about direct elections occurred in December 1976, when the Prime Minister came into the Second Chamber to explain his report on the meeting of the Council of Ministers, which had just decided to have early direct elections.[36] Proudly he declared that the Council, 'this time under our leadership', had cut the Gordian knot.[37]

In the years 1975-1976, only one written question concerning direct elections was posed. In Summer 1976, the Leader of the Opposition VVD party, Mr Wiegel, questioned the Prime Minister on whether he preferred a constituency system to the proportional representation election system, which is the rule in the Netherlands.[38] In particular, the many small parties in the Dutch Parliament were concerned about the constituency idea. The Prime Minister denied that a bill would be introduced to establish such a system.

In summarising the 1975—1976 period, we can conclude that, firstly there was a systematic change of parliamentary attitudes and behaviour over time: at first there was mostly apathy, then the issue received some minor attention in Parliament; secondly the Government, time and again, expressed its self-confidence and its praise for the Parliament's attitude, to which accolade only some Communist MPs objected; and finally in terms of legislation, 'normalcy' had returned: the Government initiated, the Parliament was passive and followed the Government's lead. How can this situation be explained?

The apathy concerning this issue which dominated the Second Chamber in 1975, was related to the frustrated experiences with the two legislative initiatives of Mr Westerterp in 1970 and 1973, the failures of which became clearly apparent in 1974. The growing attention in 1976 was not caused by interior factors or initiatives within the Netherlands, but by positive developments at the Community level. In fact, in 1975 the European Parliament itself had taken over the issue and the initiative. Also the Council of Ministers appeared to be responsive to it in 1976. What seemed completely unrealisable in 1974, both at the national and the Community levels, appeared realisable in the following years at the EC level and this stimulated MPs attention.

The Government's propaganda concerning its own performances on this issue seems to have also had the specific function of making clear, to both Parliament and the public, that it was still in a 'democratic mood' and that actions which might interfere with the Cabinet's behaviour, were unnecessary; in fact, the Government demanded and obtained discreet congratulation. In addition, the Cabinet's praise for the Parliament's actions before 1975 also provided a palliative for parliamentary feelings, frustrated by the lack of progress. Thus, our psychological explanation for the second conclusion can be fully related to the political climate within Parliament.

The return to legislative normalcy is also related to the EC 'take-over' of the direct elections issue. After the European Parliament's demand for such elections in early 1975, the issue was placed on the agenda of the Council of Ministers. This gave the full legislative initiative to the national governments: as in most other affairs the Dutch Parliament accepted the Cabinet's lead.

The year 1977: ratification and other developments

In February 1977, the bill to ratify the European Direct Elections Act, was presented to the Second Chamber.[39] The legislative process went very quickly: within four months the proposal was adopted by the Second Chamber and one week later by the First Chamber. Only one meeting of the parliamentary Committee was held in each Chamber; the Second Chamber's Committee convened in a public session for half a day, the First Chamber's Committee convened one hour before the Chamber's plenary debate. The plenary debates in the Second and First Chambers took three and a half hours and one hour, respectively. In each Chamber only a few MPs participated in the debates; in the Second Chamber, 9 MPs (7 as party spokesmen, of which 5 also belonged to the relevant Committee) and in the First Chamber only 4 (all party spokesmen and Committee members). The process of parliamentary decision-making took place through the routinised system of a division of labour, in which each party had a trustee in the Committee who provided his party with a voting-cue which was usually accepted by his fellow party members. This method of decision-making indicates that the bill was not a matter of political conflict, since both party leaders and the parties as a whole remained inactive.

The only objections to the bill came from the four small left- and right-wing parties, which together held seven seats (less than 5 per cent of all seats) in the Second Chamber (see table 10.1). Their main objection was that the quota for the European elections would not give them a chance to have an MEP elected. The left wing objected that the EC was too capitalistic, and would remain so after the direct elections. The small right-wing parties disliked the EC idea and preferred a more international confederation. One of their MPs, Mr Verbrugh (GPV), even brought forward a motion demanding an addition to the European Elections Act so that it would become clear how each national delegation of MEPs voted in the European Parliament; this was rejected by the other parties.

In the debates, both in the Committee and on the floor, two types of issues were raised. The first related directly to the Act. The main

Table 10.1
Parties in the Second Chamber, May 1977

Party	Abbreviation	Votes %*	Seats†
Communists (Communistische Partij van Nederland)	CPN	1	2
Pacifists (Pacifistische Socialistische Partij)	PSP	1	1
Radicals (Politieke Partij Radicalen)	PPR	2	3
Socialists (Partij van de Arbeid)	PvdA	35	53
Democrats '66 (Democraten '66)	D'66	5	8
G Christian Democrats (Christen Democratisch Appel)	CDA	32	49
Democratic Socialists (Democratische Socialisten '70)	DS'70	1	1
G Liberals (Volkspartij voor Vrijheid en Democratie)	VVD	18	28
Reformist-Calvinist (Gereformeerd Politiek Verbond)	GPV	1	1
State-Calvinist (Staatkundig Gereformeerde Partij)	SGP	2	3
Farmers (Boeren Partij)	BP	1	1
Total		100%	150
Turnout		87.5%	

*Share of valid votes cast in General Elections, May 1977.
†Seats in the Second Chamber, May 1977.

G   Party forming the Government from December 1977.

questions were the following:[40]

1 What would be done if one or more of the Member States should abstain from the elections because, for example, the implementation of its direct election legislation was delayed? The Government's expectation was that all Member States would participate in the elections.

2 When exactly would the elections be held? For the Government that was also still an open question.

3 According to Dutch Law, were the direct elections constitutional, as after them the electorate would be represented twice? The Government's position was that the national Parliament does not have an exclusive right of representation.

194

4 Were the twenty-five seats for the Netherlands a fair share in the European Parliament? The Government replied that the Netherlands was over-represented in relation to the large Member States but under-represented in relation to the smaller ones and concluded that it was correctly represented.

The second type of issue raised was not directly related to the Act, but anticipated the national regulations for implementation which were still under interdepartmental preparation. The Government declared that it welcomed being asked such questions because it facilitated governmental adaptation to parliamentary demands.[41] Previously, these demands had received a mainly negative response from the Suffrage Council. In this instance the following demands were forwarded:

a) franchise for all Dutch adults, wherever they may live in the Community;[42]

b) a proportional representation election system, without constituencies;

c) choice of election day so that both the polling day (which was not to be a Sunday) and the publication of the results was acceptable;

d) some regulation of national incompatibilities for MEPs;

e) an early introduction of the Implementation Bill.

These demands were met by positive promises from the Government.

On two other questions there was some disagreement, even among the MPs. Firstly, the smallest parties demanded a quota electoral system so that they would have the chance to elect an MEP. The application of a strictly proportional election system for European elections would result in a threshold six times larger than that for national elections. However, neither the large parties nor the Government supported their demand. Secondly, some MPs asked for the dual mandate to be banned, while others saw some value in it. The Government's position was twofold: firstly, Article 5 of the Act of 20 September stated that it was prohibited to ban the dual mandate; secondly, such an interdiction would imply an incompatibility of membership of the two Parliaments, for which a change of the Constitution would be required — such a change would not be initiated by the Government. Some MEPs had proposed a third alternative — granting MEPs advisory status in the national Parliament[43] — but the objection against this was that it too would require a change of the Constitution.

Thus, insofar as the parliamentary demands remained within the existing constitutional order and, as in the threshold case, were not objected to by many other MPs, they received a positive response from the Government. Its negative attitude to changing the Constitution was related to the necessity of having new elections if such a change was to be made. Given the electoral instability of the country and the fact that, just one month before, new elections had been held because of the premature fall of the Cabinet, hardly anybody liked the idea of new elections, even if there had been a majority in support of these demands.

On two occasions later in the year, some of the above demands were repeated to the Government. Firstly, there was the Government's report on EC developments in 1976, presented in June, 1977. The Government declared the direct elections to be 'the most important decision of that year' and, in its best tradition of self-esteem, added that 'partly thanks to the Dutch leadership of the Council of Ministers' during that period, the budget powers of the European Parliament had also been strengthened.[44] In public sitting the Committee for Foreign Affairs discussed this report as well as the 1975 one, which still had to be debated.[45] Concerning direct elections, the Committee raised only a few matters of implementation.

The main question concerned the date on which the Implementation Bill could be expected. The Under-Secretary's reply was 'within a few weeks', and certainly in time for the elections, which were still planned for May—June 1978.

On the second occasion a related question was posed. During question-time in the Second Chamber in September 1977, Mr Berkhouwer (VVD, also an MEP) asked the Minister for Foreign Affairs about the possibility and acceptability of the United Kingdom holding direct elections after May—June 1978, as it appeared it was having severe problems in the preparation of its direct elections legislation.[46] The Minister replied that the British Government was sticking to the appointed date and that, consequently, the question was out of order. In its report on the European Council's meeting in Brussels, December 1977, the Government noted that of all Member States only the United Kingdom was experiencing serious delays in preparing for the elections.[47]

The year 1978: implementation

In the middle of January the new Cabinet — which had been formed after nearly seven months of negotiations between the main political parties — presented itself to Parliament. In his first declaration the new Prime Minister, Mr van Agt (CDA) posed a rhetorical question concerning the day on which direct elections would be held.[48] This was the first official sign of the Government's feeling of uncertainty about the realisation of the direct elections in 1978.

In the delayed processing of the 1978 Budget Bill the Minister of Foreign Affairs declared in February 1978 that, because of the problems of implementation in the United Kingdom, the direct elections would most probably have to be postponed to 1979, and that progress was being made on the Implementation Bill.[49] In the debates, Mr Patijn (PvdA) by then a member of the Opposition, replied that the Dutch Government had also become a cause of the delay: it still had to promulgate the Ratification Bill, accepted by the Parliament the year before, and the Netherlands was the only Member State whose Government still had to present an Implementation Bill to its Parliament.[50]

In the meeting of the European Council in Copenhagen in April, a new date for the direct elections was agreed on, 7-10 June 1979. In the parliamentary debates on the Government's report on that meeting the new Minister of Foreign Affairs, Mr van der Klaauw, expressed his satisfaction with this more realistic date.[51] At this, Mr Patijn, the spokesman of the Socialist opposition, commented sarcastically that there was more cause for enthusiasm than satisfaction, for the Netherlands would now also have a chance to participate in the elections. The Dutch Government — the last of all the Member States — still had to present its Implementation Bill to Parliament. Other MPs, also from the Government coalition, joined Mr Patijn in his call for an early presentation of the bill. One week later Mr Patijn posed, during question-time, some more detailed questions about the precise nature of the implementation legislation and about the implementation itself.[52]

On 26 May — about the date originally planned for the elections — the 'great moment' arrived with the presentation of the Implementation Bill and the related Bill on Incompatibilities for MEPs.[53] The two bills can be considered as one legislative 'package' and were processed as such in Parliament.

The contents of the bills can be divided into two categories. The first category concerns the procedures for the election. The Government's main proposals, deviating from the national Election Law which for other related matter applied, were that Dutch citizens outside the Netherlands but within the EC, as well as citizens from other EC countries living within the Netherlands, have the franchise; MEPs would be chosen for a five year term of office; the election would be on Thursday, 7 June; there would be an electoral deposit of 18,000 guilders; the election system was to be based on proportional representation, with the whole country being considered as one constituency.

The second category concerned the rules for being elected. The main

197

proposals were, that it would be left to the Second Chamber to judge whether or not an elected person met the legal conditions; and membership of the European Parliament was incompatible with some specifically mentioned national political positions, which already applied to MPs.

The two bills were processed rather quickly. Within about three months, including the summer recess, they passed the Second Chamber. Compared with the normal time-ratio between the Second and the First Chamber, (about 9:1) the First Chamber processed the bills much more slowly, in two and a half months. The Cabinet was mainly responsible for this delay, as it took more than five weeks to reply to the comments of the First Chamber's Joint Committee.

The proposals met several objections in the Second Chamber, which has the right to amend legislation. Ten amendments were brought forward: one was withdrawn, five were rejected, and four were passed (see table 10.2). The table also gives summary information about the contents of the amendments, the parties which introduced them, and their success. Mr Patijn — an active propagandist for the direct elections in the European Parliament — was particularly active and successful. He also proposed the only motion accepted by the Chamber, which concerned the simultaneous publication of the election results in all the Member States.

The proposals were not only changed by parliamentary action, but also by the Cabinet itself. Twice it introduced formal reconsiderations of the bill, mainly of a technical and partly of a stylistic nature. One major change was the incorporation of the possibility for elected persons who — according to the Second Chamber's judgement — did not meet the legal requirements for membership of the European Parliament, to appeal against that judgement to the Council of State. [54] These reconsiderations must be viewed as expressions of implicit parliamentary influence, anticipating possible amendments.

During the discussions, both in parliamentary committee and in plenary session, many other questions were put and remarks were made, although none resulted in amendments or motions. They were almost a complete repetition of the comments made during the earlier debates.

The debates on the floor took about one day in the Second Chamber, and half a day in the First Chamber. The bills were passed with a large majority. However, all seven small parties, totalling twelve seats (8 per cent), voted against the bills, in protest against the high threshold for the European elections. The processing of the bills was almost entirely a matter for the party specialists — the trustees of the parties in the relevant Committees (two Standing Committees in the Second Chamber, one Joint Committee in the First Chamber). All

Table 10.2
Amendments to Implementation Bills,
with proposing party and outcome

Proposing Party	Withdrawn	Rejected	Passed	Total
Government Parties	–	Each list of candidates must be nominated by at least 450 electors	–	1
Opposition (Mr Patijn)	Registration of competing parties has to be permanent	Extension of polling to 20.00 hours	a) Retirement from the European Parliament must be reported to that Parliament's Chairman b) Any political group with the name of a national political party needs that party's permission to use it c) No electoral deposit required for parties which already have an MEP	5
Other parties (right wing)	–	a) Co-operating parties in the elections be considered as one party b) The possibility to combine lists c) Another electoral system to allocate the remaining votes after the quota application	No deposit for parties with one MP already	4
Total	1	5	4	10

nine MPs who participated, as party-spokesmen, in the Second Chamber's plenary debates, were also members of the related Committees; in the First Chamber seven out of the nine party-spokesmen were members of the Committee.

During the processing of the bills, direct elections were debated on two other occasions. Firstly, there was the Cabinet's report on EC developments in 1977 in which the Minister of Foreign Affairs blamed the postponement of the direct elections from 1978 to 1979 solely on the United Kingdom.[55] In the debates on the report some remarks were made about the significance of the direct elections. Most sceptical was the Catholic spokesman, Mr Mommersteeg (CDA, and a former

MEP) who warned against too high expectations of the political effects of a directly elected European Parliament; its effectiveness, he argued, would be more dependent on the MEPs' activities and courage than on their direct election.[56]

The second occasion was at the end of November when, during question-time, questions concerning the direct elections were twice posed. Mr Berkhouwer (VVD and also an MEP) asked about the implementation of the franchise for Dutch citizens outside the country.[57] On another occasion, the former EC fonctionnaire, Mr van der Linden (CDA), asked about the French attitude towards the direct elections, especially towards any further enlargement of the directly elected European Parliament.[58]

The direct elections as a national political issue

In our discussion of the period 1970-1974 we described several aspects of an exceptional legislative process. Initially there seemed to be wide political support in the national Parliament for the establishment of direct elections to the European Parliament. The end result of this was two legislative failures. Somewhere and somehow, after 1970, the overwhelming support for the idea given by nearly all the main political parties as well as the main parliamentary party and its spokesman, Mr Westerterp and, to a lesser extent, the Cabinet became completely ineffective. The two legislative initiatives did not even reach the floor of the Parliament. To explain this we concluded that, especially at Cabinet level, support was more verbal than real; that other, more dramatic, issues drove out the direct elections issue; and that the changing status of Mr Westerterp was also a factor.

In the next two years, the political atmosphere in the Parliament was different. Direct elections were supported, but this did not have an obvious effect, and eloquent self-satisfaction and mutual congratulations on the Dutch role in the EC was expressed. The policy-making concerning the direct elections shifted from the national to the Community level, at first to the European Parliament, and then to the Council of Ministers; this also implied a shift in the national policy-making system, from the Parliament to the Cabinet. When these resulted in progress on the issue, the national Parliament's attention and interest in direct elections recovered.

Thus in this second period neither the issue of direct elections, nor the decision-making concerning it, appeared to be independent or isolated from other issues or decision-making processes. The history of the issue of the direct elections, as it proceeded in the national Parliament, remained strongly determined by environmental factors,

200

some of which had nothing at all to do with direct elections.

The main decision-making concerning direct elections did not take place in the national Parliament, but elsewhere: partly in the European Parliament but mainly in the Council of Ministers. The national Parliament had only to ratify the Council's decision and, together with the Cabinet, to work out the details of implementation.

The Ratification Bill passed smoothly and quickly which, after so many years of verbal support, was scarcely a surprise. Indicative of the supportive atmosphere was the impatience with which the Implementation Bill was awaited. Mainly because of the same environmental factors, namely the enduring cabinet-formation crisis, the Dutch Government was the last Member State to present its bill.

The Implementation Bill also passed quickly, but less smoothly. There were several objections to some details of the proposed legislation. Some of these objections were successful: the bill was also altered by the acceptance of amendments and by the Cabinet's voluntary changes to the bill. Besides, the first draft of the bill was already much influenced by Parliament's demands which, at the Cabinet's request, were advanced during 1977, especially during the debates on the Ratification Bill.

Comparing the legislative outcomes not only with the 1977 demands but also with those of 1970 and the following years which received such a critical response from the Suffrage Council, we can conclude that even some of the earlier demands, which had a negative response in the early seventies, had a positive result in 1978. This applies, notably, to the quota rule which discriminates between large and small parties, and to the legal possibility of combining the European elections with a national election.

In terms of the general characteristics of the process of legislation, as it normally proceeds in the Netherlands, we have seen a return to 'normalcy' since 1974. The main decision-making and initiatives were made by the Cabinet, not by the Parliament. The MPs debated, the Cabinet decided, but in concert with the ruling mood in Parliament. When there was no clear ruling mood, but instead dissension within Parliament the decision was taken by voting on amendments. The Parliament itself delegated its decision-making to a committee; the parties to their specialist members of the committees. In the plenary debates these specialists acted as spokesmen and cue-givers to their parties: several of these MPs were also MEPs or former MEPs. In addition, and what is more important, this 'normal' system of legislation was much more effective than the exceptional approach of the early seventies.

The national Parliament is a dependent part of a larger and more complex system. In that position it can exert some influence; it can scarcely do this by efforts to change that position and to become an independent centre of the political system which initiates legislation. Concerning direct elections, the Parliament had some influence on the Cabinet's role and its impetus in EC decision-making, as well as on many details of the Implementation Bill. The channel of influence is indirect and the domain of influence seems limited to details, but nonetheless the Parliament did exert influence on the direct elections legislation.

Notes

1 See also M.P.C.M. van Schendelen, *Parlementaire informatie, besluitvorming en vertegenwoordiging* (Universitaire Pers, Rotterdam, 1975).
2 See also L. Prakke and G. Craenen, *Demissionaire Kabinetten in Nederland en België* (Tjeenk Willink, Zwolle, 1975).
3 For more indicators and additional explanations, see M.P.C.M. van Schendelen: 'Verzuiling en restauratie in de Nederlandse Politiek', *Beleid en Maatschappij*, 1978, 2, pp 42-54. One explanation is provided by Lijphart's thesis on accommodation and its changes; a second by the theory of political control.
4 See M.P.C.M. van Schendelen, 'The Activism of the Dutch Second Chamber', European Consortium for Political Research paper, Louvain, 1976.
5 Politicians have become aware of the political significance of this variable. In the Government's coalition pact of 1977, some points explicity concerned dates before which some agreement (notably on abortion) had to be fulfilled.
6 A full discussion of the time variable can be found in M.P.C.M. van Schendelen and H.T.J.F. van Maarseveen, *Het proces van wetgeving* (Tjeenk Willink, Groningen, 1976).
7 See note 1. Summarised information is in M.P.C.M. van Schendelen, 'Information and Decision-making in the Dutch Parliament', *Legislative Studies Quarterly*, 1976, pp 231-50 and 'Informationsund Entscheidungsprozessen im Nierländischen Parlament', *Zeitschrift für Parlamentsfragen*, 1977, pp 252-65.
8 L. de Bruyn, *Partij kiezen*, (Samson, Alphen aan den Rijn, 1971), p.175. For the nineteen sixties, see *Documentation*, published by the European Parliament, September 1969.
9 *Hoofdlijnen van het regeringsbeleid* (Kabinet Biesheuvel) (The Hague, 1971). See also the former Policy Plans of Cabinets.
10 Wetsvoorstel, 10.696.
11 Wetsvoorstel, 10.696, 7, p.3.
12 Wetsvoorstel 12.307.
13 Wetsvoorstel 12.307, 6, p.3.
14 M.P.C.M. van Schendelen, 'The Dutch Second Chamber as a career channel', Political Studies Association paper, Lanchester, 1978.
15 M.P.C.M. van Schendelen, *Regering en parlement in crisistijd*, (Tjeenk Willink, Alphen aan den Rijn, 1979).
16 Wetsvoorstel 13.100, V.
17 Handelingen Tweede Kamer, 26 February 1975.
18 Wetsvoorstel 13.600, V.
19 Handelingen Tweede Kamer, 11 November 1975.
20 Wetsvoorstel 14.100, V.
21 Wetsvoorstel 14.100, V, 2, p.25.
22 Wetsvoorstel 14.100, V, 18.
23 Wetsvoorstel 14.100, V, 31 and 43.
24 Handelingen Tweede Kamer, 2 November 1976.
25 Kamerstuk 13.143.
26 Openbare Commissie vergadering, 24 February 1975, p.556.
27 Kamerstuk 13.498, p.3.
28 Openbare Commissie vergadering, 22 March 1976, p.693.
29 Kamerstuk 14.119.
30 Wetsvoorstel 13.672. Debates on 18 December 1975.
31 Handelingen Tweede Kamer, 18 December 1975, p.2200.
32 Wetsvoorstel 13.817.

33 Kamerstuk 13.426. Debates on 9 September 1976.
34 Kamerstuk 13.859.
35 For the political relevance of this, see M.P.C.M. van Schendelen, 'Cue-processes and the relationship between the European Parliament and the Dutch Parliament' in V. Herman and M. van Schendelen (eds), *The European Parliament and the National Parliaments* (Saxon House, Farnborough, 1979), pp 279-93. See also M.P.C.M. van Schendelen, 'The EEC and the way between the European and Dutch Parliaments', European Consortium for Political Research paper, Berlin 1977.
36 Kamerstuk 14.275.
37 Handelingen Tweede Kamer, 2 December 1976, p.1808.
38 Handelingen Tweede Kamer, Appendix, 1975-76, Question 1558, p.3095.
39 Wetsvoorstel 14.383.
40 Some minor questions related to the financing of competing parties; and why, in the Act, the Parliament has been called an Assembly.
41 Openbare Commissie vergadering, 21 March 1977, p.682.
42 See note 22.
43 See also note 34.
44 Kamerstuk 14.513, 1-2, p.4.
45 Openbare Commissie vergadering, 22 August 1977.
46 Handelingen Tweede Kamer, 1 September 1977.
47 Wetsvoorstel 14.800, V, 14, p.4.
48 Handelingen Tweede Kamer, 17 January 1978, p.360.
49 Wetsvoorstel 14.800, V, p.25.
50 Handelingen Tweede Kamer, 23 February 1978, p.1124.
51 Report 14.800, V, 31. Debates on 13 April 1978.
52 Handelingen Tweede Kamer, 20 April 1978, p.2144.
53 Wetsvoorstel 15.044 and 15.045.
54 This explains why the bill after passing the Second Chamber had an extra clause.
55 Kamerstuk 15.095.
56 Openbare Commissie Vergadering, 1 September 1978, pp 912-3. See also the report on the direct elections by the Dutch European Movement (The Hague, 1979) which argued that (1) the European Parliament can make a fuller use of its present powers and (2) the European Parliament has more resources to influence than its formal powers.
57 Handelingen Tweede Kamer, 23 November 1978, p.1647.
58 Handelingen Tweede Kamer, 30 November 1978, p.1890.

The Dutch Parliament: some readings

J. Kooiman, *Over de Kamer gesproken* (Staatsuitgeverij, Den Haag, 1976). A survey of MPs' attitudes.

J. Th. v. d. Berg and J.J. Vis, *Parlement en Politiek* (Staatsuitgeverij, Den Haag, 1976). A juridical introduction to the Dutch Parliament and political system.

E. van Raalte, *Het Nederlands Parlement* (Staatsuitgeverij, Den Haag, 1977, 6th ed.). An inside view of the working and functioning of the Parliament.

U. Rosenthal, et al, *Ministers, ambtenaren en parlementariers in Nederland* (Tjeenk Willink, Groningen, 1975). A collection of empirical studies on Dutch political elites, including MPs.

M.P.C.M. van Schendelen, *Parlementaire informatie, besluitvorming en Vertegenwoordiging* (Universitaire Pers Rotterdam, Rotterdam 1975). A comparative analysis of decision-making in the Dutch Parliament.

A Lijphart, *The Politics of Accommodation* (University of California Press, Berkeley, 1968). This develops the theme of 'consociational democracy' in the Dutch political system.

11   The United Kingdom: The Reluctant Europeans

Mark Hagger

Introduction[1]

The 'making of direct elections' in the UK was a tortuous and extra-ordinary process, that produced a bill of a mere nine clauses and two schedules, at the end of two and a half years of intermittent but bitter wrangling. The legislative process was unusual in a variety of ways; not the least significant was the substantial cross-party majority that re-appeared to back the policy against the vigorous and equally cross partisan anti-Market opposition — an apparent resurrection of the 1972 debate on joining the Economic Community. The Government was also critically divided, and the conventional process based on government initiative was thus severely hampered. In the country, public indifference marked a policy that had been conceived in Paris and Rome, and that was elaborated in the absence of public influence. Finally, an issue that was treated in some of the nine countries — though by no means all — as a very minor, 'normal' and unimportant issue became in the UK a major issue of 'constitutional' importance.

The suggestion that the policy-process was 'unusual' raises immediately the question as to what features characterise a 'normal' legislative process. In the next section the principal characteristics of the legislative process are defined, and their incidence is evaluated. From this it is possible to locate the features of this particular case within the panorama of legislative processes ranging from the 'short, non-partisan, technical administrative bill' to the 'extensive, far-reaching, contentious bill'. The legislative process itself is examined through an essentially descriptive analysis focussing particularly on the more salient elements of the pre-legislative stage, the Second Readings and the Committee process.

The 'normal legislative process'

In order to provide a yardstick against which to measure the case of direct elections, it is necessary to define the principal characteristics of the legislative process.[2] It is immediately apparent that the conception of a singular 'normal process' is of no great utility or meaning: attention is therefore focused on the *range* of processes that exist, the *frequency* with which they occur and the *power structure* in evidence.

The formulation of policy and of legislation is, except in rare cases, an activity that escapes Parliament. Specialised committees have not (as yet) been fully and systematically developed in Westminster for pre-legislative work[3] and it is only in exceptional cases that Select Committees are used for this purpose. Whilst the bureaucracy and interest groups dominate in the case of 'administration' and 'consolidation' bills, party and government play a central role in the formulation of 'policy' bills;[4] the process naturally varies in its duration, but is normally within the range of a half to three years.

A major policy is first introduced by the Government into the legislative arena by its inclusion in the Queen's Speech at the beginning of the parliamentary session.[5] For central items of Government policy it has become common for governments to present a Green Paper for preliminary discussion of the issue area, and/or a White Paper as a preliminary draft of the legislation. The formal initiation of the legislation in Parliament comes with the presentation by the Government of the text of the bill at First Reading — a purely symbolic stage at which no debate occurs — before the lower chamber in the case of policy bills.

The legitimation of the principle is normally achieved at Second Reading, the first major debate on the bill, in which front-bench spokesmen for the political parties present the major arguments for and against the bill. The average duration of the debate (table 11.1) is about three hours,[6] though this conceals a significant variation between minor bills and major policy measures (table 11.2). For contested policy bills, debate is terminated by a vote which marks the formal acceptance of the government's proposal. The conventional analysis of debate and division is that they are structured strictly in partisan terms, and these 'major divisions' also serve to acknowledge continued support for the Government.[7]

The scrutiny function is implemented at the Committee stage, for which bills are normally 'sent upstairs' to a Standing Committee. However, bills of 'constitutional importance' are taken in a 'Committee of the Whole House' (CWH) having plenary membership but a more relaxed procedure. The implication of this procedure is a briefer consideration (tables 11.1-11.2) but a much tighter parliamentary control. At this stage, a number of amendments may be incorporated into the bill, with a mean of five introduced by the Government — though they may be in response to amendments originally moved from elsewhere[8] — and a mean of one amendment moved from the back-benches. However, these statistics do not reveal the substantial deviation about the mean; and half of the bills survive a CWH without amendment.

Table 11.1
Mean duration of Commons Legislative Debate 1967-71
(hours per bill)

Second Reading	3.0
Standing Committee or CWH	18.2 (N = 85)
	7.4 (N = 98)
Report	2.8
Third Reading	0.4
Lord Amendments	0.8
Total Commons debate	19.5
Number of bills	183

Source: Analysed from Griffiths, op.cit.[6]

Table 11.2
Frequency of grouped durations of Commons Debate 1967-71
(nos. of bills)

	Plenary + Committee	CWH only
5 hours	74	63
5—10 hours	29	13
10—20 hours	33	10
20—50 hours	26	1
50 hours	21	—

Source: Analysed from Griffiths, op.cit.[6]

The Report Stage provides an opportunity for the whole House to review Committee amendments, for the Government to introduce further amendments,[9] and it is therefore usually a significant phase (table 11.1). However, the practice has emerged that 'a bill committed to the Whole House and not there amended shall not be considered on report', and the Government sometimes resists all amendments until after this stage in order to 'save time or political difficulty';[10] in practice about half of government bills escape a Report Stage. The Third Reading, which provides the final opportunity for parliamentary consent, has generally diminished further in importance, both in formal procedural terms — under S.O.56 more than half of bills are not debated — and in terms of its mean duration of less than half an hour, and strong arguments have been adduced for its complete abolition.[11]

Table 11.3
Duration of Lords Debate after Second Reading
(nos. of bills)

	1968-69	1970-71
No debate	26	50
0–1 hours	9	9
1–5 hours	8	9
5–10 hours	5	3
10+ hours	2	2
Total	50	73

Source: Analysed from Griffiths, op.cit.[6]

Table 11.4
Guillotine motions in the House of Commons 1961-78

1961-62	5	1967-68	2	1973-74	0
1962-63	1	1968-69	1	1974-75	3
1963-64	0	1969-70	1	1975-76	5
1964-65	0	1970-71	1	1976-77	1
1965-66	0	1971-72	3	1977-78	3
1966-67	1	1972-73	1		

Source: House of Commons Information Office.

The bill then passes to the House of Lords, for a review or 'second look', which is often peremptory. Only a small proportion of bills are debated fully in the Lords; partly as a result of the constitutional exclusion of 'financial' measures, partly as a result of Lords' choice not to pursue debate after the second reading of some bills (table 11.3). Nevertheless, this phase enables a considerable number of drafting and technical amendments to be introduced — on average 7.5 amendments per bill — as well as providing an opportunity for significant political pressure, delay and even amendment on an extreme minority of bills.[12]

The bill thus completes its legislative path and receives the Royal Assent, in the same parliamentary session in which it was first proposed in the Queen's Speech, after an average twenty-five hours debate in the Commons. It is extremely rare for a bill to fail, though under minority governments between 1974 and 1979 the probability of this occurrence increased,[13] and there were a few cases of policies being re-submitted in the ensuing session.

The power of delay is a more general weapon available to the Opposition and to oppositional groups within the Parliament. The flow of legislation is orchestrated by the Leader of the House, with the active co-operation of Government and Opposition Whips, Opposition Leaders and the Speaker, acting through the 'usual channels' that interconnect these actors. But inter-party or intra-party conflict on rare occasions causes the normal process of reciprocity to be strained, and the Government may be forced to move the premature 'Closure' of the debate, or to introduce a 'Time Table' or 'Guillotine' motion to restrict the duration of debate. The latter device is used only rarely (table 11.4), since the House does not appreciate such formal constraint, and it takes time to debate its introduction, whilst the opposition may also withdraw its 'usual channels' co-operation in protest.[14]

The typical legislative process for major policy bills therefore shows the following summary characteristics: policy is drawn up outside Parliament, announced to Parliament in the Queen's Speech and the principles debated and legitimated at Second Reading; on rare occasions, there may be some pre-legislative debate in the House — but not in Committee. Partisan cleavage characterises debate and vote both at Second Reading and in the scrutiny stage, which is taken in CWH for 'constitutional' bills. Subsequent stages are of limited importance, and a small number of amendments are introduced by the Government either in Committee or at Report; scrutiny by the upper chamber is selective, but leads to a significant number of technical amendments. The whole process is completed within the annual cycle of the parliamentary year, and it is only in most exceptional cases that procedural devices need to be resorted to in order to accomplish this time schedule. Finally, the primacy of government is evident throughout the legislative process, even though the extent of its dominance is a matter of scholarly dispute, and in the context of minority government is also politically in question.[15]

The complexities of the socio-political background

The history of Britain's relations with the Common Market is most tortuous. In the formative period 1956-58 Conservative Governments kept Britain out, whilst through the 1960s Labour Governments sought to join Britain to the Six. It was the Conservatives who ultimately signed the Treaty of Accession in 1972, but two years later Labour began renegotiating the Treaty and then submitted the decision to a referendum. Policy towards the Community was contested both within and between the parties, and a vigorous anti-Market oppositon drew from both major parties as well as individuals in the minor parties.[16]

Whilst the balance of forces in Parliament changed over time as a result of two new electoral generations of Members, of some movement in attitudes, and of different response to new facets of the policy area, essentially the arguments remain the same as each new EC measure comes before Parliament. The principal explanation for this is that anti-Market MPs perceive every EC decision as a question that threatens (at least potentially) the authority and the unimpeachable sovereignty of the House of Commons. Yet these 'threats' are never proven, since constitutional change in an evolutionary context occurs gradually and imperceptibly over the medium/long term.[17] The second explanation for the static nature of the European issue is that the dispersion of attitudes along the 'European ideological dimension', ranging as it does from extreme demands for withdrawal from the Community to strong commitment to federalist principles, presents a bi-modal distribution that fails to encourage the assimilation of the issue in the classical pattern of moderate, gradual incrementalism typical of the policy process in the UK.[18]

The existence of a second ideological dimension, that did not coincide with the normally dominant left–right dimension, complicated a political map that was simultaneously threatened by minor parties, which commanded 25 per cent of the electorate though only 6 per cent of the parliamentary seats (table 11.5). It presents difficulties for a political system that is adjusted, both in terms of political culture and in terms of institutional arrangements, toward the two-party system.

The complex divisions exist not only at the parliamentary level, but also amongst the electorate. Attitudes towards the European Community have been extremely volatile, and therefore characterised more by uncertainty than by conflict.[19] For the 1975 Referendum, it is argued[20] that the public's primary motivation is the apparent connection between increasing food prices and EC membership; or according to one psychological analyst, the British public had not yet attained a 'post-acquisitive' outlook on life.[21] Whilst the trend in attitudes towards the Community showed a sharp upturn during 1975 and prior to the referendum campaign — though falling subsequently — the strength of support for direct elections (see Appendix to chapter 2) shows a much slower growth, and it is not until late 1976 that a marked swing in favour of direct elections occurs.

Until late in 1976, the balance of mass opinion was very evenly divided between those who favoured direct elections and those who

Table 11.5
Parties in the House of Commons, October 1974

	Party	Abbreviation	% Vote*	Seats†
G	Labour Party	Lab	39.3	319 (−5)
(G)	Liberal Party	Lib	18.3	13
	Scottish Nationalist Party	SNP	0.6	11
	Plaid Cymru (Welsh Nationalist Party)	PC	2.9	3
	Conservative Party	Con	35.8	276(+5)
	United Ulster Unionist Coalition (Ulster Unionists: N. Ireland)	UUUC	2.4	10
	Others		0.6	3
Total			100.0	635
Turnout			76.1%	

*Share of valid votes cast in General Election, October 1974.
†Seats in House of Commons, October 1974 (± changes at November 1977)

G Party forming the Government (Liberal Party gives support from 23 March 1977).

opposed them;[22] the 'don't know' response was very consistent at 18 per cent ± 5. It was not until the autumn of 1976, when the pre-legislative parliamentary process was well in hand, that a dramatic shift in public opinion brought UK support for direct elections to a level in excess of that of her more committed partners. The new level of support was subsequently sustained, and was obtained as a result of a decline in attitudes *against* direct elections. Whereas prior to the change, the ratio of support:opposition was about 50:50, subsequent to the change that ratio became 76:24.

The Conservative Party had been converted to support for Europe largely as a result of the

> personal commitment to Europe on the part of (Edward Heath)
> ... when on all the evidence the majority of the local associations
> and a very large section of the Parliamentary Party were distinctly
> cool or hostile.[23]

The hard-core of anti-Marketeers established a record of vigorous and unabated parliamentary opposition in the 1960s, in the debates on entry to the Common Market in 1971; in the referendum campaign;[24]

and in all debates bearing on the European Community. However, they were unable to persuade the Party's annual conference to support their views, neither in regard to joining the European Community nor in regard to direct elections.[25] The right wing of the parliamentary party, around its new leader, Margaret Thatcher, took a pragmatic view — welcoming the economic and political benefits to be derived from a limited and confederal Europe — whilst the ideologically moderate group associated with the former party leader, Edward Heath, formed a faction that was both more committed and more federalist. MPs not involved in either camp gradually moved into support of the Community and certainly were not willing to oppose its 'democratisation'. The Conservative electorate has always been very strongly supportive of Community membership,[26] and this may well have been a factor influencing both leaders and parliamentarians.

The Labour Party has always been more antagonistic toward the Community, as has its electorate. In 1966, the Prime Minister, Harold Wilson, changed suddenly to a supportive attitude[27] and the 1970 manifesto included the goal of membership after a lukewarm Party Conference decision in the previous year. But anti-Market forces used the National Executive Committee (NEC) as a means of resisting the pro-European swell, and forced the policies of renegotiation and referendum on a reluctant leadership.[28] After the 'yes' decision in the referendum, the Party appeared to accept membership, and sent a full delegation to the European Parliament — carefully representing regional, ideological and European differences of opinion,[29] and since 1977 holding an internal election to select MEPs. However, successive Conferences opposed direct elections, and the conflicts within and between parliamentary party, NEC and Cabinet raged until the situation was defused by an exchange of letters between the new Party Leader and Prime Minister Jim Callaghan, and the Party General Secretary, Ron Hayward, in which the 'neo-Gaullist' policy was firmly stated.[30] In the country, the Labour electorate provided the primary source of anti-Market feeling.

The fiercest and most critical conflict raged within the Labour Government itself. About a quarter of the Cabinet was hostile to direct elections, as was demonstrated in the first formal vote on the principle on 7 July 1977,[31] and this division of opinion existed at all levels of Cabinet hierarchy. The existence of this conflict, together with the pressure on the Government to tend to some pressing parliamentary and governmental problems — particularly the devolution issue and the consequences of the economic and oil crises — enabled the anti-Market opposition to successfully 'filibuster' in the Cabinet. Indeed so successful were they that the issue did not appear in the Government's programme as outlined in the Queen's Speech, until the autumn of 1976.

The Liberal Party (table 11.5) has been committed to a pro-European policy for longer than either the Labour or the Conservative parties, and its orientation is also more internationalist and more federalist. Party conferences have endorsed the policy, and the small 'Liberals Say No' movement in 1965 acted discreetly in order not to 'embarrass the party'.[32] The Liberal policy on direct elections was therefore not in question; but its strategy was complicated by two features: its strong commitment to electoral reform; and its relationship with the government, institutionalised in the March 1977 'Lib-Lab pact'.

The Scottish Nationalist Party had long opposed European Community membership, and was the only party to activate the issue seriously in the 1970 election campaign.[33] It had supported the idea of a referendum, as a reflection of its general attitude towards self-determination; but whilst Scotland was less supportive of membership than any other region, the referendum vote was still a clear 'yes'. The party therefore accepted membership as an interim situation until Scotland could determine its own relationship with the EC at independence. It welcomed the principle of direct elections as an extension of its populist ideas, and as a means of strengthening the strategic potential of Europe as a lever on the UK.[34] Nevertheless it vigorously opposed the unjust distribution of seats between countries and between regions, and opposed the plurality electoral system.

Plaid Cymru had an established policy criticising the European Community as representing '. . . a centralised European staff, a military power bloc and a remote bureaucratic system'.[35] It therefore abstained or opposed the principles of direct elections in Parliament, and strongly criticised both the electoral system and the number of seats allocated to the Principality.

The Ulster Unionist view was expressed most eloquently and vigorously by its adopted parliamentarian, Enoch Powell: he was hostile to the constitutional implications of Community membership, fearful of its implications for relations with Eire, and critical of the Roman Catholic super-state into which the Community might develop,[36] in spite of the surprising strength of pro-European attitudes amongst the electorate.[37] Whilst the anti-Market resolve of the Ulster Unionists in Parliament had weakened through the 1972 debates,[38] their opposition to direct elections was more rigorously sustained (with the exception of Wm. Craig).

Faced with the bitter internal conflict between institutions of the Party and between factions within the Party, when the issue was discussed in the Council in December 1974, the Labour Government:

. . . made absolutely clear that it could not take up a position on

212

the proposal before the process of renegotiation had been completed and the results of renegotiation had been put to the British people.[39]

In parliament, the Government made a number of contradictory statements prior to the referendum about the existence (or not) of an obligation to introduce direct elections. During the referendum campaign, the issue was scrupulously avoided by the Government and the 'yes' campaign; it was not illuminated by the media; and it is therefore difficult to deny the critique by the anti-Marketeers that the issue was kept extremely 'close to the ground'.

Through 1976, as the Government struggled to reach some internal consensus in the Cabinet, conflicting statements were made by Ministers about the improbability of meeting the original target of May/June 1978, and about the commitment, which it had made when the Act was signed[40] to use its best endeavours to achieve direct elections by the target date. The extended pre-legislative debate provided an opportunity for the Government to resolve these problems, and reconcile them with other difficulties arising from its legislative programme (in particular devolution) and from its minority status in parliament.

The long haul to the start

Avoiding activity

The pre-legislative stage lasted from the first Commons debate in March 1976 — on the Green Paper — to the publication of the bill in June 1977. It was thus an abnormally long gestation, punctuated in December 1976 by the inclusion of the policy in the Queen's Speech for the 1976/77 session. The failure of the Government to pass the bill during that session is a further unusual characteristic of this legislative process. A third and more constructive feature was the move on from the principle to the electoral system after the debate and vote on Second Reading in July 1977.

Prior to the present legislative process, the issue of direct elections was raised, at least by the anti-Market forces, during the parliamentary and public debates on entry to the Community in 1972. Whilst to them it presented a 'threat' to their conception of sovereignty, at that juncture it was sufficiently abstract for the Government to side-step the issue with ease. Later, when it emerged as an issue of public policy after the Paris meeting of the European Council, Ministers hid behind the shield of the referendum. Prime Minister Wilson had stated that:

> . . . our position was entirely reserved on all these matters until after the referendum.[41]

During the referendum campaign itself, whilst the anti-Market 'opposition' had raised the matter repeatedly, there was not a single mention of direct elections in the pro-Market propaganda, and the issue was discreetly suppressed in public meetings. Thus in response to Parliamentary questions in the first half of 1975, the Government refused to make a positive commitment:

> Walker-Smith (Cons, pro): 'Is it not the plain and simple fact that under the Treaty it is obligatory, at some time, to have direct elections to the European Parliament?'

> Hattersley (Minister): 'I think there is nothing plain and simple about the issue at all.'[42]

In this curious dialogue was enshrined the preliminary issue as to whether the principle of direct elections ensued from the Treaty of Rome, and had therefore been accepted in the previous decisions, in Parliament and in the referendum, to join the Community.

In 1974-75, six Questions were posed to the Government, primarily from pro-Market members urging the Government to greater action; in the following session, twelve Questions were asked, and during 1976-77 some forty-four Questions were tabled, as the saliency of the issue increased. Subjected to this pressure the Government published in February 1976 — eight months after the referendum decision — a Green Paper that laid out the issues and alternatives in an exceptionally open manner. A distinction was drawn between the four issues to be negotiated in the Council of Ministers (size and distribution of seats; election date and period; the status of MEPs in relation to the National Parliament; and the question of incompatibility) and a number of issues to be resolved at the national level; the only notable feature was the implicit assumption that a plurality (i.e. single member constituency, single ballot) electoral system would be utilised.

The two-day debate that followed publication provided the first major discussion of the principle of direct elections — though the Foreign Secretary endeavoured to by-pass this issue. In order to stress the openness of the decision process, Callaghan offered the Commons a Select Committee to examine the issues thoroughly, with a Minister included in its membership. The debate on principle largely followed established pro and anti-Market lines,[43] which was the cleavage that explains more of the interventions in the debate than partisanship (see table 11.6). However, the dichotomous classifications conceal a richer variation in attitude to both the Community and direct elections, which underlay the primary arguments for and against the principle.

The front-bench spokesmen of the Labour, Conservative and Liberal Parties were as one in supporting not only the principle of introducing direct elections, on various interpretations of commitment; but also on the policy of distribution of seats to the four nations of the UK in proportion to population; on a fixed inter-election period of four or five years; and on a voluntary dual mandate. They were also more or less united in rejecting essential federal implications for the issue, and in arguing that any increase in powers would be controlled, '. . . would require the specific approval of the UK Parliament',[44] yet would in all probability eventuate.

Table 11.6
Structure of the Green Paper Debate
(nos. of speeches)

	Pro-EC	Anti-EC				Lab.	Con.	Other
pro-DE	26 10L 15C 1O	2C 1O	3		pro-DE	10	17	2
anti-DE	1 1L	7L 2C 3O	12		anti-DE	8	2	3

Nos of Speeches,

L = Labour
C = Conservative
O = Other

The issues *between* the parties were therefore secondary matters not yet at stake: the choice of electoral system, the use of Boundary Commissions, and the question of institutional links between the two Parliaments. However, it was clear that party policy was not fully developed on these issues, as a result of intra-party cleavages on the first problem.

The nationalist parties had less easily identifiable positions. The SNP, Plaid Cymru and Ulster Unionists all expressed their opposition to the distribution of seats in proportion to population, drawing comparison with the smaller independent nations of the Community which would obtain a much higher ratio of representation. Whilst the Welsh and Irish Members were opposed to the principle, the SNP welcomed the element of democratic control introduced by direct elections, though it warned of the dangers of over-government.

The pro-Market spokesmen stressed some further issues. First, Michael Stewart argued that we '. . . must avoid a lengthy period during which other nations of the Community had gone over to direct elections and we as yet have not done so',[45] and the Government was therefore urged to implement direct elections (though some argued nevertheless that the target date was not of critical importance). Secondly, there was concern about links between the Parliaments, with a variety of positive suggestions being put forward. In addition, various degrees of support were expressed for '. . . a more positive and direct commitment to a democratic, outward-looking, responsive Community',[46] whose future shape was seen by some as a federalist union, by others as the existing confederation, but by the more perspicacious as an unknown quantity.

The anti-Market participants presented a more cogent and vehement set of arguments. The Treaty obligation to direct elections in their present form was rejected, and doubts were expressed as to the capability of the 'European Assembly'[47] to effectively control either the Commission or the Council of Ministers; it was feared that the powers of the Assembly would be increased at the expense of national Parliaments, '. . . and that this development should go on without people realising what is happening'.[48] The 'consequent slide to federalism' was thus seen not only as inevitable and automatic, but also as the deliberate goal of the European Movement, the Commission, the Tindemans Report and federalists in general, whose testimony was clearly cited by anti-marketeers and occasionally confessed in the debate by pro-marketeers.[49] But at times, the anti-Market argument focussed on two more realistic strategies, in arguing that the time was not right for direct elections; and that the system of democratic control should be based on an improved Commons mechanism, rather than a directly elected 'European Assembly' that merely duplicated and confused the channels of control.

Although a formal decision was scrupulously avoided by the Government at this stage, the balance of argument in the debate indicated a strong majority in favour of direct elections. Nevertheless, powerful opposition was raised to the principle, by a cohesive anti-Market group, representing bi-partisan elements without any common denominator other than their attitude to Europe. Whilst this group was small in numbers, it had sufficient access to positions of power within party organisations and more particularly in the Cabinet, and sufficient mass support, to command respect.

This first debate on direct elections was of critical importance in determining the 'class' into which the direct elections bill would be assigned. The underlying theme of the debate was the question of principle, which had already been exposed during preliminary skirmishes through Parliamentary Questions and the correspondence columns of *The Times*. Whilst the Government had previously attempted to argue that an obligation existed in Article 138 of the Treaty of

Rome, this position was now abandoned.[50] The Government conceded that its commitment to direct elections was political; it thereby acknowledged that the decision to be taken by Parliament was to determine (or ratify) the principle of holding elections. When it is also conceded that the powers of the European Parliament would in all probability increase in the future, it acknowledged the 'constitutional importance' of the bill. It should be noted that in the UK there was no requirement to pass a 'ratification bill' on this (or any other) issue: the sovereignty of parliament implies that the 'implementation bill' ratifies the principle of a measure – in practice the vote at Second Reading establishes the principle and therefore provides ratification – until such time as parliament chooses to revoke its consent.[51]

The anti-Market oppositions were in no doubt as to its constitutional significance: 'The accession of authority . . . would be instantaneous, for the whole of the Assembly would be transformed . . .'.[52] The avowed federalists clearly argued for and welcomed the constitutional change. In this debate, it was only the moderate spokesmen who were less convinced of the nature and extent of the change – some argued for example that increases in the power of the European Parliament would be at the expense of the other European institutions and not the National Parliaments.

It was thus clear from the debate that the House considered this to be a bill of 'constitutional significance'. Any previous thoughts by the Government of slipping the legislation through as a legal obligation consequential on an existing 'constitutional' act – the 1972 EC Act – were soon abandoned. Certain procedural consequences ensued, in particular the passage of the bill to CWH after Second Reading. But more generally, it was established that the issue was 'of constitutional importance', and its legislative process would therefore be conditioned by this characteristic.[53]

Furthermore, the Government made a number of formal concessions to Parliament – it confirmed national parliamentary control over changes in the European Parliament's powers; it expressed scepticism about the likelihood of a uniform electoral system in the next fifteen years; it proposed the establishment of a Select Committee to investigate the issue; and it intimated that Parliament would have a considerable degree of decisional power free of party control. Thus there was a shift from the normally attributed practice of government domination over the policy process, toward a situation wherein Parliament was of considerable influence.

Winding up for action

After the Green Paper debate there ensued a period of more than a year

217

marked principally by non-activity. Two months after the debate, following some wrangling over composition and terms of reference, a Select Committee was established.[54] Its membership was predominantly pro-European, and the four or five anti-marketeers made little attempt to develop their policies, after their failure to postpone the implementation and limit the size of the Assembly during the first phase of the Select Committee meetings.

The Committee was characterised by a narrow vision, a failure to search out and investigate real alternatives, and an overwhelming concern to meet the June 1978 'indicative target date'. In the space of six months, it reviewed a collection of evidence that had been submitted precipitously by a variety of predominantly pro-European sources; and it inquired of a number of representatives of the administration, who were able to advise on the workings of the plurality electoral system, and on such issues as the franchise. The internal decision process was dominated at times by a coalition of the two major parties to preserve the plurality electoral system and a proportional distribution of seats to the four nations; and at times by a Labour–Conservative conflict in regard to implementation aspects.

As an example of detailed pre-legislative investigation, strongly advocated by some critics of Westminster,[55] the experience of this Select Committee is hardly to be commended. Nevertheless, it enabled Parliament to begin to grapple with the real problems of implementation, and in doing so it assisted the evolution of the legitimation process by focussing attention on matters 'beyond' the principle. As an example of Government/specialised committee relations, this case epitomises the unsatisfactory previous experience[56] and offers little hope for the successful implementation of the 1978 recommendations of the Select Committee on Procedure.[57] The Direct Elections Committee's initial report was not debated until the very day of the European Council's meeting to determine the basic issues. Its subsequent two reports were not debated at all, and the parliamentary vacuum was filled only by the continuing flow of parliamentary questions and by an adjournment debate some twelve months after the Green Paper debate. Moreover, as a mechanism to assist conflict reduction, the Select Committee was a signal failure, as subsequent developments show.

In part the absence of debate may be attributed to the general activities of the Parliament and the Government. The legislative load in 1976/77 was unusually low in quantitative terms (see table 11.7), representing about half the normal quantity of policy measures; but in qualitative terms the load was extremely heavy:

   . . . the agenda gradually became dominated by constitutional

218

issues — devolution and direct elections, plus a distant prospect of House of Lords Reform.[58]

There were also a number of contentious policy bills on price regulation, development land tax, etc., apart from the bill to nationalise sectors of the aircraft and shipbuilding industries that had been defeated in the previous session. In terms of the ranking of these measures, it was the clear priority of the Government to place the Devolution Bill before all others — and this decision can be seen to be consistent with established party policy, and therefore a result of party domination of the policy process and not merely a device of the anti-marketeers in the Cabinet.

Table 11.7
Government Bills introduced (nos.)

	1974/75	1975/76	1976/77	1977/78
Policy	40(7)	34(5)	18(5)	18
Administration	18	25	20(1)	16
Finance etc.	2	4	4	5
Other	0	1	0	0
Consolidation	22	13	8(2)	12(2)
Total	82(7)	77(5)	50(8)	51(2)

Figures in parentheses are numbers of bills which failed.

Source: Adapted from Burton and Drewry, 1977, 1978, 1979, 1980, see note 4.

The second feature of the session was the political marginality of the Government. The narrow majority arising from the October 1974 election withered to a minority during 1976. Apart from generating some well publicised difficulties in the Finance Bill, this situation contributed to the failure of an unprecedented eight bills in the session. Ironically the failure of the most important of these — the Devolution Bill — enabled the Direct Elections debate to rise to the top of the agenda at this juncture.

To ease their parliamentary difficulties,[59] the Government announced an agreement between the Labour and Liberal Parties, which provided for:

a) the introduction of direct elections legislation in the 1976/77 session;

b) 'consultation' between the parties in the choice of electoral system;

c) 'recommendation' by the Government on the electoral system after considering the Liberal Party's views;

d) a free vote in the Commons on the choice of electoral system.[60]

The legislative process was thereby relaunched with the focus shifted from the principle to the electoral mechanism.

The commitment of the Government was indicated by the rapidity with which a White Paper was published a week later. But *prior to* its publication, the new state of parliamentary opinion was revealed by a five-hour debate on a Private Member's Motion: pro-Market forces dominated the debate and established a new pressure for governmental action, whilst anti-Market force was both quantitatively weaker and more isolated. Moreover, the focus of attention was on the new issue of the electoral system, to which this cleavage was not relevant (table 11.8). The White Paper contained the first formal statement of the Government's shift towards proportional representation. After reviewing the general arguments on the principle, the document reviewed the advantages and disadvantages of three types of electoral system: the plurality system, the regional list system and the single transferable vote, as well as describing the electoral systems used for legislative elections in the other eight Member States. The opening up of the electoral system issue marked an important development in the legislative process, which was to dominate the debate for the ensuing eight months, and at the same time terminated the argument on principle, which virtually disappeared from the debates that followed.

The extended pre-legislative phase closed with the publication of the first bill on 24 June 1978, some eighteen months after the introduction of the issue into the parliamentary forum, and after a phenomenal total of thirty-four hours of parliamentary debate and twenty-one meetings of the Select Committee. Whilst the Government had scrupulously avoided any parliamentary vote, the analysis of debate shows the shift of argument from the principle to secondary issues.

The early decision by Parliament and Government that the issue was of constitutional importance assured a more hazardous and protracted pre-legislative process than might otherwise have been the case. Thereafter the cleavages within the major parties rendered it impossible for the conventional party-focussed policy process to operate, and the

Table 11.8
Structure of the PMM Debate, 25 March 1977
(nos. of speeches)

a) Party/DE

	pro-DE	anti-DE
Cons.	9	0
Lab.	4	3
Other	1	0

c) EC/DE

	pro-DE	anti-DE
pro-EC	13	0
anti-EC	0	3

e) Timing/DE

	pro-DE	anti-DE
Urgency	8	0
Delay	0	3

b) Party/Electoral System

	Plur.	Indiff.	PR
Cons.	4	2	3
Lab.	4	1	1
Other	0	0	1

d) EC/Electoral System

	Plur.	Indiff.	PR
pro-EC	5	3	5
anti-EC	3	0	0

divisions within the Cabinet prevented the Government from leading a government-focussed process. The gradual acceptance by a bi-partisan parliamentary majority, together with the weakening of the bitter antagonism of the anti-Market faction in parliament, enabled the Government to lean on parliamentary legitimation in order to overcome its internal divisions.

The central feature of the pre-legislative phase was the procrastination and delay by the Government — explained only in part by the parliamentary difficulties in other areas. Whilst parliamentary divisions through 1976 restricted the influence of this body, in March 1977 the situation changed. On the one hand the Government was obliged to make concessions in exchange for Liberal support in Parliament. On the other hand, Parliament itself started to exert pressure for action more firmly than before, and indeed began to debate the post-principle issue of the electoral system.

The passage of the bill

The bill was eventually presented to Parliament at the end of June 1977, the failure of the Devolution Bill having left a vacuum in the parliamentary timetable.[61] Although it was not now intended to com-

Table 11.9
Structure of the Second Reading Debates
(nos. of speeches)

1976-77 Second Reading: 6-7 July 1977

---

a) Party/DE

	pro-DE	anti-DE
Lab.	15	8
Con.	16	3
Other	3	1

c) EC/DE

	pro-DE	anti-DE
pro-EC	30	2
anti-EC	2	12

b) Party/Electoral System

	PR	Plur.
Lab.	10	6
Con.	2	10
Other	2	1

d) EC/Electoral System

	PR	Plur.
pro-EC	12	14
anti-EC	2	3

1977-78 Second Reading: 24 November 1977

---

a) Party/DE

	pro-DE	anti-DE
Lab.	5	7
Con.	8	2
Other	3	1

c) EC/DE

	pro-DE	anti-DE
pro-EC	13	2
anti-EC	3	8

b) Party/Electoral System

	PR	Plur.
Lab.	3	1
Con.	1	5
Other	2	2

d) EC/Electoral System

	PR	Plur.
pro-EC	4	6
anti-EC	2	2

---

plete the legislative process in that session, it was possible to spend some time on a Second Reading debate, whose ultimate effect would be to accelerate the process when re-started in the following session; whilst at the same time satisfying the commitments to the Liberal Party and to the European Community. The principal feature of the text of the bill was the inclusion of both the plurality *and* the regional party list electoral systems — one of which was to be struck out after a free parliamentary vote in December, 1977.

The anti-Market leaders were both present and vigorous at Second Reading, and argument about the principle of direct elections was more clearly predicted by attitude toward the Community than by party (table 11.9). But whilst it is the conventional function of the Second Reading to determine (or legitimise) the principle of a bill, in this case attention was already focussed on the consequent question of the electoral system. Attitude toward the EC is not a factor that was salient in determining electoral system preference, and although partisanship is a far from perfect guide, it provides a better indicator of Members' orientations toward this issue. When the bill was re-introduced in the 1977-78 session, a similar debate-structure was in evidence, although by this time the issue-focus was on the electoral system and on other implementation issues — future powers, timing, salaries and links between Westminster and Luxembourg/Strasbourg.

The divisions that marked the conclusion of these two Second Readings demonstrated the strength of support for the issue in Parliament: 60 per cent of the House supported direct elections in each vote; and 23 per cent and 16 per cent respectively, voted against (table 11.10). Whilst specific opposition at the vote came essentially from one half of the Labour participants, there were also about one hundred non-voters who may have absented themselves to indicate their opposition to direct elections. The Welsh and Northern Irish regional parties were the only groups to support the hard-core Labour and Conservative antagonists.

After a record fifty-two hours of debate, the bill passed to Committee. Since it had been clearly established that this was a measure of 'constitutional importance', the Committee Stage was to be taken on the floor of the House, so that all MPs would have an opportunity to participate in the detailed scrutiny of the bill. The organisation of this phase was dominated by the obstructionalist tactics of the anti-Market minority who used a variety of procedural devices to block and protract debate (table 11.11), and ultimately obliged the Government to introduce a 'guillotine' motion to limit debate on each remaining part of the bill to an agreed timetable.

Table 11.10

(a) Partisanship in Second Reading Divisions
(nos. of votes)

		Lab.	Con.	Lib.	SNP	PC	UUUC	DSLP
7 July 1977:	AYE	132	240	12	9	0	1	1
	Absent	59	29	0	2	2	3	0
	NO	126	15	0	0	1	6	0
24 Nov. 1977:	AYE	133	229	11	9	0	1	1
	Absent	111	37	2	2	0	1	0
	NO	73	17	0	0	3	8	0

(b) Consistency of behaviour on Second Reading Divisions
(nos. of votes)

		24 November 1977		
		Aye	Absent	No
	Aye	**352**	42	0
7 July 1977	Absent	28	**50**	18
	No	4	61	**83**

An exceptional number of amendments had been tabled by the various groups competing on this issue — 246 in total, although many were similar in content (table 11.12) — with a dominance of anti-Market amendments designed to obstruct the legislative process in the same way as they had done for the Devolution Bill.[62] The Chairman, Oscar Murton, who had also chaired the ill-fated devolution CWH in the previous session — had the unenviable task of rejecting a large proportion of them each day on procedural grounds, and then of selecting and grouping amendments so that by the end of the Committee stage some fifty amendments had been directly or indirectly debated, and many more were taken into consideration.

Nevertheless the majority of the time was devoted to constructive discussion, and a number of important issues were debated and decided, with a notable absence of pressure from party leadership. The most important of these issues was the choice of electoral system: after an

Table 11.11
Committee Debate, December 1977/January 1978

Day	Duration	Issue	Proposer
1 Dec.	0h.45m	Points of order — filibustering tactics	Anti-market
	1h.55m	Am.1: 'To terminate Act if EP powers increased'	Lab-anti
	1h.45m	Clause 1 — filibustering	Government
12 Dec.	3h.08m	Clause 1 cont. — filibustering	Government
	1h.03m	'That Clause 3 (Electoral System) be taken before Clause 2'	Government
13 Dec.	5h.31m	Am.24: 'To use plurality electoral system'	Lab.
12 Jan.	0h.48m	Points of order — filibustering	Anti-market
	3h.04m	Am.121 and others: 'Use of Alternative Vote electoral system'	SNP and PC
	1h.50m	Am.26 and others: 'Replace STV by plurality electoral system in N. Ireland'	UUUC
26 Jan.		(Plenary debate to introduce 'Guillotine' timetable)	
2 Feb.	1h.15m	Am.26 cont.	
	1h.50m	Am.17 and others: 'Increase numbers of MEPs for Scotland and Wales'	SNP and PC
	4h.00m	New Clause 8: 'Safeguard on increase in EP powers'	Government
8 Feb.	2h.43m	Am.183 and others: 'Extend franchise to British residents in EC'	Cons-pro
	2h.11m	Am.195: 'EP candidate expenses NP candidate expenses'	Lab-anti
	1h.57m	Am.186: 'Increased numbers of sponsors for candidates'	Cons-pro
	0h.08m	Am.194: 'Parliamentary approval required for electoral regulations'	Lab-anti
	0h.51m	Am.196: 'No dual mandate'	Lab-pro

Table 11.12
Amendments tabled, by origin (nos.)

	Ulster-U anti-EC (Powell gp)	Labour anti-EC (Jay gp)	Cons PR	Cons Plurality	SNP/PC	Other Cons.	Other Lab.
Clause 1	9	13	0	7	2	1	15
Clause 3	2	3	1	2	1	2	7
Clause 2	4	6	1	0	4	0	4
Other clauses	1	3	10	13	0	0	5
Schedules	22	15	31	19	8	14	21
Total	38	40	43	41	15	17	52

extensive debate, attended by a modest quorum of forty to sixty members, a decisive and bipartisan majority of about one hundred was found for the plurality electoral system (table 11.15.a) on a free vote but against the Government's recommendation. The debate itself was dominated by critics of the Party List electoral system (table 11.13), a few of whom expressed sympathy with some form of PR, but were unwilling to endorse a system 'discovered by a Liberal professor in the Forests of Finland'.[63] Even the Liberal Party argued that the Party List system was a second-best solution, and it was unable to persuade the SNP to give its support (table 11.15.a), for the SNP favoured the Alternative Vote system (see below and table 11.15.b).

Table 11.13
Structure of the Electoral System Debate, 13 December 1977

		Regional pro	Party List anti		Regional pro	Party List anti
EC	Pro	5	10	Lab.	3	7
	Anti	0	5	Con.	1	6
				Other	1	2

The only other eventual modification to the bill was conceded on the first day of Committee — though its origins lie in the Second Reading debate — when the idea of introducing a legislative check on any future expansion of the powers of the EP was first mooted.[64] In that debate the Home Secretary, Merlyn Rees, was most impressed by the weight of parliamentary feeling on the matter; but perhaps more important, the support for such an amendment was expressed by members from both pro- and anti-Market groups, and from across the party spectrum, and from the overwhelming majority (80 per cent) of those who indicated an opinion on this matter (table 11.14). In Committee a similar pattern of support is evidenced — even though participation in the debate was dominated by anti-marketeers — and at the end of the debate the Foreign Secretary, David Owen, committed the Government to introducing an amendment.[65]

Table 11.14
Structure of Debate on Amendment on 'Future Powers'
(nos. of speeches)

2nd Second Reading			Committee 1st Day		
a) Party/Amendment	pro-Amt	anti-Amt	c) Party/Amendment	pro-Amt	anti-Amt
Lab.	8	3	Lab.	5	0
Con.	5	1	Con.	2	1
Other	1	0	Other	1	0
b) EC/Amendment	pro-Amt	anti-Amt	d) EC/Amendment	pro-Amt	anti-Amt
pro-EC	5	3	pro-EC	2	1
anti-EC	9	1	anti-EC	6	0

The failure to indicate its precise content led to further filibustering from the anti-Market group. But when the new clause 8[66] was eventually introduced on the penultimate day of debate, its compass was more extensive than had previously been suggested by the Government, since it required explicit Westminster legislation for *any* change in European Parliament powers, even if they were not at the expense of Westminster. The Labour anti-Market group still stressed the possibility of 'creeping powers' in the European Parliament, whilst the more committed Europeans were opposed to any limitation at all. Nevertheless, at the vote, only a handful of pro-Europeans opposed the amendment, which was designed to appease Labour Members (table 11.15.e).

Table 11.15
Partisanship in some Committee Divisions

		Lab.	Con.	Lib.	SNP	PC	UUUC	SDLP
a) Regional party list electoral system:	FOR	148	62	13	0	2	0	0
	AGAINST	115	198	0	0	0	8	0
b) Alternative vote electoral system:	FOR	1	1	8	10	3	1	0
	AGAINST	164	55	0	0	0	8	0
c) Guillotine Motion (taken in plenary):	FOR	152	152	9	0	0	1	0
	AGAINST	63	62	0	6	0	8	1
d) Plurality electoral system for N. Ireland:	FOR	4	139	0	0	0	8	0
	AGAINST	214	14	9	1	2	0	1
e) Amendment to limit 'future powers' of EP:	FOR	83	15	2	0	0	3	0
	AGAINST	0	8	0	0	0	0	0
f) Extend franchise to EC residents:	FOR	6	134	9	0	0	1	0
	AGAINST	140	10	0	4	1	8	0

The question of electoral system was raised again on two further occasions. The SNP argued for the use of the Alternative Vote, and they obtained the support of Plaid Cymru for this proposal. Despite some support in debate from the diffuse ranks of the proponents of electoral change, there was little enthusiasm for this measure from outside minor parties (table 11.15.b) although this system had been recommended by the Conservative-dominated Hansard Committee on electoral reform in 1977. Subsequently the Ulster Unionists unsuccessfully endeavoured to change the electoral system for Northern Ireland to the plurality system as for the rest of the UK — rather than the

Single Transferable Vote system that the Government had proposed, and which had been used for local elections in the province since 1973, though not for elections to the Westminster parliament. The Conservative leadership supported the amendment, and partisan lines provided the basis for the vote (table 11.15.d).

In response to extensive obstructionalism by the bi-partisan anti-Market group, which had succeeded in consuming a third of the Committee time up to this juncture, at the end of January the Government introduced a 'guillotine motion' to 'time-table' the remainder of the debate. It was carried at the end of a long debate, with cross-party support from 314 members — 259 of whom had indicated their support for direct elections at Second Reading (table 11.15.c).

The time-table provided for two further days of debate, for a bill with six clauses and two schedules still to be scrutinised. In this time, consideration was given to three major issues. The SNP-Plaid Cymru amendment sought to increase representation for the peripheral nations,[67] but it failed to obtain wide support beyond the nationalist parties. The devolution issue, which was being debated in parallel with this bill, provides an explanation for this lack of support. In any case the principle of representation for the component nations of the UK in proportion to population appears to have been widely accepted since the Select Committee first expressed their view — in spite of the broad acceptance of peripheral over-representation for Westminster, which was to be reaffirmed for Northern Ireland in January 1979.[68] The second measure, to safeguard any increase in the powers of the European Parliament, has been discussed above. The third issue was the proposal by Select Committee member Douglas Hurd (Cons, pro-EC) to extend the franchise to British citizens resident in European Community countries. Both the debate and the ensuing division were structured along party lines, and the amendment was defeated by a small margin (table 11.15.d).

In the closing hours of debate, four minor issues were raised. Douglas Jay (Lab. anti-EC) moved an amendment to limit candidates' election expenditure to the level prevailing for national elections. This represented a very modest demand, and after a broad consensus had been expressed, the Government spokeswoman was able to give assurances that similar procedures would be used, and limits determined 'after discussion with the political parties'. Another Labour anti-marketeer, Select Committee Member Bryan Gould, also obtained an assurance that the electoral regulations would be the subject of an affirmative resolution of the House. A Conservative Member unsuccessfully sought to increase the number of signatures required to sponsor a candidate, in order to discourage 'frivolous' candidatures. Finally, an MEP, Dr Colin Phipps (Lab. pro-EC), failed to make the dual mandate illegal in the final hour of the debate.

Despite the disruption caused by the anti-Market faction, which had decided that the issue was too important to allow for compromise, the Committee Stage demonstrated a remarkable responsiveness to parliamentary opinion. Without party discipline and in the absence of Government pressure, the House of Commons had reached unfettered decisions on the electoral system, and had obtained an important amendment constraining extension of the powers of the European Parliament. Nevertheless to achieve these decisions it had been necessary for the Government to over-rule the anti-Market faction through use of the guillotine motion.

During the lengthy Commons process, the House of Lords had not been idle. Indeed its highly effective Select Committee on European Legislation[69] had made recommendations on the main issues of direct elections in March 1976 in its report: HL119, 1975-76. It debated both the Green and White Papers at some length, and its principal goal at that stage was to urge the Government to more speedy action. The participants' orientation was almost exclusively pro-European and many were past or present MEPs. These same Peers were responsible for a number of questions used as a means of urging the Government to greater action; and Lord Banks (Lib. pro-EC) tabled a Private Member's Bill on direct elections as a further incentive, though this was not pursued.

When the bill arrived from the Commons with its proportional electoral system removed, it consisted of a mere nine clauses and two schedules. In Committee, their Lordships debated the electoral system, and rejected the Regional List system, and then the Additional Member system by a smaller margin, in spite of a strong Liberal Lobby (see table 11.16). Lord Banks then sought to extend the franchise to British citizens resident overseas, but withdrew the amendment after a promise of a Speaker's Conference to examine such aspects of electoral reform before the second round of elections. Although this concession is not due to the Lords alone — for the Commons had narrowly defeated the same issue shortly before — the existence of second chamber pressure to reinforce that of the lower House was an important element in forcing the Government to concede. But in formal terms, of twenty-eight amendments tabled, not a single one was carried — presenting a very different picture from the 'usual' role of technical amendment.

The Lords process was thus quite extensive, as befits a bill of 'constitutional' status, and included a full Committee scrutiny. Despite a strong lobby for a more proportional electoral system, no attempt was made to force a conflict with the Commons, largely because of the strong pro-European feeling in the House that preferred to expedite the bill to the Royal Assent.

Table 11.16
Divisions on PR in the House of Lords, 13 April 1978

	Regional List		Additional Member	
	For	Against	For	Against
Labour	9	33	2	30
Conservative	15	69	8	50
Liberal	28	0	30	0
Crossbench	7	7	11	0
Independent	9	14	10	5
	68	123	61	85

The passage of the Direct Elections Bill through the parliament was both stormy and long — particularly given that parliamentary consent had already been mobilised prior to the Second Reading debate. The CWH was severely disrupted by the anti-Market opposition, which eventually forced the use of a guillotine. Nevertheless, the bill spent almost thirty-five hours in Committee, or four hours per clause of the eventual bill, which must place it as the most intensively scrutinised piece of legislation of the decade. Despite this careful scrutiny, the bill underwent only minor alternation, the Government having conceded only one amendment,[70] though this was of considerable importance in terms of policy change.

Whilst the attitudes toward the principle of direct elections had been structured largely on the basis of attitudes toward the EC the central issue in the passage of the bill — the choice of the electoral system — was affected more by partisanship, though even this is inadequate to explain either debate structures or votes. The one amendment that was conceded was based on a support structure that was not merely bi-partisan, but also included all except the most federalist of members.

The conflict within the Government and the majority had led it to grant unusually extensive decisional powers to the Parliament. This was particularly important in the decision on electoral system, which was made by a bi-partisan majority against the Government's recommendation, though there were signs of a traditional partisanship in the debate and vote. However, the anti-Market groups were unwilling to forego their right to obstruct and delay the process — even though responsibility had been transferred from Government to Parliament — and they forced the Government to take responsibility at least for procedural aspects of the process. Moreover, the Government was effectively able to *evade* decisions on changes in the franchise, on relations between the European Parliament and Westminster, and on the status of MEPs, through the exercise of the guillotine forced on it by the minority. It is also important to note that the Lords deferred to the Government's Bill, and did not seek to introduce any changes.

Conclusion

It is clear that the legislation of direct elections was an extraordinary process that cannot even be neatly classified at the 'constitutional' end of a unidimensional typology of legislative processes. The pre-legislative process involved negligible extra-parliamentary activity, extensive parliamentary debate in plenary, followed by a rather hasty Select Committee scrutiny: it was thus the complete reverse of the normal pattern, in addition to having an exceptional duration.

In the passage of the bill, the principle became accepted by a bi-partisan majority at an early stage, whereas in major policy issues it is normal for party to be the basis of policy-making. But the anti-Market minority obstructed the bill, taken in CWH, to such an extent that a time-table motion had to be introduced. In Committee it was decided on a free vote to adopt the plurality electoral system, and one further amendment was introduced from the vast numbers that had been tabled; for a major measure, this extent of amendment places the bill in the ranks of those pieces of legislation that are more affected by the parliamentary process — particularly when the brevity of the text is recognised. The Report Stage was insignificant, but Third Reading provided both a final demonstration of the conflict over fundamentals, and a further concession by the Government, both of which distinguish the process from normality (table 11.17).

The process is further marked by a thorough scrutiny in the Upper House which ultimately deferred to the Government's policy; by the extension of the legislative cycle over two sessions; by the (extremely rare) utilisation of a time-table procedure; and by the exceptional duration of parliamentary debate. Whilst it is difficult to define precisely the features of a 'constitutional' bill, it is clear that not all of the characteristics described here would fit the pattern. The process was thus exceptional both insofar as the policy, that was considered in some countries as relatively low-key, was raised to the level of a 'constitutional' issue; and insofar as some of its characteristics were still differentiated from those typical of constitutional bills.

A number of different explanations for this extraordinary legislative process have been developed in the course of this chapter. Firstly, in

Table 11.17
Duration of legislative debate on direct elections

		Commons	Commons Totals	Lords
Pre-Legislative:	Green Paper	11 hrs 40 m		6 hrs 00 m
	SC Report	5 hrs 50 m		
	PMM	4 hrs 53 m		
	White Paper	11 hrs 40 m	34 hrs 03 m	4 hrs 06 m
Second Reading:	First	12 hrs 21 m		
	Second	5 hrs 50 m	18 hrs 11 m	4 hrs 00 m
Committee:	Day 1	4 hrs 25 m		
	Day 2	4 hrs 11 m		
	Day 3	5 hrs 31 m		
	Day 4	5 hrs 42 m		
	Day 5	7 hrs 05 m		
	Day 6	8 hrs 00 m	34 hrs 54 m	3 hrs 25 m
Procedure:	Time-table motion	3 hrs 15 m	3 hrs 15 m	
Report:		0 hrs		0 hrs
Third Reading and Consideration:		7 hrs 41 m	7 hrs 41 m	0 hrs 10 m
Total:			98 hrs 04 m	17 hrs 41 m

the absence of a legalistic means of defining 'constitutional', an analysis was made of the attitudes of two groups of political actors, on whom the procedural decision of a 'constitutional passage' depended — viz. the Government and the parliamentary cue-givers in debate. It was found that the decision on constitutionality was reached at the earliest stage in the process, as a result of significant expression of parliamentary opinion, and as a result of cleavage within the Government.

Secondly, attention must be focussed on the lack of partisan cohesion. The development of parliamentary support was based on a substantial cross-party majority in the Commons. This unusual feature had important consequences for the pattern of governmental leadership, which is normally able to relate its action to a majority party in Parliament. The divided Government was unable to provide this leadership, and was only able eventually to mobilise the policy process as a result both of cross-party support in Parliament and of agreements between party leaders. But the long delays through the 1976-77 session can be more directly attributed to division within the governing party, and the slow development was experienced in spite of the substantial cross-party majority that was available. During the passage of the bill, the existence of a bi-partisan minority opposition seriously threatened the pace at which the bill moved on its course; however the bill was amended not in response to this pressure, but only as a result of a broad parliament-based influence. The absence of a single-party majority therefore affected this legislative process, though it should be observed that the same is true to some extent for the whole range of policy-making since February 1974. The consequences were important in terms of delaying the process, and in terms of non-decision-making; but the policy changes emerged for other reasons.

The effect of a cross-party cleavage in parliament interacts with the third explanation for the nature of the policy process — the dominance of political forces in the policy process. In the pre-legislative phase, it was found that the Government dominated the policy-process in a negative way, and was able successfully to resist the pressures for action from the still diffuse cross-party parliamentary majority; the creation of a Select Committee was a cover behind which Government control was being exerted. During the passage of the bill, real gestures were made toward parliamentary control over the choice of the electoral system, but in the event traditional party cleavages were significant, if not predominant; and the Government was able to use the action of the anti-Market opposition to avoid making decisions on some issues. Thus the policy process remained substantially in the hands of the Government and its Party, despite the apparent dominance of Parliament.

The legislation of the European Assembly Elections Act was a thoroughly unusual process, even by the standards of major policy and constitutional bills. It was evidently the desire of members to treat it in this exceptional manner, and in deliberating thoroughly on the issue — and thus delaying its passage — they were reflecting the initial popular indifference. The process appeared to be dominated by Parliament, and indeed the legitimation of the issue arose from the expression of a substantial majority support. But the process was in reality controlled primarily by Government, which used the semblance of parliamentary-control as a front, to coerce the dissident minority in Cabinet and to appease the vociferous forces in the Labour Party machine.

The implications of the direct elections legislative process

A month before the direct elections were held in June 1979, the minority Labour Government was defeated in a general election which swept in a majority Conservative Government. In the analysis of this political change, the contribution of divisions within the Labour ranks has been emphasised. Although the factional disputes between left and right within the Labour Party are a perennial 'problem', the twin conflicts over direct elections and devolution in the 1974-79 Parliament provided a major demonstration of internal conflict played out not only in Westminster, but also in the electoral campaigns for both the devolution referenda and the direct elections themselves. As a factor contributing to dissatisfaction with the Labour Party in Government, these divisions cannot be ignored.

However this legislative process provided an opportunity for the 'anti-marketeers' — and it is important to stress again that this concept embraces a set of attitudes ranging from 'withdrawal' to 'reform' — to polish their brasses and parade their troops. The movement thus maintained its momentum and demonstrated its importance to party leaders and to the public. As it turned out, this was significant for the period May-June 1979: for revelations about the British contribution to the Community budget helped to raise the EC as an electoral issue, and both major parties were obliged to express orientations that signified a clear 'confederalist' approach to European integration, making no concessions to the demands of the more committed Europeans.

The electoral system used in Great Britain failed to demonstrate any particularly attractive characteristics in the first direct elections. Indeed the gross distortion of representation, affecting the balance between the two major parties as well as ensuring the virtual non-representation of the minor parties, can only enhance the pressure for change. However in 1977-78, the parliamentary opposition to such change was profound, as the structure of debates and votes on electoral systems indicate (tables 11.13, 11.15.a, 11.15.b). It is difficult to envisage an increase in the willingness of the Commons to accept a more proportional system in the near future for European or indeed any other elections in Great Britain. It is also important to note that the former Prime Minister, Callaghan, expressed his conviction that a uniform system would not be seen within fifteen years. Whilst his successor, Margaret Thatcher, has not been so explicit, she has clearly indicated both her attachment to the plurality system even in this context, and her unwillingness to contemplate any further steps toward integration in Europe.

Hindsight enables us to observe very precisely the low level of mass support by the British electorate for the Community, when measured in the behavioural terms of the direct elections (turnout = 33 per cent) rather than the attitudinal terms of surveys (see chapter 2, Appendix). Whilst the absence of mass support in June 1979 is not *ipso facto* a barrier to change in the electoral system, it is evident that there is at this time no 'mandate' for new ventures in integration.

Finally, the legislative process itself, and the first experience of direct elections arising from it, have reiterated the divisions of opinion in Britain at both mass and elite levels on the European issue. The weakness in the commitment to supranationalism and to further integration in this broad sense places the future development of the Community in a new perspective. It is indeed ironical that the very measure propounded by pro-Europeanists as a means of enhancing the legitimacy of the European Community has in Britain served to clarify the limits to integration, at least in the short term.

Notes

1 I am indebted to the many Members of Parliament, party officials and Library and Information Officers of the Palace of Westminster who helped the research for this study, and to Dr Paul Cousins for comments.
2 J.A.G. Griffiths, *Parliamentary Scrutiny of Government Bills* (Allen and Unwin, London, 1977); S.A. Walkland, *The Legislative Process in Great Britain* (Allen and Unwin, London, 1968); S.A. Walkland and M. Ryle (eds) *The Commons in the Seventies* (Fontana, London, 1977).
3 B. Crick, *The Reform of Parliament* (Weidenfeld and Nicholson, London, 1970); Study of Parliament Group, *Committees in the House of Commons* (PEP, London, 1978); *First Report from the Select Committee on Procedure*, 1977-78, HC588-I (HMSO, London, 1978).
4 I. Burton and G. Drewry, 'Public Legislation: A Survey of the Sessions 1976/76 and 1976/77', *Parliamentary Affairs*, vol.31, 1978, pp 140-73; see also preceding articles in the series by these authors.
5 V. Herman, 'What Governments Say and What Governments Do: An Analysis of Post-war Queen's Speeches', *Parliamentary Affairs*, vol.28, 1974, pp 22-30; Burton and Drewry, op.cit.
6 The data cited in this section are drawn primarily from Griffiths, op.cit., in order to provide a consistent analysis: it is based on the same sessions 1967/68, 1968/69, 1970/71. Caution should be exercised in interpreting means, in view of the considerable dispersion of bills about the mean. Whilst some change has occurred since 1974, the overall distributions are not substantially affected.
7 A 'Major Division' is defined as one in which there are fifty or more votes against the main question or for an amendment (Drewry in Walkland and Ryle, op.cit., p.82). For the nine Sessions 1968-1976, Drewry found on average ten Major Divisions per annum. Cross-voting has increased, particularly since 1970, see P. Norton, *Dissension in the House of Commons, 1945-74*, (Macmillan, London, 1975), p.609, though it has not affected 'Major Divisions' seriously.
8 V. Herman, 'Backbench and Opposition Amendments to Government Legislation' in R. Leonard and V. Herman, (eds), *The Backbencher and Parliament* (Macmillan, London, 1972), p.153.
9 Approximately half of all amendments are moved at Report Stage, see Griffiths, op.cit., p.146.
10 Griffiths, op.cit., p.145.
11 Griffiths, op.cit., pp 192-3.
12 Griffiths, op.cit., p.229, cites a number of examples from the session 1970-71, when substantial amendments were introduced by the Lords to the Industrial Relations Bill and to the Immigration Bill.
13 See Burton and Drewry, op.cit.
14 J. Palmer, 'Allocation of Time: the Guillotine and Voluntary Timetabling', *Parliamentary Affairs*, vol.23, 1970, pp 232-47.
15 M. Hagger, 'Legislating for Direct Elections: the Passage of a Constitutional Bill', forthcoming.
16 A. King, *Britain Says Yes* (American Enterprise Institute, Washington DC, 1977); U. Kitzinger, *Diplomacy and Persuasion* (Thames and Hudson, London, 1973).
17 T. Nairn, *The Left Against Europe* (Penguin, Harmondsworth, 1973).
18 R. Rose, *Politics in England Today* (Faber, London, 1974).
19 R. Jowell and G. Hoinville, *Britain into Europe* (Croom Helm, London, 1976).
20 A. King, op.cit.
21 R. Inglehart, *The Silent Revolution* (Princeton U.P., Princeton NJ, 1977).
22 Data are drawn from the Biennial Eurobarometer, published by the European Commission. See also note 26.
23 U. Kitzinger, op.cit., *passim*.

24 P. Norton, op.cit., no.196; and D. Butler and U. Kitzinger, *The 1975 Referendum* (Macmillan, London, 1976).
25 In a letter to J. Mendelson, a 'senior Conservative' wrote: 'I must express . . . my profound disappointment with my own party organisation, because every attempt I have made to have a proper motion against direct elections debated at our annual conference has been ruled out of order by the Standing Orders Committee of my own party'. (J. Mendelson, vol.939, HC Deb., c.1855, 24 November 1977).
26 Attitudes to the EC have been highly volatile, and party electorates are particularly affected by the presence of their party in government. Nevertheless, Conservative mass support has always been significantly stronger than its Labour counterpart. See: R.G. Shepherd, *Public Opinion and European Integration*, (Saxon House, Farnborough, 1975).
27 U. Kitzinger, op.cit., pp 280-2.
28 P. Byrd, 'The Labour Party and the European Community', *Journal of Common Market Studies*, vol.13, 1975, pp 469-83.
29 M. Hagger and M. Wing, 'Legislative Roles and Clientele Orientations in the European Parliament', *Legislative Studies Quarterly*, vol.4, 1979, pp 165-95.
30 *The Times*, 1 October 1977, p.4.
31 Cabinet votes *for* Second Reading, 7 July 1977:
    J. Callaghan†, D. Healey†, M. Rees†, D. Owen*, S. Williams*, E. Varley†, R. Mason*, J. Morris†, F. Mulley≠, D. Ennals*, E. Dell*, J. Barnett*, R. Hattersley*, W. Rodgers*, H. Lever*.
Cabinet votes *against* Second Reading:
    M. Foot†, A. Benn†, P. Shore†, A. Booth†, J. Silkin†, S. Orme†.
Not voting: Lord E. Jones†, Lord Peart, B. Millan†.
(* = Aye, † = No, ≠ = Abstain; in vote on joining EC, 28 October 1971).
32 D. Butler and U. Kitzinger, op.cit., p 81n.
33 D. Butler and M. Pinto-Duschinsky, *The British General Election of 1970* (Macmillan, London, 1971), p.440.
34 Vol.934, HC Deb., c.1332, 6 July 1977.
35 Dafydd Wigley, vol.908, HC Deb., c.988, 30 March 1976.
36 D. Butler and U. Kitzinger, op.cit., p.156.
37 Eurobarometre, *passim*.
38 P. Norton, op.cit.
39 Cmnd. 6003.
40 The commitment to use 'best endeavours' to implement direct elections by the original target date of May/June 1978 was made during the negotiations by the Council in the summer of 1976. It was cited in the preamble to the White Paper, Cmnd. 6768, April 1977.
41 Wilson, reply to parliamentary question by Marten, vol.888, HC Deb., c.1478, 18 March 1975.
42 Vol.892, HC Deb., c.1404, 21 May 1975.
43 Attitude to the European Community was defined both by analysis of this speech and by their vote on the principle of joining the Community (8 October 1971), and by the two votes on Second Reading of this bill. In most cases of inconsistency, Members declared their change of position, and the contemporaneous attitude was taken.
44 R. Hattersley, Minister, Foreign and Commonwealth Office, vol.908, HC Deb., c.1230, 30 March 1976.
45 M. Stewart, vol.908, HC Deb., c.927, 29 March 1976.
46 R. Jenkins, vol.908, HC Deb., c.1143, 30 March 1976.
47 The more vigorous anti-marketeers insisted on the use of the term 'European Assembly' as a symbol of inferiority to the term 'Parliament' which they reserved for the Westminster Parliament. It also happens to be the official title used in legislative texts, since the English translation of the Treaty of Rome employs the term in Art. 138.
48 G. Barnett, vol.908, HC Deb., c.980, 29 March 1976.
49 Vol.908, HC Deb., cc.900-1036, 1119-1240, *passim*, 29, 30 March 1976.
50 Legal advice in fact suggested that it might be *illegal* for direct elections to be held under a *non-uniform* electoral system!
51 Most other Parliaments were obliged to pass two separate Acts — one for ratification and one for the electoral system. See chapter 13.
52 E. Powell, vol.908, HC Deb., c.1145, 30 March 1976.
53 In *procedural* terms the decision to treat a bill as of major constitutional importance is taken by the Government, after negotiation in the 'Usual Channels' through the Whips' Office (Griffiths, op.cit., pp 31-4). Nevertheless the structure and orientation of parliamentary opinion are significant elements in the political equation. We were inclined to describe the method based on the analysis of MP's speeches as *reputationalist*; but debate may be affected not only by attitude, but also by *strategy*. In practice the validity of the analysis is not threatened, for it is only the anti-Market faction(s) which are affected by strategic action, and their 'strategic' obstructionism reinforces their basic 'attitude' that 'direct election' was a constitutional issue.

54 For a full analysis, see: M. Hagger, 'Investigation by Committee: the case of the Select Committee of Direct Elections', forthcoming.
55 See especially B. Crick, *The Reform of Parliament*, 2nd ed. (Weidenfeld and Nicholson, London, 1970), and Select Committee on Procedure, First Report, HC 588 I-III, 1977-78.
56 N. Johnson, 'Select Committees as Tools of Parliamentary Reform: some further reflections' in S.A. Walkland and M. Ryle, op.cit., chapter 9.
57 HC 588-I, 1978. The specialised committee system was implemented in 1979.
58 I. Burton and G. Drewry, op.cit., p.160.
59 David Steel, leader of the Liberal Party, argued that the Labour Government was in most desperate straits: see D. Steel, 'An Experiment in Power', *The Observer*, 8 April 1979, p.33.
60 *The Times*, 23 March 1977.
61 The bill failed as a result of delay and obstruction tactics by a bi-partisan opposition. See G. Duncan, 'The Committee Stage of the Scotland and Wales Bill (1976-77)', The Waverley Papers, no.1, University of Edinburgh, n.d.
62 See G. Duncan, op.cit.
63 D. Hurd (Con, SC) 13 December 1977: vol.941, HC Deb., c.319.
64 The demand for such a clause was inspired by the Amendment introduced by the Gaullist leader, Debré, into the French text.
65 The analysis of this and other issues suggests the following relationship between debate and outcome in the legislature:

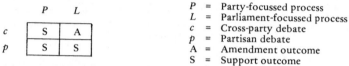

	P	L
c	S	A
p	S	S

P = Party-focussed process
L = Parliament-focussed process
c = Cross-party debate
p = Partisan debate
A = Amendment outcome
S = Support outcome

66 The 'New Clause 8', which became Clause 6 of the Act, reads: 'i. No treaty which provides for any increase in the powers of the Assembly shall be ratified by the United Kingdom unless it has been approved by an Act of Parliament. ii. In this section "treaty" includes any international agreement, and any protocol or annex to a treaty or international agreement'.
67 The distribution of seats to the four nations in proportion to population was not left merely as an instruction to the Boundary Commission, but was specified in the bill in terms of the number of seats assigned to each nation.
68 See the debate on increasing the representation of Northern Ireland in the House of Commons: vol.960, HC Deb., cc 1741-1916; House of Commons (Redistribution of Seats Bill).
69 D. Brew, 'National Parliamentary Scrutiny of European Community legislation: the case of the UK Parliament' in V. Herman and R. van Schendelen (eds), *The European Parliament and the National Parliaments* (Saxon House, Farnborough, 1979).
70 A minor second amendment was in fact conceded, prior to the Third Reading, to the First Schedule of the bill. The Government provided that Statutory Instruments regulating electoral procedures be the subject of affirmative resolutions of both Houses (Schedule I.2(6)).

The United Kingdom Parliament: some readings

S.A. Walkland and M. Ryle (eds), *The Commons in the Seventies* (Faber, London, 1977). A useful study of a number of different areas of the operation of the Parliament and its Members.

S.A. Walkland, *The Legislative Process in Great Britain* (Allen and Unwin, London, 1968). An excellent account emphasising the political context in which legislation is made.

R. Leonard and V. Herman (eds), *The Backbencher and Parliament* (Macmillan, London, 1972). A collection of short articles by academics and Members.

J.A.G. Griffiths, *The Parliamentary Scrutiny of Government Bills* (Allen and Unwin, London, 1974). A systematic analysis of three parliamentary sessions.

B. Crick, *The Reform of Parliament* (Weidenfeld and Nicholson, 2nd ed, London 1968). A critique of the unspecialised approach to parliamentarism in Britain.

S.A. Walkland (ed.), *The House of Commons in the Twentieth Century* (Oxford University Press, Oxford 1979). An historical account of recent change.

12 Direct Elections: Outcomes and Prospects

Valentine Herman and Juliet Lodge

The impact of direct elections to the European Parliament on the European Community and its Member States has been felt at two levels: the national and the supranational. Most immediately and obviously, the decision to hold direct elections initiated political processes in the Member States which culminated in the formulation and passage of a series of national electoral laws facilitating the holding of direct elections according to national electoral provisions especially adapted for the purpose. However, the way in which some Member Governments feared that direct elections would affect the balance of power among the EC's institutions both conditioned aspects of the national electoral laws drafted for direct elections and stimulated a search for means of ensuring that the European Parliament did not develop into a separate, and possibly, rival base of political allegiance and authority.

Our objectives in this penultimate chapter are twofold. Initially, we will undertake a comparison of the main characteristics of the Member States' direct election legislation with a view to highlighting their complexity and the discrepancies between them.[1] Subsequently, we will consider the prospects for the European Community adopting a 'uniform electoral procedure' for direct elections in 1984.[2]

The Member States' direct election legislation[3]

Article 2 of the Act of 20 September, 1976, distributed the seats in the enlarged European Parliament among the Member States. From table 12.1 it can be seen that some countries further distributed their seats in various regions: in Belgium, between the French- and Flemish-speaking colleges; in the United Kingdom, between constituencies in England, Scotland and Wales, as well as between Northern Ireland in which a multi-member constituency was established. The Federal Republic of Germany and Denmark also made special provisions for West Berlin (whose three MEPs were appointed by the Berlin House of Deputies) and Greenland, respectively.

In France, Luxembourg and the Netherlands the whole country formed a single electoral area, as to all extents and purposes did

Table 12.1
Seats, constituencies and electoral systems

Country	Number and distribution of seats	Number of constituencies	Electoral system
Belgium	24[1] 11 French-speaking colleges (incl. German-speaking college) 13 Flemish-speaking colleges	3[2]	Proportional representation: d'Hondt system, in each of the two electoral colleges. Inhabitants of Brussels vote for one of the colleges. Each voter gives a single vote to a list or to a candidate. Voting is compulsory.
Denmark	16 15 Denmark 1 Greenland	2[3]	1. Proportional representation in Denmark: d'Hondt system. Each voter gives a single vote to a list or to a candidate.[4] 2. Simple majority system in Greenland. Each voter gives a single vote to a candidate.
Federal Republic of Germany	81[5] 78 Germany 3 West Berlin	1[6]	1. Proportional representation: d'Hondt system amongst party lists for the Federal area and different regional lists for the Länder.[7] Lists receiving fewer than 5 per cent of the votes are not allotted seats.[8] Each voter gives a single vote to a list of candidates. 2. The Berlin Members are nominated by the House of Deputies of Berlin.
France	81	1[9]	Proportional representation: d'Hondt system. Lists receiving fewer than 5 per cent of the votes are not allotted seats.[10] Each elector gives a single vote to a list of candidates.
Ireland	15	4[11]	Proportional representation: single transferable vote system. Each voter votes for one candidate and indicates his or her preference for the other candidate.
Italy	81	5	Proportional representation: natural quotient system.[12] Each voter gives a single vote to between one and three candidates.[13]
Luxembourg	6	1	Proportional representation: d'Hondt system (Hagenbach-Bischoff variation). Each voter has as many votes as there are candidates to be elected. The votes can be given to one list, distributed among the candidates on one list, or distributed among other lists. Voting is compulsory.

Table 12.1 (cont.)

Country	Number and distribution of seats	Number of constituencies	Electoral system
Nether-lands	25	1	Proportional representation: d'Hondt system. Each voter gives a single vote to a list or to a candidate.
United Kingdom	81 66 England 8 Scotland 4 Wales 3 N. Ireland	79 78 Great Britain 1 N. Ireland	1. Simple majority system in 78 single-member constituencies in England, Scotland and Wales. Each voter gives a single vote to a candidate. 2. Proportional representation: single transferable vote system in Northern Ireland (3 MEPs elected from a single constituency). Each voter votes for one candidate and indicates his or her preference for the other candidates.

Source: See note 6.

NOTES:

1 Belgium: inhabitants of Brussels can decide individually which college to vote in.
2 Belgium: one for each of the French and Flemish-speaking colleges, and one for Brussels.
3 Denmark: one for each of Denmark and Greenland.
4 Denmark: the 15 seats are first allotted to the different parties (election alliances count as a single party) by the d'Hondt method. The seats for each party are then allocated among the candidates on the list on the basis of the preferences. Where a preference is not expressed, the vote is allocated on the basis of the order of candidates on the list.
5 Federal Republic of Germany: to be nominated by the House of Deputies of West Berlin.
6 Federal Republic of Germany: parties can submit lists for the individual Länder, or one single list for the whole of the Federal Republic.
7 Federal Republic of Germany: all the votes for the national list, or the separate Land lists, of each party are added together. (A party can, however, decide to have one or more Land lists treated as a separate party.) Seats are then allocated proportionally to the parties by the d'Hondt method. The seats allocated to a party which has presented Land lists are distributed among the different Länder, again proportionately. Candidates are elected in the order in which they appear on the list. A candidate elected twice (for more than one Land) is deemed elected in the Land where he or she appears highest on the list.
8 Federal Republic of Germany: parties receiving more than 0.5 per cent of the votes have their election expenses reimbursed by the Federal Government at the rate of DM 3.5 per voter.
9 France: the constituency — 'the territory of the Republic' — includes all overseas departments and territories.
10 France: lists of candidates receiving more than 5 per cent of the votes have their expenditure on posters, leaflets, etc., reimbursed by the State.
11 Ireland: with 5, 4, 3 and 3 Members, respectively.
12 Italy: in the 5 constituencies votes are counted and seats allocated at the national level according to the natural quotient (Hare) system.
13 Italy: in one constituency voters can give their vote to three candidates of their choices, in three other constituencies to two candidates, and in the fifth constituency for one candidate. There is also special provision for preferential votes in areas with linguistic minorities.
14 United Kingdom, Members from England, Scotland and Wales are elected from single-member constituencies. The 3 Members from Northern Ireland are elected from one constituency.

Table 12.2

Electoral systems for national and European elections

Country	National electoral system	European electoral system
Belgium	Proportional representation: d'Hondt system in multi-member constituencies	Proportional representation: d'Hondt system in multi-member constituencies
Denmark	1. Proportional representation: St Lague system at constituency level for 135 seats. 2. Additional distribution of 40 supplementary seats at national level to ensure proportionality	Proportional representation (in Denmark): d'Hondt system in which the whole country forms one constituency
Federal Republic	1. Simple majority system in 248 single-member constituencies. 2. Proportional representation: d'Hondt system at Land level among party lists for remaining 248 seats. 5 per cent 'threshold clause'.	Proportional representation: d'Hondt system amongst party lists for the Federal area and different regional lists for the Länder. The whole Federal Republic forms one constituency. 5 per cent 'threshold clause'.
France	Absolute majority on first ballot, simple majority on second ballot in single-member constituencies.	Proportional representation: d'Hondt system in which the whole country forms one constituency. 5 per cent 'threshold clause'.
Ireland	Proportional representation: single transferable vote in multi-member constituencies	Proportional representation: single transferable vote in multi-member constituencies
Italy	1. Proportional representation: d'Hondt system at constituency level. 2. Additional distribution by highest remainder method of supplementary seats at national level to ensure proportionality.	Proportional representation: natural quotient system in multi-member constituencies
Luxembourg	Proportional representation: Hagenbach-Bischoff and highest quotient (modified d'Hondt) systems in multi-member constituencies	Proportional representation: d'Hondt system (Hagenbach-Bischoff variation) in which the whole country forms one constituency

Table 12.2 (cont.)

Country	National electoral system	European electoral system
Netherlands	1. Proportional representation: electoral quota system at district level. 2. Additional distribution of seats at national level by d'Hondt system.	Proportional representation: d'Hondt system in which the country forms one constituency
United Kingdom	Simple majority system in single-member constituencies	1. Simple majority system in single-member constituencies in England, Scotland and Wales. 2. Proportional representation: single transferable vote in one Northern Ireland multi-member constituency.

Sources: See notes 6 and 8.

Entries for the national electoral system refer to the systems used for the lower – or only – chamber in the Member States.

Denmark (with the exception of Greenland). In the Federal Republic, although the whole country (except for West Berlin) formed one constituency, the parties could submit lists of candidates for individual Länder or single lists for the whole Federal area.

Three other countries elected their MEPs in multi-member constituencies: in Belgium, there were three constituencies — one constituency for each of the French- and Flemish-speaking colleges, and one for Brussels' (which is officially bilingual, although in practice predominantly French-speaking) — and two electorates; and in Ireland and Italy, constituencies were drawn up on the basis of a combination of regional and population criteria. The seventy-eight MEPs elected from England, Scotland and Wales were each elected from a single-member constituency by a simple majority system, whereas in Northern Ireland, three MEPs were elected by single transferable vote from one constituency.

With the exception of the United Kingdom (but excluding Northern Ireland) all of the Member States adopted a system of proportional representation. Five of them — Belgium, Denmark, the Federal Republic, France and the Netherlands — used the d'Hondt electoral formula.[4] Luxembourg adopted a variant of the d'Hondt method, the Hagenbach-Bischoff system. In Italy, seats were allocated at the national level according to the natural quotient (Hare) system, and in Ireland the electoral formula was the single transferable vote. In the latter country voters ordered their choices between candidates and parties: in the other Member States they chose a single party list or candidate. In the Federal Republic and France, the order in which candidates appeared on a party list could not be changed by the voters. Belgian, Danish, Italian and Dutch voters had the possibility of altering the order of names on the party list. By contrast, in Luxembourg, each voter had as many votes as the number of candidates to be elected, and could distribute these votes among the candidates on one list, or vote for individual candidates on another list ('panachage'), or simply vote for a list.

The major difference between the electoral systems that the Member States use for national elections[5] and European elections can be seen from table 12.2. Perhaps the greatest change from the system used for national elections was made by France, which replaced a two-ballot majority/plurality system in single-member constituencies, with a proportional representation system in which the whole country formed one constituency. In addition, it adopted a 5 per cent 'threshold clause'. Six other countries (Denmark, Ireland, the Federal Republic, Luxembourg, Italy, and the Netherlands) increased the 'proportionality' of existing proportional representation systems by either changing the nature of the electoral formula through which votes were converted into seats; distributing the seats over the whole country; or increasing the size of the constituencies. The aim was to ensure a more equitable distribution of seats among the parties — especially the smaller parties — than might otherwise have been obtained, while the French and German 5 per cent 'threshold clauses' disqualified the smallest parties from winning seats. The election laws of the other Member States had a similar in-built 'threshold' effect: for a party to have won a seat in the Netherlands and Denmark (excluding Greenland, and the possibility of forming electoral 'alliances') it needed to have polled a minimum of 4 per cent and 6.7 per cent of the votes, respectively.

Establishing the whole country as one constituency also increased the proportionality.[6] In part, the holding of European elections in a single nation-wide constituency was a consequence of the smaller number of seats each Member State has in the European Parliament compared to their own national parliaments. But it also reflected a desire to minimise the 'wastage' of votes in individual constituencies, and increased the chances of small parties achieving representation. The latter was a particular concern in one particular area when the United Kingdom passed its direct election legislation. Although the simple majority system in single-member constituencies (the first-past-the-post system which maximises the wastage of votes in individual constituencies and reduces the chances of minor parties from winning seats) used for general elections in England, Scotland and Wales was retained for elections to the European Parliament, the single transfer-abel vote system was introduced in Northern Ireland in an attempt to ensure the election of a representative of the minority Roman Catholic community to the European Parliament.[7]

In all Member States, candidates for election to the European Parliament had to be citizens of the country in which they stood for election. Furthermore Belgian candidates had to deposit a 'linguistic declaration' containing their confirmation of being Dutch-speaking — if presenting a nomination for the Flemish electorate — or French- or German-speaking — if presenting a nomination for the French electorate. In four countries candidates had to be at least twenty-one years of age (Belgium, Ireland, Luxembourg and the United Kingdom). In two, Italy and the Netherlands, the minimum age was twenty-five. For the Federal Republic and Denmark it was eighteen, and for France twenty-three. With the exception of Denmark and the Federal Republic, the minimum age for candidature was higher than the minimum voting age. Only Belgium changed the minimum age for candidature in the European elections (twenty-one years) compared to that in national elections (twenty-five for the House of Representatives, forty for the Senate).

Table 12.3

Candidates, votes and vacancies

Country	Eligibility for candidature: age	Nomination of candidates by	Entitlement to vote: 1. Age	2. Other	Filling of vacant seats
Belgium	21	List nominated by: 1. Members of Parliament 2. 5,000 registered voters	18	Belgian citizens resident abroad, but with a domecile in Belgium can vote by proxy	Substitutes
Denmark	18	Lists (maximum 20 candidates) nominated by: 1. Political parties currently represented in the Folketing; 2. Political parties not represented in the Folketing supported by at least 2 per cent of the voters at the last general election	18	Danish citizens resident in other EC countries[2]	Next-in-line of the party which previously held the seat
Federal Republic of Germany	18	List nominated by:[3] 1. Political parties (for the whole of the Federal area, or separate lists for each of the Länder); 2. Political associations organised on a membership basis within the EC.	18	German citizens resident in other EC countries	Substitutes[4]
France	23	Nominations must be submitted by the candidates at the head of the list or their representatives. Election deposit: 100,000Fr; returnable if more than 5 per cent of votes polled.	18	French citizens resident abroad at French consulates	Next-in-line of the party which previously held the seat
Ireland	21	Candidates may nominate themselves, or be nominated by a third party. Election deposit, £1,000: returnable if more than 33 per cent of votes polled.	18	Citizens of other EC countries resident in Ireland	Appointed by the Dail.[5]

Table 12.3 (cont.)

Country	Eligibility for candidature: age	Nomination of candidates by	Entitlement to vote: 1. Age	Entitlement to vote: 2. Other	Filling of vacant seats
Italy	25	Candidates nominated by: 1. Political parties; 2. Individuals supported by 30,000 voters	18	1. Italian citizens resident in other EC countries at Italian consulates. 2. Italians resident in non-EC countries may return to Italy to vote.	Next-in-line of the party which previously held the seat
Luxembourg	21	Lists (signed by 100 electors) nominated by: 1. Political parties; 2. Individuals	18	None	Next-in-line of the party which previously held the seat
Netherlands	25	Lists (maximum 40 candidates) nominated by political parties (and supported by 25 signatures). Election deposit, 18,000 Fl., if the list is submitted by a party neither represented in the Second Chamber nor the European Parliament; returnable if more than 0.75 per cent of the votes are polled.	18	1. Dutch citizens resident in other EC countries (personal or proxy vote) 2. Citizens of other EC countries resident in the Netherlands.	Next-in-line of the party which previously held the seat
United Kingdom	21	Candidates (supported by 30 electors from each constituency) nominated by: 1. Political parties; 2. Individuals. Election deposit, £600; returnable if more than 12.5 per cent of votes polled.	18	Irish citizens resident in the United Kingdom	By-election

Source: see note 6.

NOTES

1 Belgium: the Members of Parliament must belong to the corresponding linguistic group: the registered voters, 1,000 in each of five provinces.
2 Denmark: voters living outside Denmark are on the electoral register for Copenhagen.
3 Federal Republic of Germany: if the party or association is not already represented in the Bundestag or Landtag with at least five seats nominations must, in addition, be supported by 4,000 signatures in the case of a Federal list, or 2,000 signatures in the case of a Land list.
4 Federal Republic: if no substitute is available, a vacancy is fixed by the next candidate on the list.
5 Ireland: if the former occupant of a seat was held by a representative of a political party, that party has the right to propose a successor to the Dail.

247

By contrast, the minimum voting age was eighteen in all the Member States. For European elections, Belgium reduced the minimum voting age of twenty-one for national elections to eighteen. According to the Government this was deliberately undertaken to bring the Belgian election law into line with that of the other Member States, and — by the granting of a basic political right — to encourage more citizens to be in favour of Europe. In Denmark, a referendum in September, 1978, resulted in the lowering of the voting age from twenty to eighteen.

In six Member States the franchise was restricted to nationals. In Ireland, resident citizens of other EC countries could vote for Irish MEPs. Citizens of other EC countries could vote in the Netherlands if they were resident there, no longer met the residence requirements of their own countries, and would otherwise have been debarred from voting. In the United Kingdom, the granting of the suffrage to other EC citizens was much more restricted; only Irish citizens resident there were entitled to vote (in the same way that they may in national elections). Contrary to the practice in general elections, Members of the House of Lords could both vote in, and stand as candidates for, direct elections to the European Parliament (as for local elections).

In Luxembourg the right to vote for Luxembourg MEPs was restricted to nationals. The same was true of the United Kingdom, with the qualification that the European franchise was extended to government officials and members of the armed forces overseas. Since British nationals working in the EC's institutions are not British government employees, the franchise was not extended to them under this provision. French citizens resident abroad could vote at French consulates, whereas their Belgian counterparts could only vote if they maintained a domicile in Belgium. Citizens of Denmark, the Federal Republic and the Netherlands resident abroad could only vote in direct elections if they were resident in an EC country: in Denmark, such voters were placed on the electoral register for Copenhagen; in the Netherlands, all Dutch citizens living abroad who have never had domicile in a Dutch community were registered in The Hague. Italian citizens resident in another EC country could vote at Italian consulates (by agreement between the Italian Government and the government of each EC country), and allowance was also made for citizens to return to their country to cast their vote.

In three countries the nomination of candidates was restricted to political parties and political organisations: Denmark, where candidates could be nominated by political parties already represented in the Folketing, or other parties with the support of at least 2 per cent of the voters (about 65,000) at the last general election: the Netherlands, where lists of candidates had to be supported by twenty-five signatures; and the Federal Republic, where parties could nominate lists for the whole Federal area or for each Länder, and where political associations organised on a membership basis throughout the EC — for example, transnational party federations — could also nominate candidates. Elsewhere nominations had to be endorsed by a specific number of signatures of registered voters — thirty for each candidate in each constituency in the United Kingdom; 5,000 in Belgium (1,000 from each province); and 30,000 in Italy. Additionally, four countries (France, Ireland, the Netherlands, and the United Kingdom) required an election deposit from candidates or parties which was returnable if more than a certain percentage of votes was polled. In the Netherlands the deposit (of 18,000 Fl.) was only required if the list was submitted by a party, not represented in the Second Chamber or the European Parliament. Regulations which required a high number of signatures from voters in support of a nomination, and/or a high electoral deposit, undoubtedly deterred parties which were nascent, small, locally-organised, or short of finance from contesting the election.

In France and the Federal Republic, the direct election legislation enabled more parties to contest the election than would have been possible under the laws applicable for national elections. In France, for example, eleven parties met the conditions necessary to offer lists of candidates: only four of them would have been able to do so had the provisions concerning political parties in the national election legislation been in effect for the European elections.

Should a seat become vacant during the European Parliament's term of office, Denmark, France, Italy, Luxembourg and the Netherlands have provided that it will be filled by the next candidate on the list of the party which previously held the seat. In Belgium and the Federal Republic, vacant seats will be filled by substitute candidates: in the Federal Republic these can be designated at the same time as each candidate on the list and, in the absence of any such substitute, by the next candidate on the list. In Ireland, the Dail will fill vacancies with the party previously holding the seat having the right to propose a successor. Only the United Kingdom provided for by-elections to the European Parliament: a process facilitated by the single-member constituency system.

Although all of the Member States have a series of special rules for national elections — covering, for example, access to the media, campaign expenditure, and the duration of the campaign — only the Federal Republic, France and the United Kingdom adopted rules similar to those in their national election legislation for the direct elections. The German election law provided that parties winning at least 0.5 per cent of the votes have their election expenses paid for by the State at the rate of 3.5 DM per eligible voter: money is distributed to the parties on the basis of their percentage vote at the last Bundestag election. The French direct election law provided, *inter alia,* that the direct election campaign officially opened a fortnight before polling day; that at the start of the campaign, committees (whose costs were met by the State) would be established in each department or territory and would be responsible for distributing all election campaign material; that lists of candidates receiving more than 5 per cent of the votes would be reimbursed expenditure on posters, leaflets, etc; and that the State would provide broadcasting time on the national and radio television networks to each list of candidates. In the United Kingdom, the campaign expenditure of each candidate was limited to £15,000 per constituency plus two pence for each registered voter.

Towards a common electoral system

The adoption of a series of national laws on direct elections by the Member States was contrary to the spirit of the Rome Treaty insofar as the original (and long thwarted) intention had been to elect Members of the European Parliament by direct universal suffrage according to a common electoral law applicable throughout the EC. As we have seen in the preceding chapters, the Member Governments' refusal to contemplate the adoption of such a law resulted in a series of national laws being adopted. The discrepancies between the individual laws resulted in some States' quotas of MEPs being less representative than others of the spread of electoral opinion in the Member State (as for example in Britain where the Liberal Party won no seats in the European Parliament in spite of polling 13 per cent of the votes). Moreover, the extent to which political expediency in the Member States influenced the content of the various laws makes the task of drafting a common electoral law for subsequent election especially problematic.

The 'nationalistic' emphasis of most electoral laws for the first direct elections to the European Parliament necessarily complicates the question of expeditiously drafting a common electoral law for the second direct elections in 1984. Quite apart from the difficulties associated with distributing seats amongst the Member States, financing the elections, the enfranchisement of voters, and the type of electoral system to be adopted, problems arise out of certain provisions incorporated into national laws governing the 1979 elections. These provisions, moreover, were designed as political expedients in response to anti-EC views in some of the Member States (notably France and the United Kingdom) and were designed to postpone the adoption of a common electoral law until such time as all the national Parliaments explicitly consent to such a measure.

The French electoral law illustrates this point well. Article 1 of the

Law on the Election of Representatives to the Assembly of the European Communities, stipulated that 'The method of electing the French representatives to the Assembly of the European Communities, as laid down in this law, may only be altered by virtue of a further law'. In the same national spirit, Article 16 restricted participation, by way of propaganda, in the direct elections to 'the French political parties and to the lists taking part'.

Article 6 of the British European Assembly Election Act, 1978, stated that 'No treaty which provides for increases in the powers of the Assembly shall be ratified by the United Kingdom unless it has been approved by an Act of Parliament'. Similar constraints on the development of the European Parliament's powers were contained in Article 2 of the French Act which ratified the Council of Ministers' decision of 20 September, 1976, to hold direct elections: 'Any alteration in the powers of the Assembly of the European Communities, as defined at the date of signature of the Act introducing elections by direct universal suffrage of the representatives of the Assembly, ratification or approval of which has not been authorised in accordance with the provisions of the Treaties of Rome and which has not, where necessary, been supported by a revision of the Constitution in conformity with the decision of the Conseil Constitutionnel of 30 December, 1976, shall be null and of no effect as regards France'.

These provisions prohibit the development of the European Parliament's powers in the foreseeable future, for they make any such development dependent not only upon the approval of the French and British Governments in the European Council and the Council of Ministers, but also on the approval of the French and British Parliaments. As long as these Parliaments see themselves as the protector of popular sovereignty, neither the supranational institutions of the EC in general, nor the directly elected European Parliament in particular will be permitted to develop their own powers in any way which might usurp the authority of the national Parliaments or undermine the foundations of national sovereignty. However, no national Parliament or Government has the ability to prevent the European Parliament exploiting either its own rules of procedure, Article 235 of the Rome Treaty, or the conciliation procedure with the Council of Ministers.

Anti-supranational sentiment expressed with respect to the drafting and passage of national legislation of direct elections derived from fears as to the scope of the European Parliament's powers after 1979, and the impact of direct elections on the EC's institutional balance. As we have seen, Anglo-French fears, in particular, were couched in terms of the preservation of national sovereignty, and its embodiment in a supreme national Parliament: they reflected concern lest changes to the EC's institutional balance be exploited by the European Parliament, possibly when drafting a common electoral law. Hence in drafting national laws for European elections some countries tried to control supranational developments through domestic legislation. We have noted that in the passage of direct election legislation, the French and British Governments inserted clauses having a different function: namely, to circumscribe the European Parliament's ability to carry out its tasks effectively by casting doubts on its right to interpret its own powers, and to seek their accretion as a matter of course. In other words, some Member Governments have seized upon the opportunity to pass direct election legislation as an excuse to prevent the European Parliament acquiring either an effective role in EC decision-making or a legislative function akin to, and possibly rivalling, those of national Parliaments in EC matters.

Notwithstanding these sentiments there remains the question of how subsequent direct elections to the European Parliament are to be conducted. Although the first direct elections took place in accordance with the electoral law independently adopted by each of the Member States, Article 138 (3) of the EEC Treaty states that 'The Assembly shall draw up proposals for elections by direct universal suffrage in accordance with a uniform procedure in all Member States', and Article 7 (1) of the 'Act Concerning the Election of the Representatives of the Assembly by Direct Universal Suffrage' requires the Assembly to 'draw up a proposal for a uniform electoral procedure'. Two interpretations of 'uniformity' are possible. Firstly, that the elections in the Member States will be carried out according to certain fundamental principles of democratic elections — that they should be free, equal, secret, direct and universal. This is in accordance with Schelto Patijn's statement that, 'The real political significance of direct European elections lies not in the extent to which they are uniform, but in the fact that they are held at all', and reinforces Mario Scelba's assertion that, 'It is easier to square the circle than to create a uniform electoral system which reconciles the proportional system with the majority one'.[9]

The second interpretation of 'uniformity' is that there is a standardised, or common, electoral law for all of the Member States. Indeed in its opinion on the 1975 draft Convention on the election of members to the European Parliament by direct universal suffrage, the Legal Affairs Committee declared that, 'The concept of "uniformity" will acquire a different value when further parallels have developed between the election procedures of the individual member states. This approach therefore requires the development of a more standardised European election system at a later date'.[10] The direct election of the European Parliament in June, 1979, was uniform according to the first of these interpretations: subsequent direct elections are expected to be uniform according to the second of them when a single Community-wide electoral system has been adopted.

It is clear that the first direct elections were not 'European' elections, but rather separate elections in each of the nine Member States organised according to nationally determined electoral laws and criteria: the 'European' aspects of these elections lay in the fact that each was held simultaneously to elect national quotas of MEPs to a unique supranational European Parliament.

For a number of reasons the supranationality of the European elections was undermined. These included:

a) the Council of Ministers' initial distribution of seats in the enlarged European Parliament into 'mega-constituencies' coinciding with national boundaries;

b) each Member State determining its own legislation for direct elections and whether or not (and if so in what way) each mega-constituency was to be further subdivided;

c) the nomination of candidates by national parties rather than the transnational European party federations of which they may have been members;

d) the election campaign being fought on national (as opposed to supranational) lines by national parties and candidates, primarily emphasising national interests rather than an overarching concept of the EC.

The national nature of the elections was determined by their *legal basis* (a) and (b) above, and by their *political conduct* (c) and (d). Only changes in the first two of the above items – or more accurately in (b), as the position of the Member State *qua* Member State in the EC is likely to remain paramount in the foreseeable future – can, in a legal sense, lead to European elections under a uniform procedure or common electoral law as envisaged under Articles 138 (3) and 7 (1). Such a law, if it were truly uniform or common (according to the second interpretation set out above), would contain a set of regulations binding on each Member State concerning items such as the type of electoral system and electoral formula; the extent and nature of the suffrage; the delineation of electoral constituencies; the provision, control and auditing of election expenses; criteria of eligibility for candidature; the form of the ballot paper; the proclamation and validation of election results; incompatibilities of occupations and professions with membership of the European Parliament; the replacement of Members should seats become vacant; etc.[11]

Until a common law covering such items is adopted by the Member States elections will not be truly uniform; given the inordinately lengthy period it took the Member States to agree to the first direct elections it is unlikely that one will be adopted by the time of the second set of elections scheduled for 1984. These elections are also likely to be carried out according to common principles of democratic elections under national laws determined by each Member State. In the absence of a uniform electoral law, elections to the European Parliament in 1984 — and, perhaps, subsequently — can come to take on an increasingly 'European' character through the way they are conducted and fought, especially by national parties and transnational party federations. At present, however, evidence suggests that any uniform electoral law eventually adopted by the Member States will be based on both existing national electoral laws and the various laws adopted for the first direct election of the European Parliament — especially as national and European election calendars come to be juxtaposed.

The European Parliament will have to confront several problems in drafting a common electoral law. The three most intractable of these concern the enfranchisement of voters, the nature of any common electoral system, and the distribution of seats in the Parliament amongst the Member States. Indeed questions concerning who will vote and how their votes will be converted into seats are basic to the development of any EC electoral law.

Concerning the definition of EC citizenship and the enfranchisement of voters, France and the United Kingdom pose particular difficulties. The French — who are sceptical of the whole notion of the European Parliament — extended the franchise in the direct elections to French subjects overseas. If France extends the vote to such subjects in future European elections, and considers them Community citizens, then nationals from Gibraltar and Manx (British passport holders not resident in the UK) and other British subjects may seek equal rights. The question of who is to be enfranchised under a common electoral law, or who is to be regarded as an EC citizen will, at a minimum, necessitate re-scrutiny of the thorny and politically sensitive issue of determining British nationality. Related to the question of citizenship is the problem of the entitlement to vote of EC citizens living outside their own Member State. The European Parliament could advocate the adoption of either of three existing arrangements when drafting a common electoral law: the Irish–Dutch solution of extending the suffrage to citizens of other EC states; the Danish–German–Dutch one of allowing their own citizens to vote in the homeland; or the French and Italian ones of allowing their subjects living abroad to vote at consulates. In each instance, the problem of British passport holders in EC states awaiting entry to the United Kingdom would have to be faced.

A second problem concerns the nature of any common electoral system. Although either the national and/or European election laws of eight of the Member States are based on proportional representation, the past and continuing hostility of successive British Governments to the introduction of proportional representation for elections in the United Kingdom, militates against the eventual adoption of a variant of it for European elections. The question becomes not whether a common electoral system is possible, but rather under what conditions the British Parliament and Government could be persuaded to accept proportional representation for direct elections, recognising the possible implication of this for national, regional or local elections.

Even if a common electoral system is to be based on a variant of proportional representation, the problem still arises as to which particular variant will be chosen. No single system of proportional representation will be able to produce in the European Parliament a mirroring of the party systems which are different in each of the Member States and which have been determined by separate and distinct historical and socio-political forces: accordingly any common electoral system would distort parterns of national representation and, in particular, disadvantage small parties who would fail to cross the threshold of votes (whether built into the electoral law or not) necessary to win seats.

The different versions of proportional representation used for the first direct elections, suggest that there are at present insufficient parallels between them to advocate the adoption of a single proportional representation system. What must also be considered is the different results that would be produced — especially concerning the representation of regional, linguistic and secular minorities — in electing each Member State's quota of MEPs, by different proportional representation systems.

The proportionality of votes to seats that may be achieved by a common electoral system based on proportional representation is likely to be undermined unless there is a major redistribution of seats in the European Parliament amongst the Member States. For the first direct elections, the ratio of members of the population per MEP advantaged the small states (especially Luxembourg, with its six seats) and led to their over-representation in the European Parliament, at the expense of the larger ones which were consequently under-represented. Unless the Member States are able to agree on a reduction in the number of seats at present allocated to the smaller countries (which would result in some political forces in them not being represented in the European Parliament), a high degree of proportionality cannot be achieved between the number of inhabitants of each country and its number of MEPs without the membership of the Parliament being considerably increased.

Given the complexities of defining who is an EC citizen, agreeing on

Table 12.4
MEPs and population by country in the European Parliament

Country	MEPs	Per cent of total	Population ('000's)	Per cent of total	Population per MEP
Belgium	24	5.85	9,772	3.77	407,167
Denmark	16	3.9	5,052	1.95	315,750
Federal Republic of Germany	81	19.76	62,041	23.96	765,938
France	81	19.76	53,780	20.74	663,951
Ireland	15	3.66	3,086	1.19	205,733
Italy	81	19.76	55,361	21.38	683,469
Luxembourg	6	1.46	357	0.14	59,500
Netherlands	25	6.1	13,450	5.19	538,000
United Kingdom	81	19.76	56,056	21.65	692,049
EC	410	100	258,995	100	631,598

Source: European Elections 'Briefing', (European Parliament) no.1, January 1977, p.2.

an electoral system, and the need to re-allocate the seats amongst the Member States, it seems highly unlikely that the 1984 direct elections will be conducted according to a common electoral law. However, it is important to note that the Council Act of 20 September, 1976, contains a number of elements of a common law which have already been accepted by the Member States. These include:

— the term of office of each Parliament and its Members: Article 3 states that 'Representatives shall be elected for a term of five years'.

— the provision under Article 5 that, 'The office of representatives in the Assembly shall be compatible with membership of the Parliament of a Member State'.

— incompatibilities of office as listed under Article 6.

— the prohibition of double voting in Article 8, 'No one may vote more than once in any election of representatives to the Assembly'.

— the periods within which elections are to be held and votes to

—   be counted. Article 9 (1) provides that elections 'shall fall, within the same period starting on a Thursday morning and ending on the following Sunday', while Article 9 (2) states that 'The counting of votes shall not begin until after the close of polling in the Member State whose electors are the last to vote'.

The country studies in earlier chapters revealed that these items were not contentious in the legislation of direct elections in the Member States.

In addition, our earlier analysis in this chapter revealed that the election laws adopted by each of the Member States for the 1979 direct elections contained a number of similar or identical provisions: proportional representation by d'Hondt electoral system in multi-member regional or national constituencies; a minimum voting age of eighteen; the filling of vacant seats by substitutes or the next-in-line candidate of the party which previously held the seat; and the nomination of candidates.

The acceptability of whatever common electoral law the European Parliament may eventually draft will be conditioned not only by its technical provisions but also by the prevailing political atmosphere. Negotiations over the EC's enlargement may, for example, lead some Member Governments to advocate postponing the adoption of a common electoral law until EC applicants have joined the Community. Others, on similar grounds, or for reasons associated with a desire to ensure a continuing 'national' bias to direct elections, may favour any common electoral law having — at least for a transitional period — limited effect, and advocate conducting the 1984 elections according either to existing procedures, or to a set of common principles.[12] For example, a provision might be adopted having the force of a directive stipulating that the elections be conducted according to a system of proportional representation: the choice of variant being left to each Member State. Even if the directly elected Parliament is able to draft a common electoral law for the 1984 elections, unless this is agreed on by the Council of Ministers in 1980 or shortly after, and then submitted to the Member States for approval, it is unlikely that there will be sufficient time for the necessary parliamentary ratification processes to be completed.

However, MEPs may not be prepared to accept that anything other than a common electoral law binding in all respects and directly applicable in all the Member States would meet the *intention*, rather than the letter, of Article 138 of the Rome Treaty. Whereas in 1975, MEPs were prepared to interpret the notion of a common electoral procedure flexibly, and to accept that the first direct elections could be considered uniform to a degree even if conducted according to national electoral systems providing certain democratic criteria were observed, directly elected MEPs may very well note that this proviso was coupled with the tacit understanding, expressed by the Legal Affairs Committee of the Parliament in 1975, that this would be but a step towards the gradual introduction of a common procedure and a uniform law applicable throughout the Community: EC case law having established the acceptability of the introduction of a legal act in stages.

In drafting a common electoral law the European Parliament is likely to be guided by recommendations advanced in its 1975 Draft Convention on direct elections replacing that of 17 May 1960. Article 7 of the former gives rise to particular difficulties with respect to the interpretation of what is meant by a 'common electoral procedure'. Whereas, in 1960, the European Parliament concluded that a 'uniform procedure' was not synonymous with a 'uniform electoral system', by 1975 its view was that it was. However, Article 7, paragraph 2, of the 'Act Concerning the Election of the Representatives of the Assembly by Direct Universal Suffrage' refers to a uniform electoral *procedure* not system. If, as seems likely, the Parliament adheres to its 1975 view then conceivably any conflict with a Member State over the interpretation of this Article, as well as any problems subsequently arising from a conflict between national and EC electoral law, will be referred to the Court of Justice.

It is apparent that a common electoral law will have to reconcile discrepancies between Member States' existing electoral systems and laws. Moreover, it may also have to incorporate special clauses to meet requirements concerning linguistic/regional/secular representation in certain Member States. Indeed, in the immediate future direct elections are more likely to be held under either national laws sharing certain common principles and embracing the provisions of the 1976 Council Act, or a common electoral law with special provisions for particular Member States, than under a uniform common electoral law.

The period following direct elections will be one of uncertainty during which the directly elected Parliament will flex its muscles, decide its rules of procedure, try to assert its influence, and stimulate both a reappraisal of inter-institutional relations and of the informal sharing — if not redistribution — of political authority within the Community. Moreover, until there is some agreement as to the European Parliament's rightful role in EC decision-making, it is unlikely that Member Governments will accept any common electoral law depriving them of the right to determine how one of the most important political processes in their states should be conducted.

It is impossible to forecast what electoral system the European Parliament will devise. The controversiality and complexity of issues involved militate against expeditious formulation of a common elec-

toral system acceptable to all Member States. Consequently, it is unlikely that an electoral system with a high level of uniformity will be
adopted before the third round of direct elections in 1989.

Notes

1 See V. Herman, 'Direct Elections to the European Parliament: Comparative Perspectives',
Common Market Law Review, vol.16, 1979, pp 205-26.
2 See J. Lodge, 'The Significance of Direct Elections for the European Parliament's Role in
the European Community and the Drafting of a Common Electoral Law', *Common Market
Law Review*, vol.16, 1979, pp 195-206.
3 This section is based on Directorate-General for Research and Documentation of the European Parliament, 'Laws (or Draft Legislation) for Direct Elections, to the European Parliament:
A Comparative Study', (P.E. 54.676/rev., November, 1978).
4 The mechanics and effects of the different varieties of proportional representation discussed here can be found in D.W. Rae, *The Political Consequences of Electoral Laws* (Yale U.P.,
New Haven, 1971, rev. ed.), chapter 2.
5 See Directorate-General for Research and Documentation of the European Parliament,
'Electoral Laws of the Member States of the European Community', (P.E. 50.159, August,
1977), and V. Herman, *Parliaments of the World: A Reference Compendium* (Macmillan,
London, 1976) Part 1.
6 Rae, op.cit., chapter 10.
7 This was successful.
8 For a discussion of the French case, see D. Simon, 'Preparations in France for Direct Elections to the European Parliament', *Common Market Law Review*, vol.15, 1978, pp 127-38.
9 Debate on 'Convention introducing elections to the European Parliament by direct universal
suffrage', *Debates of the European Parliament*, D.J. Annex no.185, 14 January 1975.
10 'Opinion of the Legal Affairs Committee of the European Parliament', 1975, para 10.
11 See Herman, *Parliaments of the World*, op.cit., part 1, for a detailed discussion of these.
12 See Lodge, op.cit.

13 Towards a Comparison of Nine Legislative Processes

Mark Hagger

General characteristics

In accordance with the methodological principles described in the first chapter, we will now proceed to a comparison of the similarities and differences between the nine legislative processes. The analysis is based on indicators whose national context has been explained fully in the preceding case studies. This chapter thus provides an overview of nine parliaments processing the direct elections legislation.

In the ensuing discussion, a major emphasis is placed on the distinction between the activities of 'ratification of the principle' of direct elections, and the 'implementation of an electoral system' in each country. On the whole, these activities were closely related to the corresponding two bills that were introduced in six of the nine countries (table 13.1.b). In the three countries where there was no implementation bill, those parts of the pre-legislative and legislative processes relevant to the approval of the principle have been abstracted for the purposes of this analysis. Conversely, there were occasions when issues of principle, or issues that were agreed in the Council Act, were raised for discussion during the implementation bill debates — for example, in Italy the allocation of seats between countries was discussed at this juncture — and due note will be made of these transpositions.

The most basic comparison between the legislative processes arises from the way in which the processing of the direct elections issue was organised (table 13.1.a, 13.1.b). In the majority of countries, two bills were introduced, one to ratify the decision of the European Council, (Act of 20 September, 1976) the other to implement the election. As indicated above, these bills corresponded essentially to the acceptance of the principle and the choice of an electoral system. The absence of a ratification bill in three countries — in the two Anglo-Saxon systems, UK and Ireland, and in Denmark — is due to the convention of parliamentary sovereignty, which implied that the principle was ratified by the process of legislating an implementation bill. Three states required a third bill: in the Federal Republic, this was necessary to define the status of MEPs; in Luxembourg it was necessary to enable national and

European elections to be held simultaneously; and in the Netherlands the third bill related to incompatibilities.[1] There was also another bill in Denmark, relating solely to Greenland. The number and type of bills used is a consequence both of the constitutional framework, and of the political system. These characteristics also reveal aspects of the relationship between parliament and the political system. But they cannot reveal the 'complexity' of the measures required, nor can they demonstrate the 'contentiousness' of the political issues arising, nor the characteristics of the procedures required to resolve them.

The complexity of the legislative measures is indicated by the length of the legislation that was introduced. In table 13.1.b, the number of articles (including schedules) is used as the index of complexity, and a comparison is made between (i) ratification, (ii) implementation, and (iii) other bills. The 'article' is used as the unit of analysis since it has broadly similar characteristics as used in each country. Two types of factors must be borne in mind as affecting the complexity of bills: national parliamentary style and constitutional requirements affect the detailing which is required for legislation;[2] secondly, the substance of the policy to be enacted, as well as the perceptions of that policy by political actors, affects the length of the text.

Ratification was accomplished with a simple bill of not more than three articles in five of the six ratifying countries. The sixth ratifying bill, in the Netherlands, was extensive because it went on to define a variety of aspects of the future election, such as the rights and duties of MEPs, incompatibilities, adoption procedures, etc. For Luxembourg, the bills made changes to the existing electoral law; the number of articles and appendices affected by the legislation is therefore indicated in parentheses as a more meaningful and comparable guide to complexity. The similar lengths of the Ratification Bills conceal one critical difference: for the second article in the French bill was designed to contain any future increase in the powers of the European Parliament, and was introduced to appease the hostile Gaullist forces.[3]

The considerable length of the Irish Electoral Bill was due both to the relative complexity of the single transferable vote electoral system, and to the conventional requirement that all details should be incorporated in the electoral law, since Governmental decrees (Statutory Instruments) are not possible in this area. In Luxembourg, on the other hand, it was necessary to 'transplant' large parts of the national electoral law, most of which was incorporated without debate or scrutiny.[4] In the UK, the abandonment of the regional party list proportional electoral system, in favour of the traditional plurality system, engendered simplification of the text from 21 to 11 clauses. Yet in France, a new electoral system — on national party lists — was introduced to replace the two-ballot single-member constituency system

Table 13.1
Some characteristics of the legislative processes: general and ratification

Variable	Indicator	Chamber	Belgium	Denmark	France	Federal Republic of Germany	Ireland	Italy	Luxembourg	Netherlands	United Kingdom
GENERAL CHARACTERISTICS											
a. Organisation of leg. process	No. of bills		2	1	2	3	1	2	3	3	1
b. Complexity of bills	No. of Articles and Schedules i.		1	–	2	3	–	2	1	16	–
	ii.		36	45	25	30	120	56	2 (21)	41	21
	iii.		–	20	–	11	–	–	3 (15)	5	
c. Focus on Principle or Electoral System	Focus of pol. debate		El	Princ	Princ	El	(El)	El	(El)	El	Princ + El
RATIFICATION BILLS											
d. Contentiousness of pol. process	Duration of plenary debate (hrs)	Lower	1¼	(6)*	11	4¼	(None)*	10	5	3½	(34)*
		Upper	1	–	12½	2	(None)*	7	–	1	(10)*
e. De-institutionalisation	Extra-Parliamentary negotiations		Yes	No	Yes	No	No	No	(Yes)	No	Yes
f. Pattern of plenary activity	Spokesmen (Nos)	Lower	8	–	9	6	–	5	9	10	–
	Others		1	–	23	7	–	21	5	2	–
	Spokesmen (Nos)	Upper	6	–	2	5	–	3	5	4	–
	Others		0	–	24	1	–	28	–	2	–
g. Deconcentration to committees	Budgets, Interior, Foreign Affairs, European Affairs, Legal Affairs, Market Relations C, Select Committee Intra-German Relations	Lower	FA+*I*+EA	(MRC)*	FA	FA, LA, B, *I*, I-G	–	FA	FA	FA	(SC)*
Main committee italicized. + = joint sitting		Upper	FA	–	FA	*I*, EA, LA	–	FA	–	EA	(EA)*

262

Table 13.1 (cont.)

Variable	Indicator	Chamber	Belgium	Denmark	France	Federal Republic of Germany	Ireland	Italy	Luxembourg	Netherlands	United Kingdom
h. Judicial Review	Court giving opinion or: No reference.	—	(Council of State)	—	Constit. Council	No ref.	—	No ref.	—	Council of State	—
i. Opposition	Parties opposing principle		PCB	(SP),(LS), (CP)*	RPR, PCF, (PS)	None	None	DP	KPL	CPN, PSP, SGV, BP	(Lab.)* (Con.)*
j. Completion	Date of final reading		23ii78	—	30vi77	24vi77	—	24iii77	3vii77	28vi77	—
k. Duration of parl. process	Months from EC Act to final reading		17	—	9	9	—	6	9	9	—
	Rank order		6th	—	4th	2nd	—	1st	5th	3rd	—

*For those countries with no Ratification Bill, pre-legislative debate on the principle is used.

() Indicates lack of major importance or relevance; or that only a part of a political party was involved.

Party abbreviations are shown in the Appendix.

used in national parliamentary elections, in a text that was amongst the shorter of the Implementation Bills; for only the principles required parliamentary approval; the details were left to be implemented by decree. It should also be remembered that France introduced the simplest possible electoral system, with one constituency and blocked party lists.[5] However, the six countries that used more than one constituency (Belgium, Federal Republic, Ireland, Italy, UK, Denmark) did not *ipso facto* have Implementation Bills that were notably more complex than elsewhere.

As a preliminary analysis of the politics of the legislative process, the national debates have been examined to determine which of the two central issues: − 'the principle' and 'the electoral system' − provided the 'focus of political debate' (table 13.1.c). In only three countries was the principle of direct elections fiercely contested. The 'unholy alliance' between the French Communists and the Gaullists transformed the legislative process into a threat to the existing presidential−majority−government system, and simultaneously aggravated the already difficult relations between the two principal opposition partners. In Denmark, the Social Democratic Party, heading a minority government, expressed reservations about the principle, and initially tried to insist on the dual mandate and simultaneous national and European elections. A minority faction vigorously opposed the issue within the party and in the Folketing, thus reflecting the views of a larger mass movement. Three small anti-EC parties − the Socialist Peoples', Communist and Left Socialist Parties − joined it in opposing direct elections on the grounds that they would enhance supranational decision-making in the Community, and therefore represented a step towards political union. The third country in which the principle became an issue was the United Kingdom, where a minority of both the Conservative and Labour Parties operated simultaneously with the Ulster Unionists to obstruct and delay the process, in order to warn of the gravity of the step toward supranationalism and of the erosion of parliamentary sovereignty. In the other six countries, the principle of holding direct elections was contested by at most a handful of parliamentarians − usually from the far left of the political spectrum, though not always: e.g. in Italy, the PCI was strongly supportive of direct elections.

Legislating the principle

We now turn to the legislation of the principle of direct elections in the Member States. The comparison is based on the passage of the ratifying bill in six countries, and the pre-legislative debate salient to this issue in the other three. The first analysis is of the 'contentiousness' of the political process, for which the duration of plenary debate provides an index (table 13.1.d). The UK had by far the most extensive debate on this issue — long even by the standards of Westminster, which sits in plenary for more days and more hours each year than any other parliament in Europe. The second position attained by France is confirmed by the qualitative analysis. In both of these countries, the debate on the principle was of fundamental importance. Italy also had a surprisingly long plenary process, but this was due to the debate ranging beyond the question of principle in both chambers. In the Federal Republic there were three debates in plenary in which the principle was discussed, as well as extensive consideration by committees: whilst the West German commitment to direct elections was not in doubt, there were important domestic issues regarding the status of West Berlin, the electoral system and the veto power of the Bundesrat (upper chamber). In the Netherlands speeches by party spokesmen supporting direct elections and explanations of Government policy account for a relatively long debate in the absence of serious conflict. Amongst those countries with a shorter debate, there was some opposition from left-wing parties in both Luxembourg and Denmark. In the former, there was vigorous opposition from the Communists alone; but more extensive opposition in Denmark was contained by the institutionalisation of the conflict within the Folketing's committee system.

There is one circumstance in which the duration of plenary debate is a negative indicator of the complexity of the political process: when the issue is so politically sensitive that the process has to be de-institutionalised, and dealt with by informal negotiation between the political forces. There were three cases in which this was of the essence during the debate on principle (see table 13.1.e), and one other in which extra-parliamentary negotiation was an important element. That parliaments 'failed' to this extent to provide a forum in which an institutionalised process could occur is a striking comment on the contentiousness of the direct elections issue, and on the impotence of West European parliaments in the face of such difficulties. It was in Belgium, France and the UK that extra-parliamentary negotiations were of vital significance; but each for different reasons.

In Belgium there was no disagreement of substance with the principle of direct elections. The extra-parliamentary negotiations occurred in the context of a larger, existing dispute over the rights of the three linguistic communities, which gave rise to the Egmont Pact. The Pact had direct implications for the Implementation Bill, but it also brought to a close the drawn out national political crisis which had prevented discussion of the Ratification Bill. A similar linkage between the European issue and national politics was evident in France, where the split between the Gaullist and Giscardian parties within the majority coalition threatened to destabilise the governmental system at a critical juncture, prior to finely balanced national parliamentary elections. Thus in Belgium, extra-parliamentary negotiation was needed to resolve a problem that originated prior to direct elections, and which was essentially unrelated to it; but in France, the principle of direct elections was precisely the problem that threatened the normal working of the political system. The third case is the UK where two types of extra-parliamentary negotiation occurred; one was the conclusion of a 'pseudo-coalition' between the minority Labour Government and the parliamentary Liberal Party, which was conditional *inter alia* on a rapid introduction of the European Elections Bill, with a proportional electoral system contained therein. The other was the negotiation between the Labour Party leadership and various organs of the Party in an effort to resolve the deadlock imposed by these institutions, and by the vigorous opposition to the EC and direct elections from within the Labour Party. Thus as in France, extra-parliamentary negotiations were necessary in the UK to resolve the conflict over the principle, which had prevented the legislative process from going forward. The use of a pre-legislative 'committee of experts' in Luxembourg should also be noted: it generated solutions to the issues relating to the principle, as well as significantly preparing the ground for implementation.

It is also clear that the primary burden of parliamentary scrutiny and appraisal of the principle of direct elections fell on the lower chamber (table 13.1.d) in all countries with bicameral systems, except for France. The explanation for this exception is clear from the case study — the pro-European French Senate was used tactically by the Government as a means of by-passing the *blocage* created in the National Assembly by the Gaullist and Communist opposition to direct elections. In contrast to this, the German Bundesrat sought unsuccessfully to impose its control over the Ratification Bill. It is also significant that, in contrast to the Implementation Bills, the Ratification Bill was first introduced in the lower chamber of each Parliament.

The contentiousness of the political process is further clarified by the pattern of activity in the plenary debates (table 13.1.f); this also illuminates the structure of the conflict. In most European countries parties are so disciplined that parliamentary activity is normally focussed on the speeches of party spokesmen, together with those of the government and committee rapporteurs described in table 13.1.f as 'spokesmen'. In France there was a large number of interventions from the floor in both chambers, as was also the case in Italy. In the French National Assembly, there was both conflict between the four major parties, and cleavage within some of those parties, on the issue of principle. The debate therefore involved not only important argument at the level of official party positions, but also an extensive critique from the backbenches. In Italy, reservations came only from one minor party, the Radical Party, but other participants began to discuss other aspects of the Ratification Bill at this juncture. In the UK, the pre-legislative debate was dominated (in quantitative terms) by back-benchers who, traditionally, play an important role in parliamentary debate, as in Italy; but the existence of cross-party cleavage on the principle (table 13.1.i) ensured an extraordinarily lengthy debate. On the other hand, in the Folketing the conflict was largely contained within disciplined parties, and the debate focussed on party spokesmen. A pattern of activity which emphasises backbenchers rather than spokesmen thus resulted not only from a high level of contention in the legislative process, but also from cleavages within the parties on the issue.

The deconcentration of the legislative process to committees is a practice deeply embedded in national parliamentary traditions. 'Continental European' legislatures focus their detailed parliamentary scrutiny of legislation in specialised committees.[6] In most cases the bill was referred to the Committee on Foreign Affairs (table 13.1.g) for the principal recommendation, since the bill arose from ratification of an international agreement. However, the Belgian Chamber of Representatives held joint meetings of the Foreign Affairs with the EC and Interior Committees, in order to obtain specialist European advice and simultaneously to measure the impact of the bill on domestic politics — in this instance the rights of the linguistic communities — and to prepare the ground for implementation. Both chambers of the German Parliament similarly involved a large number of committees in scrutiny, including the Committee on Budgets and the Committee on Intra-German problems, to appraise the financial implications and the position of Berlin, respectively.[7] There is little direct evidence available about committee consideration of the ratification legislation, given the privacy of most committees in European parliaments, and the absence of public records of their proceedings. However, it is clear that no committee — except for those of the Bundestag — met for more than one sitting, and that the meetings all lasted only an hour. The other exception was the Dutch Second (lower) Chamber, which held a public meeting for six hours at which the discussion focussed on questions of timing, whether the constitution needed to be amended, and the question of incompatibilities.

Thus most national parliaments treated the Ratification Bill according to the procedures that they normally employed, deconcentrating scrutiny to a specialised committee, which then relied heavily on the work of a single rapporteur. Mention should also be made of the UK parliament, which is exceptional in European terms in having had a lower level of specialised committee institutionalisation.[8] In this case, an ad hoc committee was appointed to advise on direct elections in the Commons, and the Lords Select Committee on the European Communities also reported at each stage. As one has been led to expect, the Market Relations Committee[9] played a vital role in resolving the dispute on principle in Denmark, by investigating issues of constitutionality and sovereignty.

Of the six countries that had ratification legislation, France, the Federal Republic, Italy and the Netherlands have a full procedure for 'judicial review' to adjudicate the constitutionality of laws (see chapter 1, table 1.1). Of these, only in France did the Constitutional Court make a specific decision on the issues arising from the principle, though the Dutch Council of State automatically gave its opinion to the Government. The referral by the French President had been designed to appease those opposing direct elections; when this opposition continued to threaten the legislation, other tactics had to be employed. However, para-judicial bodies intervened in Belgium and the Netherlands. In Belgium the opinion of the Council of State was a formality of no legal or political significance. The Dutch Suffrage Council advised on the implications of the Council Act prior to the legislative process on ratification; its views were important in excluding certain issues from debate, since the Government did not wish to include any measure that implied constitutional amendment.

The process of ratification was disturbed in several cases by national political events. National elections occurred in four countries during the passage of direct elections legislation (Belgium: 17 April 1977; Denmark: 15 February 1977; Ireland: 16 June 1977; Netherlands: 25 May 1977). In the latter, difficulties in forming a government following these elections were responsible for the long delay before introduction. But in Ireland, even though there was no bill, the election had no impact at all on the acceptance of the principle. The conflict between the linguistic communities in Belgium, and the ensuing political and governmental crises, brought about the exceptional delays in this country. Whilst in the UK, domestic parliamentary difficulties over an issue similar to that in Belgium — the devolution proposals — were combined with the difficulties of minority government in a country accustomed to majorities. The conflicts in France are also attributable to the interaction of direct elections with domestic politics, for the proximity of critical national elections affected the strategies employed in this legislative process. The national political 'environments' therefore played a vital role in controlling the progress of legislation on the principle.

Primarily for this reason, the overall duration of the legislative passage, which is usually taken as a rough general indicator of the complexity of legislation, proves an unsatisfactory measure of the complexity of the ratification process (table 13.1.j, 13.1.k). The majority were accomplished within the relatively short time between March and July 1977, or five to eight weeks after the signature of the Act. This overall demonstration of speed – which one should observe is normal in regard to the ratification of governmental agreements in foreign affairs – marks a contrast to the highly differentiated pace of the Implementation Bills. Moreover, the duration of the legislative passage on ratification bears no positive correlation to the difficulties encountered in those parliaments.

Choosing an electoral system

The national parliaments then turned their attention to the implementation of direct elections. Our analysis commences with the pre-legislative phase. Generally, government law-making begins with a process of negotiation between various political forces – such as interest groups and political parties – and the government. The process may occur through consultations prior to the introduction of the text, and such consultations may be institutionalised to an extent that depends on the extent of deconcentration of political institutions; or it may continue into the parliamentary stages; or indeed it may be the intention of the government to have its own way, and therefore not to accommodate any views other than its own. We will begin by examining the general character of the pre-legislative phase, through a comparison of the duration of extra-parliamentary activity preceding the formal introduction of the legislative text – it being understood that any non-formalised activities conducted by parliamentarians outside the chamber or its committees are classified as 'extra-parliamentary'.

Four alternative explanations for variations in the duration of the pre-legislative stage are possible. First, that it is short because of an absence of conflict. Second, that it is short because of a failure to accommodate conflict, which is therefore transferred to the parliamentary arena for resolution. Third, that the pre-parliamentary stage is long, in order to prepare agreements which are so difficult to achieve that they could not be reached in the public and/or formalised setting of a parliament. Fourth, that the pre-parliamentary stage is long because the government is preoccupied with other policies or problems, and therefore does not expedite the bill in question.

Three countries had a short pre-parliamentary process (table 13.2.a), with the Government introducing the Implementation Bill within a year of the European Council's agreement (20 September, 1976). In France and the Federal Republic it was decided to introduce the Implemen-

Table 13.2
Some characteristics of the legislative process: implementation

Variable	Indicator	Chamber	Belgium	Denmark*	France	Federal Republic of Germany*	Ireland	Italy	Luxembourg*	Netherlands*	United Kingdom
a. Pre-parliamentary negotiation	Delay prior to Intro. (months)		15	13	8	8	13	22	18	20	9
b. Pre-legislative Parl. negotiation	Committee		–	MRC	–	–	Select C.	–	–	–	Select C.
c. De-institutionalisation	Extra parl. negotiation		Language Communities	No	No	No	Boundary C.	Party	Experts C.	Suffrage C.	Party
d. Introduction	Chamber	L/U	L	L	L	Upper	L	Upper	L	L	L
e. Contentiousness of pol. process	Duration of plenary debate (hours)	Lower	11	4	6	2	6¼	13	6	8½	29
		Upper	3¼	–	8½	2½	3½	5	–	2½	4
f. Pattern of plenary activity	Spokesmen (nos.)	Lower	12	24	6	12	4	13	9	11	few
	Others		19	5	8	3	19	15	5	0	many
	Spokesmen (nos.)	Upper	2	–	3	11	4	7	–	11	few
	Others		7	–	10	1	13	7	–	2	many
g. Deconcentration to committees	See table 13.1.g, and: Finance, Conciliation, C. of Whole House Constitutional, Elections, Laws	Lower	FA+I+EA	MRC	Laws+Concil	I,LA,B,F,E,I-G	CWH	Const	Special	I	CWH
		Upper	IA	–	Laws+Concil	I,LA,EA	CWH	FA+Const	–	I+EA	CWH
h. Emphasis on Committees	Committee duration (no. of meetings)	Lower	14	4	3	12	1	1	4	2	6
		Upper	1	–	3	4	1	4	–	3	1

Table 13.2 (cont.)

Variable	Indicator	Chamber	Belgium	Denmark*	France*	Federal Republic of Germany*	Ireland	Italy	Luxembourg*	Netherlands*	United Kingdom
i. Amendments in plenary	Nos. moved: nos. succeeding	Lower	151:18	23:0	12:1	3:1	24:11	–	33:10	10:4	250:2
		Upper	1:0	–	19:11	4:2	2:0	2:0	–	–	28:0
j. Opposition	Elect. system – parties opposing†		PRLW, PL,PVV, PCB		PCF, RPR	CDU/CSU	none	PCI,small parties	KPL	CPN, PSP, PPR, GPV,SGV,BP	(Lab.) (Con.)
	Final vote – parties opposing†		PRLW, PL,PVV, VU	SP,JP, CP,LS	none	none	none	PR,PLI, MSI	KPL	CPN, PSP, PPR, GPV, SGV,BP	(Lab.) (Con.)
k. Duration of parl. process	Months from EC Act to final reading		26	15	8	20	13	22	29	27	20
l. Completion	Rank order		6th	2nd	1st	5th	3rd	8th	9th	7th	4th

*Two bills were required for implementation

†Parties abstaining or voting against

() indicates that only part of a party was involved.

271

tation Bill at the same time as the Ratification Bill, so that the two issues could be debated together. In France this conjunction was itself a response by the President to the opposition movement; in the Federal Republic it was merely a rational strategy for an apparently non-controversial issue. In the UK there had been no ratification bill as such, but both pre-parliamentary and extra-parliamentary debate on the principle proceeded at a somewhat protracted pace through the two year preceding introduction; the early British start is nevertheless surprising given the pressures of national policy-making at the time, and it belies the critique, popular amongst politicians within and outside the UK, that 'Britain was delaying direct elections' in 1977.

A second group of countries comprises Belgium, Denmark and Ireland, where the pre-parliamentary debate was longer, lasting from twelve to eighteen months. In each, the delay can be explained by difficulties of national politics, which culminated in a parliamentary election; though each decision to hold an election was entirely independent of the direct elections issue. The third group comprises Luxembourg, Italy and the Netherlands, each taking between eighteen months and two years to introduce the Implementation Bill. Each of these countries is strongly pro-European, and the delay cannot in any sense be attributed to obstruction by anti-market forces. The Luxembourg Government was concerned to evade franchise extension, and the delaying tactics helped to reduce the parties' opportunities in the Chamber. Moreover, the threatened postponement of direct elections to 1979 introduced the additional problem of simultaneous national and European elections. The delay may be attributed to domestic politics in the Netherlands and specifically to difficulties over the formation of a Government, which occupied the whole period from June 1977, until January 1978; though the Dutch socialist, S. Patijn, was far from satisfied with this explanation at the time. Only in Italy can the delay be genuinely attributed to the complexity of pre-legislative discussion between the parties in the fragile government majority, and it is clear that the negotiations on the various aspects of the Italian Implementation Bill were complex and hard fought.

Alongside this quantitative comparison, it is important to consider the manner in which the pre-legislative stage was handled. In three of the nine parliaments, the pre-legislative debate was institutionalised in an existing or special committee (table 13.2.b). The Folketing's Market Relations Committee had an established reputation for powerful control over Danish EC affairs; it involved itself closely with the Government's formulation of direct elections legislation. Contrary to usual British practice, the House of Commons was involved in extensive pre-legislative consultation through a special Select Committee, which invited written submissions and held hearings on the implementation issues. In addition, the active Lords Select Committee on EC Legislation reported on the matter at an early stage. However the Committees' views were not influential on the drafting of the legislation, and their role was more that of a safety valve. The third case was the Joint Committee on EC Secondary Legislation of the Irish Parliament, which considered direct elections at an early stage, and made important recommendations that were incorporated in the eventual bill. Elsewhere there is no evidence of an important pre-legislative stage concerned with the formulation of legislation and institutionalised in a parliamentary committee, despite the frequent emphasis on this function in the literature on 'continental European' parliaments. Exception should perhaps be made for Italy, where the major reformulation by a sub-committee occurred *after* introduction of the bill, but nevertheless the activity resembled an institutionalised pre-legislative stage in most characteristics.

Conversely, we find that extra-parliamentary negotiations were important in most countries (table 13.2.c). In the UK, these were necessary to resolve the disputes within and between the various parts of the Labour Party, and the pact with the Liberal Party was the catalyst that relaunched the legislative process. In Belgium, the extra-parliamentary negotiations were, strictly, about relations between the linguistic communities, as mentioned above, but the incorporation of these communities into the organisation of the Belgian political system provided the basis for the electoral system for direct elections. In Italy the negotiations were between the various parties supporting the Government, and were of considerable importance. In Luxembourg institutionalised consultation took place between the Parliament, the Government and the administration in an *ad hoc* Committee of Experts. It is also necessary to take into account the role of the Irish Boundary Commission, which was used for the first time for these elections and which made recommendations prior to the main plenary debates — unlike that of the UK which could not (at least officially) start work until the legislation was completed. Finally, the Dutch Suffrage Council played a decisive role in establishing limits constraining policy choice in regard to implementation.

Three countries remain in which no special extra-parliamentary negotiation occurred. But that is not to say that all activity was contained within the respective legislatures. In France, important negotiations took place between the parties, which led to agreement on the national party list system at a pre-legislative stage. In the Federal Republic, the accommodation process was based on a difficult series of negotiations between the parliamentary parties regarding the use of a Land — or Federal — based electoral system. It is only in Denmark that no evidence was found of inter-party negotiations — though it is difficult to imagine the complete absence of such contacts.

The contentiousness of the parliamentary process, evaluated in the first instance by the duration of plenary debate (see table 13.2.c), shows that the majority of lower chambers spent between four and eight hours on the issue. This duration is above the average for government bills in each parliament, but it is perhaps 'normal' in the context of a bill dealing with an electoral matter. In two countries, the parliamentary debate was more extensive. In Italy, the Chamber of Deputies spent thirteen hours in plenary debate, and this is directly attributable to the sensitivity of parties to the electoral system issue. In the UK, twenty-nine hours were spent in plenary debate because filibustering by the anti-market faction continued alongside a second conflict, with a different cleavage structure, which developed over the choice between a plurality and a party list electoral system; and this despite the fact that the decision on the electoral system was taken in the equally extensive Committee stage.

It is also clear that, as for the Ratification Bills, the main burden of the plenary parliamentary process was borne by the lower chamber, except in France and Italy. As it is broadly accepted in most European countries that the lower chamber has more right to jurisdiction over electoral matters, this is not a surprising finding. The Italian Senate was the principal exception to this rule, though its French counterpart, despite its own indirect electoral basis, was not averse to seeking influence over the legislation. In France, given the procedure adopted to avoid a vote in the National Assembly, the Senate had already had to shoulder the burden of legitimation on the Ratification Bill. It now took up the offensive and proposed refinements to the electoral rules.

The role of the upper chamber is not revealed solely by analysis of the debates themselves: the sequence in which the two chambers take the bill can also be of considerable importance. As we have indicated previously, the lower chamber is usually more important than the upper in European parliaments, particularly when electoral matters are at stake, and it usually takes legislation before the upper chamber. However, in Italy the two chambers are of equal status; the bill could therefore be introduced in either assembly, and for tactical reasons it was debated first in the Senate (table 13.2.d). In the Federal Republic also, all three bills were introduced together into the Bundesrat, before consideration in the lower house, specifically to resolve the question of the power of the Bundesrat relative to the Bundestag on these bills.

In the case of the Ratification Bills, our analysis showed that the debate was clearly articulated by the party system in most countries, and in consequence the discussion in the legislature was dominated by party, government or committee spokesmen. In the case of the Implementation Bills the usually more extensive debates in the lower

274

chamber were more frequently dominated by such spokesmen (table 13.2.f). In the Federal Republic, Luxembourg and the Netherlands, the capability of the party system to regulate the debate on implementation were demonstrated as clearly as they had been on ratification; though in Luxembourg, it was more a case of consensus amongst EC specialists in the Chamber, than of a party-structured debate. In Denmark, the fragmented party system accounts for the dominance of spokesmen, and their large number. But in France, in contrast to the ratification debate, spokesmen dominated because there were no fundamental issues at stake. On the other hand in upper chambers, backbenchers (i.e. non-spokesmen) dominated the debates, except in the Bundesrat and the Dutch First Chamber; the balance of power between spokesmen and rank-and-file evidenced in the upper chambers is different from that which exists in lower chambers, where members defer more readily to their spokesmen.

The deconcentration of parliamentary control to committee is more clearly depicted in the case of the Implementation Bills than for the ratification, and in a manner that follows ascribed national practices (table 13.2.g). The two Anglo-Saxon parliaments (UK, Ireland) stand out with their use of the Committee of the Whole House in both chambers for the committee stage of the consideration. The CWH was used in each Parliament because of the constitutional importance of the issue, both because it was an electoral law, and because neither country used a distinct ratification procedure. The Luxembourg Chamber created a special committee, whose membership was composed of deputies with high party status, together with a number of past and present MEPs to provide EC expertise. Two other parliaments gave the bill constitutional treatment at the committee stage: Italy has a specific 'constitutional' committee, whilst France has broad committees, one of which specialises both in constitutional laws, and in other general legislative and administrative matters. In three other parliaments, in Belgium, Denmark and the Federal Republic, the scrutiny was deconcentrated to the Committee specialising in EC affairs, but only in Denmark was it the sole scrutinising body. In the Federal Republic, the legislation was referred to a number of committees for their specialist advice; whereas the Belgians added the expertise of the Committees on Foreign and European Affairs to the Interior Committee by meeting in joint session, though only the Interior Committee members were entitled to vote.

However, the characteristics of the committee stage in the upper chamber were different in certain respects from those in the lower chamber. The Anglo-Saxon parliaments used the Committee of the Whole House again; and in Italy, the Constitutional Committee was again mobilised but on this occasion in tandem with the Foreign Affairs

275

Committee. Elsewhere, Interior or Foreign Affairs Committees were used — in the Netherlands, both of these Committees met in a joint sitting — except in the Federal Republic, where the legislation was referred to a large number of committees, in accordance with normal practice. With regard to the Committees consulted, there was a tendency for the upper chambers to interpret the legislation in a Foreign Affairs context, whereas the lower chambers were more concerned with the Constitutional and Interior implications of the bills. However the strategies of individual chambers were evidently much influenced by national traditions.

The way in which these committees operated is largely concealed from the public gaze. Our only systematic evidence concerns the collective activity of the committee. (Often it is the case that the individual activity of the rapporteur is critical — for example, he may be involved in negotiating with party spokesmen on the issue, to try to generate a compromise that may provide the basis of his eventual rapport.) These data show the considerable variation in the extent of collective committee work carried out in the lower houses, as indicated by the number of meetings (table 13.2.h). Although evidence is not generally available on the duration of meetings, it is unlikely that the UK's total of thirty-five hours was met even by the Belgian Parliament's joint Committee. Both the UK and Belgian Committees had protracted sittings, in part because of the filibustering of determined and skilful opponents, and in part because of the policy innovation involved. In all the other Member States, the committee stage was relatively short, and the data available are not sensitive enough to allow us to distinguish much of the intensity, the politics or the issues at stake.

In most instances, the committees of the upper chambers were less actively involved than those of the lower house. One exception to this was the Italian Senate, which bore the brunt of the electoral system debate, since it considered the bill before the lower chamber. A second was the Bundesrat, which was in conflict with the lower chamber both over the constitutional status of the bill, and over the Federal versus 'Land' (region) basis of the electoral system. But the German practice of systematically referring to all possible committees exaggerates the significance of committee activity; for some of the committees did not consider that the matter warranted a report, whilst others presented only the briefest of texts. The third exception was the French Senate, which took it upon itself to scrutinise the Implementation Bill with more assiduity than did the lower chamber, and recommended a large number of amendments, many of which were successful.

It is commonly argued that the strength of many European parliaments lies in their specialised committee systems, and that a primary function of such committee systems is the detailed scrutiny of legislation. Following this theory, two measures are used to evaluate the efficacy of the committee stage. One is the extent to which amendments were proposed in committee[10] — a measure of activity; the other is the ultimate success of those amendments — a measure of the influence of the committee recommendations in the legislative process (table 13.2.i). In terms of activism, the Westminster parliament once again claims the prize, though the amending-influence of the Commons was only moderately successful. In Belgium, the enlarged Committee was both active and highly successful in amending the bill, as was the Irish Dail. By comparison with national norms, and in contrast with the 'decline of legislatures' thesis, the rate of successful amendment by the parliaments of France, the Federal Republic, Luxembourg and the Netherlands were also at par. It was only in Denmark that no amendments were passed at all. But taking quality into account, significant changes were made to the Government's Bill through a parliamentary process of amendment only in the UK, the Federal Republic and France.

In Italy, the influence of Parliament was still more important. The bill was substantially modified in a sub-committee of the joint Senate Committee, and this virtual redrafting provided in effect a new text. The Committee itself did not seek to change it, in view of the delicate political balance achieved. The Italian case should therefore be considered as an instance of a sub-committee drafting a bill, rather than amending it.

The analysis of amendments also throws light on the role of second chambers. An established debate continues as to whether it is the function of the second chamber to delay legislation or to amend it. It is clear that in the case of direct elections, the German Bundesrat and the Italian Senate were the only upper houses to play a major amending role directly. The French Senate adopted an unusual Government-support function, abetting the Government in its conflict with its divided majority in the National Assembly, and seeing a large number of its own amendments implemented. Elsewhere, upper chambers did not play a very important role in amending the legislation — indeed in the Netherlands, the upper chamber does not have this power. Nor indeed was the legislation delayed by upper chambers for the debates were rapid and overwhelmingly supportive, except in the Bundesrat. In part the electoral character of the legislation determined a secondary role for the upper chambers, as we have suggested above. In part also, the chambers were endorsing the legislation, which they supported and therefore did not wish to delay.

In most countries, the cleavage structure in the implementation stage was different from that on the principle. The two most important divisions were about the electoral system, and about the Implementation Bill as a whole. On the former, there was a common tendency for the small parties to oppose the governmental proposal (see table 13.2.j), seeking better opportunities for small parties which are often discriminated against by electoral systems. A second characteristic was for Communist Parties and other left-wing parties to oppose the electoral system, either acting in their own interest as a small party, or — as in Italy — siding with the smaller parties, in order to threaten the Christian Democratic hegemony most successfully.

However, in France, the principles of national lists and the d'Hondt quota were agreed at the beginning of the legislation, and the argument in the Assembly was a logical extension of the dispute on the principle: the Communists and Gaullists advanced a number of amendments designed to enhance national control over French representation in the European Parliament. In Britain, the division on the electoral system brought the smaller parties (except for the Ulster Unionists) together with a minority drawn from the Labour and Conservative Parties to back the Government's proposal for a regional party list electoral system; but the bipartisan majority rejected this in favour of the traditional plurality system. Whilst in Germany, the opposition came from the major Christian Democratic Party, which pressed for a regional (Land) basis for the electoral system — which the FDP had succeeded in removing from the bill during the pre-legislative stage.

On the final vote on implementation, there was a remarkable gesture of unanimity in four of the nine Parliaments, indicating the high level of acceptance of the chosen electoral systems and support for the implementation of direct elections amongst the parliamentary elites. Moreover such opposition as there was came from a small minority of each chamber concerned (Belgium, Chamber: 128 vs 1, 15 abst; Denmark, 120 vs 25, 9 abst; Italy, Chamber: 290 vs 17, 17 abst; Luxembourg, 50 vs 0, 4 abst; UK, Commons: 159 vs 45, unwhipped) which was drawn essentially from either end of the ideological spectrum.

Finally, we can compare the complexity of the whole implementation process, using the duration of the legislative process from the Council Act to the final parliamentary reading, as an indicator (see table 13.2.k). Only France completed the legislation within twelve months — a marked contrast to the ratification process, which was completed within six months in all six ratifying countries — and this speed was a true reflection of the lack of implementation difficulties. Both Denmark and Ireland completed the legislation within eighteen months; the latter might have been quicker, given the virtual absence of conflict over the issue, had it not been for an election intervening; there was more Danish conflict over the principle than over the implementation, and such conflict as emerged on the Implementation Bill was contained within the parliamentary institution. In the Federal Republic, there was a low level of conflict, and it is difficult to explain why the process was so extended. In Italy, and more particularly in the UK, there were important conflicts about implementation issues; the obstructionism of the anti-market group at Westminster exasperated the situation further. But the last to complete the legislation, taking between two and two-and-a-half years after the Council Act, were Belgium, Luxembourg and the Netherlands. All three have a strong commitment to the EC, to further integration and to direct elections; and all three had the essential structures of the electoral system pre-determined by established traditions of proportional representation. In none of these three countries can the long delay be directly attributed to political dispute over any aspect of direct elections, and these cases therefore demonstrate the care with which this overall index of complexity must be used. The Belgian delay was due to domestic political problems, and the Dutch lateness is due mainly to this same cause. But apart from the Government's delay in order to avoid franchise extension, and the problems arising from simultaneous elections, the late arrival of Luxembourg can only be attributed to the lack of urgency with which an uncomplicated issue was treated.

Nine issues in nine legislative processes

The final stage of the comparison is the analysis of the issues that became prominent in each country. In the context of any subsequent move toward a uniform electoral system, examination of the issue-structure is fundamental. It is also central to any evaluation of how changes to the powers of the European Parliament might be introduced, where these require the consent of the national parliaments. But our approach is *not* to trace the elements or extent of substantive commonality between the systems adopted. Such an approach we consider ineffectual, since the nine sets of legislation adopted were directed towards national problems in the full and explicit knowledge that a debate on a common electoral system would be carried out in the context of different assumptions and propositions, and with a different set of ground-rules and constraints. Instead, our goal is to identify the patterns of conflict over issues, in order to trace the political obstacles facing alternative policy strategies.

In comparing the nature of issues salient in each country, we will also be concerned to evaluate the extent to which these issues were significant, within the national political system. In table 13.3, a three point scale has been used to indicate the saliency of each issue, evaluated by the size and intensity of the conflict — irrespective of whether it was

Table 13.3

Issues in the legislative processes: conflict and partnership

Issue	Belgium	Denmark	France	Federal Republic of Germany	Ireland	Italy	Luxembourg	Netherlands	United Kingdom
a. Principle	B	B	A	C	C	B	B	B	A
Parties contesting	PCB	LS,CP,SP JP(SD)	PCF,RPR, (PS)	–	–	DP	KPL	CPN,PSP, GPV,SCV,BP	(Lab.), (Con.), UUUC
b. Constitutional change	C	B	A	C	C	C	B	B	A
Parties contesting	–	SP,LS, JP,CP	PCF,RPR	–	–	–	KPL	CPN,PSP,BP, GPV,SGV, PvdA	(Lab.), (Con.), UUUC
c. Sovereignty	C	B	A	C	C	C	B	C	A
Parties contesting	–	LS,CP,RL, JP,CPP,SP	PCF,(PS), RPR	–	–	–	KPL	–	(Lab.), (Con.), UUUC
d. EP-NP links	B	A	C	C	C	B	C	B	C
Parties contesting	(PSB)	SD,C,(CPP)	–	–	–	x	–	PvdA,CDA	–
e. Electoral formula	C	C	C	C	C	B	C	B	A
Parties contesting	–	–	–	–	–	(CD)	–	CPN,PSP, GPV,SGV, PvdA	(Lab.), (Con.), UUUC

Table 13.3 (cont.)

Issue	Belgium	Denmark	France	Federal Republic of Germany	Ireland	Italy	Luxembourg	Netherlands	United Kingdom
f. Constituencies	A	B	B	A	B	A	B	C	B
Parties contesting	PRLW, PVV,PL, (all parties)	PP,AL,JP	UC	CDU	(FF)	DP,PCI, PR,PSDI, PRI,(DC) PLI,MSI	KPL,SDP, CSV	—	(Lab.), (Con.), UUUC
g. Franchise	B	C	C	B	C	A	A	C	B
Parties contesting	(PRLW)	—	—	CDU/CSU	—	PCI	all	—	x
h. Finance for (campaign salaries)	B	C	A	C	B	C	B	C	B
Parties contesting	FDF	—	PCF,PS, RPR,UDF	—	(FG)	—	SDP,KPL	—	(Lab.), (Con.), UUUC
i. Conditions for candidates	B	B	C	C	B	C	C	B	C
Parties contesting	PCB,PVV	CD,CP,PP, SP,RL,JP, CPP	—	—	(FG)	—	—	PvdA,CDA, BP,GPV, SGV,VVD	—

A = major conflict
B = minor conflict
C = no conflict
() indicates that only part of a party was involved.
x = cross-party.

281

institutionalised or informal — that was provoked at any stage in the legislative process. Distinction is made between a major conflict (*A*), a minor dispute (*B*) and an insignificant, or the absence of, dispute (*C*), with each country treated as a single unit of equal importance. The ratings thus provide a cross-national scale of issue-salience, measured in relation to the national context.

In most West European polities, the party system has generally been found to be an effective mechanism for the articulation of well-aggregated policy demands. Indeed an important explanation for political behaviour at both mass and elite levels, and in a variety of institutions and contexts, is attributed to partisanship. Both in order to evaluate this general proposition in the context of the direct elections legislation, and in order to indicate the structure of partisan conflict on the various issues, we have cited in the table those parties which opposed their Government's policy on each issue (the party labels are defined in a table at the beginning of each national case study). It should be noted that since the policies of the nine Governments on these various issues are not identical, and since the parties themselves had different policies, it should not be assumed that all parties contesting an issue had similar positions — neither in absolute terms nor relative to their Government. To analyse party positions in absolute terms is beyond the scope of this comparative inquiry, and might lead to false conclusions regarding the potential for a common electoral law. The appropriate context for such analysis is to be found within each national case study.

The first issue to be considered is the question of principle: whether there was agreement on the proposition to hold direct elections at all (table 13.3.a). In some contexts the argument against the principle was articulated as a demand for direct elections to be delayed until their presence was considered necessary. Only in Ireland and Germany was there no opposition at all to the principle. In five other countries the opposition was small in scale, either because it was confined to parties with modest mass support and parliamentary representation, such as the Luxembourg Communist Party, whose voice though vigorous was constrained by the small size of the party; or because parties, like the Belgian Communist Party, felt that the issue was a *fait accompli* and that it was not worth the effort (and perhaps the cost in terms of influence over other policies) of an opposition to the last ditch. In all five countries, the opposition came from the extremes of the left—right ideological[11] spectrum — which included the Communist Party in all countries where it was represented in parliament, except for Italy where the PCI has long been supportive of the EC and direct elections. It is more rare for parties of the far-right to be represented in European parliaments and their opposition is therefore less pronounced in a legislative process that was in general highly institutionalised. In any event, the few representatives of the far-right did not vociferously oppose the principle.

However, attribution of opposition to extremist parties is an inadequate explanation, given the presence of parties of a quite moderate left–right ideological positioning amonst the opposition in Denmark. Moreover, in the two countries with the most vigorous and extensive conflict on principle, France and the UK, the opposition came from parties, or factions, not normally considered to be 'extremist' in ideological terms, though nevertheless positioned at the extremes of their national ideological spectrum. In the UK, the opposition came from individuals, who are generally associated with the ideological extremes of both major parties, whose collective behaviour on the EC issue has long resembled that of loosely organised and ill-disciplined factions. In France, with a more fractionalised party system, the opposition came from the major parties at either end of the ideological range in parliament — the Communists and the Gaullists — though the latter were not entirely cohesive on the issue, which was spear-headed by the Debré-faction of Gaullistes-de-foi. The complexity of the relationship between ideology and attitude to the principle is indicated in table 13.4, where the left is examined more closely.

Table 13.4
The European left and the principle — a schematic representation

		Attitude to Principle		
		Pro	Anti	Very anti
	Communist	It	B Lux Dk NL	Fr
	Socialist	Fr – – – – NL It (PSI) Lux (LSAP) B –	– – – Fr – Dk	– – UK
Ideological Tendency	Social-Democrat	B – – Dk – – – – UK – – – – Ire FRG It (PSDI) Lux (SDP)		

The question of principle gave rise to two related issues – the constitutionality of the proposals and the implications for national sovereignty. The former arose principally in terms of the consistency of direct elections with national constitutional provisions (table 13.3.b). The implication was that the constitution might have to be amended – involving such procedures as referral to the constitutional court, referendum or special parliamentary procedure – to permit direct elections to be held. In the event, no country required – or all countries avoided – constitutional amendment. The justifications varied: it was argued that direct elections were implicit in the existing national constitutional structure ensuing after the signature of the Treaty of Rome (France, Luxembourg, Netherlands, UK), that the consultative powers of the 'European Assembly' did not threaten the existing constitutional order (Denmark, France, Luxembourg, UK), or that the national parliament did not have an exclusive right to representation (Netherlands). Nevertheless, the issue was raised in six of the nine countries.[12] In France and the Netherlands, the matter was subjected to a form of judicial review – in France by the Constitutional Council and in the Netherlands by the Suffrage Council – as a result of which the need for constitutional amendment was rejected in both cases. However, the French Council indicated that an increase in the powers of the European Parliament, or the introduction of a uniform electoral system, would require constitutional change.

It is striking that in the UK, the absence of a written constitution did not in any sense reduce or modify the nature of the debate, except insofar as the absence of constitution logically precluded judicial review. Of the two countries where the constitutionality of direct elections became a major issue, in France there is a written constitution and the issue was referred to the Constitutional Council for review; whereas Britain has no written constitution and therefore no judicial review procedure, yet the argument was still more bitter.

In Denmark, Luxembourg and the Netherlands, the issue of constitutionality was raised, but only to a moderate extent. In the Luxembourg Chamber, it was only the five Communist deputies who presented this argument as part of their opposition of principle to direct elections, for the issue had been examined and defused by the *ad hoc* 'committee of experts' before introduction of the bill. In the Netherlands, the same issue was raised by the small parties at the ideological extremes of the party system; but, in addition, a second constitutional issue subsequently arose, which sought various forms of linkage between the European Parliament and the national Parliament, all of which were opposed by the Government on the grounds that they entailed constitutional amendment. Whilst in Denmark, the investigations of the Market Relations Committee provided for the

284

Government a rebuttal of the claim from left and right that direct elections were unconstitutional in their present form.

Another aspect of constitutionality arose in the UK, where it was argued that to hold direct elections on a non-uniform electoral system was contrary to the provisions of the Treaty of Rome. The Council's view

> . . . followed the European Parliament's recommendation of 14 January 1975 (Patijn Report), that a uniform electoral procedure could be said to exist if "elections in all member states were carried out according to the same basic principles" . . . if they were equal, free, universal, direct and secret.[13]

Finally, in the Federal Republic, minor constitutional debates arose in two different areas. One question concerned the right of the Bundesrat to pass the Ratification Bill; the Bundesrat's power varies according to the policy area in which a bill is considered to fall — in this case the choice between Foreign Affairs and Interior was critical. The other concerned the representatives for West Berlin. The disagreements were not taken to the Constitutional Court, nor were they allowed to escalate in the political arena, as a result of the underlying consensus between the two chambers on the substance of the bill.

The second issue arising from the principle was the implication of direct elections for national sovereignty (table 13.3.c). Many of the anti-market forces were concerned about the growth of supranational authority which would either arise directly from the implementation of direct elections, or would develop with the 'inevitable' subsequent accretion of the European Parliament's powers. This neo-functionalist analysis was important in France and UK, where the anti-direct elections argument was most vigorous. It was also an important element in the argument of the Danish opposition, but its impact was cushioned by the report of the Market Relations Committee mentioned above. The Luxembourg Communists were also concerned by the issue, but elsewhere it was not significant.

The acid-test for the importance of the supranational and constitutional issues was provided by three parallel decisions in different countries. These decisions arose as a response to political pressure from those concerned about the implications of direct elections. In France, a second article was introduced into the Ratification Bill, rendering 'null and void' any increase in European Parliamentary powers that have not given rise to a change in the Constitution (where necessary). In the UK, a similar clause required an explicit Act of Parliament to ratify any increase in the European Parliament's powers. Whilst in Denmark, the Government gave similar assurances to the Market Relations Committee. Although there is some doubt as to the legal effectiveness of these measures, they provide a formidable set of political commitments which will be weighed carefully in the future.

The three issues discussed above were all provoked by conflict between opponents of direct elections and their Governments. They mark the basic ground of the opposition to the elections — though some of the later implementation issues discussed below derived from these fundamental arguments. There was a considerable degree of interaction, in the majority of countries, between the three issues — in Germany and Ireland, where none of the issues were salient; in Luxembourg and Denmark, where they achieved a low level of saliency; and in the UK and France, where the issues of principle were fundamental. In the remaining three countries, not all of the issues emerged. Similarly, it can be seen that in most countries the cleavage structure carried through from one issue to another. The most interesting exception was France, where a subtle pattern of divisions emerged across the three issues, demonstrating the complexity of the political scene and explaining the lack of cohesion of the oppositional forces.

In contrast, the fourth issue was frequently introduced by those supportive of direct elections and further supranational integration. The issue arose from the failure of the Council either to require or to forbid the dual mandate, and from the failure of national Governments, Parliaments and parties to develop linkages between the European Parliament and the national Parliaments.[14] The issue tended to be raised by past and present MEPs who were sensitive to the need to co-ordinate the work of the nationalised European parliaments, and to strengthen the European Parliament's role (table 13.3.d). The argument was also adopted by some of the anti-market parties in Denmark, after it had been proposed by the Social Democratic Government as a response to the anti-market minority within its own party. It was also promoted by both anti-marketeers and 'Westminster supremacists' in the UK. On the other hand, many deputies, for example within the ranks of the Italian Christian Democrats and the Belgian Socialists, wanted to forbid the dual mandate by law — despite the Council decision to permit it. On the whole, this important issue was abandoned as readily by the political parties as it had been by the Council of Ministers.[15]

Turning to the implementation, the fifth issue concerns the choice and nature of electoral system. Here disputes centred around the type of electoral system (i.e. party list, single transferable vote and plurality system), and the 'formula' used to assign seats from votes under List systems (i.e. d'Hondt, Hagenbach-Bischoff, St Lague or natural quotient), and the opportunities for modifying the ordering of lists (preferential vote). The choice of electoral system and formula is of fundamental concern to all parliamentarians, who inevitably regard themselves as experts on a matter so close to their hearts and salary cheques. Each Government took care to present an electoral system which was broadly acceptable to the major political forces. In most cases this meant following national electoral traditions (see chapter 12, especially table 12.2), with a tendency to increase the size, by reducing the number, of constituencies (see below). In France, a major change was made from the two-ballot plurality system operated in national elections to a national party list system, without generating any dissent (table 13.3.e). The only site of major conflict was again the UK, where the Labour Government, constrained by its Liberal allies, introduced a regional party list electoral system that was rejected by a majority drawing from both Labour and Conservative Parties. In Luxembourg, Denmark, the Netherlands and Italy there was some minor dissent from the small parties about the method of allocating seats.

An issue that was more important in cross-national terms arose over the designation of constituencies. Given the choice of a party list electoral system in all countries except the UK and Ireland, and after the decision about the formula for assigning seats had been taken, the question of the number of constituencies was the next issue with a direct bearing on the proportionality of the representation (table 13.3.f). The rule is in principle simple: the smaller the number of constituencies, the less the distortion in representation. However in reality the problem is much more complex — indeed for parties that are regionally concentrated, the law is reversed.[16]

The first type of conflict therefore arose from minor parties which sought to enhance their potential representation by using a single national constituency, as in Luxembourg — this was also the case in Italy, where the small parties were benevolently supported by the PCI. The debate in Ireland, though low key, was essentially supportive of the newly established Boundary Commission's work, and also cast reflections on the delineation of the four proposed constituencies: it therefore concerned the same issue. Similarly, whilst the minor Dutch parties had argued for a single national constituency at an early stage, this solution was never really in dispute. The German case was slightly more complex. Both the minor parties favoured a single federal constituency, in order to maximise their representation; but the CSU also wanted to measure its electoral stature against its opposition partner, the CDU. They won the support of the SPD prior to introduction of the bill, but the CDU and the Bundestag fought vigorously to re-introduce the Land basis.

In two countries, the argument was reversed in defence of regional interests or parties. In France, centrist Senators argued for a regionally based electoral system, both in response to their own interests, and in sympathy for the interests of regionalist movements. In Denmark, the issue was similar: should Greenland (*qua* region) form a separate constituency, and thus enjoy a privileged existence, and a chance of its own representation?

In the remaining two countries, the debate was conditioned very much by national particularities. In Belgium, the debate about constituencies focussed on the new 2-college, constituency system: whether some linguistic minority regions should be added to the Brussels bi-communal constituency, so that their citizens could vote in either linguistic 'college', and the precise boundaries of the constituencies. In Britain, the debate was spread over the widest range of possibilities, from the Government's twelve regional constituencies for the party list proposal to the seventy-eight single member constituencies used for the plurality system, with subsidiary debate on the methods for drawing boundaries, and on their location. The conflict was less intense than on other issues, because of the tradition of devolving boundary problems to a 'non-political' Boundary Commission, though even this practice did not pass unquestioned.

Moving from aspects of electoral mechanics, we come to the debate over the franchise (table 13.3.g). In substantive terms, there was consensus on the minimum age for voting — eighteen years — and a fair degree of uniformity in terms of entry to the register for those near the marginal age. But in terms both of residence, and especially of nationality, qualifications, there was a surprising variation (see chapter 12, table 12.3). The problems of whether 'resident nationals of other EC countries', or 'own nationals resident in other EC countries' should be eligible to vote became minor issues in Germany and the UK. But the franchise was extended beyond its normal range in a number of countries — often without conflict, as in Belgium, Denmark, the Netherlands and Ireland. Whilst the German Christian Democrats successfully amended the bill to enfranchise German citizens resident elsewhere in the EC, in the UK the difficulties over other problems effectively precluded serious consideration of the issue, though the Government promised an inquiry later.

On the other hand, the Italian Communist Party fought a major battle to contain the overseas franchise, which was normally administered through consulates presumed to exercise bias against likely PCI voters. The Luxembourg Communists also opposed franchise expansion, but in the Committee stage a modest provision had been 'negotiated' with the Government, for Luxembourgers resident in the EC; attempts in the plenary to extend this further received support from the Chamber, but were resisted by the Government. Thus an issue that had been strongly advocated by Eurocrats, amongst others, achieved successful implementation with relatively little opposition in most Member States. However, it should be noted that the issue had been under active consideration for some years in a number of Parliaments, and some had already enfranchised various classes of overseas residents.[17]

The question of the financing of European elections arose in a number of different contexts. The cost to the state of the elections varied essentially according to the extent of its subsidy of political campaigning. In Britain, it was estimated at ten million pounds. Surprisingly, the central cost of holding the elections — the organisation of polling booths, the administration of the count, and the provision of broadcasting time — was never in question; even the anti-market forces did not seriously oppose the elections on the grounds of cost. But two issues did emerge quite strongly: one was the provision of state and EC funds for subsidising party campaigns; the other was the salary to be paid to MEPs.

The most vigorous debate arose in France, prior to the introduction of legislation, and in its bill the Government was obliged — against its will — to limit state funds to parties represented in the French Parliament; modifications were subsequently introduced by Government sympathisers in the Senate. The eventual solution, a 5 per cent threshold, was ultimately to effect the Ecologists most seriously, since their vote fell just below this level. In contrast, several small parties without existing representation in the European Parliament felt that they would be disadvantaged by the support given to its official Party Groups by the European Parliament: the Brussels Federalist Party (FDF) pressed this argument in Belgium, as did the Social Democrats and Communists in Luxembourg. MPs in the UK were also concerned about campaign expenses, and they pressed strongly and successfully for the level of expenses permitted for constituency campaigns to be fixed at a level corresponding to that used for national elections, and to be controlled by parliament.

French deputies were also concerned that MEPs should be subject not only to the same election campaign expense rules as themselves, but also to the same salary measures and taxation principles. In Ireland there was a similar concern over the likely disparity between the salaries of national and European representatives. Concern had also been expressed about MEPs salaries in the UK; but by the time that the Implementation Bill reached the Committee Stage, the Council of Ministers had announced, after its meeting in December 1978, that national parliamentary salaries and taxation would apply to MEPs.[18]

Another issue of moderate saliency concerned the qualifications for candidates. Most countries restricted candidacy to party lists, with various additional requirements in terms of deposit and signatures. Such conditions clearly discriminated against smaller parties, several of which were vocal in their opposition — though given their small size they could not usually make a significant impact on the parliamentary process. Given the fractionalised party system, this conflict was able to emerge in Denmark — whereas the dominance of the four major parties in France contained the issue entirely. In Ireland, there was a small amount of conflict about the level of deposit required, which reflected once again the problem of establishing relativities between national and European elections.

Conclusion

The preceding pages and chapters have put forward a plethora of facts and a myriad of ideas about nine legislative processes. It is now time to draw together these fragments, and to reach some conclusions about the performance of the political systems in the making of these laws. Before doing so, we wish to stress three *caveats*.

First, as discussed in the introduction, this is a single legislation issue with many unusual characteristics. Any general inference about law-making should be made only with the greatest care. Second, in these European polities, the mutual interdependence of the party, parliamentary and governmental systems creates a symbiosis, whose dynamics are clearly depicted in the nine national studies. This interdependency makes it extremely difficult to analyse, for example, the independent role of parliaments. Thirdly, many of the differences in institutional behaviour are due to the differences in the postures of political parties toward the various issues at stake, and not to the efficacy of the institution itself. Inferences about institutional efficacy and the performance of functions should therefore be made with caution.

Let us therefore begin by considering the analysis of conflict over issues. Firstly, a methodological point: this is the first systematic cross-national analysis that has been made of legislative issues. It demonstrates clearly the utility of this approach for analysing the political process. Whilst we do not wish to be involved in debates about the utility of political science in forecasting and futurology, we nevertheless would argue that the comparative analysis has important lessons for those concerned with future policy making in this area.

Secondly, we wish to draw attention to the essential similarity of the issue structure in the nine countries. Apart from the question of the 'pace' at which the national legislative process was progressing — which emerged sporadically and almost 'qualified' as an issue — the set of nine issues delineated above is a remarkably complete circumscription of the arguments that arose over direct elections. We may reasonably infer that *ceteris paribus* the issue-structure of future debate on direct elections will focus on these nine issues.

Thirdly, on each issue — with the single exception of 'conditions for candidates' — there was at least one country in which a major conflict emerged about the solution proposed by the national government. Moreover there were only two countries — Ireland and the Netherlands — in which there was no major conflict on at least one issue. Given the variation in the actual systems proposed, it seems highly improbable that any uniform system could be found that would provoke a lower level of conflict in the national arenas than emerged in 1974-1979. The implications depend on two separate factors: the way in which decisions can be made at the European level, and the influence which opponents can wield at a national level. If Ministers can genuinely exercise a veto in the European Council, then progress toward a really uniform system is improbable. But if the process of bargaining and exchange in Council can generate compromise on these issues, then such progress is not only possible at the European level, but also likely given the small proportion of countries in which each issue became of major importance. However, there remains the problem of consent by national parliaments, which have clearly demonstrated their powers — indeed, powers greater than many people have credited to them — over this legislative process.

Fourthly, the issue of 'constituencies' was clearly the most controversial element in the whole legislation. It arose in some form in every single country, and was a major issue in one third of them. The fact that the solutions adopted varied so greatly further exasperates this problem, when it is expressed as a cross-national issue. After this came the principle, which was an issue in seven countries. But in equal third place in the cross-national ranking of importance came most of the other issues — 'constitutionality', 'sovereignty', 'EP-NP links', 'the franchise' and 'finance'. This even dispersion of importance demonstrates the intractability of the problem.

Fifthly, we must note the saliency of issues relating to the principle of direct elections — in France and the UK in particular, and on the left of the partisan spectrum in general. It may be that the actual experience and performance of the directly elected Parliament may mollify the opposition in the future (though the immediate response to the European Parliament's rejection of the budget has confirmed this opposition). But at the very least, the opposition of principle has left behind vestiges of its activities that will provide obstacles to future change — notably the various requirements for the amendment of national constitutions — if the powers of the European Parliament are increased. These same issues of principle may well be regenerated in the event of such a change, to complicate the national processes of amendment of the EC Treaties.

Finally, we must note the efficacy with which parties articulated the issues. In the whole panorama of conflict displayed in table 13.3, in a political context where there is a total of sixty-three parties with more than 1 per cent of the seats in the national parliament, there are only ten parties which were divided, and this includes a number of cases of small parties or one-issue splits. The performance of European parties has been questioned in recent years, in the context of assertions about the weakening of ideological structures.[19] In these legislative processes, the policy positions of the political parties were clearly and effectively established — the UK being the only real exception — and their role in the law-making process was both constructive and efficient.

Having considered the way in which issues were articulated, let us now consider the manner in which the law-making process was organised, and in particular the role of the parliament[20] in passing the law. In our analysis of the passage of the Ratification and Implementation Bills, emphasis was laid on the extent to which the legislation process was 'institutionalised', or contained within the parliament. Whilst the Ratification Bills were moderately well institutionalised in the parliaments — with only Belgium and France dependent on party/government negotiation — the same was not true of the Implementation Bills, for in six out of nine countries an important step in the implementation process was carried out outside the parliamentary arena. In some cases the de-institutionalisation was in favour of bodies pretending to political neutrality — the Irish Boundary Commission or the Dutch Suffrage Council — whilst in other cases, it was explicitly a problem for political negotiation. Just as the party system articulated the issues, so also it tended to wrest from parliament some critical stages of the legislative process.

As the 'direct elections' policies passed into the parliaments, they were received in different ways. Pre-legislative scrutiny was carried out by committees in the two Anglo-Saxon Parliaments, which do not have a reputation for committee investigation; and in Denmark, which has a reputation for effective scrutiny by committee. In contrast, in the Committee stage, the Anglo-Saxon Parliaments used Committees of the Whole House, whereas the other parliaments deconcentrated scrutiny to one or more specialised committees. Thus the reputation for emphasis on the plenary in the Dail and Westminster was borne out by the legislative process, whilst other parliaments brought Interior or Constitutional expertise to bear in committees.

As befits an electoral matter, it was the lower chambers which bore the weight of the legislative process. There were two exceptions to this rule — France and Italy — both of which have been explained in their respective chapters in terms of the national political equation. But, whilst the French Senate is not generally noted for its power, and was mobilised for reasons of Government tactics, the Italian Senate has both constitutional and political equality with the Chamber of Deputies, and this helps to explain its important role (see chapter 1, table 1.1). However, both Belgium and the Federal Republic have generally powerful second chambers, yet they did not achieve the same influence.

In relation to governments, parliaments were generally subordinate partners. Given the political relationships binding the two together this is hardly a dramatic finding. But it is also clear that parliaments played a significant role of influence. In order to determine the nature of that role, we will now examine further the law-making function, in the light of theories of legislative behaviour.

Firstly, each parliament was responsible for passing the electoral law(s). In an era when executives have been blamed for usurping the prerogatives of legislatures, this is a notable feature. But further, in all countries except France — where constitutional limits constrained the parliament's scope for intervention — parliaments jealously guarded their control over elections against outside (governmental) interference by insisting on the detailing of legislation to an extent greater than that used for other laws. The opportunity for governments to intervene through decree, ordinance or other form of delegated legislation was therefore reduced.

Of course the legislative initiative was invariably vested in the hands of the government. However, two important constraints have been noted: on the one hand, the extensive activity by private members of the national parliaments to stimulate the governmental initiative (chapter 2, table 2.1), which was bolstered by parallel activity by parties; and on the other hand, the important role of various EC actors in influencing the initiative. It would be quite wrong to generalise from this case to the initiative of all legislation. But it is notable that, whilst the power of initiative is conventionally so clearly ascribed to governments, in this instance those governments were circumscribed (even if in part by their own collective decision in European Council).

Control over the passage of the bills varied greatly. In many countries with low levels of conflict, there was considerable deference to government — the Netherlands provides a clear example — and the normal governmental dominance over the legislative passage ensued. In contrast, in Britain and France, governments had to resort to coercive procedural devices to ensure the passage of the legislation in the face of virulent obstructionist opposition from substantial minorities. But the process of building a majority in Italy in a sub-committee which reworked the Implementation Bill, and the drawing up of a solution to the community conflict in Belgium, both demonstrate the sensitive interaction of parties, deputies and parliament in an accommodation process.

The power of amendment is a prerogative of parliaments, but many doubt that it is significant in practice. Three of the nine parliaments successfully introduced amendments which significantly changed the legislation; whilst in all others (except Denmark), some change was made during the passage of the Implementation Bills. The Ratification Bills remained largely unamended, partly as a result of constitutional, procedural or conventional restrictions, partly through acceptance of the principle. The French case, where an additional article was inserted before introduction in response to the demands of the parties, is a timely reminder of the political opportunities within an apparently restrictive constitutional framework.

It is clear then that the function of 'legitimation' is an underestimate of the law-making role of most of these European parliaments. In two countries, in both of which the level of conflict over the various issues was relatively low, the parliamentary role did not greatly exceed this level: for in both the Netherlands and Ireland, not only was there extra-parliamentary activity at the pre-legislative stage, but also during the passage there was little constructive criticism of the governmental bills. At the other end of the scale, the Italian parliament, which substantially rewrote the Implementation Bill in its Committee stage, stands out as performing a maximal law-making function. It is difficult to distinguish between the performances of the other parliaments which fall in the intervening category, for they are influential in different aspects of the law-making function.

The other goal of the legislative process was the resolution of political conflict over the European elections, and the integration of disputant political forces. There was a large conflict in France and the UK: the parliamentary process contributed to the resolution of the conflict in France, but in the UK the essential steps took place outside the parliamentary forum. In neither country did the political parties abandon their antagonistic positions after the legislative battle, and therefore the integration function was not successfully performed.

In countries of intermediate conflict, the Danish, Italian and Luxembourg parliaments played central roles in conflict management; whilst in Belgium and the Federal Republic it was more a matter of negotiation between parties that resolved the difficult issues. For Ireland and the Netherlands, it is not that the parliament was unsuccessful at conflict management, but rather that there was no real conflict to be managed.

At a time when the 'decline of parliaments' argument is still accepted — despite an intuition that in the 1970s parliaments have played a more important role than was ascribed to them in the 1960s — it is significant that our attention has focussed ultimately on the multi-faceted law-making role of these European parliaments. The established view about parliaments has tended to emphasise the legitimation function, which is a minimum contribution to law-making that one would associate particularly with the adversary style of parliamentarism typical of traditional British politics. But this study has emphasised the simultaneous and complementary functions of the *accommodation* of the diffuse demands of political forces, and the *adjustment* of governmental policy proposals. Variation occurs both in the balance between the roles of the party system and the parliament in performing these functions; and in the extent to which these functions are performed at all. Nevertheless it is clear that European parliaments are alive and well, and performing important functions in conjunction with the party and governmental systems with which they are intertwined.

Notes

1   A third bill was in fact passed in Belgium. It dealt with minor, technical matters relating to the conserving of ballot papers until the start of the count. It has therefore not been taken into account here. See chapter 3, note 36.
2.   For a comparison of national styles of legislative drafting, see: W. Dale, *Legislative Drafting*, (Butterworth, London, 1977).
3   A similar clause was introduced in the UK, and some other countries indicated that constitutional change would be necessary before an increase in powers could occur. See the final 'issues' section of this chapter.
4   In most countries, the national electoral law formed the basis for the European legislation; indeed in most cases, a similar electoral system was used.
5   By 'blocked' party lists is meant that voters are not able to modify the ranking of candidates on a party list.
6   For a review, see: M. Wing and M. Hagger, 'Committees in the European Parliament and Committees in the National Parliaments', *ECPR*, Grenoble, 1978. For a more detailed case study, see M. Hagger and M. Wing, 'The Deconcentration of Legislative Power: the Development of Committees in the European Parliament', *European Journal of Political Research*, vol.7, 1979, pp 117-46.
7   The emphasis on committees in the German Parliament has been noted by G. Loewenberg, *Parliament in the German Political System*, (Cornell U.P., Ithaca, 1967). The tendency has increased since the 1960s.
8   Although 'specialised' Select Committees have existed for a long time in the UK, notably in relation to financial matters, their extension to new policy areas in the 'Crossman Reforms' of 1966 has had limited impact. A major extension is in progress in 1979/80.
9   The capability and performance of the Market Relations Committee is discussed in J. Fitzmaurice, 'The Danish system of parliamentary control over EC', chapter 9 in: V. Herman and R. van Schendelen, *The European Parliament and the National Parliaments* (Saxon House, Farnborough, 1979).
10 The analysis of the amendment of legislation in parliament is fraught with complication at a national level; hence at a comparative level, interpretation must be cautious. For an introduction to the problem, see D. Hearl's discussion in chapter 3 of this book; V. Herman, 'Backbench and Opposition Amendments to Government Legislation' in D. Leonard and V. Herman, *The Backbencher and Parliament* (Macmillan, London, 1972); and J.A.G. Griffiths, *Parliamentary Scrutiny of Government Bills* (Allen and Unwin, London, 1974).
11 We assume the salience of the left—right ideological dimension in all countries. This has repeatedly been defended, see especially: I. Crewe, J. Farlie and I. Budge, *Party Identification and Beyond* (Wiley, London, 1976).
12 In Belgium and Luxembourg, there are specific constitutional provisions for the temporary delegation of legislative executive and judicial powers to 'institutions of international law' (Belgian Constitution: Article 256; Luxembourg Constitution: Article 496). See E. Wall, *Europe: Unification and the Law* (Penguin, Harmondsworth, 1969), at p.110.

13 G. Hand, J. Georgel and C. Sasse, *European Electoral Systems Handbook* (Butterworths, London, 1979) at p.235.
14 V. Herman and R. van Schendelen, *The European Parliament and the National Parliaments* (Saxon House, Farnborough, 1979).
15 The UK Labour Party decided to forbid its candidates from holding a dual mandate.
16 D.W. Rae, *The Political Consequences of Electoral Laws*, 2nd ed. (Yale U.P., New Haven, 1971).
17 Notably in France, where there are comprehensive arrangements for postal, proxy and embassy voting by non-resident French citizens. See chapter 12.
18 However, there are expense provisions, which are tax exempt.
19 On 'catch-all parties', see O. Kirchheimer, 'The Transformation of European Party Systems' in: J. La Palombara and M. Weiner, (eds), *Political Parties and Political Development* (Princeton U.P., Princeton, 1966). For a recent critical appraisal of one dimension of this thesis, see: S.B. Wolinetz, 'The Transformation of Western European Party Systems Revisited', *West European Politics*, vol.2, 1979, pp 4-28.
20 A distinction is sometimes made between the terms 'parliament' and 'legislature'. We have adopted the former term here in order not to imply any functional interpretation. See K. Wheare, *Legislatures* (Oxford U.P., London, 1968), p.2.

Appendix: Results of the first Direct Elections, June 1979

The following tables show the results of the direct elections to the European Parliament in June 1979 in each Member State, together with the overall distribution by Party Group in the European Parliament. Votes are recorded in absolute terms, and as a percentage of the votes cast. Turnout is recorded as a percentage of the electorate.

Belgium

Party	Abbreviation	Votes	Vote %	Seats (N)	E.P. Group
Communist (Walloon)	PCB	106,033	1.9	0	—
Communist (Flemish)	KPB	39,771	0.7	0	—
Socialist (Walloon)	PSB	698,892	12.9	4	S
Socialist (Flemish)	BSP	575,886	10.6	3	S
Walloon Regionalist) Brussels Francophone)	FDF-RW[1]	414,412	7.6	2	NI
Ecologist (Walloon)	ECOLO	107,837	2.0	0	—
Ecologist (Flemish)	AGALEV	77,984	1.4	0	—
Flemish Regionalist	VU	324,569	5.9	1	I
Christian Social (Walloon)	PSC	445,940	8.2	3	PPE
Christian Peoples (Flemish)	CVP	1,607,925	29.6	7	PPE
Liberals (Walloon)	PRL[2]	372,857	6.9	2	L
Liberals (Flemish)	PVV	512,355	9.4	2	L
Others		138,404	2.6	0	—
Total		5,422,865		24	
Invalid votes		789,616			

Turnout as per cent of electorate = 91.4[3]

1 The two Francophone Regionalist Groups operated an electoral alliance.
2 The Liberals regrouped since the April 1977 Election.
3 Compulsory voting.

Denmark

Party	Abbreviation	Votes	Vote %	Seats (N)	E.P. Group
Folke Bevaegelsen mod EF	FME	365,760	20.8	4	I
Left Socialist	LS	60,964	3.5	0	—
Siumut (Greenland)	S[1]	5,118	—	1	S
Socialist Peoples	SP	81,991	4.7	1	COM
Social Democratic	SD	382,487	21.8	3	S
Radical Liberal	RL	252,767	14.4	3	L
Justice	JP	59,379	3.4	0	—
Centre Democratic	CD	107,790	6.1	1	ED
Christian Peoples	CPP	30,985	1.8	0	—
Agrarian Liberal	AL	56,944	3.2	0	—
Conservative	C	245,309	14.0	2	ED
Progressive	PP	100,702	5.7	1	DEP
Others (including Atassut Greenland)		4,654	0.3	0	—
Total		1,754,850		16	

Turnout as per cent of electorate = 47.1

1 Includes a reserved seat for Greenland.

Federal Republic of Germany

Party	Abbreviation	Votes	Vote %	Seats (N)[1]	E.P. Group
Social Democratic	SPD	11,370,045	40.8	34+1	S
Free Democratic	FDP	1,662,621	6.0	4	L
Ecologist	G	893,683	3.2	0	—
Christian Democratic Union	CDU	10,883,085	39.1	32+2	PPE
Christian Social Union	CSU	2,817,120	10.1	8	PPE
Others		220,555	0.8	0	—
Total		27,847,109		81	

Turnout as per cent of electorate = 65.7

1 Includes three MEPs for Berlin.

France

Party	Abbreviation	Votes	Vote %	Seats (N)	E.P. Group
Communist	PCF	4,153,710	20.4	19	COM
Socialist and Left Radical	PS + MRG	4,763,026	23.4	21	S
Ecologist		891,683	4.4	—	
Trotskyist		623,663	3.1	—	
Centrist/Independent Republican (UFE)	UDF	5,666,984	27.9	26	L/EPP[1]
Gaullist (DIFE)	RPR	3,301,980	16.2	15	DEP
Others		930,394	4.6	—	
Total		20,331,440		81	

Turnout as per cent of electorate = 81

1 Nine UFE members belong to the Liberal Group, seventeen to the EPP.

Ireland

Party	Abbreviation	Votes	Vote %	Seats (N)	E.P. Group
Sinn Fein	SF	43,943	3.3	0	—
Labour Party	LAB	193,893	14.5	4	S
Independent	IND	189,499	14.2	2	(I[1] (L
Fianna Gael	FG	443,652	33.1	4	PPE
Fianna Fáil	FF	464,450	34.7	5	DEP
Other		3,630	0.3	0	—
Total		1,339,072		15	

Turnout as per cent of electorate = 63.6

1 One independent belongs to the Liberal Group, the other to the Independent.

Italy

Party	Abbreviation	Votes	Vote %	Seats (N)	E.P. Group
Democratic Party for Proletarian Unity	PDUP	404,989	1.1	1	I
Proletarian Democrats	DP	250,577	0.7	1	I
Communist[1]	PCI	10,343,991	29.6	24	COM
Radical	PR	1,282,841	3.7	3	I
Socialist	PSI	3,857,670	11.0	9	S
Social Democratic	PSDI	1,511,562	4.3	4	S
Republican	PRI	896,526	2.6	2	L
Christian Democrat	DC	12,753,350	36.5	29	PPE
South Tyrol People's Party	SVP	196,199	0.6	1	PPE
Liberal	PLI	1,269,612	3.6	3	L
National Democracy	DN	141,745	0.4	0	–
Italian Social Movement	MSI	1,907,505	5.4	4	NI
Aosta Valley Union	UV	165,285	0.5	0	–
Total		34,981,852		81	

Turnout as per cent of electorate = 85.5

1 'Communist' includes 'Left Independents' who were included on the Communist list.

Luxembourg

Party	Abbreviation	Votes[1]	Vote %	Seats	E.P. Group
Communist	KPL	48,813	5.0	0	–
Socialist Workers	LSAP	211,106	21.7	1	S
Social Democratic	SDP	68,289	7.0	0	–
Democratic	DP	274,307	28.1	2	L
Christian Social	CSV	352,296	36.1	3	PPE
Other		20,180	2.1	0	–
Total		974,991		6	

Turnout as per cent of electorate = 88.9[2]

1 Each voter had six votes.
2 Compulsory voting.

Netherlands

Party	Abbreviation	Votes	Vote %	Seats (N)	E.P. Group
Communist	CPN	97,343	1.7	0	—
Pacifist	PSP	97,243	1.7	0	—
Radical	PPR	92,055	1.6	0	—
Socialist	PvdA	1,722,240	30.4	9	S
Democrat '66	D'66	511,567	9.0	2	NI
Christian Democrats	CDA	2,017,743	35.6	10	PPE
Liberals	VVD	914,787	16.1	4	L
Reformist-Calvinist	GPV	62,610	1.1	0	—
State-Calvinist	SGP	126,412	2.2	0	—
Others		24,903	0.4	0	—
Total		5,666,903		25	

Turnout as per cent of electorate = 57.8

United Kingdom[1]

Party	Abbreviation	Votes[2]	Vote %	Seats (N)	E.P. Group
Labour	Lab	4,234,137	31.6	17	S
Social Democratic and Labour	SDLP	140,622	1.0	1[1]	S
Plaid Cymru	PC	83,399	0.6	0	—
Liberal	Lib	1,693,229	12.6	0	—
Scottish National	SNP	247,836	1.9	1	DEP
Democratic Unionist	DUP	170,688	1.3	1[1]	NI
Ulster Unionist	UUP	125,169	0.9	1[1]	ED
Conservative	C	6,466,090	48.4	60	ED
Other		224,096	1.7	0	
Total		13,385,266		81	

Turnout as per cent of electorate = 33.0

---

1 Includes three Ulster MEPs elected under single transferable vote proportional system for a single three member constituency.
2 The voting figures are adjusted to take account of the void election result and consequent by-election in London South West.

301

Composition of European Party Groups by Member State

European Party Groups	Abbreviation	Belgium	Denmark	France	Fed. Rep. Germany	Ireland	Italy	Luxembourg	Netherlands	United Kingdom	Total
Communist and Allies	COM		1	19			24				44
Socialist	S	7	4	21	35	4	13	1	9	18	112
European Peoples Party	PPE(EPP)	10		9	42	4	30	3	10		108
European Democrat	ED		3							61	64
European Progressive Democrat	DEP(EPD)		1	15		5				1	22
Liberal and Democrat	L	4	3	17	4	1	5	2	4		40
Independent Group 2	I	1	4			1	5				11
Non-attached	NI	2					4		2	1	9
Total		24	16	81	81	15	81	6	25	81	410

1 The French abbreviations are shown (with the English usage in parentheses).

2 During the first session of the directly elected Parliament eleven independent MEPs combined together to form a new European Party Group, to take advantage of the privileges and status enjoyed by recognised groups of more than ten members. As the title of the group indicates (Group for the Technical Co-ordination and Defence of Independent Groups and Members), the grouping is purely tactical and makes no pretentions to ideological consistency.

Select bibliography

From the wealth of material that has been published in recent years about the European Parliament and direct elections, the following items have been selected as making *significant contributions* to the understanding of the *legislative processes* in the nine nations and in the supranational arena of the European Community. For works on the European Parliament itself, the European Parliament has published an extensive bibliography in 1979 (cited below). The bibliography below was compiled by Sue Robertson, Kingston Polytechnic Library, in consultation with the research group.

Allen, David and Morgan, Roger, 'Les élections directes au Parlement européen: le dilemme britannique' (Direct elections to the European Parliament: the British dilemma), *Politique étrangère*, vol.43, 1978, pp 5-20. Also in: *Europa Archiv*, no.24, 1978, pp 798-804.

Ambris, M. de, 'Elections au Parlement européen; modes de scrutin et systèmes électoraux chez les Neuf' (Elections to the European Parliament: electoral systems in the Nine), *Revue politique et parlementaire*, no.874, 1978, pp 52-65.

Armand, L. and Drancourt, M., *Le Pari Européen* (Fayard, Paris, 1968).

Bangemann, Martin, 'Preparations for direct elections in the Federal Republic of Germany', *Common Market Law Review*, vol.15, 1978, pp 321-37.

Bangemann, Martin and Bieber, Roland, *Die Directwahl-Sackgasse oder Chance für Europa? Analysen und Dokumente* (Direct elections — cul-de-sac or opportunity for Europe?), Nomos, Baden-Baden, 1979.

Baumann, Carol Edler, 'Direct elections to the European Parliament (possible impact on the future powers of the Parliament and on the domestic policies of member states, particularly France and Britain)', *Millenium*, vol.7, 1978, pp 20-35.

Baviera, F. Saverio, 'Preparations for direct elections in Italy', *Common Market Law Review*, vol.15, 1978, pp 199-206.

Beavan, John, 'Labour, Tories and the European election', *Political Quarterly*, vol.50, 1979, pp 219-28.

Benn, Hilary, 'Direct elections to the European Parliament', *Labour Monthly*, no.60, 1978, pp 349-54.

Bonvicini, G. and Solari, S. (eds), *I partiti e le elezioni del parlamento europeo*, Il Mulino, Bologna, 1979.

Bosscher, R., 'Preparations for direct elections in the Netherlands', *Common Market Law Review*, vol.15, 1978, pp 465-73.

Boulouis, J., 'Observations sur la décision du Conseil Constitutionnel (France) décision du 30 décembre 1976' (Observations on the decision of the French Constitutional Council on 30 December 1976), *Cahiers de Droit Européen*, no.4, 1977, pp 458-81.

Bourdet, C., *L'Europe Truquée*, Seghers, Paris, 1977.

Buck, K.H., 'Die Haltung von KPI und KPF gegenüber Direktwahl und Fünktione des Europaparlaments' (The attitudes of PCI and PCF on direct elections and the functions of the European Parliament), *Zeitschrift für Parlamentsfragen*, vol.7, 1976, pp 209-19.

Burban, J.L., 'La dialectique des élections européennes' (The dialectics of European elections), *Revue Française de Science Politique*, vol.27, 1977, pp 377-406.

Burban, J.L., 'La France et les élections européennes de 1978' (France and the 1978 European elections), *Revue du Marché Commun*, no.209, 1977, pp 337-43.

Burban, J.L. 'Les communistes et l'élection du Parlement européen au suffrage universel' (The Communists and the direct election of the European Parliament), *Revue du Marché Commun*, no.199, 1976, pp 373-80.

Burban, J.L., 'Les gaullistes et l'élection du Parlement européen au suffrage universel direct' (The Gaullists and the election of the European Parliament by direct universal suffrage), *Revue du Marché Commun*, no.193, 1976, pp 75-85.

Burban, J.L., 'Le nouveau project d'élection du Parlement européen au suffrage universel' (The new plan for direct elections to the European Parliament), *Cahiers de Droit Européen*, vol.11, 1975, pp 453-63.

Burban, J.L., 'Les socialistes et l'élection du Parlement européen au suffrage universel' (The Socialists and the direct election of the European Parliament), *Revue du Marché Commun*, 1977, pp 87-96.

Capurso, Marcello, 'La decisione del Consiglio della Communità europee per l'elezione dei componenti dell'Assemblea a suffragio universale diretto' (The decision of the Council of the EC to elect the Assembly by direct universal suffrage), *Rivista Trimestrale di Diritto Pubblico*, 1977, pp 1079-94.

Chiroux, René, 'Les partis politiques et l'élection du Parlement européen' (Political parties and election to the European Parliament), *Revue politique et parlementaire*, no.876, 1978, pp 27-45.

Cocatre-Zilgien, André, 'De l'élection du "Parlement européen" au suffrage universel direct. La "décision" et l'"acte" du Conseil des Communautés européennes du 20 Septembre 1976' (On direct elections to the European Parliament. The 'decision' and the 'act' of the Council of the European Communities of 20 September 1976), *Annuaire Française de Droit International*, vol.22, 1976, pp 787-804.

Colard, Daniel, 'La France et l'élection du Parlement européen' (France and the election of the European Parliament), *Studia Diplomatica*, vol.130, 1977, pp 213-26.

Cook, Chris, *The first European elections*, Macmillan, London, 1979.

Coussirat-Coustère, Vincent, 'Le Conseil constitutionnel et l'élection au suffrage universel direct de l'Assemblée européenne' (The constitutional Council and the direct elections to the European Assembly), *Annuaire française de droit international*, vol.22, 1976, pp 805-21.

Crebo, Etienne, *Etudes sur le Parlementarisme*, Marcel, Paris, 1930.

Debré, Michel and Debré, Jean-Louis, *Le Pouvoir Politique*, Seghers, Paris, 1978.

Dabezies, P. and Portelli, H., 'Les Fondements de la Querelle Politique' (The basis of the political conflict), *Pouvoirs*, 1977, pp 67-88.

Dehousse, F., 'Réflexions à propos des élections européennes de demain' (Reflections concerning future european elections), *Revue du Marché Commun*, no.182, 1975, pp 49-56.

Dehousse, F., 'Vers des élections européennes' (Towards European elections), *Studia diplomatica*, vol.29, 1976, pp 65-86.

Dell'omodarme, M., 'Ruolo e azione del Parlamento europeo per l'elezione a suffragio universale diretto dei suoi membri' (The role and action of the European Parliament in favour of direct elections), *Il Politico*, vol.36, 1971, pp 775-841.

Dessloch, Hubertus, 'Europäische Wahlen 1978?' (European elections in 1978?), *Politische Studien*, vol.28, 1977, pp 117-26.

Election au suffrage universel direct des membres de l'Assemblée européenne [décision des 29 et 30 décembre 1976] (Direct election of the European Assembly: decision of 29-30 December 1976), *Revue du Droit Public et de la Science Politique en France et à l'étranger*, no.1, 1977, pp 129-80.

European Parliament, Directorate-General for Information and Documentation, *The European Parliament: Bibliography, 1970-1978*, European Parliament, Luxembourg, 1979.

European Parliament, *Elections to the European Parliament by direct universal suffrage*, European Parliament, Luxembourg, 1977. (Also in other languages).

Favoreau, Louis and Philip, Loic, 'Election au suffrage universel direct des membres de l'Assemblée européenne' (Direct elections to the

European Assembly), *Revue du Droit Public et de la Science Politique*, vol.93, 1977, pp 129-66.

Fitzmaurice, John, 'Direct elections and the future of the European Parliament', *West European Politics*, vol.1, 1978, pp 208-26.

Forman, J., 'Preparations for direct elections in the UK', *Common Market Law Review*, vol.15, 1977, pp 347-59.

Foschi, Franco, 'Il voto europeo' (The European election), *Affari esteri*, July 1978, pp 388-99.

Grabitz, Eberhard and Laeufer, Thomas, *Handbuch der Europawahl* (Handbook of European elections), Europa-Union Verlag, Bonn, 1979.

Guizzi, V., 'L'azione del Parlamento italiano in favore dell'elezione a suffragio universale del Parlamento europeo' (The action of the Italian Parliament in favour of direct elections to the European Parliament), *Il Politico*, vol.36, 1971, pp 782-91.

Habsburg, Otto von, 'Europa-Wahlen' (European elections), *Zeitbühne*, no.2, 1976, pp 8-11.

Herman, Valentine, 'Direct Elections to the European Parliament: comparative perspectives', *Common Market Law Review*, vol.16, 1979, pp 209-26.

Hollick, J.C., 'Direct elections to the European Parliament: the French debate', *World Today*, vol.33, 1977, pp 472-80.

Hrbek, Rudolf, 'Das deutsche Wahlgesetz zum europäischen Parlament in der Parteikontroverse' (Party conflict on the German electoral law for the European Parliament), *Zeitschrift für Parlamentsfragen*, 1978, pp 168-78.

Jackson, Robert and Fitzmaurice, John, *The European Parliament – a guide to direct elections*, Penguin, Harmondsworth, 1979.

Jacque, Jean-Paul, 'The institutional problem in the programs drawn up by the political parties for the election of the European Parliament by direct universal suffrage', *Lo Spettatore Internazionale*, April-June, 1978, vol.13, pp 131-42.

Kovar, Robert and Simon, Denys, 'A propos de la décision du Conseil constitutionnel français du 30 décembre 1976 relative à l'élection de l'Assemblée parlementaire européenne au suffrage universel direct' (Some reflections on the decision of the French Constitutional Council of 30 December 1976), *Revue trimestrielle de droit européen*, October-December 1977, pp 665-720. Also in English in: *Common Market Law Review*, vol.14, 1977, pp 525-60.

Krenzler, Horst Günter, 'Das Programm der europäische liberalen Demokraten (ELD) im Vergleich' (The programme of the European Liberal Party in comparative perspective), *Liberal* (Bonn), 1978, pp 412-21.

Kundoch, H.G., 'Le recours en carence comme moyen juridique de promouvoir l'élection directe du Parlement Européen' (An action for 'failure to act' as a judicial means of expediting direct elections), *Cahiers de Droit Européen*, vol.11, 1975, pp 425-52.

Kundoch, H.G., *Allianz der Bürokraten oder Ohnmacht der Demokraten: warum brauchen wir europäische Direktwahlen?* (Alliance between bureaucrats or vanishing democrats: why do we need the direct European elections?), Akademie Sankelmark, Sankelmark, 1976.

Kyle, Keith, 'Bringing democracy to Brussels: towards a directly elected European Parliament', *Round Table*, no.264, 1977, pp 323-30.

Laprat, Gérard, 'Institutions communautaires: instruments de la supranationalité ou expression de la démocratie?' (Community institutions: supranational or democratic?) *Cahiers du Communisme*, February 1979, pp 90-101.

Laufer, Th. (ed.), *Europa-Wahl — Pro und Contra* (For and against European elections), Europa Union Verlag, Bonn, 1977.

Laurent, Pierre-Henri, 'European elections and the making of Europe (implications of the election of representatives to the European Parliament to take place in 1978)', *World Affairs*, no.140, 1978, pp 273-83.

Legrand-Lane, R., 'Elire des députés européens' (Electing European deputies), *Etudes* (Paris), June 1976, pp 789-807.

Legrand-Lane, Raymond, '1979, Année européenne. L'élection des parlementaires européens' (1979, a European year. The election of the European parliament), *Etudes* (Paris), February 1979, pp 165-83.

Lesguillons, Henry, 'Scénario de l'élection du Parlement européen au suffrage universel' (A scenario of direct elections to the European Parliament), *Pouvoirs*, 1977, no.27, pp 53-65.

Levi, L. and Pistone, S., *L'Elezione Europeo* (The European election), Fondazione Agnelli, Torino, 1979.

Liguori, R., 'L'elezione del Parlamento europeo a suffraggio universale' (Direct elections to the European Parliament), *Communità internazionale*, vol.31, 1976, pp 689-95.

Lodge, Juliet, 'The significance of Direct Elections for the European Parliament's Role in the European Community and the Drafting of a Common Electoral Law', *Common Market Law Review*, vol.16, 1979, pp 195-208.

Lucker, Hans August, 'Die Bedeutung der Direktwahl zum Europäischen Parlament' (Significance of direct elections to the European Parliament), *Politische Studien*, 1978, vol.29, pp 11-19.

Manning, M., 'Direct elections to the European Parliament: some implications for Irish politics', *Administration* (Dublin), vol.22, 1974, pp 384-99.

Marquand, David, 'Towards a Europe of the Parties', *Political Quarterly*, vol.49, 1978, pp 425-45.

Meloncelli, Achille, 'L'elezione diretta del Parlamento europeo: note sul progetto di legge della R.F.A.' (The direct election of the European Parliament: notes on the West German bill), *Rivista Trimestrale di Diritto Pubblico*, 1977, pp 1604-12.

Mira, Giuseppe, 'Elezioni dirette del Parlamento Europeo; i problemi per l'Europa e per l'Italia (Direct Elections to the European Parliament: the difficulties for Europe and for Italy), *Studi Economici e Sociali*, no.3, 1977, pp 165-77.

Morelli, Vincenzo, 'La lunga marcia verso il Parlamento europeo' (The long march toward the European Parliament), *Nord e Sud*, 1978, pp 138-51.

Morgan, R. and Allen, D., 'The European Parliament: direct elections in national and community perspective', *World Today*, vol.34, 1978, pp 296-303.

Moxon-Browne, Edward, 'Irish political parties and European integration', *Administration* (Dublin), vol.25, 1977, pp 519-32.

Müller-Graff, Peter-Christian, *Die Direktwahl des europäischen Parlaments, Genese und Perspektiven* (Direct election of the European Parliament, genesis and perspectives), J.C.B. Mohr, Tübingen, 1977.

Neels, L., 'Preparations for direct elections in Belgium', *Common Market Law Review*, vol.15, 1978, pp 337-47.

Neunreither, Karl Heinz, 'Legitimationsprobleme in der Europäischen Gemeinschaft (Problems of legitimacy in the European Community), *Zeitschrift für Parlamentsfragen*, no.2, 1976, pp 245-58.

O'Gadhra, Nollaig, 'Re-thinking the Proportional Representation system (concerning Northern Ireland's representation in the European Parliament)', *Social Studies* (Ireland), no.6, 1977, pp 57-63.

Palmer, M., 'The Role of a directly elected European Parliament', *World Today*, vol.33, 1977, pp 122-30.

Papisca, Antonio, 'I partiti politici europei, ovvero: il "fronte dell' Europa" ' (Political parties in Europe: the 'European front'), *Il Mulino*, 1977, pp 805-44.

Papisca, Antonio, 'Communità europa: dal consenso permissivo alla partecipazione politica' (European Community: from permissive consent to political participation), *Rivista Italiana di Scienza Politica*, vol.6, 1976, pp 289-330.

Partsch, K.D., 'Das Wahlverfahren und sein Einfluss auf die Legitimation der europaischen Parlament' (Direct elections and their influence on the legitimacy of the European Parliament), *Europarecht*, no.4, 1978, pp 293-310.

Patijn, Schelto, 'Elezioni dirette del parlamento europeo' (Direct elections to the European Parliament), *Biblioteca della Liberta*, vol.64, 1977, pp 39-55.

Patijn, Schelto, 'De Europese verkiezingen en wat dan?' (Whither the European Community?), *Socialisme en democratie*, no.12, 1977, pp 575-645.

Paulin, Bernard and Forman, John, 'L'élection du Parlement européen au suffrage universel direct' (The election of the European Parliament by direct universal suffrage), *Cahiers de Droit Européen*, vol.12, 1976, pp 506-36.

Pohle, M., 'Direktwahl des Europäischen Parlaments: Ein Ablenkungsmanover? Zehn skeptischen Thesen zu den möglichen Wirkungen', (Direct elections to the European Parliament – a divisive manoeuvre? Ten sceptical theses about possible developments), *Zeitschrift für Parlamentsfragen*, 1976, pp 222-6.

Pridham, Geoffrey and Pridham, Pippa, 'The new European party federations and direct elections', *World Today*, vol.35, 1979, pp 62-70.

Rabier, Jacques-René, 'Les attitudes du public à l'égard de l'élection du Parlement européen au suffrage universel direct' (Public attitudes toward direct elections to the European Parliament), *Revue d'Integration européenne*, September 1977, pp 47-62.

Rambaud, Patrick, 'L'approbation par la France des dispositions sur l'élection du Parlement européen au suffrage universel direct (The approval in France of the procedure for direct elections to the European Parliament), *Annuaire Française de Droit International*, 1977, pp 884-901.

Rattinger, Hans, 'Bundesliste oder Landeslisten bei der Direktwahl zum Europäischen Parlament: Auswirkungen auf die Stärke der Parteien' (Federal or regional lists for the election of the European Parliament: their consequences on the strength of the parties), *Zeitschrift für Parlamentsfragen*, vol.8, 1977, pp 189-96.

Rengeling, Hans-Werner, 'Die Wahl des Europäischen Parlaments und neue Entwicklungen im Europäischen Gemeinschaftsrecht' (The election of the European Parliament and recent changes in the European Community Law), *Offentliche Verwaltung*, vol.30, 1977, pp 622-26.

Rifflet, Raymond, 'Options et alternatives européennes dans la perspective des élections européennes au suffrage universel direct' (European options and alternatives concerning direct elections), *Bulletin du Centre Européen de la Culture*, vol.16, 1976, pp 69-79.

Robinson, Mary, 'Preparations for direct elections in Ireland', *Common Market Law Review*, vol.15, 1978, pp 187-99.

Rulli, G., 'Grandi manovre per le elezioni del Parlamento europeo' (Manoeuvres for the elections to the European Parliament), *Cività cattolica*, no.3074, 15 July 1978, pp 192-9.

Sadurska, R., 'Znaczenie wyborów powszechnych do Parlamentu Europejskiego' (The significance of direct elections to the European Parliament), *Państwo Prawo*, vol.31, 1976, pp 67-78.

Salvini, Gianpaolo, 'Verso le elezioni del Parlamento europeo' (Toward the election of the European Parliament), *Aggiornamenti sociali*, March 1978, pp 161-76.

Sasse, Christoph; Georgel, Jacques and Hand, Geoffrey (eds), *Das Wahlrecht der Neun*, Nomos, Baden-Baden, 1979; *European Electoral Systems Handbook*, Butterworths, London, 1979; and in other languages.

Schondube, Claud, 'Die Vorteile des direkt gewählten Europäischen Parlaments' (The advantages of a directly elected European Parliament), *Die neue Gesellschaft*, September 1977, pp 742-78.

Schwed, J.J., 'Parliament and the Commission', *American Academy of Political and Social Science Annals*, no.440, 1978, pp 33-41.

Schwed, J.J., 'Le Parlement européen et son élection au suffrage universel' (The European Parliament and direct elections), *Revue du Marché Commun*, no.192, 1976, pp 20-7.

Schweitzer, C.C., 'Election du Parlement européen au suffrage universel' (Direct elections to the European Parliament), *Documents* (Cologne), vol.30, 1975, pp 26-35.

Seiler, Daniel L., 'En marge de l'élection du Parlement européen: le problème des familles politiques en Europe occidentale' (A by-product of direct elections to the European Parliament: the problem of political movements in Western Europe), *Revue de l'Integration Européenne*, 1978, pp 143-90.

Sidjanski, Dusan, *Europe élections: de la démocratie européenne* (European elections: European democracy), A. Stanké, Paris, 1979.

Simon, Denys, 'Preparations in France for Direct Elections to the European Parliament', *Common Market Law Review*, vol.15, 1978, pp 127-38.

Spenale, G., 'Les élections au suffrage universel direct du Parlement européen' (Direct elections to the European Parliament), *Studia diplomatica*, vol.29, 1976, pp 427-42.

Steed, Michael, *Proposals for a sensible voting system for the European Parliament. Fair elections or fiasco?*, National Committee for Electoral Reform, London, 1977.

Stewart, M., 'Direct Elections to the European Parliament (with special reference to the UK)', *Common Market Law Review*, vol.13, 1976, pp 283-99.

Streiff, Gérard, 'Europe de crise et enjeu des élections (Europe in crisis and the problem of direct elections), *Cahiers du Communisme*, 1978, pp 74-85.

Strizek, Helmut and Strizek, Gisela, 'Christdemokraten und Konservative vor der EG-Wahl' (Christian-Democrat and Conservative attitudes to direct elections), *Die neue Gesellschaft*, September 1977, pp 742-78.

Taylor, P.J. and Johnston, R.J., 'Population distributions and political power in the European Parliament', *Regional Studies*, vol.12, 1978, pp 61-68.

Thill, J., 'Preparations for direct elections in the Grand Duchy of Luxembourg', *Common Market Law Review*, vol.15, 1978, pp 473-503.

Traversa, Silvio, 'L'elezione del Parlamento europeo a suffragio universale e la legge elettorale Italiana' (The election of the European Parliament by universal suffrage and the Italian electoral law), *Rivista Trimestrale di Diritto Pubblico*, no.4, 1977, pp 1577-1603.

Troccoli, Giuseppe, 'L'elezione a suffragio universale diretto del Parlamento europeo' (The election of the European Parliament by direct universal suffrage), *Rivista Trimestrale di Diritto Pubblico*, no.4, 1977, pp 1535-76.

Vedel, G., 'Les Racines de la Querelle Constitutionelle' (The origins of the constitutional debate), *Pouvoirs*, 1977, pp 23-37.

Vedovato, Giuseppe, 'Elezioni europee e politica Italiana' (European elections and Italian politics), *Rivista di Studi politici internazionali*, January-March 1978, pp 7-17.

Weydert, Jean, 'Election au Parlement européen, faux débats, vraies questions' (Elections to the European Parliament — pseudo issues and real problems), *Projet*, 1979, pp 283-6.

Willame, Jean-Claude, 'Le rapport Tindemans et les élections européennes' (The Tindemans report and the European elections), *Res Publica*, vol.19, 1977, pp 345-71.

Special issues of journals:

Biblioteca della Libertà, January 1977.
Les Communistes Français et l'Europe: Bulletin, nos.1, 2, 1978.
Eurobarometer, twice yearly report on public opinion, passim.
Europa Archiv, vol.24, December 1978.
European Journal of Political Research, vol.8, March 1980.
Das Parlament, no.49, December 1976.
Pouvoirs, no.2, 1977.
West European Politics, vol.1, no.2, 1978.
Zeitschrift für Parlamentsfragen, no.2, 1978.

Index

References from Notes indicated by 'n' after page reference

Comparative legislative behaviour, characteristics of 5-9, 260-4; and committees 3, 167, 274-7; focus of 3-4; methodology of 3-5

Constitutions 7-8, 10-11, see also country studies

Coppieters, F. 34n

Cot, P. 119

Cotta, M. 144-67

Council of Ministers, 16, 18-27, 200-1, 251, 253

Craenes, G. 183n

Craig, W. 212

Crebo, E. 204-38, 260-96

Crewe, I. 282n

Crick, B. 205n, 218n

Criddle, B. 106n

Dahlerup, D. 58n

Dale, W. 201n

Damamme, D. 2n

Damgaard, E. 55n, 56n, 58n

Damseaux, A. 42, 44, 48

Davison, W.P. 79n

Debré, M. 109-10, 111-3, 283

Decentralisation 7-8

Decline of legislatures 4, 290-5

De Gasperi, A. 152

de Gaulle, General C. 10

Dehousse, B. 14-15, 21

Deloncle, H. 103

Delvaux, M. 170n

Denis, J. 107n

Denmark, and corporatism 57-8; and dual mandate 66-8, 70, 286; and EC 10, 54, 58-9, 60-2, 64; and EC institutions 20-21, 63-4, 68-9, 70-1, 72-3, 285-6; and election system 69, 239-45; and electoral behaviour 55-6, 62; and filling of vacant seats 246-9; and foreign policy 54-6, 60-2, 63-9, 72-3; and franchise 245-8, 288; and Greenland 69-70, 71-2, 261; and Implementation Bill, 69-72; and legislative amendments 71-2; and Market Relations Committee 58-60, 66, 68, 69-73, 272, 275-7, 284-5; and minority government 9, 54, 61, 65, 264; and NATO 61-2, 65; and national elections 55-7, 242-4; and nomination of candidates 246-7; and Nordic countries 54, 64, 65; and 'normal' legislative process 55-6, 58, 59-60, 72-3; and parliamentary committees 58-60; and People's Movement Against the EC 61; and political parties 60-4, 65-72; and principle of direct elections 65-9; and public opinion 54, 62, 64; and reservations on direct elections 22-4; and UK 63

Dewachter, W. 46n

Direct elections, and comparative legislative behaviour 1-3; and draft convention 14-16, 21-3, 102-3; and single election period 24-6. See also direct election system and uniform electoral system

Direct election systems, and constituencies 239-44; and electoral formulae 244-5; and electoral thresholds 244-5; and franchise 245-8; and national election systems 242-5; and nomination of candidates 246-9; proportionality of 245; and vacancies 249

Di Palma, G. 147

Dogan, M. 5n

Draft convention 14-16, 21-3, 102-3
Drewry, G. 205n, 208n

Eisenstadt, S.N. 5n
Electoral systems, choice of 269-79; in EC 7-8; uniform 11-12, 250-9
Elklit, J. 62n, 64n
European Coal and Steel Community, 14, 26, 30
European Communities, and decision-making 1-3, 14-27; enlargement of 20-21
European Council 10, 22-5, 32, 37, 105, 251, 260, 269
European Defence Community, 106, 119
European Parliament, and direct election legislation 14-29; powers of 191, 227; resolutions of 18-20; size of 14, 19, 25-6
Extra parliamentary negotiations 169-74

Farlie, D. 282n
Faurby, I. 56n
Faire, M. 15
Fisichella, D. 157n
Fitzgerald, G. 24
Fitzmaurice, J. 59n, 64n, 65n, 268n
Flesch, C. 170n, 178
Fouchet Plan 102-3
France, and Committee of Presidents 100; and Constitution 109, 112-3; and Constitutional Council 100, 110-3, 121, 268; and draft convention 16; and dual mandate 109; and early direct election measures 102-3, 107, 108-10; and election system 239-44, 250, 261-4,

277-8; and EC 101-3, 111, 119; and EC institutions 21, 26-7, 111-2, 118, 120-1, 250-1, 261; and five per cent clause, 111-2, 117, 245; and foreign policy 9-11; and franchise 245-8; and Gaullism 101, 103-5, 106, 109, 111, 113, 266; and Implementation Bill 110-8, 119-22; and institutionalisation of conflicts 103-5; and legislative amendments 115-9; and 'Liberal Europe' 103-5; and motions of confidence 113, 121-2; and national elections 242-5; and national sovereignty 10, 101-3, 108, 111, 112-3, 116; and nomination of candidates 246-7; and 'normal' legislative process 99-101; and parliamentary opposition 105-8, 118-9, 283-90; and parliamentary procedures 115-6; and political parties 116-7, 120, 266; position of majority in 100-1, 119-20; and Ratification Bill 110-8, 120-22, 264-9; and role of parliament 104-5; and tax status of MEPs 116-7, 289

Genco, S.J. 4n
Gérard-Libois, J. 46, 49, 51
Germany, Federal Republic of, and Arbitration Committee 79, 87; and Basic Law 78, 82-3, 84, 89, 95; and dual mandate 85-6, 93, 94; and early direct election legislative measures 79-81; and electoral system 81, 84, 88-9, 91-5, 239-44; and eligibilities 88; and EC 77, 79-80, 96; and EC institutions 80, 83, 84-5, 96;

mentation Bill 144, 150, 154-5, 160-5; and legislative amendments 150, 164-5; and minority government 9; and national elections 148-9, 156, 159, 242-4; and nomination of candidates 247-8; and 'normal' legislative process 145-51; and parliamentary agenda 146, 160-1; and parliamentary committees 145-6, 153, 160, 162-4, 275-7; and parliamentary process 160-5; and political parties 144, 148-9, 152-4, 161-3; and preference votes 157-8, 159, 161, 162; and pre-parliamentary legislative process 155-60; and public opinion 152, 162; and Ratification Bill 144, 150, 154-5, 160, 165, 264-9; and representation of minorities 158

Jay, D. 229
Jewell, M.E. 4n
Johnson, N. 218n
Jonassen, L.N. 58n
Jørgenson, A. 54
Jowell, R. 209n
Judicial review 7-8, 268

Karapa, J. 107n
Katz, R.S. 157n
Keatinge, P. 139n
King, A. 24n, 209n
Kirchheimer, O. 292n
Kirk, P. 23-4
Kitzinger, U. 24n, 209n, 210n, 211n, 212n
Klepsch, E. 80

Lautenschlager, H. 21-3
Lecaneut, J. 104
Lees, J.D. 4n

Lijphart, A. 2n, 5n, 144n, 159n
Lodge, J. 77-98, 239-59
Loewenberg, G. 4n, 267n
Lomé Convention 190
Lulling, A. 171n
Luxembourg, and coalition government 170-1; constituencies in 176, 177, 287; and Council of State 6, 168, 173, 175, 180; and early direct election legislative proposals 172-3, 180-1; and election system 239-41; and EC 172, 174, 178-9, 279; and EC institutions 174; and filling of vacant seats 247-9; and franchise 175-6, 180, 245-8, 272; and Implementation Bill 175, 177-80, 180-1; and legislative amendments 178; and national elections 171, 242-4; and nomination of candidates 247-8; and 'normal' legislative process 168-70, 176; and political parties 170-1; and postal voting 177-8; and public opinion 172-3; and Ratification Bill 173-4, 179, 181, 264-9; representation of 91, 174, 176; and simultaneous national elections 173, 175, 177-81; and site of European Parliament 176-7

van Maarseveen, H. 185n
Macridis, R.C. 4n
Marin, P. 102n
Manning, M. 139n
Manzella, A. 145n
Marjolin Report 191
Mawoy, P. 107
Meynaud, J. 34n
Mezey, M.L. 4n
Minority Governments 9, 264

317